D1250762

THE BROOKLYN MUSEUM ARAMAIC PAPYRI

Publications of the Department of Egyptian Art

The Brooklyn Museum
Aramaic Papyri

New Documents of the Fifth Century B.C. from the Jewish Colony at Elephantine

Edited with a historical introduction by

EMIL G. KRAELING

THE BROOKLYN INSTITUTE OF ARTS & SCIENCES

Published for THE BROOKLYN MUSEUM

by the YALE UNIVERSITY PRESS, NEW HAVEN, 1953

London: Geoffrey Cumberlege, Oxford University Press

PUBLISHED THROUGH THE GENEROSITY OF

LOUIS M. RABINOWITZ

FOR THE BROOKLYN MUSEUM

COPYRIGHT, 1953, BY YALE UNIVERSITY PRESS.

PRINTED IN THE UNITED STATES OF AMERICA BY MAURICE JACOBS, INC.

COLLOTYPE PLATES BY THE MERIDEN GRAVURE COMPANY.

ALL RIGHTS RESERVED. THIS BOOK MAY NOT BE REPRODUCED, IN WHOLE OR IN PART, IN ANY FORM (EXCEPT BY REVIEWERS FOR THE PUBLIC PRESS), WITHOUT WRITTEN PERMISSION FROM THE PUBLISHERS.

LIBRARY OF CONGRESS CATALOG CARD NUMBER: 53-7777

Ref 220.9 Kr 545

KRAVIT MEMORIAL LIBRARY
of Park Synagogue

55-2230

GRATEFULLY INSCRIBED

TO MY FRIEND AND COLLEAGUE

JULIUS A. BEWER

FOREWORD

In terminating my labors for this book on the Aramaic papyri of the Brooklyn Museum I am conscious of the debt I owe to others. I must first of all express my gratitude to Mr. Charles Nagel, Director, and the Trustees of the Brooklyn Museum for entrusting me, a native son and life-long resident of that borough, with the task of editing the papyri. Next I must stress my deep indebtedness to members of the Museum staff: to Mr. John D. Cooney, Curator of the Department of Egyptian Art, who placed all facilities at my disposal in the most hospitable manner; to Mrs. Elizabeth Riefstahl, Assistant Curator, and to Mr. Anthony Giambalvo, technician of the department, for their willing cooperation; and to Mr. Anthony Caruso for his excellent photographs. But various scholars who cooperated in one way or another also deserve mention here. I am particularly obligated to Professor Franz Rosenthal (University of Pennsylvania) who checked texts and commentary and made valuable suggestions, many of which I have cited. Professor William F. Albright (Johns Hopkins University) not only made some philological suggestions which have been noted but gave helpful criticism of the introductory chapters. Mr. Thomas O. Lambdin, member of the Oriental Seminar at Johns Hopkins University, kindly rechecked and retyped the entire second part of the book and showed true scholarship in critical observations of his own. Professor Richard A. Parker (Brown University) worked out the dates of the papyri for me and willingly furnished advice on chronology where questions concerning it arose. Professor Siegfried H. Horn (Washington) recently offered further chronological suggestions, some of which could still be utilized. On Iranian words and names Professor Bernhard Geiger (Columbia University) advised me. Counsel on Egyptian words or names came from Professors William F. Albright, Hermann Ranke (Heidelberg), W. Erichsen (Copenhagen), Rudolf Anthes (Pennsylvania), and H. J. Polotsky (Oriental Institute). On the Hellenistic side Professor William L. Westermann (emeritus, Columbia) was most helpful. Others who answered questions include Professors Walter Baumgartner (Basel), Alfred R. Bellinger (Yale), Elias Bickerman (Columbia), H. L. Ginsberg (Jewish Theological Seminary, New York), Albrecht Goetze (Yale), Cyrus H. Gordon (Dropsie College), Louis H. Gray (emeritus, Columbia), Benno Landsberger (Oriental Institute), Isaac Mendelsohn (Columbia), Otto Neugebauer (Brown), A. Leo Oppenheim (Oriental Institute), Jacob J. Rabinowitz (Jerusalem), Keith C. Seele (Oriental Institute), Charles C. Torrey (emeritus, Yale), Ernst Vogt, S.J.

Pontifical Biblical Institute, Rome). Last but not least I must thank my brother Professor Carl H. Kraeling, Director of the Oriental Institute, for the interest he took in this project.

EMIL G. KRAELING

New Canaan, Connecticut
April 13, 1952

CONTENTS

ILLUSTRATIONS

FIGURES

PLATES

(following p. 319)

ABBREVIATIONS

I. Periodicals and Serials

ABAW — *Abhandlungen der Bayerischen Akademie der Wissenschaften*
AfO — *Archiv für Orientforschung*
AJSL — *American Journal of Semitic Languages and Literatures*
APAW — *Abhandlungen der Preussischen Akademie der Wissenschaften*
AR — *Archiv für Religionswissenschaft*
ASAE — *Annales du Service des Antiquités de l'Égypte*
ASAW — *Abhandlungen der Sächsischen Akademie der Wissenschaften*
BA — *Beiträge zur Assyriologie*
BASOR — *Bulletin of the American Schools of Oriental Research*
BEUP — Babylonian Expedition of the University of Pennsylvania
BIE — *Bulletin de l'Institut de l'Égypte*
BSAW — *Berichte der Sächsischen Akademie der Wissenschaften*
CRAI — *Comptes Rendus des Séances de l'Académie des Inscriptions et Belles Lettres*
GGA — *Göttingische Gelehrte Anzeigen*
IFAO — *Institut Français d'Archéologie Orientale du Caire*
JA — *Journal Asiatique*
JAOS — *Journal of the American Oriental Society*
JBL — *Journal of Biblical Literature*
JEA — *Journal of Egyptian Archaeology*
JNES — *Journal of Near Eastern Studies*
JRAS — *Journal of the Royal Asiatic Society*
MAI — *Mémoires présentées par Divers Savants à l'Académie des Inscriptions et Belles Lettres*
MGWJ — *Monatschrift für Geschichte der Wissenschaften des Judentums*
MVAÄG — *Mitteilungen der Vorderasiatisch-aegyptischen Gesellschaft*
NGGW — *Nachrichten der Gesellschaft der Wissenschaften zu Göttingen*
OIC — *Oriental Institute Communications*
OLZ — *Orientalistische Literaturzeitung*
PSBA — *Proceedings of the Society of Biblical Archaeology*
RA — *Revue d'Assyriologie et d'Archéologie Orientale*
RB — *Revue Biblique*
RÉJ — *Revue des Études Juives*
SBAW — *Sitzungsberichte der Bayerischen Akademie der Wissenschaften*
SPAW — *Sitzungsberichte der Preussischen Akademie der Wissenschaften*

UMBS — University of Pennsylvania Museum. Publications of the Babylonian Section
WVDOG — Wissenschaftliche Veröffentlichen der Deutschen Orient-Gesellschaft
WZKM — Wiener Zeitschrift für die Kunde des Morgenlandes
ZA — Zeitschrift für Assyriologie
ZÄS — Zeitschrift für Ägyptische Sprache und Altertumskunde
ZAW — Zeitschrift für die Alttestamentliche Wissenschaft
ZDMG — Zeitschrift der Deutschen Morgenländischen Gesellschaft
ZDPV — Zeitschrift des Deutschen Palästina-Vereins

II. *Others*

Ant. — Josephus. *Antiquities of the Jews.* Paragraphs of Niese, H. St. John Thackeray and Ralph Marcus, trans. Loeb Classical Library. 1926.
A. P. — A. E. Cowley. *Aramaic Papyri of the Fifth Century B. C.* Oxford, 1923.
A. V. — Authorized Version of the Bible.
Aimé-Giron, *Textes* — Noel Aimé-Giron. *Textes araméens d'Égypte.* Le Caire, 1931.
B. A. — Biblical Aramaic.
BL — Hans Bauer and Pontus Leander. *Grammatik des Biblisch-Aramäischen.* Halle, 1927.
Bauer-Meissner — Hans Bauer and Bruno Meissner. "Ein aramäischer Pachtvertrag aus dem 7. Jahre Darius I," *SPAW*, 1936, 414 f.
CAH — Cambridge Ancient History.
CIS — Corpus Inscriptionum Semiticarum, 2, 2. Inscriptiones Aramaicae. Paris, 1888.
GK — Wilhelm Gesenius and Emil Kautzsch. *Hebrew Grammar.* 28th ed. tr. A. E. Cowley, 2d ed. Oxford, 1910.
Gesenius — Wilhelm Gesenius. *Hebräisches und aramäisches Handwörterbuch.* 16th ed. Leipzig, 1915.
Honroth and others, "Ausgrabungen" — Wilhelm Honroth, Otto Rubensohn, and Friedrich Zucker. "Bericht über die Ausgrabungen auf Elephantine in den Jahren 1906–1908," *ZÄS, 46,* 1909–10, 14–61.
J. A. — Jewish Aramaic.
Justi, *IN* — Ferdinand Justi. *Iranisches Namenbuch.* Marburg, 1895.
L — Pontus Leander. "Laut- und Formenlehre des Ägyptisch-Aramäischen," *Göteborgs Högskolas Arsskrift, 34,* 1948, 4.
Levy — Jacob Levy. *Neuhebräisches und chaldäisches Wörterbuch über die Talmudim und Midraschim.* 4 vols. Leipzig, 1876–89.
Lidzbarski, *Epigraphik* — Mark Lidzbarski. *Handbuch der nordsemitischen Epigraphik.* Pts. 1, 2. Unless specified Pt. 1 is meant. Weimar, 1898.
Lidzbarski, *Ephemeris* — Mark Lidzbarski. *Ephemeris für Semitische Epigraphik.* 3 vols. Giessen, 1900–15.

M. T. — Masoretic Text of the Old Testament.

Meyer, *Geschichte* — Eduard Meyer. *Geschichte des Altertums.* 2d ed. *2–3.* Berlin, 1928–37.

Meyer, *Papyrusfund* — Eduard Meyer. *Der Papyrusfund von Elephantine.* 2d ed. Leipzig, 1912.

NSI — George A. Cooke. *A Text-book of North Semitic Inscriptions.* Oxford, 1903.

Noth, *IP* — Martin Noth. *Die Israelitischen Personennamen im Rahmen der gemeinsemitischen Namengebung,* Beiträge zur Wissenschaft vom alten und neuen Testament, Folge 3, Heft 10. Stuttgart, 1928.

Pauly-Wissowa — *Pauly's Real-Enzyklopädie der klassischen Altertumswissenschaft.* Neue Bearbeitung begonnen von Georg Wissowa. Herausgegeben von Wilhelm Kroll und Kurt Witte. Stuttgart, 1894– .

Peiser, *Texte* — Felix E. Peiser. *Texte juristischen und geschäftlichen Inhalts.* Keilinschriftliche Bibliothek, *4.* Berlin, 1896.

Ranke, *ÄP* — Hermann Ranke. *Die ägyptischen Personennamen. 1.* Glückstadt, 1935.

RÉS — *Répertoire d'épigraphie sémitique.* Paris, 1900–18.

S.-C. — Archibald H. Sayce and A. E. Cowley. *Aramaic Papyri Discovered at Assuan.* London, 1906.

Sach. — Eduard Sachau. *Aramäische Papyrus und Ostraka aus Elephantine.* 2 vols. Berlin, 1911.

Schaeder, *Beiträge* — Hans Heinrich Schaeder. "Iranische Beiträge I," *Schriften der Königsberger gelehrten Gesellschaft, 6,* 5, 1929–30.

Schorr, *Urkunden* — Max Schorr. *Urkunden des altbabylonischen Zivil- und Prozessrechts.* Vorderasiatische Bibliothek, *5.* Leipzig, 1913.

Spiegelberg, *Sprachgut* — Wilhelm Spiegelberg. "Ägyptisches Sprachgut in den aus Ägypten stammenden aramäischen Urkunden der Perserzeit," *Orientalische Studien Theodor Nöldeke zum 70 Geburtstag gewidmet.* Carl Bezold, ed. Giessen, 1906, *2,* 1093 f.

Tallqvist, *NBN* — Knut L. Tallqvist. *Neubabylonisches Namenbuch . . .* Finska Vetenskaps-Societeten, Acta. *32,* No. 2. Helsingfors, 1906.

Tallqvist, *APN* — Knut L. Tallqvist. *Assyrian Personal Names.* Ibid., *43,* No. 1, 1914.

Ungnad — Arthur Ungnad. *Aramäische Papyrus aus Elephantine.* Leipzig, 1911.

Vincent, *Religion* — Albert Vincent. *La religion des judéo-araméens d'Éléphantine.* Paris, 1937.

I. HISTORICAL INTRODUCTION

1. THE RECOVERY OF EGYPTIAN-ARAMAIC DOCUMENTS

IN 1947 the Egyptian Department of the Brooklyn Museum, which owes its existence to the heirs of the American Egyptologist Charles Edwin Wilbour, received from the estate of his daughter, Miss Theodora Wilbour, the important collection of Ara naic papyri from Elephantine in Upper Egypt, which are the subject of this publication. These papyri, the largest single collection in the Western world, are significant not only because they add considerably to our store of Egyptian Aramaic documents but because they contribute to our knowledge of Jewish men and women who lived in a remote Aramaic-speaking colony[1] at the southernmost frontier of Egypt in the days of Nehemiah (the second half of the 5th century B.C). Before proceeding to translate and elucidate these texts it may be useful to give a general account of Egyptian Aramaic studies and then, on the basis of all existing records, both old and new, to outline what we know of the life and customs of the Elephantine colony in its historical setting.

ARAMAIC AND THE ARAMAEANS

The general reader may not be quite clear as to what is meant by "Aramaic."[2] He may, perhaps, have read that Jews at the time of Jesus of Nazareth spoke this language, of which a few words and phrases are reported in the New Testament writings. But he will scarcely have passed beyond that point. The word Aramaic has not gone deep into educational tradition, for it has been in widespread use only about a century. Had the Bible translations employed it where it is found in the Hebrew Old Testament it would have been familiar, but in all renderings from the Septuagint down to the King James version and its revisions the term was avoided and replaced by other expressions. It is, however, the true ancient name for the language of which we are speaking, as given, for example, by the ancient

[1] Cowley, in *A.P.* 118 f., and Schaeder, *Beiträge*, 225 f., think the Elephantine Jews used Aramaic in official documents only. But that position is rendered untenable by private letters and ostraca, which certainly have nothing official about them.

[2] Cf. on the following the useful and informative article of Raymond A. Bowman, "Arameans, Aramaic, and the Bible," *JNES*, 7, 1948, 65 ff.

Hebrew editor who in Dan. 2:4 introduced a section composed in it. Ignoring that fact the scholarly world, following St. Jerome's commentary on Daniel, long called the language Chaldee, because the Chaldeans of Dan. 2:4 are described as speaking it. Now, however, under the influence of modern Semitic studies, that term has been abandoned and replaced by "Aramaic."

To realize fully what Aramaic stands for and to see where the language of our papyri belongs, we must glance at the total scheme of modern Aramaic philology. On the one hand we may differentiate between the "Old Aramaic," which is illustrated by the language found in early inscriptions, papyri, and ostraca, as well as in the so-called Biblical Aramaic of the Old Testament, and carried further in the Nabataean and Palmyrene inscriptions,[3] and, on the other hand, the more recent Aramaic, which is divided into Western and Eastern dialects. The former are represented by the Jewish-Palestinian Aramaic of the Targums (Aramaic translations of biblical books) and the Palestinian Talmud, the Samaritan, the Christian Palestinian, and the Western Neo-Aramaic that still survives today in some villages in Syria. To the Eastern group belong Syriac (the language of a large early Christian literature), the Aramaic of the Babylonian Talmud, Mandaic, and the Neo-Aramaic still spoken in the extreme north of Mesopotamia in recent times.

It is the Old Aramaic language as it was used before the dialects went their separate literary ways that concerns us here. This language had become rather well standardized by the 5th century B.C., when the Brooklyn papyri were written, for there is no very great difference between the language of the papyri and the so-called Biblical Aramaic.[4] We owe most of our knowledge of the latter to the Jewish scholars of Babylonia and Palestine who provided the Aramaic portions of the Old Testament with a vocalization representing the traditional pronunciation. And while that pronunciation may not give us the exact speech of earlier times, it provides an assured starting point from which to operate.

A language is carried abroad by a people, and its prevalence is proof of a people's numbers and influence. Behind the Aramaic language stand the Aramaeans.[5] In the classic Bible translations their name has unfortunately been replaced

[3] See especially the survey of the Old Aramaic field in Franz Rosenthal, *Die aramäistische Forschung seit Theodor Noeldekes Veröffentlichungen*, (Leiden, 1939).

[4] For studies putting Biblical Aramaic in the background of the inscriptions, see Harold H. Rowley, *The Aramaic of the Old Testament* (London, 1929); Walter Baumgartner, "Das Aramäische im Buche Daniel," *ZAW*, *45*, 1927, 81 ff. The best grammar is Hans Bauer and Pontus Leander, *Grammatik des Biblisch-Aramäischen* (Halle, 1927), hereafter BL. A new lexicon by Baumgartner will complete Ludwig Köhler's *Lexicon Veteris Testamenti* (Leyden, 1945–).

[5] See Emil G. H. Kraeling, *Aram and Israel* (New York, 1918); Sina Schiffer, *Die Aramäer* (Leipzig, 1911). For an up-to-date popular presentation with some learned notes see André Dupont-Sommer, *Les araméens*, L'Orient ancient illustré, No. 2 (Paris, 1949). Most recently, Abraham

by "Syrians." They appeared on the stage of history in Mesopotamia and Syria at about the time the Hebrews appeared in Palestine. The Hebrew story tellers, who like the Greeks try to express international relationships in terms of genealogical theories, claim a kinship between the two peoples. No such kinship is sensed by the prophet Amos, however, who, after the rise of Damascus and the bitter wars between Aram and Israel, was conscious of the two peoples having come from opposite poles: when he says (9:7), "Have I not brought up Israel out of the land of Egypt? and the Philistines from Caphtor and the Syrians from Kir"?[6]

The Assyrian inscriptions give us what is known of the early history of the Aramaeans of Mesopotamia.[7] They invaded that region in the time of Tiglathpileser I in the 12th century B.C., but many also made Syria their promised land and gradually gained the upper hand in some of its principalities — a situation made vivid by inscriptions from those areas.[8] Damascus in particular became "the head of Aram" (Isa. 7:8). No doubt it was in Syria that the Aramaeans evolved their own adaptation of the Phoenician alphabet, and it was probably in the kingdom of Damascus that the language became a literary medium with a standard spelling and phraseology, for literature goes hand in hand with rising political power. The destruction of Damascus by Tiglathpileser III in 732 involved the deportation of its people. According to II Kings 16:9 they were carried back to Kir, their ancient homeland, as prophesied by Amos 1:5. If Kir designates an area north of Assyria that removal may have helped to spread the Aramaic language farther in Mesopotamia and have led to its literary use in that area. In the declining years of the Assyrian empire it was evidently very widely spoken and written there. Tablets from Tell Halaf in Mesopotamia give evidence that it was in use there in the 7th century, and an Aramaic ostracon from Assur shows an Assyrian leader of that period communicating with a Babylonian colleague by this medium.[9] In Babylonia, too, Aramaean tribesmen, who had presumably

Malamat, *The Aramaeans in Aram Naharaim and the Rise of Their States* (Jerusalem, 1952), in Hebrew. Roger T. O'Callaghan, *Aram Naharaim. A Contribution to the History of Upper Mesopotamia in the Second Millennium B.C.* (Rome, 1940) Analecta Orientalia, *26*.

[6] The early narratives made Harran the home of the patriarchal family. Kir (*Ḳīr*) is linked with Elam as an Assyrian auxiliary in Isa. 22:6; the name is hardly that of a principality, since it is not found in Assyrian sources. Perhaps it is the name of a mountain region and survives in *el-Ḳaiyāra*, a range that, according to Emil Forrer, *Die Provinzeinteilung des assyrischen Reiches* (Leipzig, 1920), 12, marks the northern boundary of Assyria.

[7] See Forrer, s. v. "Aramu" in *Reallexikon der Assyriologie*, (Berlin and Leipzig, 1928–), *1*, 131–139, for the new light from texts found at the old Assyrian capital of Assur.

[8] See especially Harold L. Ginsberg, "Aramaic Dialect Problems," *AJSL*, *50*, 1933, 1–9, *52*, 1936, 95–103, and further his "Aramaic Studies Today," *JAOS*, *62*, 1942, 229 ff.

[9] Friedrich, in *Die Inschriften vom Tell Halaf: Keilschrifttexte und aramäische Urkunden aus einer assyrischen Provinzialhauptstadt*, herausgegeben und bearbeitet von Johannes Friedrich, G. Rudolf Meyer, Arthur Ungnad, Ernst F. Weidner (Berlin, 1940), 70 ff., Beiheft *6*, *AfO*. Mark Lidzbarski,

pressed into that country and occupied areas depopulated by war, waxed numerous during the era of Assyrian rule.[10] Meanwhile in the extreme south of Babylonia, in Chaldea, newer Aramaean groups were even able to establish some political power.

With the fall of Assyria and the destruction of the Assyrian aristocracy, the Aramaeans virtually took over Mesopotamia. Probably it was through the Median dealings with the population of Mesopotamia that Aramaic became a sort of official language for communication on the part of the non-Semitic conqueror with Semites in general.[11] The Persians, after their conquest of Media, merely accepted the existing arrangement and on conquering Babylonia evidently extended it to that country, where they had very good reason to favor the Aramaic-speaking elements. As a young and vigorous people the Aramaeans increased in numbers in the Neo-Babylonian and Persian periods, while older populations were declining. All in all, then, their distribution over wide areas, thanks to Assyrian deportation policies, refugee immigration, and royal Persian favor, helped to spread their language so that it actually became a lingua franca.[12]

The theory of ancient relationship between Hebrews and Aramaeans, which, we have already noted, was advocated by early Hebrew writers, came to the fore again among the Jews after both Aram and northern Israel had fallen and the Assyrian empire, too, was disintegrating. The Deuteronomic law bids the worshiper, when sacrificing the first fruits, confess: "An Aramaean ready to perish was my father" (Deut. 26:5).[13] The so-called Priestly Source in Gen. 11:21 makes Abraham start his migration from Ur, a city that in his time was the center of the Aramaic-speaking "Chaldees."[14] Such conditioning of the Jewish mind for the thought of kinship with the Aramaeans made it rather easy for Jews in foreign communities

Altaramäische Urkunden aus Assur, WVDOG, *38* (Leipzig, 1921). The most recent discussion is by André Dupont-Sommer, "L'Ostracon araméen d'Assour," *Syria*, *24*, 1944–45, 24–65.

[10] See Forrer, "Aramu," 132.

[11] Presupposing that the Persians first adopted Aramaic for official use, Josef Markwart, *Ungarische Jahrbücher*, *6*, 1927, 91 coined the term "imperial Aramaic" ("Reichsaramäisch": see Schaeder, *OLZ*, *31*, 1928, 610), which is used by Schaeder, Rosenthal, and others. Ginsberg, in his articles cited above (*AJSL*, *50*, 1933, *52*, 1936), converts this into "official Aramaic" and makes the Assyrians rather than the Persians inaugurate it. It might be better, however, to speak of "standard Aramaic" to avoid entanglement in hypotheses.

[12] It was hardly a lingua franca in the situation of 701 B.C. described in II Kings 18:26, as most writers seem to assume. Since both Assyrians and Jews had to deal with the people of Aram at this time they were both conversant with this tongue and so might well use it. But the papyrus referred to below in n. 69 below may prove that it was a lingua franca by 600 B.C.

[13] The Aramaeans, after the destruction of their states by the Assyrians, had a miserable existence, so that "Aramaean ready to perish" evidently became proverbial in the 7th century.

[14] Ur of the Chaldees was glossed into the older version in Gen. 11:28 to harmonize it with that of the Priestly Writer.

like Elephantine to join with Aramaeans residing there, to adopt their language and even to style themselves as belonging to that nationality, without being conscious of any disloyalty to their own past.

In the revived Jewish community at Jerusalem the Hebrew language was spoken after the exile had ended. The prophets Haggai and Zechariah at the time of Darius I use this medium, as do authors such as Trito-Isaiah, Joel, Malachi, etc. But during the 5th and 4th centuries Aramaic began to make inroads. Aramaisms in the latest Hebrew writings[15] suggest that their authors are writing the old national tongue while actually speaking another. Outside of the Jewish community Aramaic evidently had long since become the chief language of Palestine. The Aramaic sections of Ezra possibly reflect the use of the language in the 5th or 4th century B.C.[16] The Aramaic materials of Daniel need not be younger than the 4th century B.C., if one will allow that some slight revision was made about 165 B.C. However one may choose to explain such Aramaic enclaves in Hebrew books, they prove this much beyond doubt: that Judaean readers of 300–150 B.C. could be expected to understand both tongues, the sacred Hebrew tongue of the past and the Aramaic language which had engulfed the whole Near East.

The progress of Aramaic in Jewish quarters became accelerated in the Hellenistic and Roman eras. Indeed, the time was to come when it would be necessary to translate the Hebrew Bible lessons extemporaneously into Aramaic in the worship of the synagogue — a situation of which the so-called Targums, which preserve such renderings, give vivid evidence.

FIRST DISCOVERIES OF EGYPTIAN ARAMAIC INSCRIPTIONS AND PAPYRI

The first vestige of Old Aramaic outside of the Old Testament came from Egypt in an inscription on a stela brought to the museum at Carpentras in southern France and first published in 1704.[17] The script was, however, regarded as Phoenician and hence was dealt with by Wilhelm Gesenius in 1837 in his great work on the remains of that language. The inscription invokes the blessing of Osiris on Tebo, daughter of Taḥpi. It remained the only known Aramaic inscription until the 19th century.

[15] See Emil Kautzsch, *Die Aramäismen im alten Testament* (Leipzig, 1902).

[16] A much later date for them was strongly urged by Charles C. Torrey, *Ezra Studies* (Chicago, 1910), 140 ff. Baumgartner, in the article cited above (n. 4, 116 ff.), reached the conclusion that the Aramaic documents in Ezra must be of more recent date than the Elephantine papyri. Schaeder, *Beiträge*, 228 ff., attempted to invalidate this.

[17] Conveniently included with text, translation, and notes in Cooke, *NSI*, 205. For the literature, cf. *CIS*, 2, No. 141.

In 1824 the first Aramaic papyrus, or rather piece of a papyrus, was brought from Egypt to Turin, Italy. It, too, was treated by Gesenius, but though he recognized it as a fragment of a letter its true meaning eluded him. Adalbert Merx in 1866 finally recognized the names of the addressee and sender, and in 1878 Clermont-Ganneau put the text in its proper historical setting, the Persian era, thereby dating all other Egyptian Aramaic texts as well, and succeeded in deciphering the meaning of the second line, so that the whole read:

> "To my Lord Mithravahisht, thy servant Paḥim, greeting:— Living, happy and prosperous may my Lord be exceedingly!"[18]

Some additional Aramaic papyrus fragments came from Saqqāra to Italy about 1825–26 and were published in 1827 by Lanci. For a time they were in the collection of the Duc de Blacas (and hence are known as the Papyri Blacasiani[19]), but after his death they were acquired by the British Museum. The four fragments seem to belong to one text, probably a 5th-century Aramaic version of an Egyptian writing containing both narrative and predictive elements.

Some pieces of a papyrus acquired in Egypt in the early 19th century by Bernardin Drovetti eventually came into the possession of the Louvre. This text, known as Papyrus Luparensis,[20] and first published by Jean Joseph Barges in 1862, is a record of daily accounts. It is thought to be somewhat more recent in date than the Blacasiani fragments, perhaps from the 4th century B.C.

A papyrus acquired by the Vatican (hence called the Vaticanus) was first mentioned by Michel Angelo Lanci in 1827 but was not actually published until 1881.[21] It, too, seems to contain accounts, and lists quite a number of Egyptian names. Another papyrus fragment, the Papyrus Borgianus, was mentioned by Lanci in 1827 but first published by Eugène Ledrain in 1884.[22] It also consists of a brief list of Egyptian personal names.

Apart from these only small scraps were known in 1888. There were the eight fragments obtained by Karl Richard Lepsius and the three papyrus fragments found at the Serapeum by François Auguste Mariette and published in 1887.[23]

[18] *CIS*, *2*, No. 144. See also Charles S. Clermont-Ganneau, "Origine perse des monuments araméens d'Égypte," *Revue archéologique*, n. s., *36*, 1878, 93–107, *37*, 1879, 21–39.

[19] Cooke, *NSI*, 206 ff.; *CIS 2*, No. 145.

[20] Cooke, *NSI*, 210 ff.; *CIS*, *2*, No. 146.

[21] Edited by C. J. Melchior de Vogüé in his *Syrie centrale, inscriptions sémitiques* (Paris, 1868), 125 ff., pl. 16, and in *CIS*, *2*, No. 147. Closely allied with this papyrus are some small fragments with but a few words or letters on each — C, D, E, F, in *CIS*, *2*, Nos. 165–166.

[22] *CIS*, *2*, No. 148.

[23] K. R. Lepsius, *Denkmäler aus Aegypten und Aethiopien* . . . (Berlin, 1849–59), T. *12*, Abth. 6, Bl. 124. They are reproduced in *CIS*, *2*, No. 149. For the Mariette find see Julius Euting, "Epigraphische Miszellen," *SPAW*, *23*, 1887, 670; reproduced in *CIS*, *2*, Nos. 150–152.

Yet another fragment preserved in Cairo was edited by De Vogüé in 1888.[24] To these papyrus fragments should perhaps be added a few Aramaic ostraca: one obtained by Adolf Erman at Elephantine in 1886, two preserved in the British Museum, and two others belonging to Vladimir S. Golenischeff.[25]

Of further Egyptian Aramaic inscriptions, of which at least some passing mention should be made, there was only a small increase between 1704, the year of the acquisition of the Carpentras text, and 1888. In 1855 Honoré, Duc de Luynes published a short four-line inscription from a libation vessel found by Mariette at Saqqāra; it recorded an oblation of Aḥiṭab, son of Banit, before Osiris-Apis.[26] In 1877 a Berlin stela from the ancient cemetery at Saqqāra, with an Aramaic (as well as a hieroglyphic) inscription, was published by Karl Richard Lepsius and Julius Euting.[27] It invokes a blessing on a deceased couple and is dated "in the month of Meḥir, the 4th year of Xerxes, king of k[ings]," (485–464 B.C.). The only other Egyptian Aramaic inscriptions found before 1888 are very brief and consist chiefly of names on seals and the like.[28]

This was the status of Old Aramaic materials from Egypt at the close of the 1880's.[29] As one surveys the meager remains in the fine plates of the *Corpus Inscriptionum Semiticarum*, one cannot help feeling that those were the days of small beginnings.

THE GREAT FINDS OF 1893–1908

The documents now in the Brooklyn Museum comprise the first really great find of Aramaic papyri ever made, though they have remained unknown to scholars for more than half a century. They were unearthed in the *kom* or ruin mound of the ancient city of Elephantine by *fellāḥīn* who were digging and carrying away the debris of the past for use as fertilizer (*sebakh*). They were acquired by Charles Edwin Wilbour between January 28 and February 12, 1893. Wilbour, who was accustomed to pass his winters in Egypt, touring the Nile in his *dahabiyyah*, "The Seven Hathors," kept notebooks in which he recorded his purchases (see fig. 1). An entry made at Assuan for January 26—February 13, 1893, records, "All these

[24] *CIS 2*, No. 153.

[25] *CIS 2*, Nos. 137–139 (the first two in Cooke, *NSI*, 202 ff.), 154–155.

[26] Cooke, *NSI*, 201; *CIS*, *2*, No. 123.

[27] *NSI*, 200; *CIS*, *2*, No. 122.

[28] Assembled in *CIS*, *2*, Nos. 124–136.

[29] Mark Lidzbarski, *Handbuch der nordsemitischen Epigraphik* (Weimar, 1898), 2 vols., contains selected inscriptions and a complete glossary based largely on *CIS*, *2*. Cf. also Stephen A. Cook, *A Glossary of the Aramaic Inscriptions* (Cambridge, 1898). George A. Cooke, *A Textbook of North Semitic Inscriptions* (Oxford, 1903) is a convenient source book for selected texts known up to that time, including the papyri in *CIS*.

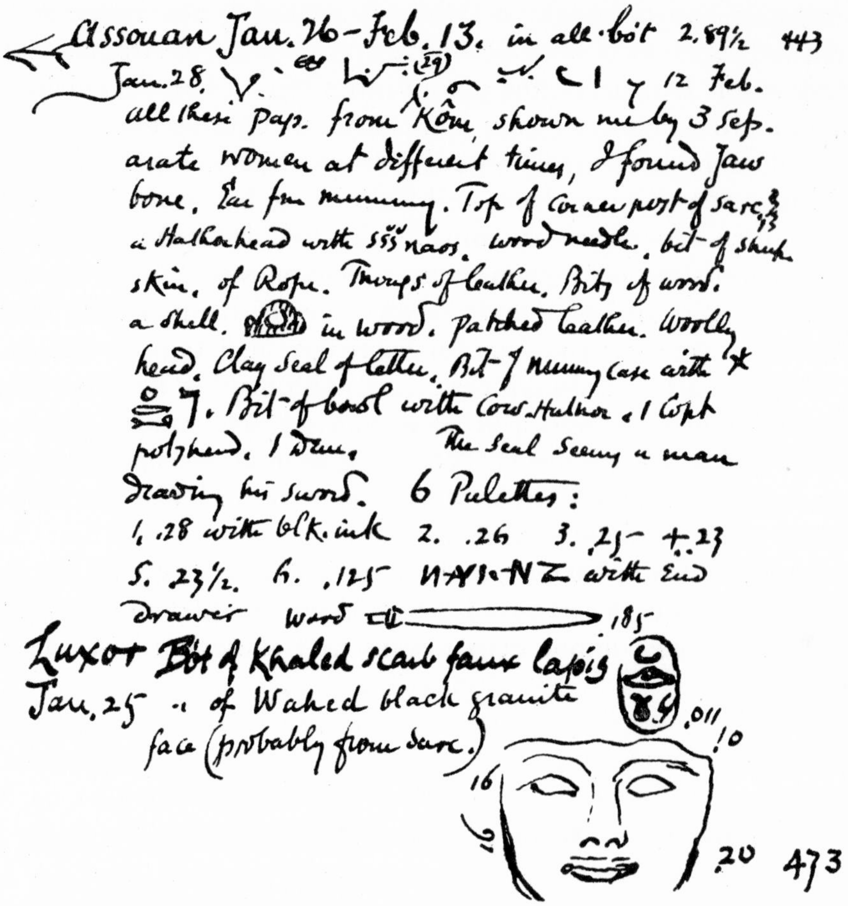

FIG. I Page from Wilbour's Notebook Recording Purchase of Papyri

papyri from *kom* shown me by three separate women at different times." He then lists other items obtained there, including a clay seal for a letter and six scribes' palettes, of one of which he gives a drawing and a partial copy of its Aramaic inscription (see fig. 1).[30] This palette (see pl. xx) came to the Brooklyn Museum in 1916, together with the greater part of the Egyptian collection made by Mr. Wilbour during his years in Egypt. It was published by Aimé-Giron in 1939.[31]

[30] Wilbour's notebooks are at the Brooklyn Museum. A volume of his letters was published by the Museum: *Travels in Egypt, December 1880 to May 1891: Letters of Charles Edwin Wilbour*, ed. Jean Capart (Brooklyn, 1936).

[31] Noel Aimé-Giron, "Adversaria Semitica," *Bulletin de l'institut français d'archéologie orientale du Caire, 38*, 1939, 47 f. A better photograph is provided below in pl. xx; we have also reproduced the inscribed sides of another palette collected by Wilbour at this time, no. 1 of his list in fig. 1. These inscriptions will be discussed in the article mentioned below in n. 58.

The Aramaic papyri bought by Wilbour consist of nine entire rolls, eight of them preserved with their original cords and sealings, and a large number of papyrus fragments. He packed the papyri in tin biscuit boxes and deposited them in the bottom of a trunk filled with other boxes containing Egyptian papyri, and there they remained, unknown, until 1947, when they were bequeathed to the Brooklyn Museum by his daughter. One roll (No. 8) he may have tried unsuccessfully to open, for it came to the museum in two separated, folded pieces. An envelope containing small fragments bore a question in Wilbour's hand: "Is not this authentic Phenician?" and, underneath, in another, apparently British, hand, the answer: "It is Aramaic passing into Palmyrene and Hebrew like the Carpentras text. It should all be carefully copied." Evidently Wilbour showed only these fragments to his informant, who, as it has recently turned out, was Archibald Henry Sayce, noted Oxford Orientalist.[32] That must have been in the following winter.

Wilbour was an accomplished linguist. Heinrich Karl Brugsch, German Egyptologist, praised his knowledge of Egyptian, and Sayce remarks that "he was not only a good Egyptologist but one of the most accurate of copyists." Perhaps he planned to study Aramaic and to work over his treasure at some future date. His death in 1896, however, cut short any plans he may have had. By keeping silent about the texts he lost a great opportunity. If he had confided in Sayce, his purchase would have received all the celebrity that was given to the later acquisitions of Lady William Cecil and Sir Robert Mond. Since these papyri provide valuable information about the location of the Jewish temple at Elephantine, early publication might, moreover, have made possible more methodical search for its site on the part of the excavators.

The first Elephantine papyrus to be published — though its provenance was not at first known as such — was the Strassburg Papyrus, which came through the antiquities market in 1898. That document was ably interpreted (as far as was then possible) by Julius Euting in 1903.[33] It was subsequently recognized by Charles Clermont-Ganneau that the "fortress of Yeb" mentioned in it was Elephantine.[34]

[32] This envelope was reproduced in my article, "New Light on the Elephantine Colony," *The Biblical Archaeologist*, *15*, No. 3, September, 1952, 53. A. Sachs, "The Answer to a Puzzle," *ibid.*, *15*, No. 4, December, 1952, 89 f., provided the solution, which was confirmed by Ernst F. Weidner. But the fact that Sayce in his *Reminiscences* (London, 1923), 289, makes no mention of Wilbour's having shown him Aramaic fragments, though he records traveling with him in the winters of 1893–94 and 1895–96, suggests that Wilbour gave no hint of having acquired complete papyri.

[33] Julius Euting, "Notice sur un papyrus égypto-araméen," *MAI*, *11*, 1903, 297 ff. A better photograph was provided by Sachau, *Aramäische Papyrus und Ostraca*, in his final plate. For the text see *A.P.* 27.

[34] See *CRAI*, 1903, 364, and Wilhelm Spiegelberg, "Zu dem Strassburger aramäischen Papyrus," *OLZ*, *7*, 1904, 10.

The further history of the recovery of Elephantine papyri is inseparably connected with the name of Sayce. In the winter of 1900 while at Elephantine he rescued a more than usually perfect roll of papyrus from the hands of the diggers for sebakh, as well as three ostraca with Aramaic writing. They came to the Bodleian Library and were published by Sir Arthur Ernest Cowley in 1903.[35] A dig was undertaken at Elephantine by Gaston Maspero, French Egyptologist, in 1902, but he found only a few papyrus fragments which were published by Melchior de Vogüé in the same year.[36] In 1904, however, more rolls of papyrus were offered for sale by dealers at Assuan. Three were bought by Lady William Cecil and five by Sir Robert Mond and given to the Cairo Museum. They were all published in a masterly manner by Sayce and Cowley in 1906.[37] Seymour de Ricci provided a valuable bibliography in which he included hand-drawn copies of three papyrus fragments in the Cairo Museum (two found at Saqqāra in 1888 and the third found more recently by Wilhelm Spiegelberg in the same locality).[38]

Since the Brooklyn papyri, then in the possession of Wilbour, were unknown, Sayce could write in his introduction to the publication:

> The find was such as had never been made before. The papyri were in a practically perfect condition; the very strings which had been tied around them were still intact and the clay seals which fastened the strings to the papyri were still unbroken. For the first time the Aramaic scholar has at his disposal a series of connected and fairly lengthy documents, clearly written and but little injured, and furnished with exact dates. A fresh light is thrown by them on the history and character of the Aramaic language as it was spoken and written in the provinces of the Persian empire in the fifth century B.C. New words and meanings are added to the Aramaic dictionary and new forms or idioms to Aramaic grammar, while the origin of Biblical Chaldee is at length explained to us.

Mark Lidzbarski, a foremost authority on Semitic epigraphy, in his review of the work wrote in a similar vein, remarking that this collection contained "Aramaic texts of such extent and in so excellent a state of preservation that — if one will

[35] A. E. Cowley, "Some Egyptian Aramaic Documents," *PSBA*, *25*, 1903, 202 ff., 264 ff., 311 ff. See *A.P.* 11. On the acquisition of the papyrus see Sayce, *Reminiscences*, 312.

[36] De Vogüé, *CRAI*, 1902, 49 ff. Cf. *RÉS*, *1*, Nos. 246–248; Clermont-Ganneau, *Recueil d'archéologie orientale* (Paris, 1904), *6*, 246 ff.; Cowley, *A.P.* 78–80 (where No. 248 is omitted); Lidzbarski, *Ephemeris*, *2*, 236 ff.

[37] A. H. Sayce and A. E. Cowley, *Aramaic Papyri Discovered at Assuan* (London, 1906); hereafter S.-C. A cheap and convenient edition with attempted vocalization and valuable annotations based on S.-C.'s commentary and on reviews by leading scholars was furnished by Willy Staerk, *Die jüdisch-aramäischen Papyri von Assuan*, Kleine Texte für Theologische und Philologische Vorlesungen und Übungen, herausgegeben von Hans Lietzmann, No. 22/23 (Bonn, 1907; 2d ed., rev., 1912).

[38] S.-C. 28–29. See Lidzbarski, *Ephemeris*, *2*, 127 ff. Cowley strangely took no notice of these fragments either in S.-C. or in *A.P.*

disregard the Babylonian-Assyrian texts — nothing in the Semitics field of pre-Christian times can be put beside them."[39]

That other papyri from Assuan or Elephantine had come into private hands had in some way, however, been learned by Sayce, presumably from Arabs or local dealers, for in the foreword to the Sayce-Cowley publication he writes, "There is reason to believe that other papyri from the same find are in existence. Any museum, library or private person into whose possession they may have passed is earnestly requested to make the find known." The only voice that could have answered was no longer able to do so. Wilbour had died in 1896. He had taken his secret to the grave with him, and his papyri were then reposing in a trunk stored in a New York warehouse.

As to the place where the papyri bought by Lady William Cecil and Sir Robert Mond in 1904 had been found, divergent accounts were received by Sayce and by Howard Carter, then inspector general of the Service des Antiquités de l'Égypte and later to win fame as the discoverer of the tomb of Tutankhamen. On the one hand they were told that the documents had been found on the Island of Elephantine, where the actual spot from which they had supposedly come was pointed out to them, and on the other hand it was said that they had been discovered at Assuan by workmen making the road from the railway station to the Cataract Hotel. Sayce (mistakenly) declared, "That this latter was the true story seems to admit little doubt."[40]

In that year of 1904, however, Otto Rubensohn of the Berlin Museum, who had been carrying on excavations in the Faiyūm at Greco-Roman sites, made a visit to Assuan. He gained the confidence of local Arabs and dealers who seem to have shown him the spot on Elephantine to which Sayce refers. He attached more credence than Sayce to the Arab story and at his suggestion the Berlin Museum authorities asked for permission to dig in that area. Maspero, who, as we have seen, had failed to find anything worth while there, granted them the western half of the kom.[41]

Within a yard of the place that the sebakh diggers had pointed out to Rubensohn he made his great find of Aramaic papyri, though not until the second campaign. The presentation in 1907 to the Prussian Academy of three of these texts by Eduard Sachau was an event of considerable importance,[42] for they were

[39] Lidzbarski, review of S.-C., reprinted in *Ephemeris*, *3*, 70.

[40] S.-C. 9.

[41] Wilhelm Honroth, Otto Rubensohn, Friedrich Zucker, "Bericht über die Ausgrabungen auf Elephantine in den Jahren 1906–1908," *ZÄS*, *46*, 1909–10, 14–61; hereafter Honroth and others, "Ausgrabungen."

[42] Eduard Sachau, "Drei aramäische Papyrusurkunden aus Elephantine," *APAW*, 1907, 7. Willy Staerk, *Aramäische Urkunden zur Geschichte des Judentums . . .*, Lietzmann, Kleine Texte, No. 32 (Bonn, 1908), speedily provided a cheap vocalized and annotated edition, including also the text

concerned with a surprising incident: the destruction of the Jewish temple (whose existence on the Island of Elephantine had already been demonstrated by the Sayce-Cowley papyri) at the instigation of the priesthood of the god Khnum, and the efforts of the Jews to enlist support for its restoration by appeals to authorities in Palestine (see below, Chapter 9). It was now apparent that Euting's papyrus referred to the same event. But the new papyri had an importance that lay beyond the factual material they provided, for they gave a glimpse of Persian administration and thus shed light on the Aramaic documents in Ezra, about which the historian Eduard Meyer had written in so conservative a vein.[43]

The French Académie des Inscriptions et Belles Lettres, in which such men as De Vogüé and Clermont-Ganneau were leading spirits, now decided to take a hand; and so the second and third German excavations were paralleled by two French campaigns on the eastern half of the kom, while a third French campaign continued for another year.[44] We shall revert again to these excavations in Chapter 6. So far as their main quest, papyri, was concerned the results of the French digs were disappointing. Only a single small fragment came to light.[45] But the large number of Aramaic ostraca found provided some compensation.[46]

In the same year in which Rubensohn found the new papyri (1906) Sayce acquired at Luxor an Aramaic papyrus of accounts, containing numerous names. It was said to have come from Ḳûs. When published by Cowley,[47] it showed that the Aramaic language was still used in Egypt in the early Greek period, from which this text, as shown by the occurrence of Greek names, must have come. Some fragments of a legal text acquired at the same time and coming from Edfu,[48] which is explicitly mentioned, did not see publication until 1915 when Cowley issued them.[49]

of the documents in Ezra. Karl Marti appended the texts to the second edition of his *Kurzgefasste Grammatik der Biblisch-Aramäischen Sprache* (Berlin, 1911).

[43] Meyer, *Entstehung des Judentums* (Halle, 1896). He claimed that if original documents with Persian royal decrees ever turned up they would be found to be exactly like those in Ezra, a statement vindicated by the Elephantine papyri.

[44] See *RB*, 1908, 261, n. 2.

[45] See J.-B. Chabot, "Les fouilles de Clermont-Ganneau à Éléphantine," *Journal des Savants*, 1944, 92.

[46] Clermont-Ganneau did not live to publish them, and Cowley, who was to take up the task in conjunction with Chabot (see *CRAI*, 1931, 333), also died before being able to pursue it.

[47] Sayce-Cowley, "An Aramaic Papyrus of the Ptolemaic Age from Egypt," *PSBA*, *29*, 1907, 260–272 (=*A.P.* No. 81).

[48] "*Ṭbh*, the fortress," l. 3, is Edfu, not Thebes, as Sayce-Cowley thought. Cf. W. F. Albright, "The Date of the Scrolls from 'Ain Feshkha and the Nash Papyrus," *BASOR*, No. 115, 1949, 16, n. 8; A. Tscherikower, "Edfu (Apollonopolis Magna)," *Kedem*, *Studies in Jewish Archaeology* (Jerusalem, 1942), *1*, 80 f., in Hebrew.

[49] Cowley, "Another Aramaic Papyrus of the Ptolemaic Age," *PSBA*, *37*, 1915, 217–223 (=*A.P.* No. 82).

Meanwhile Eduard Sachau in 1911 republished his papyri of 1907 with revised text, translation, and commentary, together with all the other papyri, ostraca, and inscribed jars that had been discovered by the Berlin expedition.[50] The collection contained numerous letters, additional legal texts like those of Sayce-Cowley and, most surprisingly, two literary texts: pieces of an Aramaic version of Darius' Behistun inscription and of an Old Aramaic Book of Aḥiḳar, a work known from younger versions in various languages. Materials other than papyri — notably ostraca and brief inscriptions on jars, many of the latter in Phoenician but a few in Aramaic[51] — were also included in the publication.

The historian Eduard Meyer contributed the most toward discovering the larger significance of Aramaic texts and their bearing on Hebrew history and on the affairs of the Persian realm. His book of 1911 contains much illuminating discussion, to which he added further valuable and more technical material in a paper of 1915.[52] Among other early attempts to give a comprehensive treatment we may mention the brochure of Norbert Peters,[53] the excellent work of Hedwig Anneler,[54] and the Schweich lectures of Albin van Hoonacker.[55] More recently C. G. Wagenaar[56] and Albert Vincent[57] have added fresh studies in Dutch and in French.

[50] Sachau, *Aramäische Papyrus und Ostraka aus einer jüdischen Militär-Kolonie zu Elephantine . . .* (Leipzig, 1911), with folio of plates. The excellence of the reproductions in the Tafeln is noteworthy. One other papyrus had been published by Sachau in advance (*A.P.* 35) "Ein Altaramäischer Papyrus aus der Zeit des ägyptischen Königs Amyrtäus," in *Florilegium: ou Recueil d'érudition dedié à M. le Marquis Melchior de Vogüé* (Paris, 1909), 529 ff. An inexpensive *editio minor* of most of the texts with a valuable independent commentary was published by Arthur Ungnad, *Aramäische Papyrus aus Elephantine . . .* (Leipzig, 1911). Willy Staerk, *Alte und neue aramäische Papyri übersetzt und erklärt* (Bonn, 1912), Lietzmann, Kleine Texte, No. 94 provided translations with annotations for many of these texts and those of his previous text editions. A similar undertaking, with improved translations, was the one of Cowley, *Jewish Documents of the Time of Ezra*, Translations of Early Documents, Ser. 1, Vol. *1* (London, 1919). Selected translations are given by Gressmann in *Altorientalische Texte und Bilder zum Alten Testament*, ed. Hugo Gressmann (2d ed., Berlin-Leipzig, 1926–27), 450 f., and by H. L. Ginsberg in *Ancient Near Eastern Texts Relating to the Old Testament*, ed. James B. Pritchard, (Princeton, 1950), 222–223, 491 ff.

[51] Restudied by Lidzbarski, "Phönizische und aramäische Krugaufschriften aus Elephantine," *APAW*, 1912.

[52] Meyer, *Der Papyrusfund von Elephantine* (Leipzig, 1911; 2d ed., 1912); "Zu den aramäischen Papyri von Elephantine," *SPAW*, *47*, 1911, 1026 ff.

[53] Peters, *Die jüdische Gemeinde von Elephantine-Syene und ihr Tempel* (Freiberg, 1910).

[54] Anneler, *Zur Geschichte der Juden von Elephantine* (Bern, 1912). Her approach deserves renewal in a series of dissertations, with comparison of similar texts in other languages.

[55] Von Hoonacker, *Une communauté judéo-araméenne à Éléphantine en Égypte* (London, 1915).

[56] Wagenaar, *De joodsche Kolonie van Jeb-Syene in de 5de eeuw voor Christus* (Groningen, 1928). Strangely enough no monograph on the subject has appeared in English, though rather full incidental treatment was given the colony by various writers, including, e. g., Albert T. Olmstead, *History of Palestine and Syria to the Macedonian Conquest* (New York, 1931), 598–610 and Rudolf Kittel, *Geschichte des Volkes Israel*, *3*. (Stuttgart, 1927), 501–519.

[57] Vincent, *La religion des judéo-araméens d'Éléphantine* (Paris, 1937).

DISCOVERIES SINCE 1914

At the end of World War I the Fathers of the Pontificio Istituto Biblico in Rome undertook an excavation at Elephantine. According to a list preserved at that institution, three Aramaic ostraca, some fragments of Aramaic papyri, and two fragments of inscriptions, one of which is in Canaanitic script, were recovered. But nothing was published at the time except a brief report to the director of the Service des Antiquités.[58] It seems probable to me that the papyrus fragments are among some of unknown origin in Cairo that were published by Aimé-Giron.[59]

In 1923, finally, Cowley published his *Aramaic Papyri of the Fifth Century B.C.*, a handbook of all the papyri then known, including one hitherto unpublished text, the Harrow School Museum Papyrus (No. 83) of which no photograph has ever been published. The ostraca, however, were not contained in the volume. He gave the texts as far as possible in a chronological order. There are 83 numbers, plus the Words of Aḥiḳar and the Behistun inscription. Cowley did not publish the grammar of the papyri he intended to bring out to carry further the pioneering sketch he had given in Sayce-Cowley. This desideratum was provided later by Pontus Leander.[60]

Some fragments of Aramaic papyri found in Saqqāra in 1913 and 1917 were published by Aimé-Giron in 1921.[61] Cowley was able to include them in an appendix to his volume of 1923. Additional materials from the Cairo Museum were edited in 1931 by Aimé-Giron with detailed commentary and excellent plates.[62] Of particular importance were the portions of an Aramaic journal page of 472–471 B.C. from the Memphis arsenal.[63] A few Elephantine fragments are of special interest to us because of their relationship to the Brooklyn papyri.

A highly important find, not of papyri but of Aramaic leather documents,

[58] A. Strazzuli, P. Bovier-Lapierre, and S. Ronzevalle, "Rapport sur les fouilles à Éléphantine de l'Institut Biblique Pontifical en 1918," *ASAE, 18*, 1919, 1–7. The published report does not say that *Aramaic* papyrus fragments were found. Rektor Josef Vogt of the Pontifical Biblical Institute in Rome kindly gave permission to publish the inscriptions mentioned above. As it was not possible to include them in this volume they will be published in an article in the *BASOR*.

[59] Aimé-Giron, *Textes araméens d'Égypte* (Le Caire, 1931), 64 ff., Nos. 76–86. The mention of [Anan]i b. Azariah (No. 78, l. 1), the man so important in the Brooklyn texts, reveals Elephantine origin for this group of fragments in view of the new texts that are published in this volume.

[60] Leander, "Laut und Formenlehre des Ägyptisch-Aramäischen," *Göteborgs Högskolas Arsskrift, 34*, 1948, No. 4. He quotes all papyri by Cowley's *A.P.* numbers.

[61] Aimé-Giron, "Fragments de papyrus araméens provenant de Memphis," *JA, 18*, 1912, 56 ff. In *A.P.* 317–319.

[62] See above, n. 59. Corrections are given and a few items added in his "Adversaria Semitica" (see above, n. 31), 33 f.

[63] This was restudied by Bowman, "An Aramaic Journal Page," *AJSL, 58*, 1941, 302–313. The dates were worked out by Richard A. Parker, *ibid.*, 295.

was acquired in Egypt by the German Egyptologist Ludwig Borchardt in 1932. Even the leather bag in which they were stored is preserved. Borchardt published a photograph of one of these documents together with a translation made for him by Eugen Mittwoch,[64] who subsequently worked on photographs of the other texts with the aid of Franz Rosenthal, H. J. Polotsky, and W. B. Henning, but did not live to publish them. He was able, however, to produce a valuable article on their contents and significance.[65] The originals were acquired from Borchardt's estate by the Bodleian Library and have now been published by Godfrey R. Driver.[66]

The Borchardt documents are not, as he thought, from Elephantine; they presumably came from the secretariat of the Satrap Arsham, or Arsames, at Memphis or from one of his estates, but they were not written in Egypt at all. The use of leather as writing material illustrates what Ctesias relates about the "royal hides" (i. e., skins produced from the vast herds on the king's domains) serving that purpose in Persia.[67] They contain thirteen letters which could be printed as complete documents, though some are not in very good condition. In Driver's opinion the collection may originally have contained twenty or more. One scroll was spoiled in the attempts made to unroll it. The most important figure in these texts is Nakht-Ḥor, an Egyptian who seems to have been steward of Arsham's estates.

From Saqqāra, but bought in the antiquities market, came the valuable papyrus acquired by Bruno Meissner and published with the aid of Hans Bauer in 1936.[68] It was up to that time the oldest known Aramaic papyrus, for it dates from June, 515 B.C. Of entirely different vintage is the Aramaic papyrus found in a pottery jar at Saqqāra in 1942 and recently published.[69] It is by far the oldest Aramaic

[64] Borchardt, "Nachricht von einem weiteren Funde aramäischer Urkunden," in his *Allerhand Kleinigkeiten* (Leipzig, 1933), 47–49.

[65] Mittwoch, "Neue aramäische Urkunden aus der Zeit der Achämenidenherrschaft in Ägypten," *MGWJ*, N. S., *47*, 1939, 93 f. The text in Borchardt's book was studied by J. Kutsher, "An Aramaic Leather Scroll of the Fifth Century B. C.," *Kedem, Studies in Jewish Archaeology* (Jerusalem, 1945), *2*, 66 f., in Hebrew; he included a brief account of all the other texts by H. J. Polotsky. A second one was published by Murad Kamil, *Bulletin of the Faculty of Arts* (Cairo) *10*, 2 f. (inaccessible to me).

[66] G. R. Driver, *New Aramaic Documents of the Fifth Century B. C.* (Oxford, 1953). See his brief account, "New Aramaic Documents," *ZAW*, *62*, 1949/50, 220 f.

[67] *Diodorus* II, 32, 4.

[68] Bauer and Meissner, "Ein aramäischer Pachtvertrag aus dem 7. Jahre Darius I," *SPAW*, *72*, 1936, 414 ff. A new study has been issued by Dupont-Sommer, "Métayage égypto-araméen de l'an 7 de Darius I," *MAI*, *14*, 1944, 61 ff.

[69] See above, n. 12. Dupont-Sommer, "Un papyrus araméen d'époque saïte découvert à Saqqarah," *Semitica*, *1*, 1949, 43–68. For an English translation see Ginsberg, "An Aramaic Contemporary of the Lachish Letters," *BASOR*, No. *111*, 1948, 24 ff. The title given to the Pharaoh is

papyrus known to date. It is a portion of a letter addressed "to the lord of kings Pharaoh" by a Phoenician tributary king who is endangered by invasion on the part of the King of Babylon and asks for help. The situation is thus somewhat similar to that of the famous Tell el Amarna Letters of 1400 B.C. The Pharaoh addressed may have been Apries (588–568 B.C.) or even Psammetichus II (594–589 B.C.).

The most recent find of Aramaic papyri comes from the western part of Hermopolis Magna, Tûna el-Gebel.[70] Here the excavations conducted by the Egyptian Service des Antiquités explored four underground galleries dedicated to the god Thoth and serving as catacombs for the cynocephalous apes and ibises sacred to him. Curiously enough, in Gallery C, in a jar like thousands of others containing only ibis mummies, was found in November, 1945, a cache of eight Aramaic papyri. These documents, according to Murad Kamil, indicate the existence of an Aramaic colony living at Ashmūnein or on the shore west of the Bahr el-Yussef. While the texts are undated they seem to be similar in style of writing and in language to those of the 5th century found elsewhere. In a chamber opposite and only a few yards away there was found a *naos* bearing the cartouche of *Intarwish* (Darius I).[71] It may well be, therefore, that these papyri are not much younger than the one published by Bauer-Meissner. According to the preliminary report six of them are private letters pertaining to one family. Four among them are addressed to persons in the town of Syene. Two are addressed to a person at a place called *'Api* (Panopolis?). One may look forward with great interest to the publication of these letters. They contain quite a few Egyptian names, and the Semitic names do not suggest that there are more than a few Jews among the people concerned. Of their formal aspects and some items of religious interest reported by Kamil we shall speak later.

rendered by him "lord of kingdoms." But the title does not reflect the ancient dual monarchy of Upper and Lower Egypt, as he supposes, but rather the Assyrian arrangement of putting Egypt under twelve kings which was ended by the rise to power of the Saitic dynasty. Titles like "king of the kings (*šar šarrāni*) of Cush and Egypt" used by Esarhaddon and Ashurbanipal are antecedent to "lord of kings" used in this papyrus. On the name of the Phoenician ruler Adon compare the equally short or abridged name of Baal of Tyre. Philistaea is an unlikely quarter in which to seek an independent kingdom at this time. A city in the plain of Acre such as Achshaph (Josh. 11:1, etc.) seems more suitable. Pharaoh Necho had this area firmly in hand and his successors doubtless held title to it till Nebuchadrezzar conquered it.

[70] See Sami Gabra, "Lettres araméennes trouvées à Touna el Gebel (Hermopolis Ouest)," *BIE*, *28*, 1947, 161–162; Murad Kamil, "Papyri araméennes découvertes à Hermopolis Ouest," *ibid.*, 253 ff. According to Kamil in *Actes du XXIe Congrès des Orientalistes* (Paris, 1949), 107 ff., they are to appear in *Publications of Fouad I University*, Cairo.

[71] See Max Burchardt, ". . . Zu den ägyptischen Namensformen der Achämeniden," *ZÄS*, *69*, 1911, 79. This form was used from the 28th year of the ruler.

OTHER EGYPTIAN ARAMAIC MATERIALS

We have paid but scant attention to the ostraca in our account. Those known before 1888 were included in the *Corpus Inscriptionum Semiticarum, 2.* De Ricci's bibliography in Sayce-Cowley gives full particulars. Important lots were published in the works of Sayce-Cowley and Sachau along with the papyri. Subsequently Sayce, Cowley, and Lidzbarski published other ostraca which may conveniently be found in the latter's *Ephemeris, 2–3* and in the *Répertoire d'épigraphie semitique, 1–3.* Some of them will engage us in the course of our study. More recently additional ones at Cairo have been published by Aimé-Giron.[72] Since 1944 the previously unpublished Clermont-Ganneau collection of the Académie des Inscriptions et Belles Lettres has been assigned to Dupont-Sommer. According to his preliminary report[73] there are only seventeen complete texts in the lot (now given as 256). Most of these ostraca are letters dealing with such matters as food, clothing, etc. Fifteen are lists of names. He has recently published some of the more interesting specimens. As we shall have occasion to refer to them below in Chapter 8 we shall not list them here. His forthcoming work will contain all the Elephantine ostraca, old and new, consisting of about 350, and will supply full bibliographical information.

Attempts seem to have been made, though perhaps only for a cryptic purpose, to write Aramaic with demotic Egyptian script. A text of this sort is now the property of the Pierpont Morgan Library in New York. Its Aramaic character was discussed by Raymond A. Bowman on the basis of photographs that were among the papers of the late Wilhelm Spiegelberg.[74] A preliminary account of it, rendered in 1944, suggests that it is a text of a magical character. We thus have an interesting counterpart to the effort to write Aramaic in Babylonian cuneiform script, as evidenced by the tablet from Warka.[75]

A few words may be added concerning Egyptian-Aramaic inscriptions discovered since 1888. Of considerable interest is the sandstone stela "from Syene" which was published by De Vogüé in 1903 but about which no information was divulged concerning the exact place of discovery.[76] It refers to something done (probably built) "in the month of Siwan, that is, Meḥir, of the seventh year of

[72] "Trois ostraca araméens d'Éléphantine," *ASAE, 26,* 1926, 23 ff., and in *Textes,* 3 *b* and 4 *bis.*

[73] *Actes du XXIe Congrès des Orientalistes,* 109 ff. They are to be published by Geuthner, Paris, under the title *Les ostraca araméens d'Éléphantine,* Bibliotheque archéologique et historique.

[74] R. A. Bowman, "An Aramaic Religious Text in Demotic Script," *JNES, 3,* 1944, 219–231.

[75] First published by François Thureau-Dangin, *Lettres d'Uruk* (Paris, 1922), No. 58. The most recent study is that of Dupont-Sommer, "La tablette cuneiforme araméenne de Warka," *Revue archéologique, 39,* 1942–44, 35–62, where full references to previous discussions will be found.

[76] De Vogüé, "Inscription araméenne trouvée en Égypte," *CRAI,* 1903, 269 ff. Cf. *RÉS, 1,* 438, *2,* 806; Lidzbarski, *Ephemeris, 2,* 221.

Artaxerxes" (June, 458 B.C.) by N. N. (name lost), "the commander of Syene." In 1931 Aimé-Giron published some Aramaic graffiti from various quarters in Egypt.[77] Noteworthy among these is that of the priest of Nabu named *Šeʾīl*, an Aramaean "Saul." The most recent Aramaic inscription to come from Egypt is that found in the Wadi Ḥammâmât in 1946 and published by Dupont-Sommer.[78] It is a curiously artificial product, containing nearly all the letters of the alphabet in their proper order. It appears to be from the 5th century B.C.

Of the Aramaic inscriptions of Asiatic provenance we can render no account here. Only the Aramaic endorsements on Babylonian tablets require mention, because they show us how Assyro-Babylonian names given in the cuneiform texts were transcribed into Aramaic letters, and thus illustrate and confirm the Babylonian names found in the papyri. Albert T. Clay published by far the greatest number of those known to date.[79] A convenient handbook of them was provided by Louis J. Delaporte.[80]

Against this background the great find of Charles Edwin Wilbour may be seen in the proper perspective. While the publication of it cannot be as sensational as it would have been fifty years ago, it still forms an immensely valuable addition to the Aramaic literature.

[77] Aimé-Giron, *Textes*, No. 99.

[78] Dupont-Sommer, "Une inscription araméenne inédite de l'Ouâdi Hammâmât," *RA*, *41*, 1947–48, 105–110.

[79] These appeared in Hermann V. Hilprecht and Albert T. Clay, *Business Documents of Murashū Sons of Nippur Dated in the Reign of Artaxerxes I*, BEUP, *9*, (Philadelphia, 1898), and Clay, *Business Documents of Murashū Sons of Nippur Dated in the Reign of Darius II*, *BEUP*, *10* (Philadelphia 1904). He made a fresh study of them in his paper "Aramaic Indorsements on the Documents of Murashū Sons," *Old Testament and Semitic Studies in Memory of William Rainey Harper*, eds. Robert Francis Harper, Francis Brown, and George Foot Moore (Chicago, 1908), *1*, 28 ff., and again with additional material in *Business Documents of Murashū Sons of Nippur Dated in the Reign of Darius II*, UMBS, *2*, No. 1 (Philadelphia, 1912).

[80] Delaporte, *Epigraphes araméens* (Paris, 1912). New ones have appeared since then, notably in Oluf Krückmann, *Babylonische Rechts und Verwaltungsurkunden aus der Zeit Alexanders und der Diadochen* (Weimar, 1931).

2. YEB AND SYENE

"YEB the fortress," "Syene (really *Sewen*) the fortress," these are the key geographical words of the Elephantine texts. The latter name has survived to this day in Assuan, the town on the eastern side of the Nile below the First Cataract. It was raised to world fame by the modern Assuan Dam constructed to flood Lower Nubia and submerging, in the interest of modern progress, the lovely Island of Philae with its ancient monuments. But remote and obscure as Syene may seem, the name was known in antiquity to people outside of Egypt. Just as "from Dan to Beersheba" described the northernmost and southernmost towns of Israel's small country, so "from Migdol to Seveneh" described the limits of Egypt, and the prophet Ezekiel could expect his hearers of the 6th century B.C. to be familiar with the phrase (Ezek. 29:10; 30:6).[1] In the first of his references we find the further definition, "and to the border of Cush." That gives the picture fully, for it is beyond Assuan that Cush begins[2] (a region called Ethiopia by the Greeks but which we call Nubia, since Ethiopia is now the name of the more easterly Abyssinia). The name *Sewen*, means "mart," "trading post," and reflects the fact that there, from time immemorial, the raw materials of inner Africa and the finished products of Egypt were exchanged. The protection of trade required soldiery. "Syene the fortress" was a garrison town in the days when it was thus described.

"Yeb the fortress" was on the narrow, palm-studded island in the Nile which

[1] The Authorized Version has "from the tower of Seveneh," but the word *migdōl*, "tower," must be taken as a place name here; Seveneh has a slight error in the last vowel, and the word should be rendered "to Sewen." The land of Sinim in Isa. 49:12 appears as "land of the *swnyym*" in the ancient Isaiah scroll. Cf. *The Dead Sea Scrolls from St. Marks Monastery*, *1*, ed. Millar Burrows with the assistance of John C. Trever and William H. Brownlee (New Haven, 1950), pl. 41; the word is wrongly transcribed *synyym* by the editors. It gives the Hebrew equivalent of Aramaic *swnknn*, *A.P.* 33:6, and thus clearly means "land of the inhabitants of Syene." The Sin of Ezek. 30:15 ff., there called "the stronghold of Egypt," is scarcely Syene but rather the Egyptian name of Migdol. See Spiegelberg, "Der ägyptische Name von Pelusion," *ZÄS*, *49*, 1911, 81–84. Cf. below Chapter 10, n. 17.

[2] Originally Cush began south of the Second Cataract and extended to Khartûm, but from the time of Amenophis I it also included the region south of the First Cataract. Dows Dunham, "Notes on the History of Kush," *American Journal of Archaeology*, *50*, 1946, 380, would restrict the term to its original country, but this is contrary to the consciousness of the people who used it in the times with which we are dealing. See, further, on "Aethiopia" and "Cush," Jozef M. A. Janssen, "Notes on the Geographical Horizon of the Ancient Egyptians," *Bibliotheca Orientalis*, *8*, 1951, 213–214.

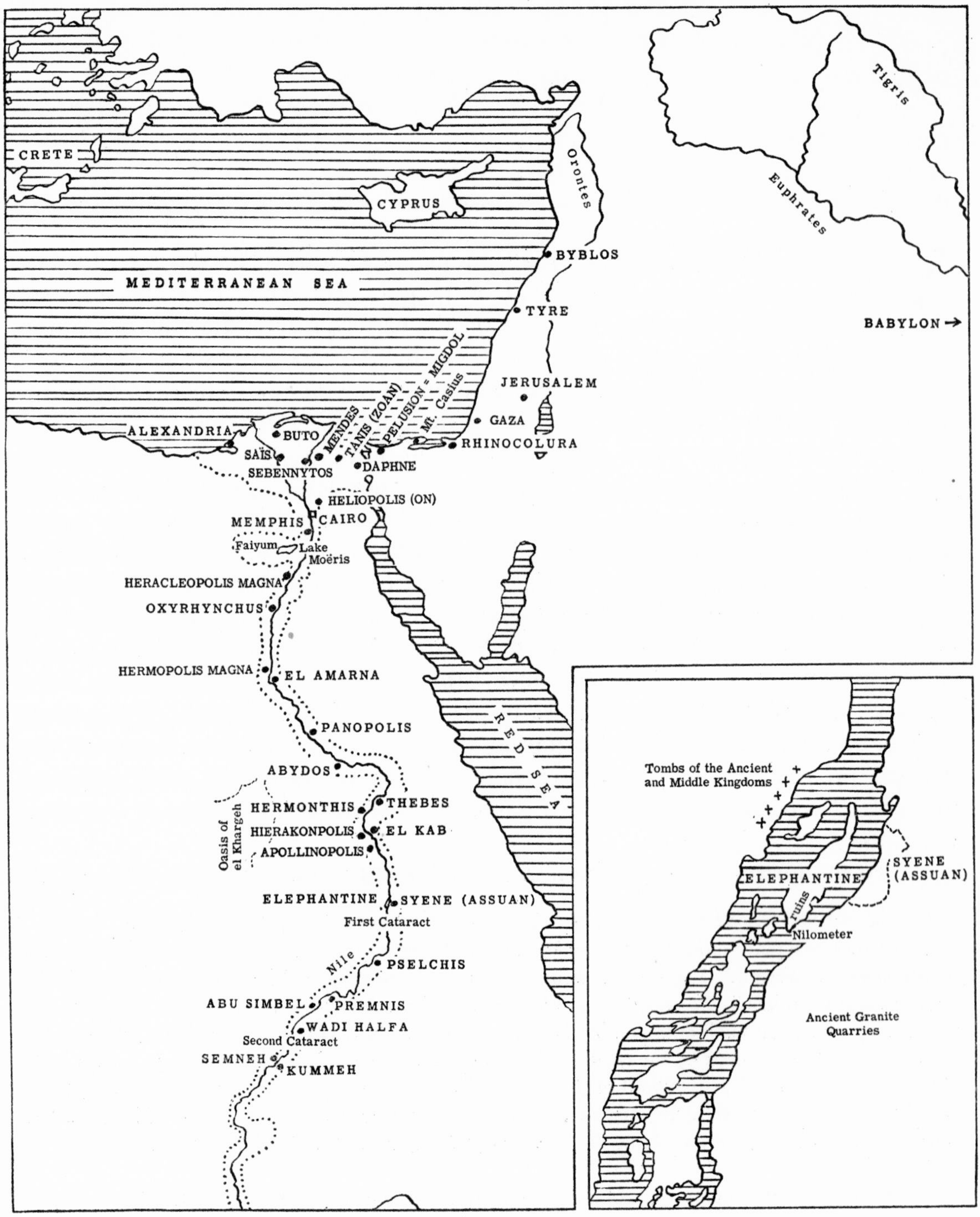

FIG. 2 Sketch Map of the Nile Valley with Elephantine and Assuan

lies opposite Assuan and extends for three kilometers parallel to the eastern shore (fig. 2). Unlike Syene Yeb has not preserved its old Egyptian name. It is known as

Gezîret Aswân, the "Island of Assuan." The Yeb of the papyri reproduces the older native Egyptian name *'Iēbew*, which means "elephant place" and in the Greek period was translated "Elephantine." According to Georg Steindorff the term *'Iēbew* applied originally to the whole Nile cataract country but later became narrowed down to the island from which that country was controlled.[3] Whether at a remote age elephants actually lived there or whether the name just reflects the fact that this was the center of the trade in ivory tusks is not known.

The visitor who goes to Elephantine today will regard it as a more or less insignificant place as compared with Assuan, but in antiquity "Yeb the fortress" was by far the more important. Here were the government buildings and the temples, including two lovely ones built by Thutmose III and Amenophis III; they were still standing when the French scholars of Napoleon's day made their great survey, but have since been destroyed. This, too, was the residential area. Protection against sudden assault by desert tribesmen was naturally better on the island than at Syene. That danger was not to be disregarded. Even in Greco-Roman times places such as Syene and Philae were subject to raids.[4] On the other hand one can well see the desirability and necessity of a supplementary fort at Syene. Life on an island was bound to be cramped and the soldiery required some elbowroom for its cantonments and exercises. Some of the colonists, like Anani b. Haggai of Brooklyn No. 11, owned houses in both places and perhaps for that reason they could at one time describe themselves as of Yeb and, at another, as of Syene. It was at Syene that the ships loaded and unloaded their freight. There too must have been important labor camps, for the quarries nearby provided the wonderful red granite from which Egyptian craftsmen created works of art. Herodotus refers to these quarries as on the east bank of the Nile.[5] In the word describing the stone "syenite" we still echo the old name of Syene.

In his description of Egypt Strabo names the cities from Thebes southward, and at the end of the list mentions Syene and Elephantine; the former, he says, is on the borders of Ethiopia and is a city of Egypt, the latter an island lying half a stadium (19.5 m.) in front of Syene with a temple of "Khnuphis" (Khnum) and a Nilometer as in Memphis.[6] With true Greek interest in scientific matters Strabo is especially concerned with the Nilometer, to which Plutarch had already referred, and with the well at Syene which reflected the sun's rays at the time of the summer solstice and had provided Eratosthenes (ca. 250 B.C.) with a starting point for his pioneer work in geography. For it had taught him that Syene was at the extremity of the Summer Tropic Zone (in the Tropic of Cancer). The well at Syene

[3] Steindorff, in *Pauly-Wissowa*, s. v. "Elephantine."

[4] Strabo XVII, 1, 54.

[5] Herodotus II, 175, tells of a "house" made of a single stone that was brought from Elephantine to Saïs in Amasis' time. It took 2,000 workmen three years to transport it. It was probably a naos, such as is portrayed in Honroth and others, "Ausgrabungen," 56, Tafel X.

[6] Strabo XVII, 1, 47 ff. Cf. Plutarch, *De Iside*, ch. 43.

is no more, but the Nilometer on Elephantine still exists. After a long period of neglect it was put into operation again in 1870.[7]

In ordinary times of peace Yeb and Syene were probably not heavily garrisoned. The Romans later kept only three cohorts there, not even at full strength.[8] That would amount at most to 1500 men. Strabo explains that large forces were not needed because neither the "Ethiopians" nor the Egyptians of those days were very warlike and could be kept in check by small garrisons.[9] However, there was evidently a danger point in the reduction of occupation forces. That was reached when they were unduly depleted to provide troops for the campaign of Aelius Gallus against the Sabaeans of South Arabia in 26–25 B.C. The Ethiopians in an unexpected attack then seized Philae, Syene, and Elephantine, and tore down the statues of Caesar. The Romans thereupon mustered 10,000 infantry and 800 horsemen and drove them out, penetrating as far as the Ethiopian capital, Napata.[10] On the last lap of the way, between Pselchis and Premnis, they passed the sandhills in which the army of Cambyses had allegedly been submerged by a sandstorm — an event still recalled 500 years later. What happened here in 25 B.C. doubtless had happened many times before in the long course of the history of Elephantine and Syene. But when the din of battle died down the garrisons dwindled again and life went its uneventful way.

In the very days in which the earliest of the Brooklyn papyri originated, a famous visitor from lands across the sea came to Elephantine — none other than Herodotus.[11] It must have been about 450 that he was there, in the reign of Artaxerxes I. According to him there were three Persian garrison centers in Egypt in his day, guarding the three vulnerable frontiers of Egypt. The one at Marea (near the later Alexandria) protected the frontier facing Libya; the one at Daphne, near Pelusion at the mouth of the eastern arm of the Nile, protected Egypt from invasion from the direction of Syria and Arabia; the third, the one that here concerns us, was on the Island of Elephantine and on the shore to the east of it at Syene and guarded Egypt against "Ethiopia."[12] Herodotus says nothing further about the life at Elephantine, which presumably was of too ordinary a nature to arouse his interest, and makes no mention of foreign elements found there. But there can be no doubt that the eyes of the Father of History saw some of the very

[7] See Borchardt, "Nilmesser und Nilstandsmarken," *APAW*, 1906, Anhang. On the (large) cubit of the Nilometer cf. Friedrich Hultzsch, *Griechische und römische Metrologie* (Berlin, 1862), 355. On the importance of Syene for Eratosthenes cf. Lloyd A. Brown, *The Story of Maps* (Boston, 1949), 29, 38.

[8] Strabo XVII, 1, 53.

[9] *Ibid.*

[10] Strabo XVII, 1, 54.

[11] See Camille Sourdille, *La durée et l'étendue du voyage d'Hérodote en Égypte* (Paris, 1910); Spiegelberg, *Die Glaubwürdigkeit von Herodots Bericht über Ägypten . . .*, Orient und Antike, Heft 3 (Heidelberg, 1926).

[12] Herodotus II, 30.

people mentioned in our papyri, and that these Jews and Aramaeans noticed with curiosity the traveler from far-off "Yawan."

Herodotus states that Elephantine was the point farthest south that he reached in his travels and that what he reports about the regions beyond depends on hearsay. He then gives us some Egyptian views about the sources of the Nile which Strabo, centuries later, regarded as most ridiculous.[13] The great fact of geography, however — that Egypt has its natural boundary at Elephantine and Syene — was apparent to both the Father of History and the Father of Geography: The end of deep-water navigation is at the First Cataract of the Nile. It was that fact which made Assuan a trading post. There the deep-water vessels had to receive or discharge their freight. The products of inner Africa had to come down by small boat or be hauled down by land to Syene, and the wares received in exchange from Egypt had to be taken southward in the same laborious manner. The interlude during which navigation was realized — through a canal bypassing the cataract — was brief, and in the times that concern us here lay far in the past.[14]

To our eye the cataracts are only stretches of rough water, such as we have in abundance on the rivers of the Occident. There is no actual "waterfall," in the full sense of the word, at any point. The cataracts are rapids, the first one ending just above the Island of Elephantine, the second above Wadi Halfa, with others at intervals up the river as far as Khartûm, about two thousand miles from the sea. Strabo, however, seems to imply that in his time there was actually a waterfall in the middle of the river above Elephantine, while near the shore boats could be taken upstream. He asserts that exhibitions of shooting the waterfall were put on here by boatmen as a spectacle for the Roman governors.[15]

In the Persian days with which we are concerned the boatmen who navigated the rapids played an important role. In the Sayce-Cowley papyri we heard of a "boatman of the rough waters," obviously an Egyptian, and in Brooklyn No. 12:20 we learn of two brothers living in Yeb who are "boatmen of the waters" and from their names also Egyptians. Herodotus observes that if one goes up farther from the city of Elephantine, then the region is steep; hence a hawser must be tied to the boat from either side, as to an ox; if it breaks, the boat shoots downward, hurled back by the power of the current. He notes that it takes four days to go through this region, for the Nile has many bends like the Maeander; twelve *schoinoi* must be traversed in this laborious manner.[16] This is evidently an allusion to the Dodekaschoinos or "Twelve-mile Country."[17]

[13] Herodotus II, 28; Strabo XVII, 1, 52.

[14] Sesostris I (ca. 1887 B.C.) cut a channel through the First Cataract. Charles Edwin Wilbour was the first to note his inscription recording the feat, as well as the one of Thutmosis III commemorating the repair of the canal. Cf. Wilbour, "Canalizing the Cataract," *Recueil de travaux relatif à la philologie égyptienne et assyrienne, pour servir de bulletin à la mission française du Caire, 13,* 1890, 202 ff.

[15] Strabo XVII, 1, 49.

[16] Herodotus II, 29.

[17] The country from Syene to Hierasykaminos (*Maḥarraḳa*). See Kurt Sethe, *Dodekaschoinos,*

The completion of the Assuan Dam in 1902, three and a half miles south of Elephantine, terminated the hauling of boats through the rapids. William C. Prime, who traveled up the Nile in a dahabiyyah in 1855, gives a rather vivid account of the way in which an agreement was negotiated with the local *reis* of that day and of how his boat was pulled up by fastening a rope to rocks farther up stream. The reis contracted to bring his party from Elephantine to Philae in the course of an afternoon.[18] The ancient predecessors of the reis mentioned in the papyri dealt with satraps, officers, and merchants.

The commerce with Nubia and the Sudan was of course much more extensive in antiquity, when the Egyptians eagerly craved imports from the south, than it is now, and hence Elephantine had a much greater importance than it has today. For the large ships that could not be hauled up through the rapids Assuan was the last port; there they were loaded with the Nubian products that had been brought down through the rapids in smaller vessels. We have a picture of such large vessels with the products of Nubia from a slightly earlier time than the one with which we are directly concerned, that of Psammetichus I,[19] but we may well assume that the Jews of Elephantine often watched vessels of that sort coming and going on the river.

As late as the 3rd century of the Christian Era Elephantine must have presented, in the words of Friedrich Zucker,

> a uniquely impressive picture, especially to anyone who approached it from the south — with the great Khnum temple rising aloft, and below it, on the east, the wonderful little sanctuary of Amenophis III; more in the foreground, the temple built by the Roman Emperor Trajan, and toward the north another small sanctuary similar to that erected by Amenophis III. It must have been a picture not unlike that which the temple-island of Philae still reveals. The cramped houses of the city dwellers occupied but a small amount of space in comparison with the extended temple areas.[20]

The scene was doubtless more typically Oriental in the 5th century B.C. than in A.D. 300. Only the ancient temples of the Pharaohs brooded over "the blooming isle," "the garden of the tropics,"[21] and lent it that charm which was characteristic of old Egypt.

das Zwölfmeilenland an der Grenze von Ägypten und Nubien, Untersuchungen zur Geschichte und Altertumskunde Aegyptens, Bd. 2, (Leipzig, 1901), and his "Schoinos und Dodekaschoinos," *ZÄS*, *41*, 1904, 58–62; and Wilhelm Schubart, "Dodekaschoinos," *ZÄS*, *47*, 1910, 154–157.

[18] W. C. Prime, *Boat Life in Egypt and Nubia* (New York, 1857), 262 ff.

[19] See Margaret Benson and Janet Gourlay, *The Temple of Mut in Asher* (London, 1899), pls. 20–22, pp. 46, 257, 370. Cf. also Torgny Säve-Söderbergh, *Ägypten und Nubien* (Lund, 1941), 206 ff.

[20] Honroth and others, "Ausgrabungen," 59 ff.

[21] Edmé F. Jomard, "Description de l'île d'Éléphantine, in *Description de l'Égypte* (Paris, 1821), Texte I, 175.

3. EGYPT UNDER PERSIAN RULE

THE Elephantine papyri reflect the period when Egypt was under the domination of the great Asiatic empire that had been established by Cyrus (559–529 B.C.). The 26th Dynasty, founded by Psammetichus I of Saïs, had reigned over the land for over a century, when its fifth ruler, Pharaoh Amasis (569–526 B.C.), was succeeded by his son Psammetichus III. The world had grown smaller and the Persian empire could not, like the earlier Assyrian empire, defer the problem of controlling the key to Africa; the restive Greeks were already on the doorstep of that continent. Early in 525 Cambyses (529–522 B.C.) undertook the invasion of Egypt.[1] Psammetichus III was defeated at Pelusion. The conqueror pushed up the Nile and besieged and took Memphis in the summer of that year. The Libyans and the Greeks of Cyrenaica now became his subjects. Psammetichus III fell into his hands.

Cambyses remained in Egypt until 522, consolidating his hold upon this valuable country. He sent an expedition westward to the Oasis of el Khargeh; it is said to have perished in its effort to penetrate still farther to the Oasis of Siwa — a fact that puts in high relief the daring nature of the journey undertaken two hundred years later by Alexander.

If tradition is to be trusted, Cambyses did not fare too well in his attempt to invade Nubia.[2] Herodotus gives a curious report of his sending for the "fish eaters" (*ichthyophagi*) of Elephantine, whom he then dispatched to the Ethiopians (Cushites) ostensibly to bear gifts but actually to spy out the land and report to him.[3] However, the true purpose of their embassy is said to have been perceived by the Ethiopians. Legend has it that Cambyses was so enraged at the scornful reception given his messengers that he began his campaign in senseless haste, without proper preparation.

There can be little doubt that the Persian ruler inspected the fortresses of Yeb and Syene and visited the temples of the Island of Elephantine in the course of his

[1] Most of our information comes from Herodotus III, 1 ff. See Meyer, *Geschichte*, *3*^{2}, 189 ff. Albert T. Olmstead, *History of the Persian Empire* (Chicago, 1948), 86 ff. A. Klasens, "Cambyses en Égypte," *Ex Oriente Lux*, *10*, 1945–48, 339 f.

[2] Herodotus III, 19 ff.

[3] What group is meant is not clear — certainly not Jews or Aramaeans. Strabo XVI, 4, 13, speaks of a similar group on islands in the Red Sea. Perhaps they were landless people who had no other way of making a living except by fishing. Those meant by Herodotus may have been of Nubian extraction and therefore able to converse in that language.

campaign. We can imagine the river full of his warships and the clang and clash of armor as his regiments disembarked at Assuan for the long trek into Nubia. Whether he got as far as Napata is uncertain. A "storehouse of Cambyses" still bore that name in Roman times in the vicinity of the Third Cataract.[4] But his army is said to have suffered heavily from privations, and the Ethiopian ruler Nastasen boasts of having turned him back.[5] Actually, the Nubians may have accepted vassaldom, for Darius I later lists them among the tributary peoples.[6]

Cambyses was forced to leave Egypt in charge of a governor, Aryandes, early in 522, when the news from the homeland made his return imperative. An impostor, claiming to be Cambyses' brother Smerdis (Bardiya), whom he had had secretly put out of the way before going to Egypt, had arisen in Persia. The king died of an accidental wound on his way to the east at Hamath in Syria.

The policy of Cambyses toward the conquered Egyptians seems to have been stern. The Bagoas letter from Elephantine asserts that when Cambyses came down to Egypt he destroyed all the temples[7]— a statement that agrees with what was related in Egypt even earlier, as shown by Herodotus.[8] It seems likely enough that the king, bent on improving the finances of the country, curbed its exploitation by priests and temples. Doubtless many temples became desolate when their incomes were cut off, and one may suppose that those dedicated to the animal gods, like that of Khnum at Elephantine, suffered most under his restrictions. According to an edict of Cambyses, preserved in a demotic text, only three temples were officially recognized by him and retained their prerogatives and incomes — one of them being that of Ptaḥ in Memphis and the other two being of uncertain identity.[9] However, it would seem that he subsequently made further exceptions, for the inscription on a statue in the Vatican reports that he recognized the importance of the goddess Neith of Saïs in the Delta and issued orders to give back her possessions.[10] He is specifically accused only of having destroyed one temple, that of Heliopolis.[11] It is quite possible that his reputation was unduly blackened.

[4] Herodotus III, 25–26; cf. Pliny VI, 35.

[5] Meyer, *Geschichte*, *3*², 191.

[6] F. H. Weissbach, *Keilinschriften der Achaemeniden*, Vorderasiatische Bibliothek, *3*, (Leipzig, 1911), 89.

[7] *A.P.* 30:14.

[8] Herodotus III, 1 ff.

[9] Spiegelberg, "Die sogenannte demotische Chronik des Pap. 215 der Bibliothèque National zu Paris," in his *Demotische Studien* (1914), Heft 7, 142 ff. On the interpretation see especially Meyer, "Ägyptische Dokumente aus der Perserzeit," *SPAW*, *51*, 1915, 310 ff. On the inscriptions cf. Georges Posener, "La première domination perse en Égypte," *IFAO*, *Bibliothèque d'Étude*, *11*, 1936, 164 ff.

[10] See Heinrich Schäfer, "Die Wiedereinrichtung einer Ärzteschule in Saïs unter Darius I," *ZÄS*, *37*, 1899, 72 ff.

[11] Strabo XVII, 1, 27.

According to the Behistun inscription of Darius I (522–486 B.C.) Egypt revolted while Darius was fighting with the Babylonian pretender Nebuchadrezzar III. It has been suggested that Darius, after he had succeeded in obtaining the sovereignty, made a campaign to put down a revolt in Egypt in the winter of 519–518.[12] It is doubtful, however, whether the words of the inscription on which the theory rests should be taken as implying a full-fledged revolt. It may merely refer to the personal disloyalty of Cambyses' satrap, Aryandes, who is reported to have given the queen of Cyrene help against the Greeks of Cyrenaica, though the thing which is said to have brought about his downfall was his revaluation of Egyptian money at a higher standard than that of the Persian mint.[13]

The story of the mighty deeds by which Darius suppressed all rebellions[14] eventually reached the Aramaeans and Jews of Elephantine — of that fact the fragments of an Aramaic papyrus found there, giving a translation of the great inscription of Darius at Behistun, give vivid testimony.[15] Perhaps such versions were circulated in Egypt at the time of his visit to impress people with the fate of revolutionaries against his power. The monarch came to Egypt in person in 519 and spent almost a year there. He inaugurated measures to increase the prosperity of the land. Among these was the completion of Pharaoh Necho's canal from the Nile to the Red Sea, enabling commerce to flow from east to west without paying tribute to Arabian chiefs. Monuments with his bilingual cuneiform and hieroglyphic inscriptions still stand along the course of that waterway.[16] He made the Oasis of el Khargeh an outpost against the Greeks of Cyrenaica; the ruins of his buildings there stand to this day. Renewed prosperity must have led to an expansion of business activity and building. Since the oldest Aramaic document from Elephantine dates from the seventh year of Darius I,[17] it may well be that the Jewish quarter from which our records are derived came into existence only at this time. But that the Jewish colony as such was older is, of course, proved by the reference in the Bagoas letter to the existence of the temple before Cambyses.

Diodorus reports that Darius was the sixth and last lawgiver of Egypt; that, in contrast to Cambyses and his acts against the temples, he had conducted himself piously, had associated with the Egyptian priests and shown interest in their sacred books, had emulated the generosity and good will of the ancient Pharaohs toward his subjects, and in return had received divine honors.[18] On the reverse

[12] Richard A. Parker, "Darius and His Egyptian Campaign," *AJSL*, *58*, 1941, 373 ff.

[13] Herodotus IV, 166.

[14] On Darius see Meyer, *Geschichte*, *3*², 192 ff.; Olmstead, *op. cit.*, 107 ff.

[15] Sach. 50; *A.P.* 248 ff.

[16] Herodotus II, 158; Weissbach, *op. cit.*, xxi ff., 118 f.; H. R. H. Hall, *CAH*, *3*, 1925, 310 ff. Posener, *op. cit.*, 180 f.

[17] Sach. 31; *A.P.* 1, from 498 B.C.

[18] Diodorus I, 95.

of the so-called *Demotic Chronicle*, already referred to in connection with Cambyses, there is a copy of regulations of importance to the temple priesthoods.[19] The material precedes that about Cambyses, cited above. After referring to the death of the latter "before reaching his own territory" and to the succession of Darius "whom the whole land obeyed on account of the excellence of his heart," the scribe records that this king in the year 3 (519 B.C.) sent word to his satrap in Egypt that the "wise . . . among the military, priesthood and scribes of Egypt should be gathered in order that they might record the former law of Egypt up to the year 44 of Pharaoh Amasis . . ." (526 B.C.). It was subsequently written "on a papyrus-roll in Assyrian (Aramaic) writing and in epistolary writing (demotic)." Eduard Meyer is of the opinion that the regulations preceding this statement were from the Egyptian law code of Darius (which was evidently a restatement of old native law) and that the account of Cambyses' edict was quoted only because it had been completely modified by Darius.[20]

That Darius ruled them with a firm hand, in spite of all concessions made to priesthood and temples, is vividly brought home by the demotic correspondence of his Satrap Pherendates with the priests of Khnum at Elephantine; we see from it that the satrap supervised priestly appointments[21] and that there was thus no inclination to let the priesthood become independent and a menace to the authority of the crown. One must hold, then, that the propaganda of his descendants portrayed the rule of Darius I as more mild than it actually was. Certainly native uprisings broke out in Egypt in the last years of his reign — a fact indicative of dissatisfaction.[22]

The reign of Xerxes (486–465 B.C.) saw the zenith of Persian power.[23] It was marked by the great attempt to safeguard the position in Asia Minor and Egypt by winning control of Greece, which was threatening both these flanks of the empire. After Xerxes had decided to embark upon that project he first undertook a campaign to Egypt, in the year after the death of Darius, to put down the revolt there. We know nothing about these events save the brief statement of Herodotus to the effect that "when he had subjected them and brought all Egypt under a worse servitude than was the case under Darius, he entrusted it to Achaemenes."[24]

[19] Spiegelberg, "Die sogenannte demotische Chronik . . .," col. c, ll. 6 ff. See especially Meyer, *SPAW*, *51*, 1915, 308.

[20] Meyer, *ibid.*, 306; Nathaniel Reich, "The Codification of Egyptian Laws by Darius . . .," *Mizraim*, *1*, 1933, 180.

[21] Spiegelberg, "Drei demotische Schreiben aus der Korrespondenz des Pherendates des Satrapen Darius I, mit den Chnumpriestern von Elephantine," *SPAW*, *64*, 1928, 604 ff.

[22] Olmstead, *op. cit.*, 227. On the inscriptions cf. Posener, *op. cit.*

[23] Olmstead, *op. cit.*, 230 ff.; Meyer, *Geschichte*, *3*, 192 ff. Inscriptional material on the successors of Darius is meager; see Posener, *op. cit.*, 191 f.

[24] Herodotus VII, 7.

This satrap was called away from his post to act as admiral of the fleet during the Greek war,[25] but must subsequently have returned to Egypt.

Xerxes was followed by Artaxerxes I (465–425 B.C.). In the early days of his reign a certain Inaros, who is described as a "son of Psammetichus" and may well have been a scion of the old Saïtic royal family, obtained control of the Delta.[26] Memphis and Upper Egypt, however, remained in Persian hands. Achaemenes was successful in maintaining himself against the rebels until the Athenians intervened on their side. The satrap fell into the hands of Inaros in a battle at Papremis and was slain by him. The Athenians defeated the Persian fleet and sailed up the Nile capturing Memphis. Perhaps the Aramaic text, Sayce-Cowley "L" (*A.P.* 11), which uses the monetary standard of Ptaḥ rather than the Persian royal weight, dates from this time and thus gives implied support to this change of regime. The erection of the sandstone stela by a commander of Syene (see Chapter 1) may also hang together with these events. But the Greek success was short-lived. The satrap of Syria, Megabyzos (in cuneiform texts called *Bagabuḫša*),[27] came down with an army and defeated the Athenians (in 455 B.C.). The revolt collapsed and Inaros was executed. A few irreconcilables, headed by an Egyptian named Amyrtaeus, are said to have remained in the marshes of the Delta. Arsham (or Arsames as he is called in Greek sources) was now made satrap of Egypt.

The numerous Aramaic documents from the reign of Artaxerxes I found at Elephantine suggest that his was a period of peace and prosperity for the colony. The main purpose of the king evidently was to build up the realm and its finances after the long and costly wars fought by his father. Megabyzos rebelled in 450 B.C., but a settlement seems to have been reached and the satrap to have retained his position.[28]

The throne of Persia now passed to Darius II (425–405 B.C.). The violent manner in which he obtained it and the subsequent uprising of his brother Arsites cannot but have had disturbing effects in the provinces.[29] Uprisings in Asia Minor, Media, and Egypt marked the period 410–408 B.C. With this general situation must be linked the persecution which befell the Jewish military colony at Elephantine in 410 and the absence of the Satrap Arsames from his post in Egypt at this time (see Chapter 9 below).

Artaxerxes II (404–361 B.C.) was the last Persian king to hold sway over the garrison at Elephantine. It had hitherto been thought that the independence of Egypt was established at the end of the reign of Darius II, but the Brooklyn papyri teach us otherwise (see Chapter 10). We see now that the rebellion of Artaxerxes'

[25] Herodotus VII, 97.

[26] Meyer, *SPAW*, *51*, 1915, 289.

[27] Cf. on him Friedrich W. König, "Altpersische Adelsgeschlechter," *WZKM*, *31*, 1924, 295 ff.

[28] See Olmstead, *op. cit.*, 312.

[29] *Ibid.*, 355 ff.

brother Cyrus, which the Greek expedition of Xenophon abetted, had a weakening effect on his position and made possible the full success of Amyrtaeus' revolt.

It will be useful to consider here some aspects of Persian rule in Egypt.[30] We must recall that the Persian state, from the days of Darius I, was organized into twenty satrapies.[31] Egypt ranked sixth among the satrapies listed and was one of the heaviest income producers for the throne, bringing in 700 talents, twice as much as all Syria-Palestine combined. It is obvious, therefore, that the satrap of Egypt, whose seat was the "white castle" or citadel at Memphis,[32] was an extremely important official.

Herodotus tells us that for the Persian garrison and its associated troops the satrapy had to furnish 120,000 rations, which were in addition to the tribute mentioned.[33] That suggests an army of 10,000 to 12,000 men. The Persian crown also laid hands on at least one income-producing industry — the fishery of Lake Moëris in the Faiyūm, which had been artificially created in ancient days. During six months it produced a talent of silver a day for the royal treasury; for the remaining six months, twenty minas daily.[34]

The satrapy was subdivided into provinces,[35] but only two are specifically named in the papyri: one is *Nï'* (so vocalized in Ashurbanipal's account of his Egyptian campaign and called *No*-Ammon — with erroneous vocalization — in Nah. 3:8) and identical with Thebes; the other is *Tšṭrs.*[36] Grain from the latter area forms an important part of the rations received for the garrison at Syene, though there is also reference to what was brought from the province of Thebes.[37]

The satrap of Egypt was chosen from the highest aristocracy. Achaemenes, satrap under Xerxes, was the king's brother, and Arsham, who held this post under Artaxerxes I and Darius II, was from the Achaemenid house. Arsham had an

[30] Cf. especially Meyer, "Zu den aramäischen Papyri . . .," *SPAW*, *47*, 1911, 1041 ff. and *Papyrusfund*, 23 f.

[31] Herodotus III, 89 ff. On this list cf. Ernst Herzfeld, *Archaeologische Mitteilungen aus Iran* (Berlin, 1929), *1*, 91 ff.

[32] Thucydides I, 104, gives this name to a part of Memphis.

[33] Herodotus III, 91. According to Greek papyri of the 2nd century B.C. the ration (*sitonion*) of grain per man per month was one *ardab*, together with a cash payment in lieu of more grain. Cf. Frederic G. Kenyon, *Greek Papyri in the British Museum* . . . (London, 1893), *1*, 55.

[34] Herodotus III, 91; II, 149; Diodorus I, 52.

[35] On the nomes cf. Diodorus I, 73; Georg Steindorff, "Die ägyptischen Gaue," *ASAW*, *25*, 1909, 25 ff. It seems unlikely, however, that the Persian provinces were as small as the nomes.

[36] *A.P.* 37:6, 27:9. Meyer, *SPAW*, *47*, 1911, 1041, and *Papyrusfund*, 12, thinks that this province extended from Elephantine to Hermonthis, south of Thebes. The name means "province of the south."

[37] *A.P.* 24. The Iranian word *ptp'* is used for "ration." In *A.P.* 43:8 a woman refers to the *ptp'* which she had received from "the house of the king." Cf. on this word Wilhelm Eilers, "Iranische Beamtennamen," *Abhandlungen für die Kunde des Morgenlandes*, herausgegeben von der *DMG*, *25*, No. 5, 1940, 71 f.

estate in Babylonia; its manager is mentioned in cuneiform texts of 413, 411, and 404 B.C., while a son of Arsham is named in 417 B.C.[38] Arsham was not in Egypt when the sack of the Jewish temple took place, but had "gone to the king." The leather documents of his aide Nakht-Ḥor (see Chapter 1) reflect the period of his absence in Asia and suggest that his authority extended over larger areas than the Egyptian satrapy.

An outstanding characteristic of Persian officialdom was that the presiding individual in every department of government had a group of "colleagues" who shared in the responsibility of decisions and actions. At the head of the chancery from which the satrap's orders were issued was an official called the "chancellor" or *beʿēl ṭeʿēm.*[39] Among the letters published by Sachau was one by this official, on the authorization of Arsham (*A.P.* 26). Ezra 4:9, where a man named Rehum, bearing the same title, sends a report to the king, is thus fully confirmed. The Persian official in the former case is "Anani the scribe" (apparently a Jew), but his scribal title is only an earmark of his earlier profession; he has a scribe of his own to do the writing for him, as does the chancellor Rehum in Ezra.[40] In the Borchardt leather documents the title *beʿēl ṭeʿēm* is not directly used, but the issuing officials are described as "cognizant of this order." Two such persons are mentioned — Bagasaru and Artaḥay — and the latter is in a position to write a letter on his own authority.[41]

The provincial setup doubtless duplicated the satrapal. At the head of the province stood a *peḳīd* or "officer." This is the term used in *A.P.* 36:6, where such an official is reviled by the Egyptians as a "Mazdaean." In the Borchardt documents there is allusion to the officers of the provinces, not only in the Egyptian but in the Asiatic sphere.[42] Such an officer had precedence over the military commander of an area and could call on him for aid. There were seeming differences of rank between persons who bore this title. Of those designated as officers

[38] Cf. on him F. W. König in *Reallexikon der Assyriologie*, *1*, 155. A Pharnaces (Prnk), son of Arsham, appears on an Aramaic seal from Persepolis; G. C. Cameron, *Persepolis Treasury Tablets*, Oriental Institute Publications, *65* (Chicago, 1948), *1*, 53.

[39] "Lord of the order," but the exact interpretation is not certain. The term is of Babylonian origin, *bel ṭēmi* "reporter (?)." Herzfeld, *Altpersische Inschriften* (1948), 147, understands it to mean "one who has a royal patent."

[40] The name Reḥum appears in Brooklyn Nos. 10:19, 11:14, 12:34, thus vindicating the biblical name. Shimshai the scribe also has an Aramaic name; cf. *Šamša-a-a* in Clay, *Legal and Commercial Transactions*, BEUP, *8* (Philadelphia, 1908), 1, 89. On the word "scribe" cf. Eilers, "Keilinschriften und antike Rechtsgeschichte," *OLZ*, *34*, 1931, 930 ff.

[41] Driver, *ZAW*, *62*, 1949, 224. Here also the other details mentioned in the next paragraph.

[42] The manager of Arsham's Babylonian estate is called "the *paḳdu* of Arsham" in Clay, BEUP, *10*, 46. The title seems to be specifically Neo-Babylonian (it is also written *paḳūdu* and *paḳḳādu*). See Raymond P. Dougherty, *The Shirkūtu of Babylonian Deities*, Yale Oriental Series, *5*, 2 (New Haven, 1923), 21 ff.

in Egyptian-Aramaic texts, three had Egyptian, one a Persian, and one a Babylonian name. It is clear, therefore, that the Persian government freely employed native Egyptians to help them administer the country. Nakht-Ḥor was apparently senior "officer" in Egypt. The title *peḳīd* (Hebrew *pāḳīd*) as designation for provincial officials of Egypt was evidently known to the Hebrew writer of Gen. 41:34, who describes Joseph as counseling the Pharaoh to appoint such men.[43] The "*azdakara* of the province" were presumably officials of the provincial chancery.[44]

The instructions of Arsham are given in letter form and under his name, though one is evidently issued by a secretary at his command; two texts containing directives are by other prominent Persians. No dates are mentioned, and so they seem more like executive orders for immediate action than communications, for which at least a month date might be expected. The salutations are short if the addressee is of lower station in life or an Egyptian, but more elaborate if he is of higher rank or a Persian. One of the texts is a letter of safe-conduct which Nakht-Ḥor took along on a journey from Asia to Egypt. In it Arsham issues orders to officials in various districts, among which Damascus is named, to give Nakht-Ḥor and his men rations "from the house of Arsham." Nakht-Ḥor evidently had the management of the holdings of his master in Egypt. Here he seems to have had his troubles, some of which were due to a recent revolt of the Egyptians that is explicitly referred to. We learn that during the revolt some of the workers on Arsham's domain had been captured and now had to be liberated; others had run away and had to be caught and punished, or a troop was mutinous and would not accept Nakht-Ḥor's orders. The *garda*, a class of artisans, evidently slaves of the satrap, were mutinous. Relations with other Egyptian officials were difficult. An official of a Persian grandee who had delayed in sending Arsham the levy due from his estate wrote about the matter to Nakht-Ḥor, who had to ascertain the satrap's position on the matter. Sometimes Nakht-Ḥor went too far. Thus he was accused of having refused an official the promised five Cilicians, of having appropriated his harvest, and of having struck the garda and taken away what did not belong to him. He was ordered by Arsham to restore what he had taken. Matters of a simpler sort,

[43] Gen. 41:34 in the Elohistic stratum. This could have a bearing on the date of the Elohistic materials. In the Yahwistic stratum, Gen. 41:43, Joseph is saluted by the Egyptians with *abrek*! The A. V. renders "bow the knee," but the word is doubtless to be explained as the Assyrian title *abarakku*, which the writer rather unrealistically puts in the Egyptian milieu. In the Assyrian sources the *abarakku* is a very exalted figure of the military hierarchy, ranking close to the Tartan (really *turtan*) and the Rabshakeh. It was originally a courtiers' title ("mixer of ointments") and continued in use in court circles in Assyria. (See *Reallexikon der Assyriologie, 1*, 461 f.) It is also found in Neo-Babylonian texts; cf. the interesting *Ḫarrimaḫḫi' mar biti ša Ḫarrimunatu, abarakku*, Clay, *BEUP, 10*, 51 — a man evidently of unfree status, with maternal name given, yet bearing this title.

[44] *A.P.* 17:5, 7. Cf. Schaeder, *Beiträge*, 272. *Azda*, "announcement," "decree," is used in Dan. 2:5. (A.V. wrongly renders, "The thing is gone from me," i. e., is forgotten; it means, "The decree has gone forth from me.") The azdakara are "those who make known" the government orders.

too, occupy Nakht-Ḥor. He must concern himself with sending articles like a cloak and some hides, or giving an assignment to a sculptor to fashion "a mare with its rider" and to send this object to Arsham, presumably at Babylon or Susa.

Two letters of an official nature, one to and one by the satrap were among the texts published by Sachau. The first, *A.P.* 17 of 428 B.C., is addressed to Arsham by several Persian officials. It is difficult to ascertain its import owing to its fragmentary condition and poor legibility, but it apparently concerns payments received. The other letter (*A.P.* 26) is dated in the 12th year of Darius (II) or 412 B.C. On behalf of the crew of a ship a man named Psamsineith, with the Iranian title of *naupat*, "captain of a ship," had reported to a man named Mithridates, bearing the same title, that a boat needed repair. Mithridates had evidently notified Arsham, who in this letter restates the case and (from line 22 on) issues an order to an Egyptian named Wahprimaḥi to have the boat repaired, after checking to see if the repairs are really necessary. The papyrus contains technical terms of the shipbuilding trade and is therefore difficult. But it shows the meticulous manner in which the satrap watched over government expenses.

There is no direct indication that the term *peḥā* (governor) was applied to Egyptian provincial heads at this time. It is used in the papyri for the Persian governor at Samaria, Sanballat, and for the governor of Judaea, Bagoas.[45] In the biblical sources relating to this period the term governor is used, sometimes for the satrap of Syria and again for the heads of provinces.[46]

The treasury department of the satrapal and provincial organizations must have been well organized. In the leather documents Nakht-Ḥor, in addition to being an officer also has the title of *knzsrm*, "chief of the treasury," and has associated with him the *hamarakara* or "treasurers."[47] The latter are mentioned in *A.P.* 26 as officials of the treasury (*ginzā*), and the recipient of the letter is told to accept their directions. With them occur the *prmnkr'* who have to inspect the boat that is to be repaired.[48] It is doubtless just accidental that we do not hear in

[45] *A.P.* 30:1, 29. Both belonged to the satrapy of *Ebir-nāri*, the region on "the other side of the river" (seen from the Mesopotamian angle). Cf., recently, Eilers, "Iranische Beamtennamen," 31 ff. Governors in Egypt are not impossible. Ashurbanipal speaks of *paḫāti* appointed in Egypt by his father, *Annals* I, 110.

[46] Cf. especially Albrecht Alt, "Die Rolle Samarias bei der Entstehung des Judentums," *Festschrift Otto Procksch* (Leipzig, 1934), 24. "Governor" means "satrap" in Ezra 5:3, 6; 6:6, 13; Neh. 3:7. It is possible, however, that the satrap of Ebir-nāri did not reside in Syria at this time. In the 3d year of Darius I, *Uštanni*, *paḫat Babili u Ebir-nāri* (here, too, "governor" for "satrap"!) evidently combined the administration of both areas and resided at Babylon. Cf. Peiser, *Texte*, 305. That the archives of the satrapy were at Babylon is presupposed also in Ezra 6:1.Before the satrapies were set up the realm was doubtless governed from Ecbatana. Ezra 6:2 appropriately mentions the discovery of a record of Cyrus there.

[47] The pronunciation is given by cuneiform texts; cf. Eilers, "Iranische Beamtennamen," 43 ff.

[48] Cf. Schaeder, *Beiträge*, 75 and Eilers, "Iranische Beamtennamen, 37. Eilers, *ibid.*, 123 f.,

the papyri of the *gizbārayyā* or "treasurers" of Ezra 7:21; the Aramaic title appears on objects from Persepolis.[49]

In the gubernatorial organization, as reflected in Ezra 4:9, the "chancellor" is followed by a list beginning with four classes of officials. The first word, rendered "the Dinaites" in the Bible translations, really means the "judges"—a fact no longer clear to the ancient editors and translators of the text.[50] This corresponds fully to the fact that the judges play an important role in the papyri. In Brooklyn No. 12:28 we hear of cases being brought "before *segēn*, lord and judge." Simplified phraseology gives the combination "*segēn* and lord," "*segēn* and judge," "lord and judge." The title segēn is derived from the Assyrian term for governor, *šaknu*, with which *bel-paḫāti* was synonymous.[51] However, it seems to be used in these late times in a very inferior sense. It appears in an Aramaic endorsement on a Babylonian text from the time of Darius II as equivalent of *ḫaṭru*, "overseer."[52] A segēn of the carpenters is mentioned in *A.P.* 26:9, 21. The use of the term in the books of Ezra and Nehemiah suggests that at Jerusalem the *sāgān* was not a foreign official but a native group leader.[53] In any case, the segēn in the judicial references is hardly more than a district head.

In the references to judicial action the name of a person is frequently joined with the judges. We hear of "*Trwḥ* and the court" or of "Damidata and his colleagues the judges." In several cases the person's title is specified: "The king's judges and Rauaka the commander," "Nephayan, the commander of Syene, and the judges

suggests reading *prmndry'* (with Sachau) instead of *prmnkry'*, as in *A.P.* 26:4, 8, but the latter is undoubtedly correct.

[49] Cf. Eilers, "Iranische Beamtennamen," 123 f., and Erich Schmidt, *The Treasury of Persepolis*, Oriental Institute Communications, *21* (Chicago, 1939), 62.

[50] On the Apharsathchites of Ezra 4:9, cf. Eilers, "Iranische Beamtennamen," 39, who explains this as *frēstak*, "messengers." In Ezra 5:6, the Apharsachites are "companions" of the governor; Eilers, 5 f., links them with the *(lù)iprasak* of Babylonian texts, an official concerned with public documents. The Tarpelites of Ezra 4:9 have not been satisfactorily explained according to Schaeder, *Beiträge*, 272, Eilers, "Iranische Beamtennamen, 39. Kurt Galling, "Kronzeugen des Artaxerxes," *ZAW*, *13*, 1951, 71, instead of seeking an Old Persian etymology, would connect the word with Greek "Tripolis." The place of that name in Syria, he believes, was the government seat of the Persian satrapy of Ebir-nari. See his "Die Syrisch-palästinische Küste nach Pseudo-Skylax," *ZDPV*, *61*, 1938, 72 ff., 90 ff. The Semitic name of the place is not preserved (Qiriath Shalosh? cf. Biblical Kiriath Arba, "city of four"). Galling supposes it was known by a Greek name exclusively. Against Eilers it should be noted that in Ezra 4:9 all the designations except "Dinaites" ought to be names of peoples (or nisbehs of regions or cities), rather than titles of officials.

[51] On šaknu cf. Eilers, "Kleinasiatisches," *ZDMG*, *94*, 1940, 201, 227. Dan. 3:2, etc., puts the "deputies" right after the satraps, an echo of the earlier importance of the title; Dan. 6:8 wrongly puts it before satrap. Cf. further the comments on No. 9:19.

[52] Cf. Clay, BEUP, *10*, 32, No. 126. Dan. 2:48 seems to know a title *rab-signīn* (plural of *sĕgēn*).

[53] Meyer, *Entstehung des Judentums*, 132 f. *Sāgān* is the Hebrew form.

of the province."[54] The commander of Syene thus exercised judicial functions. Perhaps he is the one meant by "lord" in the phrases quoted above. In one case we find a suit brought before *Rmndyn* the *prtrk* (*A.P.* 20) and Widrang the commander in "the court of Nepha (?)", without mention of judges, and an adoption is arranged before the commander who is given the additional title *hptḥpt'*, likewise acting without associate or colleagues.[55] On one occasion we hear of three judges going up to Syene especially to try a case that has been appealed.[56] When a matter like the sack of the Jewish temple is to be investigated it can be requested that the judges, the *tīftāyē* and the *gūškāyē* who are appointed over the province of *Tšṭrs*, be sent to investigate and report to the high official.[57] The former are the sheriffs of Dan. 3:2. The *gūškāyē* are "the listeners." A class of officials attached to the commander in his police or judicial functions were the [*p*]*rtky'*.[58]

The trial of cases and claims must have been an important part of the activity of the lower courts. The contending parties had to produce contracts, deeds, or agreements, and on the basis of these their claims were weighed. When the facts could not be ascertained from documents and when statements for which no witness could be adduced had to be resorted to, an oath was imposed — not upon the accuser but upon the accused. He had to swear by a god designated by the accuser or by the court that the charge was untrue, and if he did so the accuser's case evidently fell to the ground. If a man refused to swear it was assumed that he was in the wrong. The oath was used especially in the case of loans made by oral agreement, a custom allegedly first introduced into law by King Bocchoris (720–715 B.C.). But evidently the principle was extended to cover all cases in which there were no records. Thus a man swears to another concerning the ownership of a humble beast of burden, and a woman, to the husband from whom she is getting a divorce concerning property to which she lays claim.[59] Diodorus asserts, however, that there was a strong tendency to avoid letting things come to a point where

[54] *A.P.* 16:3; 6:6; 1:2; 16:6.

[55] *A.P.* 20:4 and Brooklyn No. 8. On reading the name *Ramman-daian* in Babylonian manner rather than as *Dmndyn*, cf. Schaeder, *Beiträge*, 258.

[56] *A.P.* 16:6.

[57] *A.P.* 27:9. Schaeder, *Beiträge*, 272, includes *tīftāyē* among the words not yet explicable. For *gūškāyē* he accepts the etymology given above, following Hübschmann, *Indogermanische Forschungen*, *1*, 1892, 264. Cf. Eilers, "Iranische Beamtennamen," 22 f.

[58] Eilers, *ibid.*, 119, reads and supplements the word in this manner; Cowley would take it as [*d*]*tky'*; cf. Schaeder, *Beiträge*, 65. Whether *ptyprs* in *A.P.* 37:2, 12 is the name of an official (the *pat-para-su* of Babylonian texts of this period according to Eilers, "Iranische Beamtennamen," 27 f.) seems doubtful. His translation, "Er ging die *patifrasa* Leute an; einer war Ǧiwaka; er ging den *patifrasa* an" is hardly satisfactory. It seems better to connect *ptyprs* with *ptp'*, "ration" (cf. n. 37, above).

[59] *A.P.* 44 and 14.

the oath had to be taken, for it damaged a man's reputation to be put in the position of having to swear, especially if that occurred repeatedly.[60] Behind such an oath, then, stands the failure to reach agreement.

An important function of government is the fixing of the monetary standard. The Elephantine texts, by revealing what denominations of money were used in business transactions, permit inferences as to the arrangements set up in the province of Egypt.

The modern reader must understand that money, in the days before the vogue of paper currencies, involved pieces of metal of certain weight which had an officially recognized value. The ancients had to be particularly conscious of this relationship of weight to worth, before minted coinage became the rule. Coins issued by mints naturally carried the assurance of governments and relieved the individual of much of the worry concerning the weight or purity of a piece offered in payment. But in many areas, even after the establishment of coinage, people continued to weigh out pieces of metal.

Our texts are quite particular in stressing the fact that a sum has been or will be paid "by stones of the king." The terminology is to be understood quite literally. The individual carried with him in a bag or pouch small stone weights ground down to the point where they accorded with official standards (=the stones of the king; compare II Sam. 14:26). There is a reference to that in Prov. 16:11, "A just balance and scales are Yahweh's. All the weights of the bag[61] are his work." We may imagine that the recipient of money always used his own stone weights, which he carried in a pouch, to check the weight of metal given him. Official stone weights of Persia have come to light in various quarters, and we may suppose that the government bureaus everywhere had such stones of the king to determine monetary values.

It is thus beyond any doubt that the reference to stones of the king in the Aramaic papyri have the Persian monetary system in mind. Only in one papyrus is a different system mentioned, and there payment is specified "according to the stones of Ptaḥ" (*A.P.* 11:2). This text, the date of which is missing, must have been written at a time when Persian rule was temporarily interrupted by an Egyptian revolution — the emphasis on Ptaḥ suggests that the standard of Memphis was used. Demotic texts from the time of Darius I also mention that standard, but it seems likely that *A.P.* 11 is of a later date, perhaps 455 B.C.[62]

The monetary system of Persia is well known.[63] The gold shekel or daric

[60] Diodorus I, 94 f.

[61] The phrase "weights of the bag" (*'abnē kīs*) doubtless goes back to Babylonian terminology. In an Assyrian list of stones we hear of an *aban kīsi* or "stone of the bag." See Weissbach, "Zur keilinschriftlichen Gewichtkunde," *ZDMG*, *65*, 1911, 635.

[62] See Meyer's note, "Zu den aramäischen Papyri . . .," *SPAW*, *47*, 1911, 1032.

[63] Meyer, *ibid.*, 1029 ff. Hultzsch, *Griechische und römische Metrologie*, 485 ff.

(weight of 8.4 grains) was basic to the system but was doubtless not in the hands of the common man. A silver shekel of two-thirds of the weight of the gold shekel (or 5.6 grains) was the ordinary medium of exchange. In value gold was to silver as $13^1/_2$:1. One gold shekel was thus worth 20 "median" silver shekels.

The subdivisions of the silver shekel in use in Elephantine were the quarter shekel (*rib'at,*) and the *ḥallur* (abbreviated a few times to *Ḥ* in Brooklyn No. 7), of which there were ten to the silver shekel. The *zuz* or half shekel does not seem to have been in use in 5th-century Elephantine but is mentioned in an Aramaic papyrus of about 300 B.C. (*A.P.* 81:22 f.). There, too, is found an abbreviation *M.* which probably stands for the *ma'ah* or one-twelfth of a shekel.[64] The monetary names bear testimony to the influence of the Babylonians on trade and commerce.

In the Persian era with which we are concerned, the most important unit above the shekel was the *karsh* (*karša* in the cuneiform texts) or ten-shekel weight. An official one-karsh weight has been found at Persepolis,[65] and a two-karsh weight (=20 shekels or one-third of a Babylonian mina or one gold daric) is also known.[66]

A peculiar formula that occurs often in the papyri continuing the phrase "silver karsh by stones of the king" is "silver 2 *R.* to the ten" (or "to the karsh"). The *R.* is here clearly an abbreviation of the word rib'at, quarter, which was chiefly in use for the quarter shekel.[67] Cowley observed that money paid by stones of the king is sometimes described as "refined silver" (*A.P.* 5:7; 28:11, 12) and inferred that this was pure silver as distinguished from silver with an alloy.[68] The latter, according to him, is meant with "silver 2 *R.* to the 10" (with 2 *R.* or one-half shekel — or 5 per cent — alloy in ten shekels). He was on the right track, but he erred in differentiating the two descriptions. Actually, they are merely different ways of saying the same thing. This is shown by a cuneiform text from the Persepolis treasury from the time of Darius I.[69] We learn from it that money offered in payment of taxes was not accepted at face value but was tested to see if the silver were first, second or third grade. The depreciation from adulteration of first-

[64] See Lidzbarski, *Ephemeris, 2,* 248.

[65] Schmidt, *op. cit.*, 62.

[66] See Weissbach, "Neue Beiträge zur keilinschriftlichen Gewichtkunde," *ZDMG, 70,* 1916, 78 ff.

[67] Meyer, *SPAW, 47,* 1911, 1031, argued that in this formula the gold standard was being applied (2 gold quarter-shekels to the silver karsh). Lidzbarski held that 2 silver quarter-shekels are meant and that this represents an agio to be paid on the karsh. Alfred R. Bellinger calls my attention to A. Segrè, "Circolazione Tolemaica et Pretolemaica in Egitto," *Rivista Italiana di Numismatica,* 1920, 6 ff.; the author assumes that the karsh was modified in Egypt to accommodate calculation in terms of Attic and Phoenican standards, which were current there, while Persian coins were not.

[68] Cowley, *A.P.*, xxx.

[69] G. C. Cameron, *Persepolis Treasury Tablets,* 200.

grade "white silver," according to George C. Cameron, varies from an almost infinitesimal 0.416 per cent to a high of 5 per cent. The ten-shekel piece, or *karša*, served as an index to classify each item. The "refined silver" of the Elephantine texts is obviously such white silver. Since a high of 5 per cent depreciation is allowable within this first grade, the statement "2 *R.* to the 10" (one-half silver shekel to the ten-shekel piece, or 5 per cent) would appear to indicate *the limit of impurity permissible*. In the standard of Ptaḥ, as given in *A.P.* 11:2, we have the rate of one sh(ekel) to ten — in other words the Egyptian money of the time was of poorer quality, with a 10 per cent depreciation permissible.

The decline of Persian power and the growth of Greek influence in Egypt is vividly illustrated by the fact that the Greek *stater* came into common use there. This was proved for the fifth year of Amyrtaeus by *A.P.* 35:4 and illustrated by the undated letter *A.P.* 37:12.[70] In Brooklyn No. 12:5, 14, we have fresh vindication of it for the fourth year of Artaxerxes II. In *A.P.* 35:4, 7, 9, the stater is given as the equivalent of two shekels. This is confirmed by the new text which also supplies the interesting and explicit identification of the stater as "money of Yawan," i. e., of Greece.[71] No doubt the stater used was Attic money, which according to Xenophon was noted both for purity of metal and exactness of weight.[72] Indeed, Attic merchants could convert their coins elsewhere at a profit and then buy more wares with the local coinage, while other foreign merchants had to give discounts to convert their money. It stands to reason, then, that it was not only the Attic political influence but the excellence of the Attic money that brought the Greek stater to the fore in Egypt at this time.

[70] It is also found in the fragment *A.P.* 67, No. 9, and perhaps in the inventory *A.P.* 61:8.

[71] See Hultzsch, *op. cit.*, 232 ff.

[72] Yawan (Javan), i. e., Ionia or the Ionians, is found in the Old Testament, Gen. 10:2, 4; Isa. 66:19; Ezek. 27:13; I Chron. 1:5, 7. The Egyptian texts have *wynn* (with metathesis of *w* and *y*) for Ionians, the final *n* being the Aramaic plural ending; see Kurt Sethe, "Spuren der Perserherrschaft in Ägypten," *NGGW*, 1916, 133.

4. NATURE AND ORIGIN OF THE JEWISH COLONY

THE Elephantine papyri draw the curtain on a scene for which the sources concerning the 5th century B.C. known up to 1906 had not prepared us. We see established in Yeb a Jewish community, having houses, families, slaves, and a temple dedicated to the god of their people. They were part of a garrison (*ḥailā*) guarding this frontier outpost. We find letters addressed "To my lords Yedoniah, Ma'uziyah, Uriah and the garrison," "To my brethren Yedoniah and his colleagues, the Judaean garrison," and a list of contributors to the temple is earmarked, "These are the names of the members of the Judaean garrison who gave money."[1] We hear also of the "Syenian garrison,"[2] but it is not immediately clear whether that is distinct from the Judaean or includes it. Indubitably, then, these papyri show the existence of a Jewish colony, the members of which were engaged in military service to the Persian crown.[3]

The garrison cannot have been very large. A fragmentary papyrus, *A.P.* 24, lists the rations issued to the Syenian garrison and the names of the persons to whom they were given. Among the names are a few Hebrew ones — notably that of Haggai b. Shema'iah, the scribe who wrote a number of the new papyri. A summary in lines 27 f. gives the total of persons listed as 54.[4] That all these men were in active service may be inferred from the fact that they received rations, for the latter were doubtlessly issued only to such and not to those living in retirement on allotments of tax-free lands.[5]

The Jews and others of the Elephantine garrison are described as belonging to the *degel* of N. N. This word, which basically means "standard," is found in that sense in the Old Testament, notably in the Book of Numbers, and appears in some late Jewish sources in the sense of "troop detachment."[6] Degels of Egyptians are

[1] *A.P.* 37:1; 21:1; 22:1. [2] *A.P.* 24:33.

[3] Aimé-Giron, *Textes*, 59, erroneously held that ḥailā, which occurs also in the fragment from Saqqāra (*A.P.* 318, l. 6), meant a "colony" or "quarter."

[4] Of these, two received 1 ½ ardab of barley, 22 received 1 ardab, 30 received 2 ½ ardab. This was no doubt a monthly ration (cf. Chapter 3, n. 33, above).

[5] Herodotus II, 168.

[6] The word was taken as *regel* (literally "foot") by S.-C. In his review in *Theologische Literaturzeitung*, *32*, 1907, 1 f., Emil Schürer urged the alternate reading *degel*, which Cowley then accepted

mentioned and we hear of Egyptian troops in action.[7] A differentiation is made at Yeb between "the men of the degel" (*ba'alē degel*) and "the men of the town" (*ba'alē ḳiryā*),[8] so that we must suppose that the members of the military group stood apart from other residents; however, the Jewish leaders refer to themselves as "men of Yeb" (*ba'alē Yeb*),[9] which would seem to be equivalent to the latter phrase. An interchangeable term for degel seems to be "hundred," and if so it reveals the numerical strength of such a unit.[10] The degels are designated by the names of their officers — invariably Persian or Babylonian. In the fragments of a journal page from the Memphis arsenal of 472 B.C. (cf. p. 16), we see that there, too, degels under Persian officers occur. Over the entire garrison stood the commander (*rab-ḥailā*), who resided in Syene. Of higher rank still is the *prtrk* in Yeb, though it is not clear whether this is a purely military title.[11]

The Jews of this garrison had lived here prior to Persian rule, which began in 525 B.C., for they state that their temple existed under the kings of Egypt.[12] They must have formed a military colony from the very outset. No other motive for their coming to such a remote outpost is discernible. They could hardly have made their living here by cultivation of the soil. At Assuan and Elephantine there was no livelihood except in trade, shipping, stone quarrying, guarding the border, and tending to taxes on incoming and outgoing goods. Moreover, some special reason for royal favor is required to account for the fact that the Jews had received the unusual privilege of having a temple of their own god close to the sanctuary of the great Egyptian god Khnum who was the official lord of the region.

When could such a colony have been established? At the latest in the middle of the 6th century, at the earliest in the 7th.[13]

in *A.P.* In the Dead Sea scroll of "The Wars of the Children of Light with the Children of Darkness" (E. L. Sukenik, *Megilloth Genuzoth* [Jerusalem, 1948], 19, in Hebrew), *'ōth*, "sign," is used for the military standards. On the use of standards in Hellenistic times, cf. Jean Lesquier, *Les institutions militaires de l'Égypte* (Paris, 1911), 109 f.

[7] *A.P.* 27:1; 30:8.

[8] *A.P.* 5:9, 13:10; 46:6; cf. *A.P.* 20:11.

[9] *A.P.* 30:22. In 33:6 some of the same men are "Syenians holding property in Yeb."

[10] In *A.P.* 22:19 the concluding names from the "hundred of Sin-iddin" are listed; in the next line is the caption for those from "the hundred of Nabu-'aḳab." Cf. also *A.P.* 2:6, 8 and 3:11; Cowley, *A.P.* p. 6, thinks the hundred a subdivision of the degel.

[11] On *rab ḥailā* cf. Assyrian *rab ḫiyāli*. Doubtless the lower officers had titles corresponding to Assyrian *rab mē*, "chief of a hundred," *rab ešrite*, "chief of ten." *Prtrk* occurs on a coin from Iran of Seleucid times, with the legend in Aramaic script, "Bgrz, the prtrk of the gods." Cf. Eilers, "Eine mittelpersische Wortform . . .," *ZDMG*, *90*, 1936, 193 ff. On the title, cf. Schaeder, *Beiträge*, 60, Eilers, "Iranische Beamtennamen," 23, 119.

[12] *A.P.* 30:13.

[13] One might argue that the soldiers of Manasseh, King of Judah, who went to Egypt with the forces of Ashurbanipal in the campaign of 667 B.C. could have been among those left behind to

A theory enjoying strong sponsorship holds that the founding of the Jewish colony took place under Psammetichus I (664–609 B.C.). We must recall that this prince from Saïs, an Assyrian protégé, had fled from Egypt when the Ethiopians seized the country, but had been restored to his position when Ashurbanipal reconquered the land in 663. When opportunity offered, because of Assyria's involvement in struggles in Asia Minor and the north, he shook off the Assyrian yoke and sought to unify Egypt. Gyges of Lydia sent him auxiliary troops, Ionian and Carian mercenaries, who helped him to establish his power and independence.[14] The warrior caste of the *Ma*,[15] which had exploited the land under Ethiopian and Assyrian rule, was doubtless his chief opponent and lost much of its power as a result of his victory. It must have been at this time and in consequence of this disaffection that the garrison at Elephantine revolted — if any credence may be attached to a report of such an event preserved by Herodotus.[16] The Egyptian soldiers, we learn, had had no furlough for three years and finally decided to rebel and go over to the Ethiopians. Psammetichus pursued them and urged them not to abandon their native gods and their wives and children (doubtless imagined as living in central or northern Egypt). But they nevertheless went over to the Ethiopians and after aiding the king of that people against certain rebels were assigned a territory of their own. Meyer would see in this tale an actual echo of the exodus of a good part of the old Libyan warrior caste, which was not willing to adapt itself to changed conditions that reduced its power and influence. Such a situation would of course provide the occasion for settling a new garrison at Elephantine, and Psammetichus I might well have induced some of his Asiatic mercenaries, including a Jewish contingent, to take over the post.

Another piece of information from Palestine lends support to such a theory. Within the time of Psammetichus I a book was published in Judaea which seems to have knowledge of the sending of Jews to Egypt. This was the so-called Deuteronomic Law (preserved in the Book of Deuteronomy), promulgated about 621 B.C. under King Josiah, as related in II Kings 22–23. In curbing the power of the future

guard the border and thus have been founders of the colony. See the inscription Cyl. C, I, l. 25, Maximilian Streck, *Assurbanipal und die letzten Assyrischen Könige bis zum Untergang Niniveh's*, Vorderasiatische Bibliothek, 7, (Leipzig, 1916), Teil II, 139.

[14] Cf. Meyer, *Geschichte*, *3*, 133, 145. The Pharaoh gave them crown lands on both sides of the Nile below Bubastis. The colonies were called "camps." Amasis later transferred them to Memphis; Herodotus II, 154, 163. A Jewish camp existed in the Delta in Caesar's time (Josephus, *Ant.* XIV, 133).

[15] Meyer, *Geschichte*, *3*, 146; *2*, 30 ff.

[16] Herodotus II, 30–31. He calls them *automoloi*, "deserters." It was a four months' journey from Elephantine to where these people lived. On the interpretation of this tale see H. Schäfer, "Die Auswanderung der Krieger unter Psammetich I . . .," *Klio*, *4*, 1904, 155 ff., and Spiegelberg, "Ägyptologische Randglossen zu Herodot," *ZÄS*, *42*, 1906, 95 f.

Jewish rulers this law says that the king is "not to multiply horses to himself nor cause the people to return to Egypt that he may multiply horses (17:16)." "People" here can hardly mean the whole nation but must just refer to a Jewish group. We must assume that a Jewish king prior to Josiah — perhaps Manasseh — had actually furnished Psammetichus I with some Jewish manpower in return for a delivery of horses for his Judaean cavalry.[17] The new constitution, looking back on this deal, forbade the Jewish kings to make such arrangements in the future.[18] It is not necessary to suppose, however, that Jewish auxiliaries went down to Egypt when Psammetichus I first seized power over all Egypt. We hear that he besieged the Palestinian city of Ashdod for twenty-nine years (said to be the longest siege on record),[19] and thus for a long time his officers were close to the border of Judaea, where they could have recruited Jewish mercenaries or obtained them by negotiation with the Jewish king.

A second view would hold that the founding of the Jewish colony of Elephantine stands in close connection with the Deuteronomic reformation itself.[20] The latter, as mirrored in the Book of Deuteronomy and described in II Kings 22–23, proceeded in puritanical fashion to purge the Jewish religion of certain old customs and institutions objectionable to the prophetic, priestly party that brought it about. All the "high places" were abolished, and hereafter there was to be only one temple where it was lawful to bring sacrifice — that of Jerusalem. Such drastic changes, effected by the instruments of political power, must naturally have evoked great dissatisfaction in those fond of the older, popular religious ways. We can imagine that many may have fled the country at this time. Many priests in particular were now jobless. Since Egypt was ever the natural haven for malcontents from Palestine, a group of Judaean religious refugees might well have sought asylum and established a temple there. The religion of the Elephantine Jews is certainly of the "pre-Deuteronomic" variety (Chapter 8). Still, the theory that a group of Jewish refugees sought religious freedom in Egypt does not explain why they should have gone to Elephantine.

A somewhat later origin of the Jewish colony, under Psammetichus II (593–589 B.C.), has also been advocated.[21] The Letter of Aristeas, of Hellenistic-Jewish origin, in referring to several occasions on which Jews had come to the land of the Nile, states: "Even before this time [i. e., that of Ptolemy] large numbers of Jews

[17] Carl Steuernagel, "Bemerkungen zu den neuentdeckten jüdischen Papyrusurkunden . . .," *Theologische Studien und Kritiken*, *82*, 1909, 98.

[18] Meyer, *Papyrusfund*, 23; *Geschichte*, 3^2, 146, accepted Steuernagel's thesis and his interpretation of Deut. 17:16.

[19] Herodotus II, 157. Jer. 25:20 in 604 B.C. speaks of "the remnant of Ashdod."

[20] Vincent, 288 ff. The idea of Van Hoonacker, *Une communauté*, 83 ff., that they were Samaritans from the Bethel neighborhood is made impossible by the designation "Judaeans."

[21] Sachau, *Aramäische Papyrus und Ostraka*, xiii.

had come into Egypt with the Persians, and in an earlier period still others had been sent to Egypt to help Psammetichus in his campaign against the king of the Ethiopians."[22] While the letter is relatively late, ca. 120 B.C. the report could conceivably rest on good information. The Psammetichus referred to can hardly be Psammetichus I, for in his day the relations between Egypt and Ethiopia were peaceful. During his reign the new Saïtic dynasty of Egypt was at first much more interested in Mediterranean and Syrian relations than in southern affairs. A campaign against the Ethiopians, however, actually took place under Psammetichus II in 589 B.C. and so he may be the one meant by Aristeas. It is now known, furthermore, that this same ruler carried on a campaign in Palestine in the year before his Nubian campaign[23] and thus could easily have been able to recruit a Jewish force. Foreign groups, including Greeks and Phoenicians, took part in the latter campaign and left record of their presence in graffiti at Abu Simbel in Lower Nubia.[24] In the light of the Aristeas letter, one may assume that a Jewish group was among the participants, and among those left behind to guard the Nubian border when the campaign was over.

Another theory possessing considerable attraction places the origin of the Jewish colony in the time after the fall of Jerusalem in 587 B.C. A new Pharaoh, Apries — called Hophra in Jer. 44:30 — had come to the throne in Egypt. The encouragement he gave to Jews and other Palestinian groups to rebel against Chaldean rule brought them disaster. Nebuchadrezzar's army came down to Palestine in the winter of 589/8 and besieged Jerusalem.

It stands to reason that the Jewish partisans of the Egyptian ruler fled to Egypt when Nebuchadrezzar's army drew near and when the Pharaoh's promised support failed to materialize. Whole detachments of Jewish soldiery, furthermore, may well have deserted from outposts in the south country and likewise have taken refuge there. It would be comprehensible, too, that a temple should be established in Egypt for the Jewish god after the one at Jerusalem had fallen. The analogy of the Leontopolis temple founded by a fugitive high priest in the Nile Delta in Ptolemaic times with the sovereign's support even suggests the possibility that Apries may have lent similar aid to a Jewish high priest of his time.[25] It may be considered only a variant of this theory of the origin of the colony after the fall of Jerusalem if it is advocated that survivors of the Chaldean invasion, finding life too severe

[22] *Aristeas*, 13. Cf. the translation in R. H. Charles, *Apocrypha and Pseudepigrapha of the Old Testament* (Oxford, 1913), *2*, 96.

[23] Cf. Alt, "Psammetich II in Palästina und Elephantine," *ZAW*, *30*, 1910, 288 ff. On the Egyptian-Jewish relations of this time cf. also Alt, *Israel und Ägypten* . . . (Greifswald, 1909), 100 ff.

[24] Cf. K. A. Wiedemann, "Die griechischen Inschriften von Abu Simbel," *Rheinisches Museum für Philologie*, *35*, 1880, 365 ff. Aimé-Giron, *Textes*, 84 ff.

[25] Cf. Otto Stähelin, "Elephantine und Leontopolis," *ZAW*, *28*, 1908, 180 ff. Josephus, *Ant.* XIII, 62–73.

in the devastated and impoverished land, went down to Egypt to seek better living conditions and that such a group, analogous to that which took Jeremiah along against his will, was settled at Elephantine.[26]

The information we get from the book of that prophet, however, does not seem to support the idea that the colony originated in the period just mentioned. It is evident from the narrative given there that a good many Jews were already in Egypt when he arrived. The prophet, in proclaiming "the word that came to Jeremiah concerning all the Jews that dwell in the land of Egypt," specifies colonies at "Migdol (Pelusion), Taḥpanḥes (Daphne), Memphis and in the country of Pathros." The last-mentioned geographical concept is of particular interest in this connection. It appears as *Patures* in a title of the Assyrian king Esarhaddon, who calls himself "King of the kings of Muṣur, Patures, and Cush,"[27] and evidently specifies a district in Upper Egypt.[28] Undoubtedly Elephantine would fall within this area, but since the island city is not specifically mentioned we cannot know whether there was already a Jewish colony there in Jeremiah's time. All we do know is that there were Jews in Pathros, whose representatives met in a convocation and heard the prophet from Jerusalem (44:15 ff.).[29] The prediction he delivered at that occasion that henceforth no Jew in Egypt would use the name of Yahweh could hardly have been uttered had the Elephantine temple already existed. The group that built that house of God cannot have been as deeply sunk in paganism as the one confronting the prophet at the occasion referred to. Possibly the inner strength of the Yahweh religion reasserted itself as time went on and the demoralization brought about by the catastrophe passed. The ministry of Jeremiah, who disappears from the scene with that prophecy, may have contributed to such a renascence. But time must be allowed for such a development.

An Egyptian inscription found at Elephantine on a statue of Nesuḥor may have a bearing on the date of the origin of the Jewish colony. Nesuḥor, a man of princely

[26] Hedwig Anneler, *Die Juden von Elephantine* (Bern, 1912), 115 f.

[27] See Luckenbill, *Ancient Records of Assyria*, 2, 553 ff.; cf. Meyer, *Geschichte*, 3^2, 79.

[28] Pathros and *Tšṭrs* are related expressions; see Spiegelberg, *OLZ*, 7, 1904, 10. Perhaps the latter designation came up with the Persian organization. Pathros is viewed as the homeland of Egyptian sovereignty in Ezek. 29:14, a view that must have come up as a result of the Ethiopian domination. On Taḥpanḥes-Daphne see Albright, "Baal Zephon," *Festschrift Alfred Bertholet* (Tübingen, 1950), 14.

[29] The question whether the mention of Pathros is original in the Jeremiah passages is raised and answered negatively by Steuernagel, *op. cit.*, 6. It seems unlikely to him that Jewish men and women of Upper Egypt would have traveled as far north as Tahpanhes (near the border city Pelusion), where Jeremiah lived (Jer. 43:7), and equall yunlikely that the prophet would have journeyed as far south as Pathros. But the Elephantine letters show Jews traveling far, and Jer. 44:15 ff. is so well confirmed by the Hermopolis papyri (see p. 86) that the assertion of Jeremiah's having addressed Jews of Pathros cannot be entirely discounted, however the actual meeting of the parties is to be explained.

rank under Pharaoh Apries, was governor of "the gate of the countries of the south."[30] Among the foreign elements at Elephantine he names Syrians (*'ȝmw*), Greek islanders (*ḥȝnbw*), and Asiatics (*styw*). There was thus quite an international colony here at the time. Since no Aramaic Elephantine text contains any Greek names we may imagine that the Greek element had left this locality by the time the papyri were written.

In lines 6 ff. of the inscription of Nesuḥor we hear that the Elephantine mercenaries were rebellious and planned to desert to Nubia, but were led by Nesuḥor "to the place where His Majesty [Apries] was" and that the latter punished them. This, it has been suggested, marks the end of the garrison settled on the island by Psammetichus I (or II). A new garrison must have been appointed and may well have contained the Jewish element.[31] Since Nesuḥor gives no date for the occurrence of the rebellion it could have taken place rather late in the reign of Apries (589–569 B.C.). However, even the latest possible date hardly allows enough time for a revival of the Yahweh religion among the Jewish exiles such as seems requisite to justify the founding of a Yahweh Temple.

But one must account not only for the presence of the Jews but for the fact that they so frequently call themselves "Aramaeans of Syene" and that they speak Aramaic. Any Jews who came to this area, either as a military force in the 7th century or as refugees in the 6th century, certainly were Hebrew-speaking. That they had abandoned their native tongue and spoke Aramaic in the days of our papyri is obvious. It is untenable to assert that they used Aramaic only in legal and other documents because the Persians used Aramaic as an official language. A language lives only through a population that speaks it. The Jews of Elephantine must have been received into an Aramaic-speaking environment and have been absorbed by it.

That Syene was not the only Aramaean colony in Egypt is known by the occurrence of Aramaic papyri and inscriptions in Memphis, Hermopolis, and elsewhere. But when did Aramaeans come to Egypt in such numbers as to establish colonies which could absorb or engulf Jews and others of Canaanitic speech?

This is as difficult to answer as is the question of the origin of the Jewish part of the colony. At the time of the fall of Damascus in 732 B.C. numerous Aramaeans may have fled to Egypt, so that Aramaean colonies there could be ancient. Some of the occasions that could have brought Jews down, and that have been described above, could also have brought the Aramaeans. The absence of Aramaic as of

[30] Cf. James H. Breasted, *Ancient Records of Egypt* (Chicago, 1906–07), *4*, 989. A detailed study is found in Schäfer, "Die Auswanderung" (see n. 16, above). On the *ḥȝnbw* see Jozef M. A. Janssen, *Bibliotheca Orientalis*, *8*, 1951, 213 ff.

[31] W. Struwe, "Zur Geschichte der jüdischen Kolonie von Elephantine," *Bulletin de l'Académie des Sciences de U. S. S. R.*, Ser. 6, *20*, 1926, 445 ff. W. F. Albright, *Archaeology and the Religion of Israel* (Baltimore, 1942), 168, gives this theory his support.

Hebrew graffiti among those at Abu Simbel would seem to suggest that neither Aramaeans nor Jews were among the mercenaries of Psammetichus II in 589 B.C. The unruly element that caused trouble at Elephantine under Apries may have been the Greek mercenaries. The Syrians Nesuḥor mentions could have been Aramaeans, but were probably Phoenicians (in view of the Abu Simbel graffiti).[32] It seems probable that replacements that may have been brought into the Elephantine garrison at this time consisted of a group of Aramaeans strong enough to dominate it linguistically. Into this community, we think, Jewish elements were introduced later, perhaps under Amasis (569–526 B.C.), and continued to serve under the Persians. Certainly the Jews were already fully Aramaized by the time the earliest known Aramaic papyrus from Elephantine, *A.P.* 1 of 495 B.C., was written.

[32] Worship of Phoenician divinities at Elephantine suggests that this element had once been stronger in the garrison. A "Tyrian camp" at Memphis is mentioned by Herodotus II, 112, thus supporting the existence of Phoenician mercenaries.

5. TEXTS REFLECTING EVERYDAY LIFE IN THE COMMUNITY OF ELEPHANTINE

WHAT knowledge we have of the manners and customs of the Jewish colony of Elephantine is derived from the papyri. In order to gain a notion of how people lived there one must, of course, read between the lines of the documents, which consist mainly of deeds and contracts interspersed with a few official and private letters. Private letters, which one might expect to furnish intimate, personal details, offer little precise information. Yet certain personalities stand out from the others in the mass of documents, and one can form an idea of how the affairs of daily life were conducted and by what laws the people of the colony were governed.

One of the chief points of interest in the Brooklyn papyri lies in the fact that they are concerned with many of the same personalities who appear in the documents published by Sayce-Cowley and Sachau. The name of Yedoniah b. Gemariah, who appears as a witness in Brooklyn No. 10:20, would be only a signature if we did not know from earlier publications that he was the head of the Jewish community, who represented it in the negotiations with the Persian authorities and who acted as collector of the temple funds (*A.P.* 30:1; 22:121). With the aid of the new texts we can likewise add greatly to the family history of such a citizen as Meshullam b. Zakkur, who figured prominently in documents previously known.

From the Brooklyn collection there also emerge new personalities, notably Anani(ah) b. Azariah, the servitor of the god Yahu, his wife Tamut, his daughter Yehoyishma, and his son-in-law Anani b. Haggai. We learn something not only of the private affairs of this family but of laws and customs of their day hitherto unknown.

Most of the papyri found in Elephantine are legal documents. These mirror a rich variety of situations and employ a precise and well-developed legal terminology. The people of Yeb were evidently accustomed to bringing suit for real or supposed rights, and they safeguarded every transaction of everyday life with agreements and contracts drawn up in accordance with well-established patterns.

When the Persians took over the Neo-Babylonian realm in 539 B.C they permited its laws, manners, and customs to continue. Since they spoke a strange

KRAVITZ MEMORIAL LIBRARY
of Park Synagogue
55-2230

northern tongue that could not possibly be forced on their Semitic subjects, there was little else for them to do but to govern with the help of those who had governed previously. Trusted Persian officials were naturally put in the highest posts and Persian innovations were of course introduced, but fundamentally the Babylonian system continued as before. The bureaucracy sent by the Persians into new provinces such as Egypt (in 525 B.C.) was composed of men who were used to the Babylonian way of doing things. It is not surprising, therefore, to find the people of Elephantine producing legal and business documents in which the Babylonian influence is as obvious as is that of the English common law in contemporary American legal documents.

The first principle of Babylonian law was that the validity of any legal act depended on its being recorded in writing and attested by witnesses.[1] That principle also prevailed at Elephantine. The papyri are often (though not always) signed by the witnesses in person. After being written they were rolled up and the two ends of the roll folded back toward the middle. A string was tied around the roll and a clay seal affixed to the knot so that it could not be opened without breaking the seal (pl. XXI). The seals used for sealing the intact Brooklyn documents were widely divergent in type, ranging from scarabs of earlier Egyptian periods to intaglios of the Persian epoch (fig. 6 and discussion by Mr. John D. Cooney below). On the outside of the roll was usually penned a memorandum ("endorsement" or "docket") suggesting the nature of the contents (pl. XIX). In some cases this amounts almost to a classification such as would be used in a filing system. The most general word for a document is *sefar*. The endorsements contain such designations as a "document of a house," "document of removal," and the texts themselves have allusions to "document of sale" and "document of marriage."[2]

The procedure followed in executing legal documents is described in the Old Testament in Jer. 32:8 ff., and there is every reason to believe that things were not done much differently at Elephantine. The prophet Jeremiah, we are told, bought a field at Anathoth from his cousin Chanamel. The former wrote the document,[3] sealed it, had it attested by witnesses, weighed out the seventeen shekels of silver constituting the purchase price, and then had the text, together with an open (i. e., unsealed) duplicate, put in an earthenware jar for preservation, in the presence of the witnesses who had signed it. It is not at all clear that papyrus was used by Jeremiah; it could have been leather, which doubtless was more readily available in alestine as writing material. The most surprising thing in the descrip-

[1] See Schorr, *Urkunden des altbabylonischen Zivil- und Prozessrechts*, Vorderasiatische Bibliothek, *5* (Leipzig, 1913), xiii.

[2] See *A.P.* 14:4; 35:5. Brooklyn Nos. 10:7; 12:9, 18.

[3] It is most unusual for the *buyer* to make out a document; ordinarily the seller does this. There must be a special reason for Jeremiah's writing the document; perhaps the claim he has to this property, according to v. 7, provides the reason. Cf. Lev. 25:25 f., 48.

tion is that the witnesses signed *after* the roll was sealed.[4] Certainly the known Aramaic papyrus rolls are too small for inscribing with names of witnesses after sealing. The preparation of an unsealed duplicate, too, seems to be distinctive. The Aramaic papyri furnish no clear evidence of that custom for the legal texts, but Greek papyri of the 4th century B.C. found at Elephantine[5] show that the custom of providing a duplicate was then current. These papyri, as well as many demotic papyri, were found in jars. Whether the Aramaic papyri from Elephantine were also originally stored in jars we do not know, but the marvelous state of preservation of the Booklyn texts makes that seem likely in their case.

Most of the Aramaic legal papyri bear double dates. The scribes were evidently obliged to give not only the date according to the Egyptian calendar, which was naturally the one used by the Egyptian people, but also that according to the Babylonian calendar, which was official in the western Persian realm.[6] The Babylonian date usually takes precedence, though in Brooklyn Nos. 1 and 6 the opposite holds true. The oldest text with a double dating is *A.P.* 5 of 471 B.C. Several earlier texts (Bauer-Meissner which, however, is not from Elephantine and *A.P.* 1) have solely the Egyptian dating and the same is true of the youngest texts of the Brooklyn collection (Nos. 11, 12, 13). It is possible, with the help of chronological tables, to convert Egyptian dates into the Julian calendar without error.[7] Babylonian dates from 626 B.C on are now also convertible, with an occasional margin of error of one day. If there is a frequent discrepancy of a day or so between the Egyptian and Babylonian dates we must bear in mind the fact that we are dealing with two different systems.[8] The Babylonian days ran from sunset to sunset, while the Egyptian days ran from daybreak to daybreak. If a papyrus was written in the

[4] This fits with what is stated in the Mishnah, *Baba Bathra* 10, 1. Cf. note on Brooklyn No. 1:10. Cowley, *A.P.* xxix, erroneously assumes a cuneiform tablet and envelope were used by Jeremiah.

[5] See Otto Rubensohn, "Elephantine Papyri," *Ägyptische Urkunden aus den Königlichen Museen in Berlin*, Sonderheft, 1907, 6 ff. In the case of these papyri the text was written twice on one sheet with a space between the two sections of writing. A slit was made in the blank space from each edge, the upper section was rolled up, strings drawn through holes made in the sheet, and seals affixed. The lower section was then also folded and rolled, remaining attached to the sealed roll for convenient perusal. On the endorsements as survivals of the more elaborate procedure just described, see Mariano San Nicolò, *Beiträge zur Rechtsgeschichte im Bereich keilinschriftlicher Rechtsquellen* (Oslo, 1931), 129, n. On Aramaean scribes see R. P. Dougherty, "Writing upon Parchment and Papyrus among the Babylonians and Assyrians," *JAOS*, *48*, 1928, 109 f.

[6] See R. A. Parker, "Persian and Egyptian Chronology," *AJSL*, *58*, 1941, 285 ff. A fresh discussion of the double dates in the Aramaic Papyri, including those here published, will be found in a forthcoming article by S. H. Horn and L. H. Wood, "The Fifth Century Jewish Calendar at Elephantine" *JNES*, *12*, 1953.

[7] Eduard Mahler, *Chronologische Vergleichungstabellen*, (Wien, 1889).

[8] R. A. Parker and Waldo Dubberstein, *Babylonian Chronology 626 B. C. — A. D. 45*, Studies in Ancient Oriental Civilization, No. 24, (Chicago, 1942). On the differences of the systems see Parker, *AJSL*, *58*, 1941, 289, n.

evening the Babylonian date would accordingly be a day earlier at Elephantine than at Babylon, because the new moon was visible forty-seven minutes sooner at the former place. When the dates are drastically out of line, as is the case with Brooklyn 8 and *A.P.* 8 and 10, some scribal error must be suspected.

Since Egypt was under Assyrian domination from 671 to 663 B.C. and under Persian rule from 525 B.C., even the native Egyptians were naturally influenced to some degree by Babylonian custom in the conduct of legal and business affairs. It is not surprising, accordingly, to find demotic texts comparable to those of the Aramaic papyri. Indeed, these two classes of texts are closer to each other than to the cuneiform which influenced both of them — a fact showing that the Elephantine colonists, while adhering to Babylonian precedent, were not unaffected by their Egyptian environment.[9]

In the following pages we shall give a brief survey of the known Elephantine texts, including those here published, grouping them according to contents. We shall begin with the documents dealing with marriage. All marriages were, in accordance with ancient and modern Eastern custom, arranged between the groom and some person acting for the bride — usually, of course, her father. The husband gave a bridal gift (*mohar*) to the person acting for the bride, and the bride brought her own possessions with her to her new home. In case of divorce the husband seems to have lost the mohar and the wife could take back her possessions to her father's house. But the wife also could sue for divorce. In that case she had to pay her husband "the money of divorce" but retained the right to her possessions. If her husband expelled her (without resorting to legal measures) he was obliged to pay a penalty.

Unique, thus far, is a text published by Sachau (*A.P.* 48) and containing part of a betrothal agreement.[10] It was made between Meshullam b. Zakkur and Maḥseiah b. Yedoniah. Meshullam contracts to marry Maḥseiah's daughter (doubtless the Mibṭaḥiah of texts that will shortly engage us) and agrees to pay Maḥseiah a compensation in event of failure to live up to the agreement. This contract was probably executed before Mibṭaḥiah had reached marriageable age.

When we next meet with that woman she is the wife of Yezaniah b. Uriah (*A.P.* 8, dated 460 B.C.). No document exists to show whether she had previously

[9] On the background see San Nicolò, "Vorderasiatisches Rechtsgut in den ägyptischen Eheverträgen der Perserzeit," *OLZ*, *30*, 1927, 217 ff. Ulrike Türck, "Die Stellung der Frau in Elephantine als Ergebnis persisch-babylonischen Rechtseinflusses," *ZAW*, *46*, 1928, 166 ff. The demotic marriage texts are of interest here, too, especially the one from Elephantine: W. Erichsen, "Ein demotischer Ehevertrag aus Elephantine," *APAW*, 1939, Heft 8. See also Spiegelberg, "Der Papyrus Libbey," *Schriften der Wissenschaftlichen Gesellschaft zu Strassburg* (1907), *1*, 9 f. Georg Möller, "Zwei ägyptische Eheverträge," *APAW*, 1918. Contrast also the oldest Greek marriage contract in Rubensohn, *op. cit.*, 18 ff.

[10] The significance of this text has not hitherto been properly emphasized.

married Meshullam b. Zakkur. Since we find her involved in divorce proceedings with Pi' b. Paḥi in 440 B.C. (see below) she must subsequently have been married to that man of Egyptian descent. However, in *A.P.* 15 of 435 B.C. she marries yet another husband, Asḥor b. Ṣeḥo.[11] He, too, as his name shows, was of Egyptian descent and bore the title, "builder(?) (*'rdkl*) of the king."[12] The contract for this marriage is a typical one. Asḥor pays the bride's father the bridal gift (mohar); the bride's possessions are enumerated. Stipulations are made concerning inheritance and divorce, and penalties are imposed if the husband should drive out his wife or acknowledge another wife or other children than hers.

Two new and extremely interesting marriage contracts in the Brooklyn collection reveal the matrimonial affairs of mother and daughter. The first (No. 2) shows Ananiah b. Azariah, the servitor of the god Yahu in Yeb, marrying Tamut, the handmaiden of Meshullam b. Zakkur, in 449 B.C. Tamut is allowed to take her son Palṭi with her. Meshullam agrees not to reclaim the child, though with the reservation that if he should change his mind he will pay Ananiah an indemnity. She has, moreover, the right to initiate divorce proceedings. In spite of her marriage to a freeman she is still bound to her owner, Meshullam, as shown in another Brooklyn document, No. 5, discussed below.

Tamut's daughter Yehoyishma appears as bride in Brooklyn No. 7, the longest Aramaic marriage contract yet known. Though there are gaps in the text nothing really essential is missing. Yehoyishma married Ananiah b. Haggai in October, 420 B.C. A unique feature of her marriage contract is that her bridal gift is paid by the groom, not to the bride's father (or stepfather?) Anani b. Azariah, who is not even mentioned, but to her "brother" Zakkur b. Meshullam, the son of her former owner, Meshullam b. Zakkur. Evidently the latter was now dead, but Yehoyishma and her mother Tamut were still obligated to his son, as is shown by the terms of the manumission document (Brooklyn No. 5).

A fragment of a marriage contract (*A.P.* 18) has an importance that has not yet been appreciated. In this document the *mother* had a prominent role in giving the bride in marriage — a most unusual situation. The mother was Yauḥan, daughter of Meshullak (b. Hosha'iah? *A.P.* 46:13), a woman occurring in an earlier loan document (*A.P.* 10) that will be discussed below. This marriage agreement shows that Yauḥan's daughter, Salluah, married a (Meshul)lak b.

[11] The text restoration of Cowley, "25 of Tishri," is convincing. S. H. Horn and L. H. Wood date this papyrus in 435, though a fair agreement of dates can also be obtained for 457 B.C. Epiphi 6 is October 15–16, Tishri 25, October 14–15. The synchronism for 435, however, is better.

[12] *'rdkl* (*A.P.* 15:2, *'rdykl*). The Persian etymologies thus far suggested are rejected by Schaeder, *Beiträge*, 263. The word is perhaps to be derived from Babylonian *arad ēkalli*, "slave of the palace," which is also a designation of an occupation (builder?). The word passed into Syriac *ardīklā*, "builder." Cf. Heinrich Zimmern, *Akkadische Fremdwörter als Beweis für babylonischen Kultureinfluss* (Leizpg, 1917), 26; Peiser, *OLZ*, *10*, 1907, 626.

(U)ri, whose name occurs in *A.P.* 22:68. There is a stipulation in lines 2–3 that what Yauḥan gave the couple as a gift she cannot reclaim. The contract associates Yauḥan with a Hosha'iah (line 4), but it seems more likely that he was a relative (brother?) than her husband, who would have acted singly.

Divorce documents are rare, even among the multitudinous Babylonian legal texts. Yet we seem to have such a document, or at least one concerned with a *phase* of a divorce, in *A.P.* 14 of 440 B.C. The husband was Pi' b. Paḥi and the wife Mibṭaḥiah, the daughter of Maḥseiah, who then must have remarried after the death of Jezaniah b. Uriah, to whom we found her wedded in *A. P.* 8 of 460 B.C. The endorsement calls this a "document of removal"— a term otherwise employed for a deed giving possession of a house. Pi' states: "In connection with (*'al*) the suit which we conducted at Syene I surrendered [13] the money and produce and clothing and copper and silver, all the goods and possessions, and the document of marriage." Evidently Pi' had denied that certain things were Mibṭaḥiah's, and so an oath was imposed on her. "My heart was content at that oath which thou didst swear to me concerning those goods," he declares. He then gives up all claims and protects her against further suit by himself or any heir with a penalty of five karsh.

As has already been stated slavery was current in the Elephantine colony. Slaves were considered chattels, to be bought, sold, or inherited, but they seem to have been treated nevertheless with a certain consideration. [14] In *A.P.* 28 of 410 B.C., two brothers, Yedoniah and Maḥseiah, are concerned with dividing the possessions of their late mother Mibṭaḥiah — more particularly her slaves. She had a slave woman named Tebo who had three male children. Yedoniah took the boy Peṭosiri, Maḥseiah took Belo. The mother and the third son, Lilu, evidently still an infant too young to be separated from his parent, remained the common property of both brothers, with a future settlement envisioned.

In the Brooklyn papyri we have our first Aramaic documents relating to the freeing of slaves. In No. 8 of 416 B.C., Zakkur b. Meshullam gives Uriah b. Maḥseiah a slave boy named Yedoniah for adoption. Uriah has to pledge that Yedoniah

[13] Cowley renders *nprt* as "Let us make a division," following Nöldeke, and rejects as "unsuitable" Halévy's "I withdrew" (based on Arabic *nafara*). We think that Halévy was right, for how could the two divide the marriage document which is one of the objects of *nprt*? The point is that the things specified were *surrendered* to the court, and thereupon the wife took the oath that brought her into possession of them and made the husband execute this "document of removal," giving up his claim. This passage is important for the understanding of the concept *'bd dīn* used in Brooklyn No. 7.

[14] The Babylonian material about slavery is studied in Isaac Mendelsohn, *Slavery in the Ancient Near East* (New York, 1949). It is interesting to contrast Oriental slavery with that in the Greco-Roman world. See William L. Westermann's forthcoming book, *The Slave Systems of Greek and Roman Antiquity* (Philadelphia, 1953).

will not be reduced to slave status again, but that he will treat him as a son. That evidently also involves inheritance rights and suggests that Uriah had no son of his own. Peculiarly interesting is Brooklyn No. 5 of 427 B.C., which concerns persons with whose affairs other documents have made us familiar. In it Meshullam b. Zakkur liberates the handmaiden Tamut, whom he had given in marriage to Ananiah b. Azariah twenty years earlier. He also liberates her daughter Yehoyishma, but nothing is said about her son Palṭi, whom he had evidently relinquished to Ananiah, though as mentioned above, with a reservation (Brooklyn No. 2). The liberation is under the arrangement well known from the Greek world as *paramone.*[15] The bondservants are freed but must continue to serve the owner and his son Zakkur after him for as long as these shall live. Highly significant is the statement that they are to be "freed to the god"[16] (compare Chapter 8).

In ancient Elephantine, as now, businessmen and women were sometimes obliged to arrange loans, and we find our prominent citizens of Elephantine active as lenders and borrowers. In *A.P.* 10 of the year 456 (?), Meshullam b. Zakkur lends money in the amount of four shekels to Yehoḥan (in *A.P.* 18, Yauḥan), daughter of Meshullak, who acknowledges the receipt and agrees to pay a rather stiff interest of two ḥallur per shekel per month or 60 per cent per annum. If the debt is not paid by a certain time the unpaid interest is to be added to the capital, and the whole sum is to draw interest at the same rate. She gives Meshullam the right to distrain her possessions at the end of the second year and makes the debt collectible from her children[17] in the event of her death. Of a similar nature but a little less clear is *A.P.* 11, written perhaps a year earlier. It is a receipt for a loan with specifications as to interest and repayment of the principal. The beginning of the text is broken away and only a portion of the name of the lender, ". . . b. Yathma," is preserved. Maḥseiah b. Yedoniah is a witness to the transaction. The loan appears to be for four shekels. It is to draw interest at the rate of two ḥallur per shekel per month until paid. If the borrower fails to pay the interest due in any given month, it shall be added to the capital and he shall be charged interest on the total sum. He promises to pay the monthly installments due out of the portion which is given him from the king's treasury. The lender agrees to give him a receipt[18] for principal and interest paid, and if he fails to pay by the month of Thoth (Egyptian New Year) of the ninth year (of Artaxerxes I), or 456, the unpaid

[15] On this concept, see Paul Koschaker, "Über einige griechische Rechtsurkunden aus den östlichen Randgebieten des Hellenismus," *ASAW*, *43*, 1931.

[16] The gift to the deity is emphasized in a Babylonian slave liberation text from Sippar from the days of Sin-muballit: "To Shamash and Aya they gave her" (Schorr, *Urkunden*, No. 25, l. 5). Perhaps in the papyrus the meaning is only that the liberation gets religious sanction and protection by the process of dedication to the god.

[17] See Schorr, *Urkunden*, 73, No. 287.

[18] The word *nbz* used here is a Babylonian loan word, *nibzu*, "document."

principal and interest shall be doubled (?)[19] and the amount due from him shall be increased against him month by month until the loan is paid.

The Brooklyn texts also contain a loan document (No. 11) of 402/1 B.C.; in it we have a loan of grain rather than of money. Anani b. Haggai borrows two *peras*, two *seah* of spelt from Paḫnum b. Bs'. It is repayable in twofold quantity in twenty days and a fine of one karsh of refined silver is imposed for failure to return it. In the event of Anani's death the debt is to be paid by his children and heirs or is collectible from his estate. The terms are very harsh. If the debt is not repaid everything of the debtor's in the house belonging to his children can be taken to satisfy the creditor.

A man who used any of his wife's money was considered a borrower and had to write her a formal promise of payment. Thus in *A.P.* 35 of 400 B.C. Menahem b. Shallum admits owing two shekels (or one stater) to his wife Salluah. He acknowledges that it represents "part of the money and the goods which are upon thy marriage document." He promises to pay it back in a little over a month but apparently without interest. The text breaks off in the midst of the consideration of what is to happen if he fails to pay.

In a different class from loans is an acknowledgment of money still due in payment of a purchase. In the fragmentary text *A.P.* 29 of 409 B.C. a (Nathan) b. Hosha' states that he owes Yislaḥ b. Gaddūl one (?) karsh, four shekels, on a house bought from him. He promises to pay this debt within nine months. The clauses dealing with penalties for failure to pay are lost.

Business contracts other than loans have been preserved. In *A.P.* 2 of 484 B.C. Hosha' b. Hodaviah and Aḥiab b. Gemariah acknowledge the receipt of a load of barley and lentils from Espemeṭ the boatman, doubtless an Egyptian. They agree to deliver the goods to several companies of troops and to render an account to "the house of the king" and "the scribes of the treasury." The two pledge themselves as liable to a fine of thirty karsh for failure to fullfil the contract. Espemeṭ is given the right to collect his payment, if necessary, from the portion due these middlemen from "the house of the king" and to seize their property until fully recompensed. Another but poorly preserved text (*A.P.* 3) was evidently very similar in content and seems to have been written on the same date; it may have been supplementary to the first and refer to the same transaction. The fragment *A.P.* 4 also concerns Espemeṭ and a grain deal.

There was a great deal of litigation in the Elephantine colony. People were accustomed to pressing claims of all kinds. A successful suit is mirrored in Brooklyn No. 1, in which Mika b. [Agur?] cedes to Anani b. Azariah, the servitor of Yahu,

[19] So Cowley, and this is endorsed by G. R. Driver, "The Aramaic Papyri from Egypt, Notes on Obscure Passages," *JRAS*, 1932, 77. But there seems to be no warrant for such a penalty here, though Schorr, *Urkunden*, 70, mentions instances.

a property described by the Egyptian (?) word *hīra*. Apparently Anani had brought suit against Mika and had succeeded in establishing his right to this property. Mika accepts the payment of five shekels for it and protects Anani against any further trouble by a penalty of five karsh.

When the plaintiff failed to establish his case he had to make out a document to the defendant. In contrast to the case about the *hīra* just referred to stands that of *A. P.* 6 of 464 B.C. Dargman b. Ḥarshin, the Chorasmian — obviously a Persian resident of Yeb — had lodged complaint against Maḥseiah b. Yedoniah, the Jew, before Damidata and his colleagues, the judges, laying claim to some land, the boundaries of which are described in detail. An oath had been sworn to Dargman by Maḥseiah, his wife and his son, three in all, to the effect that the land no longer belonged to Dargman. The latter declares that he accepts their sworn statement and protects their title against any future suit by imposing a penalty of twenty karsh on anyone who shall bring such suit.

An occasion for all manner of claims was naturally provided by the death of a person. Thus *A.P.* 20 of 420 B.C. was apparently written after the death of Asḥor. Two brothers, Menahem and Ananiah, "sons" of a Meshullam (the former of the two is mentioned in the name list *A.P.* 19:7), had sued Yedoniah and Maḥseiah, Asḥor's sons, concerning certain articles which their grandfather, Shelomem b. Azariah, had deposited with Asḥor but which had not been returned before the latter's death. Yedoniah and Maḥseiah had been interrogated by the judges and had cleared themselves. Menahem and Ananiah renounce all further claims. The wife of Asḥor, Mibṭaḥiah, was still living at this time but is not mentioned in the text. In *A.P.* 25 of 416 B.C. Yedoniah and Maḥseiah are concerned with a matter of their mother's estate. Mibṭaḥiah had held possession of the house of a former husband, Yezaniah b. Uriah. The property had passed to her sons. But a nephew of her first husband — a brother's son, Yedoniah b. Hosha'iah b. Uriah — had put forward a claim to the property. He lost the suit and in *A.P.* 25 he renounced his claim.

Other occasions on which suits failed are mirrored in the papyri. Thus *A.P.* 7 of 461 B.C. deals with an accusation leveled against Malkiah b. Yoshibiah by a man with a Persian name, Phrataphernes b. Artaphernes. Malkiah is accused of having invaded the latter's house and of having struck his wife and carried off goods.[20] The court imposed an oath on Malkiah denying that he had done what he was accused of. He repeats in detail the oath that he swore, but unfortunately the text breaks off in the midst of it.

The undated text *A.P.* 44 deals with an accusation made against Menahem b. Shallum by Meshullam b. Nathan. The latter has attacked Menahem's half

[20] Cowley, *A.P.* 19, supposes that Phrataphernes had boasted of trespassing, and that Malkiah requires him to retract under oath. This seems unlikely.

ownership in an ass. Whether an inheritance is involved is not entirely clear, owing to the gaps in the text and the uncertainty of restorations. But supposedly Menahem had been given a he-ass in return for his share. An oath was evidently imposed. The text is unusual in that it begins with a caption: "The o[ath of] Menahem b. Shallum b. H[odaviah which] he swore, etc."[21] The religious aspects of this oath will be discussed in Chapter 8.

The fragmentary text *A.P.* 45, probably from the reign of Artaxerxes I, indicates that Maḥseiah b. Shībah had claimed that fish had been stolen[22] from him by the writer of the document (whose name is not preserved). An oath was demanded of the latter, which he apparently did not swear, for he speaks of paying back the fish in produce or the equivalent in value. If he fails to do so within a given time he is to pay at the rate of one *ḳab* barley to one peras (see on No. 11:2) every month.

No leases of property are preserved in Elephantine papyri[23] but we have a text acknowledging a grant of privilege with respect to property. This document, *A.P.* 5, is dated 471 B.C. It reveals Maḥseiah as having given his neighbor Ḳoniya (permission to infringe on?) the gateway of his house in building a wall (*'gr*). This wall is to begin at the upper (northern) corner of Ḳoniya's house and run along the side of it to the house of Zekariah (b. Nathan). Ḳoniya, in making out the document, agrees that the wall is to be the legal property of Maḥseiah. Neither Ḳoniya nor his heirs can restrain him from building on it if he chooses to do so and furthermore Ḳoniya cannot assert that the gate does not belong to Maḥseiah and refuse him exit by it into the street that lies opposite between their two houses and the house of Pefṭonith, the boatman. Evidently Maḥseiah accepted no money — that might have established rights which he had no intention of conceding.

Homes were naturally bought and sold in a community such as Yeb, and real estate transactions were of course recorded. Some persons owned a number of houses. No rental agreements concerning houses have been preserved, however. Our documents record only purchases or transfers by gift. The documents recording such legal actions are very similar in style and follow a pattern found also in demotic texts.

No deed of sale of a house was known from the Sayce-Cowley or Sachau texts. The Brooklyn texts, however, give several instances. In No. 3, of 437 B.C., Bagazušt and Ŭbīl, his wife, sell their house in Yeb to Anani b. Azariah, the servitor of the god Yahu. The document is a "document of removal," evidently made out when

[21] Wolfgang Kunkel, "Griechische und ägyptische Elemente im Eidesrecht der Ptolemäerzeit," *Zeitschrift der Savigny-Stiftung für Rechtsgeschichte, 51*, 1931, 229 ff., thinks that this oath was set up prior to the actual swearing.

[22] In l. 3 *ḥmst* should be rendered "I stole." Cf. Assyrian *ḫamāsu*.

[23] The Bauer-Meissner papyrus (cf. Chapter 1, n. 69) deals with a lease of a field but comes from a different locality.

the old owner relinquished actual possession, and also a receipt for the price paid — one karsh, four shekels. An exact description of the location of the property is given. The new owner is guaranteed possession and protected against future suits, except such as might be brought by the person from whom the vendor had originally bought the house. Similar is the sale in Brooklyn No. 12 of the year 402 B.C. (Parker, 401) of this very same house by Anani and his wife to their son-in-law Anani b. Haggai. They gave him the original deed received from Bagazušt and Ūbīl. The purchaser has full liberty to dispose of the house and is protected against suit by a fine of twenty karsh imposed on the suer.

Gifts are also frequently the subject of documents and gifts of houses are common. In the previously published materials there is a fragment of a text which records a gift of a house by Shelomem b. Hodaviah to his wife Abiḥi (*A.P.* 44).

A man might even give his wife a part of a house.[24] In Brooklyn No. 4 of 434 B.C. Anani b. Azariah gives his wife Tamut, the handmaiden he had married in 449 B.C., a portion of the house he had bought from Bagazušt and Ūbīl, but with the proviso that their two children, Palṭi and Yehoyishma, are to inherit it from her, as they are also to inherit his own share.

Daughters seem to be the favored recipients of gifts of houses. In Brooklyn No. 6 of 420 B.C. Anani b. Azariah gives Yehoyishma, his daughter, a house adjoining that in which he himself is living. This apparently was some months before her marriage to Anani b. Haggai (Brooklyn No. 7). In Brooklyn No. 9 of 404 B.C. Anani b. Azariah again gives Yehoyishma a part of a house he had formerly bought. The gift was to become effective at his death and was given in recognition of her taking care of him in his old age. In Brooklyn No. 10 of 402/1 B.C. Anani b. Azariah gives Yehoyishma still another house (or the remainder of the house of which he gave her a part in Brooklyn No. 9?). In Brooklyn No. 15 we have the endorsement of a papyrus which Anani (b. Haggai) b. Meshullam made out to Yehoyishma — perhaps a gift of the house he had bought from her parents (in Brooklyn No. 12).

Mibṭaḥiah, whose marriage contract was discussed above, was also the recipient of the gift of a house. In *A.P.* 8 of 460 B.C., Maḥseiah states that he has given a property (along with Dargman's surrender of his claim, doubtless a document much like Brooklyn No. 1) to his daughter Mibṭaḥiah, when she married Yezaniah b. Uriah. Mibṭaḥiah is guaranteed possession of it for herself and her children. She may build on it or give it to whom she will. In *A.P.* 9, made out on the same day, Maḥseiah established the position of Mibṭaḥiah's husband Yezaniah with respect to this property. It stipulates that he shall have the right to build on it and occupy

[24] A situation we find paralleled in demotic papyri; cf. Spiegelberg, *Die demotischen Papyri der Strassburger Bibliothek* (Strassburg, 1902), 25; "Demotische Papyrus von der Insel Elephantine," *Demotische Studien*, Heft 2, Bd. 1 (Leipzig, 1908), 26.

it but shall have no power to sell it; only his children by Mibṭaḥiah can inherit. In the event of her divorcing him she cannot take it to give to others — only her children by Yezaniah can inherit in return for the work he has done.[25] If he divorces her she may keep half the house and he shall have power over the other half, but only her children by Yezaniah are entitled to his half.

On November 19 of 446 B.C. Maḥseiah, according to *A.P.* 13, conveyed to his daughter (whose name is here spelled Mipṭaḥiah) another house, which he had bought from Meshullam b. Zakkur. This gift seems to have been in the nature of payment of a debt, for he states that he gives the house to her in return for certain unspecified goods she had given him in the value of five karsh, when he was in the fortress for mustering (?). He resigns all future claims for himself and his descendants and gives her liberty to dispose of it as she chooses.

In several gift documents we find women in the role of donors. In *A.P.* 43, the date of which is lost but which is probably early, Mipṭaḥiah, daughter of Gemariah, gives her sister Asori six shekels in return for support received from her. She renounces the right to bring suit to recover this gift, and imposes a fine of two karsh on any attempt to do so from her part or that of any other person. She also refers to having received from her sister the ration from the house of the king and of being content with it. She will not make any future claim on her sister either for this ration or her gift.

What is unmistakably an exchange is recorded in *A.P.* 1 of 495 B.C., where the contracting parties are likewise women. The two sisters Salluah, daughter of Ḳoniah, and Yethoma declare to Yeho'or, daughter of Shelomem, that they have given her the half share that was granted them by the king's judges and Rauaka, the commander, in return for the half share which had come to her *with Ne'ehebeth* (feminine name). They renounce any right to reclaim the "gift" or any possibility of future suit over it. A fine of five karsh is imposed on any attempt at such suit by anybody. It is not clear what sort of property was involved in this exchange.

To this survey of the legal and business documents we may add a brief account of the letters and other materials which give us information concerning the Jewish Aramaean colony. From a formal point of view the Elephantine letters all have much in common. But the Arsham correspondence and the unpublished Hermopolis papyri suggest that at different levels of society or at different times and places the forms of Aramaic epistolography could vary considerably. We have devoted some brief space to the former material above (Chapter 1). For the latter we may here adduce some of the facts given out by Murad Kamil. The letters follow a characteristic pattern. They begin with salutations to the temple of the deity, are

[25] In *A.P.* 9:5 Cowley's rendering is unacceptable. One cannot raise cattle on a patch 13 x 11 cubits. The verb is *'tr*; the preposition *b* is before the object *hmyt'* (plus suffix): "enrich its neglected condition (?)." Cf. the Syriac *hm'* and its derivatives.

followed by mention of the addressee ("my sister," if a woman, or "my lord"), continue with the name of the writer ("from your brother(s)" or "from your servant") and with the blessing or wish that God may permit seeing the face of the addressee in peace. Then after more polite phrases comes the request of the sender that something be bought for him or the declaration that he has bought something for the addressee. The objects in question include such things as wool, olive oil, balsam ointment, clothing (linen or woolen), skins, boxes (for which the word *'rn*, "ark," is used), wood, and several kinds of containers. The letters invariably end with, "For your well-being I send this." On the outside of the roll is the address, "To N. N. from N. N. to be sent to (place N.)." The destination given is Syene or Thebes.

A number of letters from Elephantine, though in a poor state of preservation, were published by Sachau and the present collection adds at least one to their number. We may disregard here the "diplomatic" correspondence and the letters relating to governmental affairs (*A.P.* 17) or events of a nature affecting the Elephantine colony (*A.P.* 34, 37, 38 and Brooklyn No. 13), since discussion is devoted to them in other chapters. *A.P.* 16, in which the name of the sender is lost, refers to a period embracing the 24th to the 31st year of a ruler (who then must have been Artaxerxes I). The writer complains of having stated his case before *Trwḥ* (name of an official) and the court, and of subsequently appealing it to Nephayan, the commander of Syene and the three judges of "the province," Megaphernes, Nephayan, and Mannuki. In this letter he addresses a man whom he calls "lord" and whose name evidently ended in *-prn* (Megaphernes?) and demands an investigation of *Trwḥ* and the court.

In *A.P.* 39 we have a letter addressed to a woman named Shalwah by her servant Hosha'. He invokes the blessing of the gods on her and sends greetings to a number of persons, including several other women. Among these is a Yehoyishma — quite possibly the woman who occurs so often in our texts. The main body of the letter, however, is missing.

In *A.P.* 40 Hosha'iah b. Nathan (doubtless identical with Hosha' of *A.P.* 39) writes to his "brother" Palṭi. Shewa' (b. Zekariah?) and his children receive greetings. *A.P.* 41 is very disconnected. In it a man writes to his brother Ṣeḥo. He complains of not having heard from the addressee since coming to Syene and bids him look after his servants and his house as he would after his own.

A.P. 42 is written by a Hosha' to a man whose name was . . . b. Haggai and who is addressed as "brother." Perhaps he was Anani b. Haggai. He bids him, among other things, to buy the house of Zakkur (Zakkur b. Meshullam?) and the house of *'šn* (compare the *'šyn* of *A.P.* 65:5). The addressee is urged to come to Memphis on receipt of the letter. But first he is to go to a man named Bethel-taddan and get certain garments and send them to the writer.

Closely linked with the letters on papyrus are the ostraca, which were frequently

used for local and unimportant messages. However, in the case of many of the ostraca so far published, the difficulties of translation and interpretation are so great that one must hesitate to make any definite statement about their content and purpose. We shall have occasion below to cite passages from those ostraca that are believed to have significance for the history of religion at Elephantine and shall not dwell further on them here. For the private life of the colony their chief interest lies in the names they mention, especially when the names happen to be those of persons also known from the papyri. Unfortunately, since only the given name is used in most instances in the ostraca, the identity of the person remains obscure.

The first Elephantine ostracon published, that found by Adolf Erman in 1886, mentions a woman named Yaḥmoliah who may, perhaps, be identical with Yaḥmol the daughter of Palṭi b. Ye'ūsh of *A.P.* 22:89.[26] An ostracon that Sayce obtained at Elephantine in 1901 mentions Gemariah b. Aḥio.[27] A Uriah also appears there, as well as in the Sachau ostracon 76, No. 1, and in an ostracon found in 1925 and published by Aimé-Giron;[28] but since his father's name is not given he cannot be identified with certainty. The same thing is true of the persons Yislaḥ, Meshullemeth, and Shema'iah of the Sabbath ostracon.[29]

We have a veritable roster of the members of the Elephantine colony in several papyri published by Sachau containing lists of persons. Of particular interest is the list of the contributors to the temple, *A.P.* 22. We shall revert to its religious aspects later in our discussion of the religion of the Elephantine colony. At this juncture we are concerned with it merely to the extent that it gives us a sort of who's who of a certain time. What time that is, is debatable. The document is dated "on the 3. of Pamenḥotep, the fifth year," but without mention of the king whose year is meant. We are inclined to think that "the fifth year" is that of Amyrtaeus (or else of Artaxerxes II) and that this text, therefore, was written June 2, 400 B.C., a few weeks before *A.P.* 35.[30] In that case the avoidance of the name of the king would be quite understandable. The Jews sympathized with the Persian regime and might well hope for its restoration. The legal document just referred to shows that the

[26] *CIS*, *2*, 137.

[27] *RÉS*, *1*, No. 492.

[28] "Trois ostraca araméens d'Éléphantine," *ASAE*, *26*, 1926, 47 ff.

[29] See Chapter 8.

[30] Sachau, followed by Meyer, *Papyrusfund*, 55, and Cowley, *A.P.*, p. 66, put this text in the 5th year of Darius II (419 B.C.). If it came from that time one would expect individuals occurring in such texts as *A.P.* 20, from the 4th year of Darius, or Brooklyn No. 7, to be mentioned. Some of those named in the list seem to be children of personages mentioned in earlier texts. Thus Maḥseh b. Uri (*A.P.* 22:65) is surely a son of Uriah b. Maḥseiah of Brooklyn No. 9. The Yehuṭal of l. 103 is probably a daughter of Yislaḥ b. Gaddūl of Brooklyn No. 7:44. J. N. Epstein, "*Jahu, AŠMbethel und ANTbethel*," *ZAW*, *32*, 1912, 139 ff., was on the right track in dating it later. Cowley's objection, *A.P.*, p. 66, is of no consequence; the dating is not by years of the revolt (so Epstein) but by the regnal years, either of Amyrtaeus or Artaxerxes.

Jewish community was still continuing its religious and social-economic life undisturbed in the fifth year of Amyrtaeus. Apparently no immediate calamity befell them or their temple at the time of the change of sovereignty.

The list seems to have arranged several groups of contributors according to their membership in "companies" (literally "hundreds") named after their leaders. Thus in line 19 the preceding names are summarized with "all the company of Sin-iddin"; then, introductory to the next set of names, follows "the company of Nabū-ʿaḳab," the contributions of which are summarized in line 31. Apparently, then, the company is a political or military entity (degel?), but one must not conclude that such a company was all Jewish or had been listed *in toto* in this text. "All the company" is simply short for "those belonging to the company." The list seems to have had a total of 123 names,[31] a considerable percentage of them names of women.

Another list, *A.P.* 24, which enumerates members of the Elephantine community, is dated in the month of Meḥir of an uncertain year. It deals with the rations issued to soldiers. Though most of the persons named in it were non-Jews, one familiar Jewish name of our papyri appears near the beginning — that of Haggai b. Shemaʿiah.

For what purpose the brief list of names in *A.P.* 23 was set up is not stated. It could have been written after the time of Uriah b. Maḥseiah who wrote the Brooklyn text No. 8 in 416 B.C. for it mentions his son. A similar obscurity of purpose attends several lists of names on Elephantine ostraca, such as some Clermont-Ganneau ostraca and the Golenischeff ostraca,[32] the first of which contains largely West Semitic names while the second seems to have only Egyptian names.

[31] So according to Umberto Cassuto, "The Gods of the Jews of Elephantine," *Kedem: Studies in Jewish Archaeology* (Jerusalem, 1942), *1*, 47 ff. (in Hebrew). Albright, in a brief review of the article, *BASOR*, *90*, 1943, 40, endorses the correctness of Cassuto's calculation of the number of Jewish contributors. Meyer, *Papyrusfund*, 55 f. thought the list totaled 130 names. Cassuto points out that the contribution for the Jewish god and temple would amount to 246 shekels (exactly two per person for the estimated number).

[32] *CIS*, *2*, 154, 155.

6. THE EXCAVATIONS AT ELEPHANTINE

WHILE the Elephantine papyri give rich information concerning the life of the Aramaic-speaking colony at the southern border of Egypt, we have still another source of knowledge concerning it in the excavations carried out on the island. Some account of those excavations seems necessary here, for they help, in a certain measure, to an understanding of the papyri, as the papyri help to an interpretation of the archaeological findings. We shall deal with these excavations under two separate aspects: 1) as they concern the residential quarters of Yeb and 2) as they concern the temples.

THE ARAMAEAN QUARTER OF YEB

Mention has been made of an archaeological investigation by Maspero on Elephantine in 1902 (see Chapter 1). There is no record of the area in which he worked. Fortunately, however, we are able to get a clear picture of the ground dug over by the German excavators in 1906–08 from their report of 1909.[1] It must be borne in mind that, as in their previous work in the Faiyūm,[2] the task set for them was to search for papyri and that everything else was subsidiary to that end. They nevertheless did the best they could to clear up the history of the site.

The situation at Elephantine was particularly difficult. As a glance at the plan made by the German expedition shows (figs. 3, 4), the excavation laid bare a confused mass of walls, from which recognizable groups of houses emerge only on the summit of the mound. In reality the confusion is greater than it appears to be on the plan, for the walls rise from different levels, representing different archaeological periods.

The city mound of Elephantine is not a natural one. The oldest settlement was established on granite cliffs, covered only by a moderately thick layer of soil. The "southern gate" — the border fortress of the Old Kingdom — doubtless lay here. Later generations, one after the other, built new houses and temples on the site.

[1] Honroth and others, "Ausgrabungen," 14–61. In all, the Berlin Museum carried on three campaigns, January 30–March 3, 1906, December 10, 1906–February 22, 1907, and the middle of October, 1907–January, 1908.

[2] See Otto Rubensohn, "Aus griechisch-römischen Häusern des Fayum," *Jahrbuch des Kaiserlichen Archaeologischen Instituts, 20*, 1905, 1 ff.

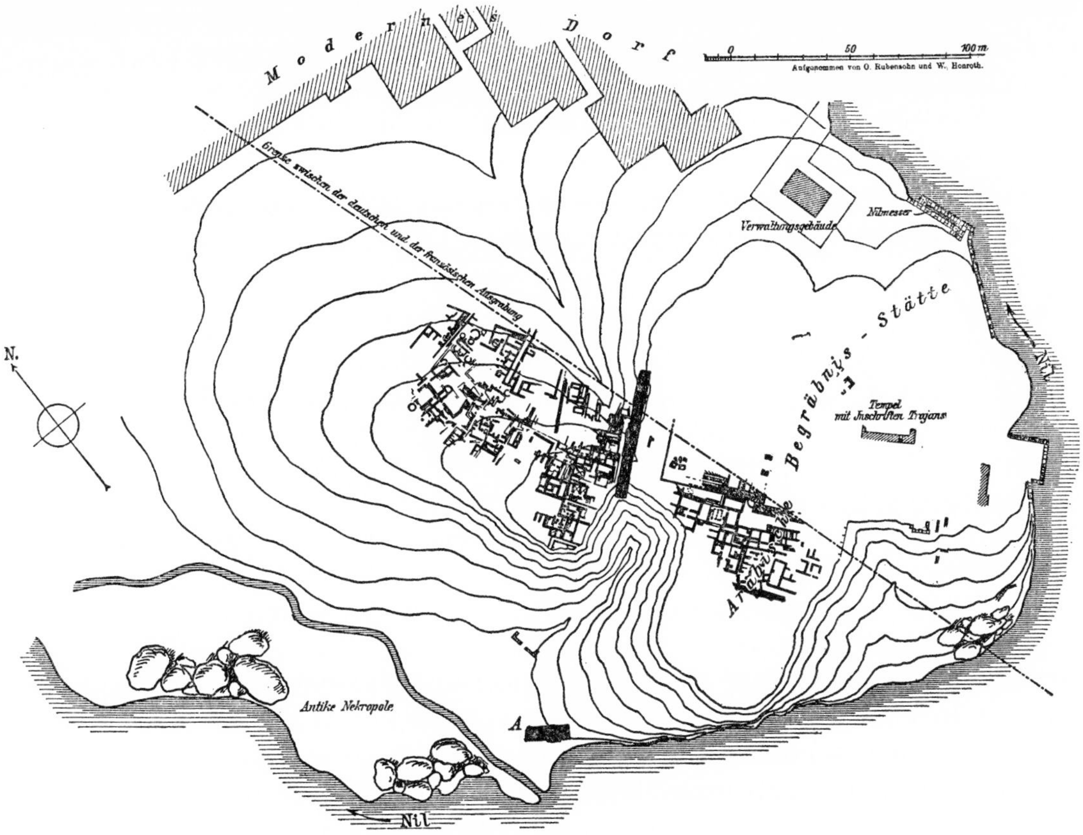

FIG. 3 Elephantine. Sketch plan of the Southern End of the Island and of the Excavations of the Berlin Museum Expedition (after Honroth and others, "Ausgrabungen"). Compare the aerial photo in the article cited in Chapter 1, n. 32.

They rarely bothered to raze existing structures before rebuilding, and the site seems to have been continuously occupied, so that no deposit separates the buildings of an earlier generation from those of a later one. Later inhabitants occupied earlier houses or rebuilt them, incorporating entire rooms or at least walls into their remodeled dwellings. The dwelling of one era usually became the cellar of another; in one instance four houses were found superimposed, one on the other. It will readily be seen from all this that it is an almost insurmountable task to reconstruct the plan of the city for any given period.[3]

Since a large number of the Elephantine documents deal with the sale or deed of houses, it is important to know what kind of house was built and inhabited by the Aramaic-speaking colonists at Yeb. The excavators state that the type remains constant down into the late Coptic and Arabic periods and is surprisingly similar

[3] Honroth and others, "Ausgrabungen," 17.

to that of Berberine villages of the present day.[4] The houses were built of bricks made from the clay of the riverbank — the only building material abundantly available. Stone was occasionally used for door and window sills and stairs. The scarcity of wood characteristic of the Nile Valley prohibited extensive use of wooden beams for ceilings and made necessary a barrel-vaulted construction.[5] Rooms were made narrow to decrease the area to be spanned by a vault, and the decreased width was compensated by increased length.

The brick walls were carefully built, usually with alternating brick and bond courses, of small bricks with four fingermarks pressed into the clay before drying, so that they might hold together better. The walls were necessarily thick (from two to two and one-half bricks deep) in order to provide support for the vaults. At older levels, the outside walls were sometimes reinforced with wooden beams — a type of building familiar in Greco-Roman houses in the Faiyūm. The vaults were constructed, as was customary in Egypt, with the narrow side of the rooms opposite the entrance. If a second story was added, as was regularly the case at Elephantine, the hollows between the vaults were filled with bricks or rubble in order to provide a level surface for the floors of the upper chambers. The upper story was usually reached by means of an opening broken through the vaulted ceiling. Ordinarily a ladder was used for access, but sometimes a narrow, inside stair led from one of the end walls up to the opening. Occasionally the upper story or the roof was reached by an outside stair leading from the courtyard. A house of the Ptolemaic period had a brick bench along the west wall of the courtyard, at the southwest end of which was a small building with a narrow stair leading from the court to its roof.

It was at *d* of the plan (fig. 4) that an important find of Greek papyri was made.[6] They were discovered in a jar rather deep under the floor of late Coptic buildings, which had mutilated the plan of the older house. The front of that house, which faced south, had furthermore been destroyed by the sebakh diggers. The clearest example of a house arrangement, though from the Ptolemaic era, is afforded by the house designated as *f*, adjoining *d* on the north.[7] Here five vaulted rooms are grouped around a court. From the court a staircase led to the upper story (largely destroyed), which was evidently the entrance to the house. The lower

[4] *Ibid.*, 18 ff. To relate the building descriptions of the papyri to the archaeological remains is difficult. For the material from papyri of the Hellenistic period on architectural terms see Fritz Luckhard, *Das Privathaus im ptolemäischen und römischen Ägypten* (Giessen, 1914); in general Alfred R. Schütz, *Der Typus des hellenistisch-ägyptischen Hauses im Anschluss an Baubeschreibung Griechischer Papyri* (Giessen, 1936).

[5] Honroth and others, "Ausgrabungen," 19, Abb. 1.

[6] *Ibid.*, 21. These were published by Rubensohn, "Elephantine Papyri," *Ägyptische Urkunden aus den Königlichen Museen in Berlin* (1907), Sonderheft.

[7] Honroth and others, "Ausgrabungen," 21.

story apparently had no door, for the walls of the five rooms rise to a height of six feet without any sign of an opening. This type of house is well-known from the Faiyūm in the Greek period.

A particular interest attaches to the row of houses that lay along the "temple street" adjacent to the Temple of Khnum. The house marked *k* in the plan contained a Greek graffito of late Roman times, "Homage of the foreigners."[8] It suggests that this house was a headquarters for strangers (foreign mercenaries?), some of whom expressed by this graffito their veneration for the god of the neighboring temple. In digging down to lower levels at this point, the excavators found three rooms, the easternmost of which extended into the French concession. The first, or westernmost, was of particular importance, for at its east wall they struck a heap of papyri, once composed of a large number of rolls,[9] so rotted by dampness that they disintegrated when touched. The few fragments saved showed that they were Aramaic. The excavators had thus struck the Aramaean stratum, as was interestingly demonstrated when the remainder of the house was cleared. The neighboring room contained a great quantity of large earthenware jars, and a few similar ones were also found in the adjacent, easternmost room.[10] These jars were broken but several could be assembled almost completely from the fragments. They were storage jars of two types, which bore inscriptions mostly in Aramaic but also in Phoenician. Jars of similar types have been found at Thebes in graves of the 21st to the 26th Dynasties and are also represented on a stela of about the same time in the Vatican, which bears a brief Aramaic inscription.[11]

The excavators were of the opinion that, in the days of the Aramaean house in which these finds were made, the "temple street" bordering it was not yet in existence, for the structure shows no consideration for it, does not lie parallel to it, and even cuts into its course with one angle.[12] They leave it uncertain whether the outer temple wall, which sits deeper than the walls of the house, had been erected at the time when the Aramaean house was inhabited. These uncertainties will weigh rather heavily when we come to discuss the location of the Temple of Yahu on the basis of the texts.[13]

The other Aramaean quarter excavated by the Germans lay several blocks of houses to the north of this district.[14] This was the area in which most of the Aramaic papyri from Elephantine so far published were discovered. Those acquired by Sir Robert Mond and Lady Cecil are said to have been found on the

[8] *Ibid.*, 25, Abb. 5 and Tafel III.
[9] *Ibid.*
[10] *Ibid.*, 25 ff.; see Abb. 6–7.
[11] See *CIS*, *2*, 142, Tab. 14.
[12] Honroth and others, "Ausgrabungen," 28.
[13] Cf. below, Chapter 7.
[14] Honroth and others, "Ausgrabungen," 28 ff.

west and immediately in front of the building marked *m* 1, on the plan. The houses *m* and *n* produced the finds that were published by Sachau. Both houses lay close to the western rim of the kom in the immediate vicinity of the area where the sebakh diggers were operating. Traces of fresh digging were discernible everywhere and were even met with in house *m*, the walls of which had been so badly destroyed that no plan could be made of it. The Germans found their first papyri on the declivity of the kom in front of wall *m* 1, the larger quantity, however, at wall *m* 2 and at the late wall *m* 3. The papyri were not stored in jars nor were there any indications that they had ever been. They lay hardly half a meter under the surface in the loose rubble. The walls of house *n* also had caved in and no plan could be established. The finds of papyri were not nearly as numerous here as at *m*.

In addition to papyri (and some ostraca) the Aramaean houses also produced terra cottas and carved wooden figures.[15] The former are of a known type, showing a nude woman lying on her bed with a small child at her side. The report discusses the possibility of this representing a goddess and her child, an interpretation made plausible by the likelihood that the crude wooden figures are foreign and presumably of an idolatrous nature.[16] A small dig, carried on in the extreme south of the kom, brought to light 25 demotic papyri.[17]

We have already mentioned the fact that a French expedition led by Clermont-Ganneau began to dig at Elephantine next to the German concession during the latter's second season and continued for a year after the German excavations were terminated.[18] Like the German expedition, the French was primarily a papyrus hunt. We shall speak subsequently of Clermont-Ganneau's work in the Temple of Khnum and of his search for the temple of the Jews. The Aramaean quarter on the kom was the main theater of his explorations. "Our removal of the Aramaean quarter has at least had the result of bringing to light a network of streets and alleys clearly enough characterized." This rather general statement in his posthumously published letters unfortunately does not help us to locate the area dug over by him. No plan of the dig seems to have been made. The most important find was a large number of Aramaic ostraca. In a letter from the second campaign Clermont-Ganneau states, "As was proper I have made our principal effort bear on the Aramaean quarter, determined by us in the course of the preceding campaign, or at least on the part of that quarter comprised in our concession. I there

[15] *Ibid.*, 30 ff.

[16] See the discussion in Vincent, *Religion*, 677 ff.

[17] Honroth and others, "Ausgrabungen," 43. See the publication of these texts by Spiegelberg, mentioned above Chapter 5, n. 24.

[18] The French dug here three times: December, 1906–March, 1907, and November, 1907–March, 1908, under Clermont-Ganneau and J. Clédat, and 1908–09 under H. Gauthier. See *CRAI*, 1908, 201 ff., and Lagrange, "Rapport: les fouilles d'Éléphantine," *RB*, n. s., *5*, 1908, 260 ff.

again recovered some Aramaean ostraca, perhaps as many as last year, . . but not in proportion to the intensity and extent of the excavations . . ."[19]

In the year 1918 Fathers of the Pontifical Biblical Institute of Rome carried on a dig at Elephantine. Only a brief report to the director general of Antiquities at Cairo was published.[20] The scientific direction of the dig was in charge of P. Sebastian Ronzevalle. The purpose was to check at certain points where previous excavations had not gone deep enough, and to dig up areas which had not as yet been touched. The latter were very limited except in the region near the Nubian village at the north. The first houses of this village, which are built on an artificial mound, undoubtedly cover a part of the ancient town of Yeb. Ronzevalle noted that this area still awaited the pick of the excavator.

But it was not there that the Fathers exerted their main efforts during this campaign. They felt that the state of the kom after the German and French excavations of 1906–10 imposed on them the obligation to rescue from the searchers for sebakh whatever might remain there. Like a century-old cancer, the report states, the incessant work of destruction of peasant diggers had spread over the western flank of the kom and had already devoured down to rock bottom a third of the ancient site; it still was proceeding under their eyes when they began their task.

Their first care was to turn to the section formerly conceded to the Germans and to investigate the ancient surfaces, still covered with the debris of the former excavation, at the edge of the group of houses *n* and *m* in the German plan. Their idea was to push their excavations, wherever it appeared possible and useful, down to virgin soil, to proceed from *n* to *m* and, having arrived at a point south of *m*, to clear completely all the space between this point and the first walls of the houses *g*, which mark the highest point of the site. They devoted more than six weeks to this work of salvage.

The principal purpose of the previous excavators, the discovery of Aramaic documents, had obliged them to neglect the examination of the strata lying below that of the Persian epoch. Some enormous piles of debris, more than three meters deep, had to be removed before the Fathers were able to reach undug surfaces. They judged it necessary to sift not only the freshly dug soil but even that removed by their predecessors, for they were convinced that the mass of rubble, which everywhere, though chiefly on the north of the site, formed veritable mountains, contained some objects or ancient fragments that had perhaps escaped the eye of

[19] J.-B. Chabot, "Les fouilles de Clermont-Ganneau à Éléphantine," *Journal des Savants*, 1944, 87 ff., 136 ff.

[20] A. Strazzuli, P. Bovier-Lapierre et S. Ronzevalle, "Rapport sur les fouilles à Éléphantine de l'Institut Biblique Pontifical en 1918," *ASAE*, *18*, 1919, 1–5. A plan of the excavations is given and the objects found are listed but not described.

previous explorers. In this they were not disappointed, and numerous interesting items turned up.

One of the most interesting finds was a metallurgical workshop of the late Egyptian period. The report also mentions papyrus fragments, but it is not clear that they were Aramaic. However, according to a list preserved at Rome, a few Aramaic fragments were found (see Chapter 1). No one today remembers what became of them. They seem to have been obtained near house *g* of the German plan, on its north side.

Of the search of the Catholic Fathers for the Temple of Yahu we will speak later. Here we shall call attention only to their last-minute dig near the Nubian village in the north, where they undertook a small investigation. They chose a slightly elevated place that looked as though it had never yet been dug. The surface to be explored formed a quadrangle of 11 to 18 by 20 meters and was far enough removed from the first houses of the village so that one did not have to fear clandestine resumption of the dig by natives. The spot was a hundred meters north-northeast of Clermont-Ganneau's supposed site of the Jewish temple. At a depth of about four meters they found that the buildings of the Persian epoch had been preceded by a necropolis of vaulted tombs of the New Kingdom, of which the previous excavators had already found traces to the south and west of this area. It was in this quadrangle, which they had not the time to explore equally in all parts, that the Catholic Fathers happened on a little fragment of an inscription, believed by Ronzevalle to be written in old Hebrew characters of the type of the Siloam inscription.[21]

In recent years the Egyptian Department of Antiquities has been protecting the ruin mounds at Elephantine, but no digging in the Aramaean quarter has been reported.

THE TEMPLES

1. The Exploration of the Temple of Khnum

The German and French excavations have uncovered much of the Temple of Khnum. While the details of its construction need not greatly concern us, its location is of importance because of its proximity to the Temple of Yahu (compare Chapter 7).

The northern and western walls of the Temple of Khnum were found by the Germans in their second campaign. Proceeding southward from the point where they had discovered the Aramaic papyri, they struck a great brick wall running west-east and a street that led along outside of it.[22] They devoted considerable time

[21] See Chapter 1, n. 31.

[22] Honroth and others, "Ausgrabungen," 15, 35 ff.

to exploring the course of the wall, though, in conformity with their instructions to hunt for papyri, they naturally devoted greater effort to digging in the block of houses lying on the hither or northern side of the street. At first the excavators believed that the wall was that of the old fortress of Yeb, but they soon saw that it stood in a relationship to the portal of Alexander II, one of the noteworthy remains of antiquity still surviving on the surface. Since this was known to be an entrance to the Temple of Khnum, they came to the conclusion that the wall they had struck was the outer wall of that temple. They informed Clermont-Ganneau, who thereupon pursued the course of the wall in the French concession.

The wall of the temple *enceinte* was revealed to have been a massive structure, about 111.50 meters long.[23] Its height, of course, was undeterminable, but in some places it was preserved to a height of more than five meters, and it was more than five meters thick at the base. It was carefully built of brick strengthened by acacia logs laid crosswise at intervals[24] and had projections which once bore towers. The age of the wall could not be deduced from its method of construction, for Egyptian building methods remained constant over long periods of time, but archaeological finds made inside the temple quadrangle indicate that it was begun by the Egyptian ruler Nektanebos II (358–341 B.C.) and completed only in the Ptolemaic period. The portal of Alexander II represents only one phase of building activity on the temple site.

In constructing the wall the builders did not seek to place the foundations on bedrock, for underneath them were found traces of older walls and buildings. This fact is of importance in determining the confines of the temple in the earlier, Persian period, the one that concerns us here.

The area within the outer wall of the temple was divided into two sections, one containing the "house" or Holy of Holies, and the portion of the *temenos* lying southwest of it. Remains of the outer wall of the house have survived. However, the destruction carried on here by the Copts in quarrying for building materials has been very thorough, for they later erected on the site a large monastery for three hundred monks and several churches, of which one very large one, dedicated to the Virgin, was converted into a mosque by the Fatimid ruler el-Hakim (996–1021).

While in the construction of the temple numerous sculptured blocks derived from a temple of the 18th Dynasty were reused, nothing was found in the portion excavated by the Germans that could be ascribed to the time with which we are dealing. The results of their work, however, permit no conclusions, for the excavations were nothing more than soundings.

Concerning the work in the area of the French concession the information is

[23] *Ibid.*, 59.

[24] *Ibid.*, 41, and Tafel VIII.

most meager. Here Clermont-Ganneau found the "Khnubeum," with several crypts containing sarcophagi of embalmed rams.[25] Allowing ten years for the age of each of the thirty-three rams, a total of 330 years would be accounted for and this, according to him, would fit the period from Augustus to Constantine.

It is apparent, then, that no knowledge concerning the Khnum Temple of the 5th century B.C. was afforded by all these excavations. Nevertheless it seems most likely that the site of the more ancient temple was the same as the site of the new Temple of Nektanebos II and the Ptolemies. The question is whether the temple was enlarged in the later period, and whether in the process of enlargement a quarter of the Aramaean city was wiped out.

2. The Search for the Temple of Yahu

The Sayce-Cowley papyri had brought to light the fact that there was a Temple of Yahu in Yeb and even gave a hint of its location in the vicinity of certain houses.[26] Of the destinies of that temple, furthermore, three papyri found in the second Berlin campaign and published by Sachau in 1907 gave surprising information.[27] It is no wonder, then, that the excavators in continuing their work kept their eyes open for some signs of this temple.

It was natural for the excavators to suppose that the Aramaic papyri were found in the houses to which they refer. Since they had come from the houses *m* and *n* on the western rim of the kom that area seemed to offer a point from which to proceed in the search for the Jewish temple. Rubensohn of the German expedition came to the conclusion that the street marked *p* on his plan was the "street of the king," to the east of which the Temple of Yahu must then have lain, but he added, "Any prospect of recovering the Yahu temple in this area is hopeless, for rebuilding and destruction have, since antiquity, been carried on here in a more radical manner than in the other quarters of the city. All our efforts at locating the temple, notably our deep excavations east of the said street, remained unsuccessful."[28]

With particular ardor Clermont-Ganneau concerned himself with the problem of the Yahu Temple. Evidently he was not acquainted with the views of the German excavators concerning the probable area where the Jewish temple was to be sought, but developed a theory of his own on purely archaeological grounds. In a letter to De Vogüé[29] he expresses the idea that the temple was to be sought in the area of the German concession at a point (apparently γ on fig. 4) the importance or

[25] See his letter, *Journal des Savants*, 1944, 89 ff.

[26] See below, Chapter 7.

[27] See below, Chapter 9.

[28] Honroth and others, "Ausgrabungen," 30.

[29] *Journal des Savants*, 1944, 136.

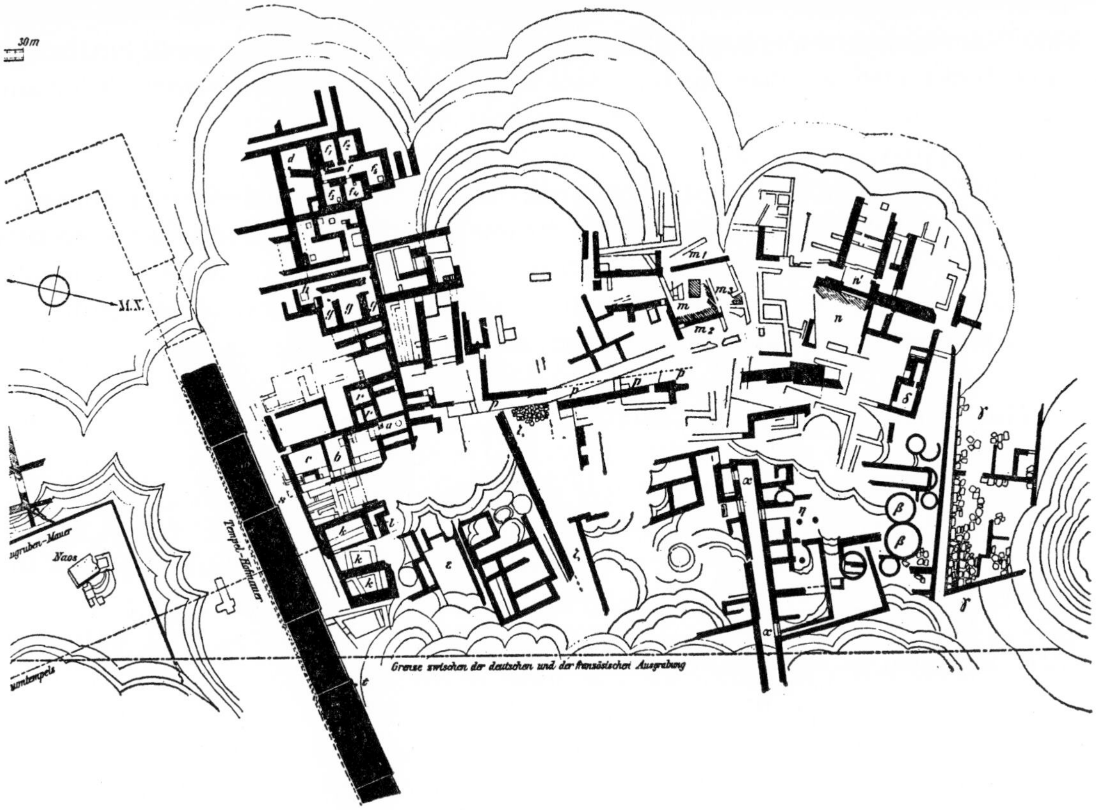

FIG. 4 Plan of Area of Significance for the Papyri (Honroth and others, "Ausgrabungen"). Solid black line marks northern wall of the court of the Temple of Khnum.

significance of which the rival excavators did not understand. Its outer limits were within two meters of the French concession: "I see the promised land. I almost touch it with my hand. And it is not given me to enter there. It is truly provoking." He does not venture to assert positively that the temple stood there, but he regards the spot as a serious candidate for the honor. He thinks that the Yahu Temple was destroyed[30] and asks, "But then, if it be so, must one lose all hope of finding the sanctuary of Jehovah?" To this he answers, "Not at all," and argues that the site of the temple is still there and can be discerned.[31]

Toward the extreme north of the kom, all along the French boundary line the German excavations had partially brought to light a *massif* of enormous blocks of unhewn granite, of gigantic rolling stones, forming a wall of a thickness yet undetermined. According to Clermont-Ganneau, the excavators were at first inclined

[30] On his explanation of that destruction, see below, p. 102.

[31] *Journal des Savants*, 1944, 138 ff.

to see in it the subbase of a street which might be identified with the "street of the king" mentioned in the papyri. But it gradually became clear that the mass was much larger than was suitable for a street. The Germans then allegedly (for their own report makes no mention of the matter) shifted to the idea of a fortress, a fortified mound, a post of observation, etc. They did not attach extreme importance to it, for instead of digging the place out completely they made it a dumping ground for a formidable mass of earth during their last dig. Clermont-Ganneau's idea was that this massif was the platform on which rose the Temple of Jehovah, like that of the Temple of Jerusalem, with a *ḥarām* in miniature. The south face of this platform was visible to a length of fifteen meters, though it was partly fallen in.

With a sort of prophetic intuition Clermont-Ganneau reconstructed in his own mind the story of the Jewish temple.[32] He believed that when the Jews had obtained permission to build a temple at Elephantine, they had been assigned a site in the northern suburb. The Jewish houses then grouped themselves around the temple, which formed the kernel of an Aramaean quarter that gradually grew up adjoining the Egyptian quarter, which lay on the south side of the temple. At first the Egyptian houses lay at some distance from the temple; little by little they filled in the intervening space until they lay close to the temple walls.

He imagines the building of the temple to have proceeded as follows: First was constructed a vast quadrangular platform of which we have the remains — remains without analogy in Egypt but, as already stated, singularly reminiscent of a Syrian or Palestinian ḥaram. Unhewn stones were used, a circumstance immediately reminding one of those of the altar of Jerusalem (Deut. 27:5). On this platform was set the temple, properly speaking "the Holy," a rectangular enclosure containing the *adyton*, the altar, and other accessories. The worshipers of the god Khnum must have pitilessly razed the whole superstructure when they destroyed the temple in order to wipe out even the last vestige of the sacrilegious cult. Clermont-Ganneau believed that a number of mutilated architectural pieces might have been discarded and could perhaps be found at the base of the platform. There might even be discovered there some fragments of Aramaic inscriptions, for example, of documents authorizing the Jews to construct or reconstruct their sanctuary. For on this point the Jews shared the customs of other peoples and set up in their temple documents of this nature (compare the Seleucid decrees, the treaties of alliance under the Hasmonaeans, etc.). The discovery of such remains is the only hope left of finding any vestiges of the Jewish temple.

In his next letter of March 19, 1908,[33] he speaks of having concentrated his

[32] *Ibid.*, 136 ff.

[33] *Journal des Savants*, 1944, 139 ff.

efforts on the side of the well-known "esplanade" where he inclines more and more to localize the Temple of Jehovah.

> I am pushing, as energetically as I am able, the trenches on the front which borders the German boundary . . . These labors of approach are extremely difficult, given the conditions under which we have to operate. All the German dumps which overhang us roll down on us as we try to push forward. I should like at least to be able to find the N. E. corner which would furnish an essential element, the length of one of the small sides of the parallelogram constituting the *hieron* or *ḥarām* . . .

But the expedition had to be terminated shortly afterward.

The expedition of the Fathers of the Pontifical Biblical Institute in 1918[34] also concerned itself with the site of the temple and was not hampered by the concession line that had existed in the days of the French excavations. Concerning this Ronzevalle reports as follows:

> The inquiry into the Jewish sanctuary led us ourselves to carry on some soundings south of the point marked *y* on the German plan. We established our second camp there for a fortnight. Our excavations which were confined to points already very deeply dug deserve to be regarded merely as a preliminary attempt. We found only formless debris and some vases, among them a jar containing the skeleton of a newborn infant. The site of the temple of Yahu, destroyed in the Persian epoch and perhaps not even rebuilt, still remains therefore a matter for research. Divers indications, however, permit one to conjecture reasonably with Maspero[35] and Clermont-Ganneau that it is indeed here that one should seek the emplacement of the Jewish sanctuary.

This last effort to obtain any exact knowledge of the temple site therefore also remained unproductive of any real evidence.

Excavations were carried on at Elephantine by the Egyptian government in 1932 and 1946, but not in the area of the Jewish-Aramaean quarter, and the valuable finds made concern the earlier history of the town.[36]

[34] See Strazzuli and others, "Rapport," *ASAE*, *18*, 1919.

[35] Gaston Maspero, *Rapports sur la marche du Service des Antiquités de 1899–1910* (Cairo, 1912), 294.

[36] See *Chronique d'Égypte*, *21*, No. 42 (1946), 200–201; and C. De Wit, "À propos de quelques statues inédites trouvée à Éléphantine," *Actes du XXe Congrès International des Orientalistes* (Paris, 1949), 87–88.

7. THE LOCATION OF THE JEWISH TEMPLE

As WE have seen, the excavations left the location of the Jewish temple of Elephantine in doubt. Before reconsidering the problem in the light of the valuable new indications contained in the Brooklyn papyri we must discuss two minor points: first, what is meant by "the street of the king"; second, what is the relation to the actual points of the compass of the designations "above" and "below," which appear so often in the papyri in giving the location of property.

There were allusions to a street without further specification in *A.P.* 5:12, 14 and *A.P.* 13:14. In addition a "road (*'rḥ*) of the king" was mentioned in *A.P.* 25:6 as lying between the house of Jezaniah b. Uriah and the Temple of Yahu. This reference to the "road of the king" was held to signify the "main street" of the town. Rubensohn would have liked to identify it with the street that ran along the north wall of the Ptolemaic Temple of Khnum.[1] He gave up that idea, however, because he reasoned that the road referred to in *A.P.* 25:6 must have run close to the houses where the Sayce-Cowley papyri were found and most of these, it will be recalled (see above, Chapter 6), came to light immediately west of the house *m*[1] (fig. 4). For the same reason he also ruled out the street marked *α*, which was found in the third campaign under Zucker. The street marked *p*, he concludes, must be the road in question. It is a narrow alley hardly a meter and a half wide. In its north-south course it passed east of the house *m* — a circumstance which, the excavator held, would agree well with the fact that in the papyri houses are described as lying west of it. That, he believed, would rule out both the temple street and *α*, which run east-west.

Clermont-Ganneau also kept his eyes open for the "rue royale," but observed that in the network of streets and alleys in the adjacent part of the Aramaean quarter excavated by him there was none that could pretend to such a dignity.[2] No plan of the French excavations seems to have been prepared, so we do not know how the streets ran in that area.

In the Brooklyn papyri the term "street," without further specification, occurs once in the fragmentary connection of No. 6:6. Otherwise we hear only of the "street of the king" (Nos. 3:8, 10; 4:10, 11; 10:4, 5; 12:19, 21), not of the "road

[1] Honroth and others, "Ausgrabungen," 29.

[2] Cf. *Journal des Savants*, 1944, 136.

of the king." These texts, as we shall see, concern houses that have the Temple of Yahu to the west of them, while the Sayce-Cowley papyri relate to houses that have that temple either "below" or to the east of them.

Terms like "road of the king" and "street of the king" have their parallels. In examples of Assyrian provenance given by Weidner the "road of the king" refers to highways between garrisons located in different towns and cities.[3] In Babylonia a field has the "road of the king" for a boundary in one instance.[4] In the demotic texts "street of the king" is common in the description of properties,[5] and the same phrase occurs in the Greek texts in the Greek equivalent. If "road of the king" and "street of the king" were synonymous the phrase manifestly could not mean the main street of the town, since they lie on opposite sides of the temple. But if they are not synonyms then one would still be uncertain which signifies the main street. In the case of the street of the king, furthermore, we find that it is used of streets on two sides of a given house (Brooklyn No. 4:9–11). That also makes it rather unlikely that the phrase designates a particularly important thoroughfare. It would seem best for the present to regard "street of the king" as a term for any public street, in contrast to alleys in which individuals owned or shared ownership of the land and which they could close to the public. In Greek papyri, too, the equivalent phrase may, perhaps, mean "public street," as does its successor, the term "fiscal street."[6]

The second point needing clarification is what is meant by "above" (literally, "the upper side") and "below" (literally, "the lower side") in the property descriptions. It was assumed by Cowley and has been taken for granted since then that above means upstream or south, and below downstream or north. The colonists, it was thought, conformed to the Egyptian way of thinking, which was supposedly governed by the fact that the Nile flowed north. But this is not entirely convincing. If, for example, the Aramaeans had previously been accustomed to use above for north and below for south, there is little likelihood that they would have changed established expressions to suit Egyptian ways of thinking.

Similar phraseology appears in the Babylonian property descriptions. There, however, the distinctions are more elaborate, for in the case of fields and houses the quadrangles specified have an upper and a lower "front" and an upper and a

[3] See *Die Inschriften vom Tell Halaf*, 15. Cf. also Heb. *derek hammelek* in Numb. 20:17, referring to the main route through Transjordan.

[4] Peiser, *Texte*, 225.

[5] See Eugène Révillout, *La propriété; ses démembrements, la possession et leurs transmissions en droit Égyptien* (Paris, 1897), 168, 322, etc. New examples are given in the Theban archive from the time of Ptolemy I, published by S. R. K. Glanville, *Catalogue of the Demotic Papyri in the British Museum*, (London, 1939), *1*, xxix and 21. A way or road of the king is likewise mentioned on p. 32.

[6] See Bernard P. Grenfell, *The Amherst Papyri* (1901), *2*, No. 97:10, and Hermann Rink, *Strassen und Viertelnamen von Oxyrhynchus* (Giessen, 1924), 20 ff.

lower "side," with the fronts designating the narrower ends.[7] It is then further specified in these texts in which direction the fronts and sides face.[8] The upper sides seem to be north and west and the lower sides south and east.[9] In the Nuzi texts, on the other hand, a more simple pattern prevails. While north and south are referred to especially, east and west are simply given as above and below.[10] The Elephantine papyri are much like this, except that east and west are the points of compass especially named, with above and below referring to the remaining two directions. It would certainly seem that above and below are regular terms for two points of the compass, else how could they be used so uniformly in the descriptions of houses lying on three sides of the Jewish temple? One might, perhaps, infer from the usage at Babylon that a predilection existed for describing north as "above" and south as "below." In any case we believe that this is the meaning of the terms in the property descriptions and that such an assumption clarifies the whole situation.

Turning now to the evidence of the papyri we shall first review the clues given by those of Sayce-Cowley concerning the Temple of Yahu. In *A.P.* 13:13–14 the house that Maḥseiah b. Yedoniah bought from Meshullam b. Zakkur and conveyed to his daughter in the year 446 B.C. is described as follows:

"Above it is the house of Ye'osh b. Penuliah; below it is the Temple of Yahu the god; on the east of it is the house of Gaddūl b. Osha' and the street between them; on the west of it is the house of Marduk b. Palṭo, priest of the gods – – –."[11] This house thus had the Yahu Temple below it. While it is not directly stated it seems likely that there was a street between the Yahu Temple and the house of Meshullam b. Zakkur.

[7] Cf. François Thureau-Dangin, *Textes mathématiques babyloniens* (Leyden, 1938), 224, 226. *Pūtu* is front; *šiddu* is side.

[8] See examples in Mariano San Nicolò and Arthur Ungnad, *Neubabylonische Rechts- und Verwaltungsurkunden* (Berlin, 1935), 68, No. 44, 69, No. 45, 71, No. 46, 76, No. 48, 83, No. 54.

[9] So according to Ephraim Sonnenschein, "Beiträge zu den Neubabylonischen Urkunden über Kauf," *Rocznik Orjentalistyczny, 3,* 1925, 188, with the statement corrected by Landsberger, who tells me that by a misprint east and west were reversed here. The usage in the Sippar texts is thus similar to that at Babylon.

[10] See Cyrus J. Gordon, "The Dialect of the Nuzu Tablets," *Orientalia, 7,* 1938, 226. The terms are *iltānu* (north), *sūtānu* (south), *elēnu* (above), *šupālu* (below).

[11] I regard it as certain that the name of the man was Marduk; the tops and bottoms of the letters are a bit out of line as a crack in the papyrus passes through them. But I consider the restoration making him priest of the gods Kh[num and Sa]ti impossible, as the space is insufficient. It is improbable in any case that a man with such a name could have been priest of Egyptian deities. It is not certain that the word god following [–]ti was plural, though the spacing makes that seem likely. If the first letter of the divine name or names was *ḥ*, as also seems probable, the god *Ḥn* of the ostracon referred to in Chapter 8 may have been meant. The [–]ti is then a remnant of another short name — perhaps 'Attī, a hypocoristic form of 'Attā according to Albright, *AJSL, 41,* 1925, 89.

Another reference to the Yahu Temple in the Sayce-Cowley papyri was afforded by *A.P.* 25:5–7 of 416 B.C. Here the house of Jezaniah b. Uriah is described thus: "Above the house of Hosha' b. Uriah adjoins it; below the house of Haṣṣūl b. Zekariah adjoins it – – –; on the east of it is the Temple of Yahu the god and the road of the king between them; on the west of it the house of Mibṭaḥiah, daughter of Maḥseiah, which Maḥseiah her father gave her adjoins it." Like Maḥseiah's house this, too, was near the Yahu Temple, except that the temple lay to the east of it instead of below it and that a road separating it from the temple is explicitly mentioned.

The Brooklyn papyri speak of the Temple of Yahu more frequently than the Sayce-Cowley papyri. Particularly instructive is the reference in No. 3:7–10, describing the situation of the house of Ananiah b. Azariah.

"Above it is the house of Satibar; below it is the *tmy* of Khnum the god and the street of the king is between them; east of it the treasury of the king adjoins it; on the west is the Temple of Yahu the god and the street of the king is between them." In Brooklyn No. 4:9–11 of the year 434 B.C. a portion of the same property is described, but with a variation in the directions; the house of Satibar has been shifted from north to west; the *tm'* (so instead of *tmy*) of Khnum to the east; the Temple of Yahu to "below"; the treasury of the king is not mentioned but must have lain "above," beyond the portion of the house here described. However, since the eastern location of the treasury of the king is confirmed in No. 10 we may rule out this variant description and regard that of No. 3, given above, as the standard one. The divergence in No. 4 need not be completely mistaken but could be due to the fact that the buildings and streets were a little off the true directions — north actually being northwest, etc.[12]

We thus have fresh clues for the location of the Temple of Yahu from a house on a different side of that edifice. It lay west of Ananiah's house, across a north-south street, while to the east of his house lay the "treasury of the king." Across an east-west street from Ananiah's corner property lay the *tmy* of the god Khnum; hence the east-west street will also have run between the *tmy* of Khnum and the Temple of Yahu.

The question what is meant by the *tmy* of Khnum becomes of crucial importance here both for determining the direction meant by "below" and for the location of the Yahu Temple. It is apparently an Egyptian loan word meaning "the town of Khnum."[13] Anything that was Khnum's should probably be sought in the close neighborhood of the Khnum Temple. Since the Khnum Temple lay south of the district where the Aramaic papyri were found it would appear rather certain that "below" in the property descriptions must mean *south* and not north as has hitherto been supposed.

[12] The same shift of directions appeared in *A.P.* 8 in describing the property bought in *A.P.* 6.

[13] See the discussion in the commentary on No. 3:8 below.

In Brooklyn No. 12:17 f. of 402 B.C. the *tmy* of Khnum is not mentioned as "below," but rather the house of the brothers Peḥi and Pemeṭ, the boatmen — men with Egyptian names. That might suggest that the *tmy* of Khnum was an Egyptian quarter. In Brooklyn No. 9:10 and 10:6, the house of Ḥor b. Petesi, gardener of Khnum, lies "below"; he may well have been living close to the Khnum Temple, just as Ananiah, the servitor of Yahu, lived hard by the temple of his god. It should be recalled here that numerous demotic papyri were found on the southern edge of the promontory west of the Khnum Temple (fig. 3), in the area of the Arab burying ground.[14] It is reasonable to suppose that this was part of the "town of Khnum." Before the wall of the Ptolemaic temple was built that district may have encircled the temple on the north as well and extended over the area of *g* later occupied by houses of Ptolemaic times.

The location of the treasury of the king clearly has an important bearing on the matter of the location of the Yahu Temple. The excavators emphasize the fact that they found no remains of buildings which could be described as public buildings. But the "treasury of the king" means nothing more than storehouse and it need not have been a large structure. One is struck by the fact that in the house marked *k* on the plan of excavations numerous jars and vessels with Phoenician and Aramaic inscriptions were found, suggesting that there was a depot of *naturalia* here;[15] furthermore, in the westernmost room of this house a great quantity of Aramaic papyri was unearthed, but disintegrated on contact with the air (see Chapter 6). It is tempting to seek here the treasury of the king and the place where the "scribes of the treasury" of *A.P.* 2:12 labored. Ananiah's house then would have lain west of *k*. The Temple of Yahu would have been a sort of chapel on the outskirts of the Khnum compound, separated from it only by a street. But archaeological uncertainties enter in here. We cannot be sure how the street passing the Khnum Temple ran at this particular time and whether a street corresponding to the one that passed west of Ananiah's house existed at this point.[16] It seems advisable, therefore, to look for the site of the Jewish temple a little farther to the north, as Rubensohn did.[17]

If one assumes with that scholar that the house of Maḥseiah b. Yedoniah lay in the area where the papyri were found, then the street *p* would be the north-

[14] See Honroth and others, "Ausgrabungen," 16.

[15] *Ibid.*, 25 f.

[16] A street, but of a later period, is noted as coming in to the temple street from the north considerably west of *k*. See *ibid.*, 23 and the photograph.

[17] In the excavations of Ronzevalle Aramaic papyrus fragments were found in the vicinity of *o* on his plan (the area adjacent on the north to *g* on Honroth's plan). In Chapter 1 we have expressed the belief that these fragments have been published by Aimé-Giron. One contains the name "bar Azariah" and could thus come from the house of Ananiah. But if Ananiah's house had lain north of *g* the street *p* would lose its bearing on the location of the temple.

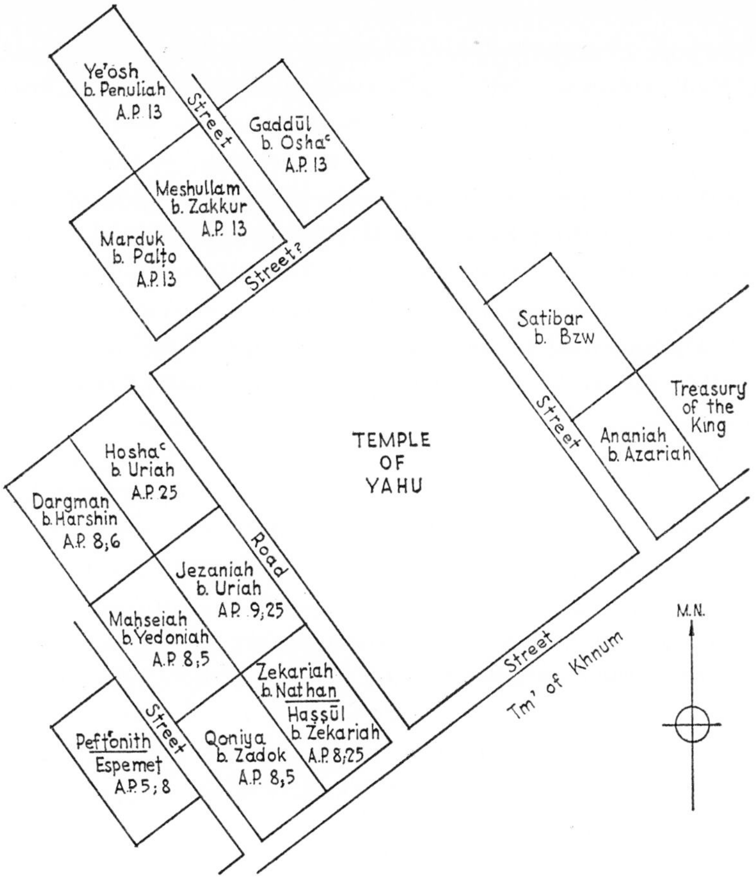

FIG. 5 Revised Plan of the Jewish District

south street of the Sayce-Cowley papyri and the Temple of Yahu would have lain east of it. The stone *empierrement* (to use Ronzevalle's term) situated where the long, impressive, sloping wall ζ coming from the east[18] reaches the street *p* would then merit especial attention as possibly within the temple area. That area, however, may have been very small, so that one cannot be too sure of this. But in general one may say that the tract east of *p* seems to be the most logical place in which to seek it. But without more precise information concerning streets, buildings, and houses, such as could only be provided by methodical excavations, it would appear to be impossible to identify the other streets and the houses of Ananiah and his neighbors on the plan of the site. Perhaps the Egyptian govern-

[18] Zucker considers the possibility that this wall may have been the boundary of a quarter of the town, but was unable to relate it to other walls, *ibid.*, 46. Ronzevalle mentions a wall 18 meters long at a point some 100 meters north-northeast of γ on the plan (fig. 4), in the direction of the Nubian village. See *ASAE*, *18*, 1919, 5. Is the wall *zeta* the one of *A.P.* 27:5 (cf. p. 103)?

ment's Inspectorate of Antiquities will see fit to undertake a small excavation, if only for the purpose of locating the "treasury of the king." It should be noted, however, that Rubensohn was extremely pessimistic about the prospects of finding any vestige of the temple if it lay in this district, for the building and rebuilding carried on here in various periods and the devastations of the sebakh diggers had created a discouraging situation already in his time[19]— a state of affairs now worsened by his own dig and the later one of P. Ronzevalle.

For the present, then, we must regretfully leave in uncertainty the localization of the Yahu Temple. But on the basis of the insight now gained — that it lay close to the Temple of Khnum or to an Egyptian quarter in the very shadow of it and thus roughly fixing its site — we may with some degree of confidence propose a revised plan of the Jewish district, with "above" and "below" taken as north and south (see fig. 5).[20]

[19] See "Ausgrabungen," 29 ff.

[20] On this plan we have taken no account of changes in the area adjoining the treasury of the king, reflected in Nos. 9:8 and 10:3. For the previous plan see Cowley, *A.P.*, p. 13, adapted from Van Hoonacker, *Une communauté*, 41; also Vincent, *Religion*, 339.

8. THE RELIGION OF THE JEWISH COLONY

THE members of the Jewish colony of Elephantine continued in a foreign land the ancient worship of Palestine. They had built a temple to their god (see below, Chapter 9). The law set forth in the Deuteronomic ordinances,[1] which recognized but a single sanctuary, that of Jerusalem, was either not known to them or else not accepted. Since the Deuteronomic law was connected, according to II Kings 22, with the religious reformation of King Josiah, which may have been as abortive as that of the ancient Pharaoh Akhenaten, it is possible that the rule proscribing any but the one sanctuary was not strictly observed for any length of time even in Palestine. Certainly the so-called Priestly Code does not repeat or restate it.

In exilic and post-exilic times, prophetic voices continue to assail the cult of the "high places" (Ezek. 20:28–29; Isa. 65:7). In Ezra 4:2 we learn that the enemies of the children of Judah and Benjamin (i. e., the Samaritans), seeking to cooperate in the building of the Temple at Jerusalem, declare, "for we seek your god, like unto yourselves; we have sacrificed to him since the time when Esarhaddon, king of Assyria, brought us hither." In II Kings 17:32 ff. the worship of Yahweh at high places in Samaria is especially emphasized.

Sanctuaries of Yahweh were thus not uncommon after Josiah's reformation. It is likely enough, furthermore, that at such sanctuaries concessions were made to what puritanical persons would have called "idolatry." In Judah itself there was a deterioration in the direction of downright paganism. Jeremiah (19:13) speaks of the cult of the "host of heaven" on the roofs, of the cakes that the women bake for the "queen of heaven" (7:18), and of rites to strange gods performed by the women in the land of Judah and in the streets of Jerusalem (44:9). Ezekiel, furthermore, describes (8:14 ff.) how these cults, including the worship of the rising sun and the mourning for Tammuz, were carried on in Jerusalem at the temple itself.

It is not the depraved type of Jewish religion that is illustrated in the Elephantine colony.[2] We may be certain that the Jews residing there were worshipers

[1] Deut. 12. The interpretation has been denied by Adam C. Welch, *The Code of Deuteronomy* (London, 1924), and others. See the critique of Karl Budde, "Das Deuteronomium und die Reform König Josias," *ZAW*, *44*, 1926, 177 ff. On recent developments, cf. Christopher R. North "Pentateuchal Criticism," in H. H. Rowley, *The Old Testament and Modern Study* (Oxford, 1951), 49 f.

[2] Vincent, *Religion*, provides an exhaustive discussion on this subject. But see also the brief

of their national god. But as a matter of insurance they were willing to give a bit of attention to several subsidiary gods, whom they might readily view as his vassals or helpers. The inducement to be liberal was all the greater because of the composite nature of the community. The Jews there lived among Egyptians, Aramaeans, Phoenicians, Babylonians, and Persians. Mutual tolerance and a willingness to recognize other deities were almost a practical necessity.

The liberal attitude of some of the Elephantine Jews is reflected in the salutations used in certain letters. In the Mazzoth Papyrus, *A.P.* 21:2, Hananiah, in writing to "Yedoniah and his colleagues (and) the Jewish garrison," says, "May the gods desire the welfare of my brethren." A similar greeting is used in *A.P.* 37 in which someone writes to "Yedoniah, Ma'uziyah and the garrison." In *A.P.* 39 Hosha' writes to the woman Salluah, "May the gods all desire your welfare at all times." In the very fragmentary letter, *A.P.* 56, Yislaḥ b. Nathan uses the polytheistic formula and so does Shewa b. Zekariah writing to his lord "Yislaḥ" in Brooklyn No. 13. Meyer, speaking of the Mazzoth Papyrus, which he characterizes as a "completely orthodox letter," asserts that the word "gods" (*ĕlāhayyā*) here is merely the equivalent of Hebrew *'elōhīm*, which in the Old Testament is plural in form and singular in meaning.[3] Since the plural of the verb is used this seems unlikely; there is no escape from the fact that the polytheistic formula was employed, however mechanically or unreflectingly, by Hananiah.

In a number of passages in the Elephantine papyri published by Sachau we find the phrase "God of Heaven" substituted for the divine name. The occurrences are restricted to the "diplomatic" documents and to two other letters, *A.P.* 38:2, 3 and 40:2. The writer of the former is Ma'uziah b. Nathan and of the latter, Hosha'iah b. Nathan, both scribes and important men of the community. Since this phrase is also found in Old Testament writings of the Persian or Hellenistic age, the predilection shown for it in the diplomatic texts may be in conformity with recent Palestinian custom, reflecting Yahweh's absorption of the title of the god Baalshamin. That Ma'uziah and Hosha'iah use it in two letters of their own suggests that they, as scribes, were emulating the style set in the homeland and that, as men of superior insight, they preferred not to employ the polytheistic formula in more common use. Certainly God of Heaven does not seem to have been a term in general use for Yahu at Elephantine.

In the Brooklyn Museum texts, as in those previously published, it is "*Yhw* the god" who is the chief object of reverence. This is, of course, the form of the name of Yahweh that is so often found in the Old Testament at the *end* of names

sketches of Meyer, *Papyrusfund*, 38 ff.; Anneler, *Zur Geschichte*, 77 ff.; Van Hoonacker, *Une communauté*, 67 ff.; Wagenaar, *De joodsche Kolonie*, 120 ff.

[3] Meyer, *Papyrusfund*, 67. It is true that there is one occurrence of the word with a singular of the verb, Aḥ. 126, but this may be regarded as a scribal error (see Cowley, *ad loc.*).

(compare Jeremiah's name, which is really Yirme-yahu). In the ostraca, however, as well as in *A.P.* 13:14 and in several personal names,[4] the writing *Yhh* is used.[5] It suggests the pronunciation Yahṓ which is found for *Yhw* (as *Yehṓ-*) in the Old Testament at the *beginning* of personal names such as Jehoshaphat. The difference is simply due to accent: *Yehṓ*, but *Yā́hū*. We transcribe the name as Yahu in accordance with our tendency to accent it on the first syllable.

The Jews of Elephantine believed that Yahu was actually present in his temple. When the Deuteronomic doctrine was formulated, it reflected an enlightened skepticism which found it impossible to believe, with earlier, more naïve generations, that God literally "dwells" in his sanctuary. Accordingly, it was said, "He caused his name to dwell" there — the "name" representing a holy emanation from the deity, who really had his dwelling place far removed in heaven. This was a formulation (of Phoenician origin?) which preserved the sanctity of the temple, so that it would not become useless to go there, but at the same time met the critical doubts of an advanced age. The colony at Elephantine had no need for such subtleties. It was satisfied with the more primitive concept. Yahu was, to them, "the god who is in Yeb, the fortress."[6] Brooklyn No. 12 makes the idea doubly clear, for in it Yahu is "the god who *dwells* in Yeb the fortress."

The ancient phrase, "Yahweh of Hosts," was used in Elephantine, appearing on ostraca found by Clermont-Ganneau as *Yhh ṣb't*.[7] The use of this epithet shows the ancient relationship of the Jews of the colony with Jerusalem, for Yahweh of Hosts was the full cult name of the deity worshiped in the Holy City (compare Ps. 24:10).

We have no evidence of the existence of other temples to foreign gods on the Island of Elephantine. There may, however, have been several in nearby Syene. In an Aramaic inscription from Saqqāra we have direct information concerning a

[4] *Yhh'wr*, *A.P.* 1:2, *Yhhdry*, *A.P.* 11:13. The latter is taken as *Yh-hdry* by Cowley, *A.P.*, p. 35. Dupont-Sommer, "Le syncretisme religieux des juifs d'Éléphantine," *Revue d'Histoire des Religions*, *65*, 1945, 23, would read *Yhh-ddy*. On the element *hdr* see W. W. Baudissin, *Kyrios als Gottesname im Judentum* (Giessen, 1926–29), *3*, 85 f.

[5] Dupont-Sommer thinks *Yhh* is a popular way of writing the name *Yahweh* and that it is perhaps more ancient than the writing *Yhw*, but that the latter recommended itself by the resemblance to *Yhwh* (the officially accepted form). There is an extensive literature on the divine name; see, e. g., Baudissin, *Kyrios*, *3*, 194 f.; G. R. Driver, "The Original Form of the Name Yahweh: Evidence and Conclusions," *ZAW*, *46*, 1928, 7 f.; Otto Eissfeldt, "Neue Zeugnisse für die Aussprache des Tetragramms als Jahwe," *ZAW*, *53*, 1935, 59 f.

[6] Even in the letter *A.P.* 30:6 the rendering should not be as Cowley has it, "the temple of Yahu the god, *which* is in Yeb the fortress," but "*who* is in Yeb, the fortress" (cf. in l. 5, "Khnub, the god who is in Yeb the fortress").

[7] Dupont-Sommer, "Yaho et Yeho Sebaot sur les ostraca araméens inédits," *CRAI*, 1947, 175 ff. Cf. Eissfeldt, "Jahwe Zebaoth," in *Miscellanea Academica Berolinensia* (Berlin, 1950), *3*.

shrine of the god Nabū at that place,[8] and the Hermopolis papyri mention the divinities, Nabū, Banīt-in-Syene, Bethel, and Malkatshamin, the "queen of heaven."[9] Since four of these documents are addressed to persons in Syene, it seems probable that all the Semitic deities mentioned were worshiped here.

Dupont-Sommer would find evidence for worship of Babylonian gods on the part of Elephantine Jews in the Clermont-Ganneau ostracon No. 271,[10] because it begins "(1) To my brother Haggai, thy brother (2) Yarḥo. The welfare of my brother (3) may Bel and Nabū, Shamash and Nergal ask at all times." He notes that these gods appear in the same order in an inscription of Sargon.[11] The same gods (though with Marduk given his real name instead of his title Bel) were also listed in the 8th century Aramaic stela of Sujin in Syria published by Ronzevalle.[12] The invoking of four Babylonian deities is certainly evidence of the presence of a Babylonian cult in this area. Since numerous men with Babylonian names are mentioned in the papyri, this seems natural enough. The Persians doubtless had many Babylonians in their service, and the situation in Samaria, where Babylonian settlers introduced Babylonian gods (II Kings 17:30), seems to have repeated itself in Egypt. The ostracon permits no certain inference as to the worship of these deities by Jews, however, for Yarḥo and Haggai were not necessarily of that nationality.[13]

Another Clermont-Ganneau ostracon, No. 70, is taken by Dupont-Sommer as revealing Jewish participation in the worship of Khnum, the Egyptian god of Elephantine.

(1) To my lord Micaiah, thy servant (2) Gaddūl. Peace and life I send (3) to thee and I bless thee to Yahoh and to *Khn.* (4) Now send me the garment (5) which is upon thee that one may sew it. (6) For thy peace (?) I have sent the letter.

The editor would regard *Khn* as abbreviation for Khnum. But it would seem more probable that the god *Ḫan* or *Ḫun* is meant, whose existence has been inferred from personal names of the Harran district.[14]

[8] Aimé-Giron, *Textes*, 98 ff., No. 99.

[9] Murad Kamil, *BIE*, *28*, 1947, 254. The goddess *Banītu* is Babylonian; she is Ishtar as "the (progeny-) begetting deity." Her name occurs prominently in the names of female slaves. See J. J. Stamm, "Die Akkadische Namengebung," *MVAÄG*, *44*, 1939, 307 f. Her worship in Syene illustrates the presence of Babylonians in the Semitic colony. The second element in Succoth-benoth, II Kings 17:30, is probably this name, provided with waw instead of yodh as *mater lectionis*.

[10] Dupont-Sommer, "Le syncretisme religieux" (see n. 4, above), 17 ff.

[11] See D. D. Luckenbill, *Ancient Records of Assyria*, *2*, 73 ff.

[12] See Hans Bauer, "Ein Aramäischer Staatsvertrag aus dem achten Jahrhundert vor Chr.," *AfO*, *8*, 1933, 1 ff.; Driver, "Notes on the Aramaic Inscription from Soudschin," *AfO*, *8*, 1933, 203 ff.

[13] Dupont-Sommer, *loc. cit.* (see n. 10 above), compares Yaroaḥ, I Chron. 5:14, Yeroham, I Sam. 1:1. However, the name *Yarḥa* in the Palmyrene inscriptions is equally comparable, and Haggai occurs at Gezer; see David Diringer, *Le iscrizioni antico-ebraiche palestinesi* (Firenze, 1934), 120.

[14] See Claude H. W. Johns, *Assyrian Doomsday Book or Liber Censualis of the District round Harran*

In *A.P.* 14:5 we find the Jewess Mibṭaḥiah swearing an oath by the goddess Sati, who with the goddess Anuki was closely associated with Khnum in the worship of the local Egyptian temple. The Egyptian Pi', however, had demanded this oath and it was imposed by the court.[15] One cannot, therefore, conclude with certainty that Mibṭaḥiah was a worshiper of Sati, for if the oath was imposed there was nothing to do but to swear it or lose valuable rights. Custom, too, may have dictated that the Egyptian slave of the Jew Meshullam be liberated to the sun-god, as Brooklyn No. 5 presupposes (but perhaps only if the manumission document was contested). This was not yet the time or the climate for uncompromising monotheism.

The chief witness for syncretism among the Jews at Elephantine has hitherto been the great list of contributors to the temple,[16] *A.P.* 22, already referred to in Chapter 5, and dating from 400 B.C. It begins:

"On the third of Pamenḥotep, the fifth year. These are the names of the Jewish force who have given silver to Yahu the God, man by man, 2 shekels." In column 7 (line 120 ff.) the text states by way of conclusion, "The money which is in the hands of Yedoniah b. Gemariah in the month of Pamenḥotep is silver 31 karsh, 8 shekels. Therein

for Yahu: 12 karsh, 6 shekels;
for Eshembethel: 7 karsh;
for 'Anathbethel: 12 karsh."

It is most interesting to find here that certain moneys were earmarked also for Eshembethel and 'Anathbethel. The collector, Yedoniah b. Gemariah, was the man who, more than any other, represented the Jewish community, as evidenced by the letter, *A.P.* 30. But the inconsistency between the opening statement that "man for man they gave money to Yahu the god," and the subsequent apportionment of funds among *three* gods, is a striking one. Some scholars have insisted that Eshembethel and 'Anathbethel were not the recipients of gifts from Jews at all. It is argued that Yedoniah was not just treasurer of the Jewish group but also handled contributions of non-Jews for their cults. That thought seems dubious, for there were more gods worshiped at Elephantine than the two referred to, and a general

in the Seventh Century B. C. (Leipzig, 1901), 16 (addendum on p. 82) and 73. Clay, BEUP, *10*, 50, n. Such names as *Ḫan-suri*, *Ḫan-dada* seem particularly convincing. On the former compare 'Atar-šuri in *A.P.* 8:27. There is also a god Ḫani; cf. Bruno Meissner and Paul Rost, *Die Bauinschriften Sanheribs* (Leipzig, 1893), 96, 100, 105, n. He is called "god of the scribes" and hence seems akin to Nabū; he is one of the attendants of Ashur. The statement of Ronzevalle on p. 68 of the contribution cited in n. 19 below, equating Ḫan with Ramman, is hardly proven by his references.

[15] Cf. the fact that in the Talmud, *Sanh.* 63b, we read that it is forbidden to have any business partnership with "a servant of the stars" lest he at some time impose an oath on his Jewish associate and force him to swear by the star-gods.

[16] For similar Egyptian lists see Vincent, *Religion*, 551 ff.

collector for all cults would seem an anomalous kind of dignitary. Of more weight seems the claim that the total given to Yahu would be accounted for by 123 two (light-) shekel contributions and that the list originally contained exactly that number of names.[17] But that need not imply that the sums earmarked for the other two gods are of non-Jewish origin. They could represent free-will offerings, requiring no listing of the donors, as did that tax which the Jewish community had evidently imposed on itself as obligatory. That we here have "a symbiosis between heretical Yahwism and a syncretistic Aramaean cult, rather than a fusion between the two (Albright)," may be the right way to describe this peculiar situation.

That 'Anathbethel and Eshembethel are deities seems indubitable. This is particularly obvious in the case of 'Anathbethel, for 'Anath, by itself, is the name of a goddess.[18] That Bethel is likewise a deity appears clear from such proper names as Bethelnathan, "Bethel has given," and is substantiated by the Hermopolis papyri in which greetings are sent to the Temple of Bethel. Such combinations of god names are illustrated for the North Semitic sphere by the 'Aštarkemosh of the inscription of King Mesha of Moab. It seems certain that this is a female deity, not the male 'Athtar of Arabia. 'Anathbethel is paralleled at Elephantine by 'Anathyahu (*A.P.* 44:3). This makes one wonder whether Bethel and Yahu were not identified and whether the Temple of Bethel in the Hermopolis papyri was not the Temple of Yahu at Elephantine. In later North Semitic usage we see god names passing at will into mere equivalents for *theos*, god. This is particularly clear in the case of 'Atar in Atargatis, which as Ronzevalle has shown, means "the god 'Attā."[19] Perhaps in the consciousness of the people Bethel was used, just as *'el* in Hebrew, in the sense of "god."[20]

[17] See Umberto Cassuto's article in *Kedem: Studies in Jewish Archaeology* (Jerusalem, 1942), *1*, 47 f. (cf. above, p. 63, n. 31). Pertinent criticisms of this article are made by Albright in a review in *BASOR*, *90*, 1943, 40. An earlier, even less tenable attempt to defend the Elephantine Jews from the charge of syncretistic tendencies was made by J. N. Epstein, in *ZAW*, *32*, 1912.

[18] On this goddess see Albright, "The Evolution of the West Semitic Divinity 'An-'Anat-'Atta," *AJSL*, *41*, 1925, 73 ff. The Ras Shamra texts have added new material. See Hans Bauer, "Die Gottheiten von Ras Schamra," *ZAW*, *51*, 1933, 90, and Albright's more recent remarks in *Archaeology and the Religion of Israel*, 195.

[19] "Les monnaies de la dynastie de Abd-Hadad et les cultes de Hiérapolis-Babycé," *Mélanges de l'Université St. Joseph*, *23*, (Beyrouth, 1940), 28 ff. A close parallel to 'Anathyahu is Anammelech (II Kings 17:31), which Ronzevalle (p. 49) explains as *'Anath-melek*. It seems probable to us that Adrammelech in the same passage is to be explained as *Adad-melek* (Assyrian form rather than Aramaic Hadad), with *d* misread as *r*. If melek (king) is not secondary in the latter instance (added under the influence of Anammelech) it is in apposition and not in the genitive as in 'Anat-melek. The melek meant in the 'Anat of melek is Adad.

[20] The use of *'ēl* "god," is restricted to the Aḥiḳar text, which is obviously of Asiatic provenance. 'El was also the name of a particular god in Phoenicia, as the Ras Shamra texts have made vivid; cf. Bauer, *ZAW*, *51*, 1933, 83 f. on the material.

If the god Bethel was a god who could be identified with Yahweh just as *'el* had been, one may well ask whether there was any precedent for the use of the name in the Hebrew past? There are believed to be traces of the existence of a god Bethel in the Old Testament.[21] A fairly convincing instance is Jer. 48:13:

> "And Moab shall be ashamed of Kemosh,
> As the house of Israel was ashamed of Bethel their confidence."

The parallelism seems to require that Bethel be considered not as the city of that name but as the god of the northern Israelitic tribes, as Kemosh was god of Moab. In the light of the widespread occurrence of a god "Bethel" this can no longer be explained as an abridged way of speaking of the idolatrous calf of the city of Bethel (I Kings 12:28). A personal name comparable to the Bethel names at Elephantine is, indeed, found in the Old Testament. If in Zech. 7:2 we translate as follows: "Bethelsharezer and Regemmelech sent," taking *Bethelsharezer* as a single personal name,[22] we have there an excellent Palestinian parallel to the Bethel names in the papyri[23] from an age only a few generations earlier. And there, too, the man with the Bethel name appears as a pious devotee of Yahweh!

Originally of course Bethel, like 'El, was a Semitic god quite distinct from Yahweh. Philo of Byblos, who calls him Baityl, makes him the second of the four brothers begotten by heaven and earth: 'El, Baityl, Dagon, and Atlas.[24] He thus holds an exalted and ancient position. The close association of Baityl with 'El suggests that the two names are artificially differentiated. Since the fact that Bethel means "house of 'El" is indisputable, we may suppose that it is simply a personification of 'El's house (in heaven) and as such a substitute expression for 'El. The Phoenician origin of the deity is confirmed by the treaty between Esarhaddon and

[21] This was first suggested by Israel Lévy, "Nouveaux papyri araméens," *RÉJ*, *63*, 1912, 161 ff. The fullest discussion is that of Otto Eissfeldt, "Der Gott Bethel," *AR*, *28*, 1930, 1 ff., who cites all the literature. Other passages where the deity is found include Amos 3:14 ff.; 5:5; Hos. 10:3, 15; 12:5. Cf. J. Philip Hyatt, "The Deity Bethel and the Old Testament," *JAOS 59*, 1930, 81 ff. Excellent discussion also in Albright, *Archaeology and the Religion of Israel*, 168 f.

[22] The King James Version renders, "When they had sent to the house Sherezer and Regemmelech." The emendation was first suggested by Julius Wellhausen, *Die kleinen Propheten*, Skizzen und Vorarbeiten, *5* (3rd ed., 1898), *ad loc.* See further on this name in n. 26, below.

[23] Among the Bethel names we find Bethel*tḳm*, *A.P.* 2:6, 10, Bethel*tdn*, *A.P.* 42:8. Eissfeldt (see n. 21, above), 21, takes *tḳm* and *tdn* as jussive 2d person singular. But names like *Bel-tattanu-bulliṭsu*, "Bel let live him who thou gavest!" suggest a different solution. Cf. Clay, BEUP, *10*, 11, Eilers, "Iranische Beamtennamen," 121.

[24] Philo of Byblos II, 16. See Carl Clemen, "Die phönikische Religion nach Philo von Byblos," *MVAÄG*, *62*, 1939, 25. One Bethel-name seems to occur in Ras Shamra: see Bauer, *ZAW*, *51*, 1933, 82. For a brief analysis of the Ras Shamra myths see Julian Obermann, *Ugaritic Mythology* (New Haven, 1948); Theodor H. Gaster, *Thespis. Ritual, Myth and Drama in the Ancient Near East* (New York, 1950).

King Baal of Tyre, in which *Baiti-ilī* is one of the Phoenician gods invoked.[25] From Phoenicia the deity was doubtless taken abroad by Phoenicians. A number of names compounded with Bethel occur in Babylonian texts and one man with such a name even inscribed it in Aramaic writing on a brick of Nebuchadrezzar.[26] In view of the known presence of Phoenician mercenaries in the Nubian area under Psammetichus II it can occasion no surprise to find the god-name Bethel used at Elephantine.

But what does the combination Eshembethel mean? Lidzbarski held that *'šm* is merely the word for "name."[27] It is believed by some scholars that *'šm* is a god-name in an old Aramaic inscription from northern Syria; but that inscription is devoted to the god Hadad and if a deity were referred to there (as does not seem certain) *'šm* might well be the Eshem of Hadad.[28] If *'šm* means "name" then Eshembethel means "name of Bethel." The inscription of the Phoenician king Eshmunazzar of ca. 300 B.C. gives us an indication of what this signifies, when it refers to the goddess 'Ashtart as "the name of Baal."[29] Eshembethel was probably an appellation of Bethel's spouse. The name arose in Syria and continued in use there, as is shown by a Greek inscription of A.D. 223. mentioning a divinity Sumbetylos.[30]

[25] See especially Ernst F. Weidner, "Der Vertrag Asarhaddons mit Baal von Tyrus," *AfO*, *8*, 1932, 29 ff.; translated also in Luckenbill, *Ancient Records of Assyria*, *2*, 229 ff. *Bit-ilī* is followed by the plural sign. This is frequent with West Semitic names ending in *'el*, "god." See Clay, BEUP, *10*, 12 f., who thought a plural with singular meaning as in Hebrew *'elōhīm*, is meant.

[26] On the brick inscription see *CIS*, *2*, No. 54, where *Byt* is falsely separated from the rest of the name (*Byt'ldlny*). A "Babylonized" Bethel name is that of Bethelsharezer (see n. 22 above). On its occurrence also in cuneiform texts see R. P. Dougherty, *Archives from Erech*, *Time of Nebuchadrezzar and Nabonidus*, Yale Oriental Series, *6* (New Haven, 1920), 108:3; cf. Hyatt, "A Neo-Babylonian Parallel to Bethelsharezer," *JBL*, *56*, 1937, 390 ff., who would even identify the individual there mentioned in 541/540 B.C. with the one in Zech. 7:2 of 518/17 B.C. This opinion could be reenforced by assuming that the delegation of which he was a member was from Samaria. People from Erech were in that colony, according to Ezra 4:9, and some may be more recent arrivals than is presupposed there (the transplanting being attributed to "Asnapper," i. e., Ashurbanipal).

[27] Lidzbarski, *Ephemeris*, *3*, 261 ff.; cf. Hubert Grimme, "Die Yahotriade von Elephantine," *OLZ*, *15*, 1912, 14 f.; Albright, *AJSL*, *41*, 1925, 93, *Archaeology and the Religion of Israel*, 171. Cf. *'šym*, "name," in Ṣafaitic, Enno Littmann, *Thamūd und Ṣafā. Studien zur altnordarabischen Inschriftenkunde*, *Abhandlungen für die Kunde des Morgenlandes*, herausgegeben von der DMG (Leipzig, 1940), 16. The idea of Ungnad that Eshem is the Babylonian deity Ishum seems unlikely, since that deity was little known in this period. The Ashima of Hamath, 2 Kings 17:30, is adduced by Meyer, *Papyrusfund*, 58. Noth, *IP*, 124 ff. would connect Eshem with Eshmun, who as god of healing is more probably to be derived from *šmn*. Emphasis on the "name" of Yahweh in the Old Testament religion of the younger period was doubtless elicited by a similar emphasis on the name of Baal or Bethel in Phoenicia and Syria generally. See above, p. 85.

[28] See Cooke, *NSI*, 160, No. 61, ll. 16, 21.

[29] *Ibid.*, 30, No. 5, l. 18.

[30] Victor Chapot, "Antiquités de la Syrie du nord," *Bulletin de Correspondence Hellénique*, *26*,

Another deity linked with Bethel is mentioned in *A.P.* 7, where a man swears an oath by the god Ḥerembethel. Personal names like Ḥeremnathan (*A.P.* 18:4), which means "*Ḥrm* has given," show that Ḥerem was a god. Scholars have almost without exception taken it for granted that the name is to be linked with Arabic *ḥarām* and means the "sacred precincts,"[31] thus providing an instance of the deification of a temple. Since in the Hermopolis papyri greetings are sent to the temples of Nabū, Banit in Syene, Bethel and Malkat Shamin, fresh support for such a view is given. But it seems more likely to me that a name combination like this links a personal figure with the god Bethel. If one vocalizes the name Ḥarīm (cf. Ezra 2:32) this could well be an appellative meaning "holy one" and referring to a son or brother of the deity.

In the oath, which Menahem b. Shallum executed by order of the court he swore by the *msgd'* (?), by Anathyahu and another deity whose name is not preserved (*A.P.* 44:3).[32] The word *msgd'*, perhaps owing to its kinship with the Arabic word for mosque (*masjid*), and because of the allusion to an oath by the temple in Matt. 23:16, has generally ben rendered "temple." But if "temple" had been meant the regular word for it used in these texts, *'egōrā*, would be in order. In the Nabataean inscriptions of the 1st century of the Christian era *msgd'* signifies a stela or pillar which is venerated and at the same time represents the person who erected it and pleads for him before the deity.[33] It seems possible that such a pillar is meant in *A.P.* 44 also. But it should not be overlooked that the reading *msgd'* is not absolutely certain. Owing to the identity of *d* and *r* in this script the word could equally well be taken as *msgr'*.[34] As for 'Anathyahu, since she is parallel to 'Anathbethel, or even identical with her, and since we have taken Eshembethel to mean the spouse of Bethel, it may be best to regard her as the daughter of the god.

Did the Jews at Elephantine observe the Sabbath? Dupont-Sommer has found what he believes to be evidence for that observance on their part in several of the Clermont-Ganneau ostraca. In No. 204, lines 4–5, there is a statement that he

1902, 182 ff.; cf. Lidzbarski, *Ephemeris*, *2*, 323 ff. and *3*, 247, where he regards Symbetulos as female.

[31] Albright, *Archaeology and the Religion of Israel*, 174, interprets "Sacredness of the house of God"; cf. also Vincent, *Religion*, 579 ff. Noth, *IP*, 129 would connect with Hebrew *ḥerem*, "ban," a possibility also considered by Albright in *AJSL*, *41*, 1925, 94.

[32] Yahu was not mentioned in l. 2. The text plainly has *bar*, "son," so that the name of the grandfather followed. A divine name may, however, have stood at the beginning of l. 4, but the space is too large for "Yahu" and too small for "Yahu the god."

[33] See Cooke, *NSI*, 238; Lidzbarski, *Epigraphik*, 152, *Ephemeris*, *3*, 247 f.; Meyer, *Papyrusfund*, 64. The stelas of the ancient Assyrian officials published by Walter Andrae, *Die Stelenreihen in Assur* (Leipzig, 1913) were certainly no mere memorials but had a religious purpose. Cf. Eduard Meyer, *Kleine Schriften* (Halle, 1924), *2*, 1 ff.

[34] The word occurs in the sense of "prison" in the Clermont-Ganneau ostraca, according to Dupont-Sommer, *Actes du XXIe Congrès des Orientalistes* (Paris, 1949), 110.

renders "I am going, and not will I come until the eve (of the Sabbath)." The word used for eve (*'rwbh*) seems to be the same as that used for the "day of preparation" in Jewish sources (*'arūbhtā*; *paraskeue* in the Greek New Testament; cf. Mark 15:42).[35] In No. 152, further supported by No. 186, Dupont-Sommer holds there is express mention of the Sabbath day. In the former ostracon the important clause occurs in lines 2–3.

"Tie up the ox tomorrow on the Sabbath lest he stray."

The word here rendered Sabbath by Dupont-Sommer is written *šbh*, and if it really means the Sabbath it compels our seeking for a different etymology than the customary Hebrew form would seem to suggest. The other ostracon referred to is very fragmentary but provides in its last line a phrase this scholar believes to have been "day of the Sabbath."[36] Since the Sabbath is ancient in Israel its observance in the Elephantine colony is quite possible.

A Cairo ostracon from Elephantine published by Sayce, but inadequately rendered or interpreted by him, is of interest because it mentions a *marzeḥā* or collective celebration (?).[37] The writer Itō addresses a man named Haggai and tells him that he has spoken with Ašian about the money for the banquet, and that worthy has replied, "I will not give it to Haggai or to Yigdol." The writer suggests that Haggai speak with Ašian and get it. This is one of the most lucid of the ostraca. As Lidzbarski pointed out, the marzeḥā had a somewhat ill repute in later times, for it is described as a place where an idol was honored.

Did the Jews of Elephantine observe any Jewish religious festivals? It seems certain that they celebrated a Mazzoth Festival, or Festival of Unleavened Bread, though the name of it does not happen to be preserved in the letter *A.P.* 21[38] of 419 B.C. that reveals this fact.

The writer was a Hananiah, who calls himself (in Egyptian style) "brother" of those addressed. The latter are "Yedoniah [b. Gemariah] and his colleagues [and] the Jewish garrison." Hananiah states that in this year word was sent from

[35] Dupont-Sommer, "Sabbat et parascève à Éléphantine d'après des ostraca araméens inédits," *MAI*, 1950, 68 ff.

[36] *Ibid.*, 71 ff., with full discussion of the problems. The text and photograph with philological commentary are in "L'ostracon araméen du Sabbat," *Semitica*, *2*, 1949, 31 ff. In my article "The Present Status of the Sabbath Question," *AJSL*, *49*, 1933, 218 ff., earlier views concerning the Sabbath are discussed.

[37] Sayce, "An Aramaic Ostracon from Elephantine," *PSBA*, *31*, 1909, 154 ff.; Lidzbarski, *Ephemeris*, *3*, 120. The word also occurs in Phoenician and Palmyrene inscriptions.

[38] The most recent discussion of this is by Dupont-Sommer, "Sur la fête de la Pâque dans les documents araméens d'Éléphantine," *RÉJ*, 7, 1946–47, 39 ff. In his text and translation he has refrained from adopting text restorations for which the text gives no direct mandate. A recent English translation by Ginsberg will be found in James B. Pritchard, ed., *Ancient Near Eastern Texts*, 491.

the king to Arsham (which he is relaying to the addressees). His name is clearly Jewish, so he must in some way have been charged by the satrap with dealing with the Jewish colonies. Sachau suggested that he might be Nehemiah's brother of that name (Neh. 1:2). If he is the personage referred to in the later text *A.P.* 38:7, he must have been from Palestine or Babylonia. The implication there is that his coming had made relations between Jews and Egyptians at Elephantine more difficult. However that may be, since an official order originating in Susa is being transmitted the Mazzoth Papyrus reveals something of the interest taken by the Persian government in the religious affairs of Jewry and thus confirms what is reported concerning the mission of Ezra to Jerusalem (Ezra 7:12 ff.).

Much is evidently missing on the left side of the recto and the right side of the verso of this document (which was written on both sides). From a comparison with other epistolary papyri it seems certain that 10 cm. or about one-third of the papyrus or 23 letter spaces in each line is broken off on the left. A portion of lines 4–10 or 22–25 letter spaces is also missing on the right. (The reader will bear in mind that Aramaic, like Hebrew, is written from right to left, so that in our translation the actual situation is reversed.) Of l. 10 only the final letter remains.

RECTO

1. [To my brethre]n
2. [Yedo]niah and his colleagues (and) the Jewish g[arrison], your brother Hanan[iah]. The peace of my brethren may the gods [desire].
3. And now this year, the year 5 of Darius the king, from the king there was sent to Arsh[am]
4. now thus shall you count: fou[rteen days]
5. [ma]ke and from the 15th day to the twenty-first day of Ni[san]
6. be ye clean and take heed. Work no[t]
7. [No]t shall ye drink and anything which leaven t[here is]

VERSO

8. [from] the setting of the sun to the twenty-first day of Nisa[n]
9. [ye shall not br]ing into your chambers and ye shall seal between the day[s]

Address: [To] my brethren Yedoniah and his colleagues (and) the Jewish garrison, your brother Hanani[ah] . . .

It is certain from line 8 that the month referred to at the end of line 5 was Nisan, and though the name Mazzoth does not occur, the days show that the Mazzoth Festival was involved — a point supported also by the reference to "leaven."

We thus have the bare historical fact that Darius II ordered the Egyptian Jews to celebrate the Mazzoth Festival from the 15th to the 21st of Nisan in 419 B.C. What led a Persian king or those empowered to issue orders under his seal to send such a message to Arsham? Was it merely, as Lidzbarski held,[39] an annual permit for Jewish government employees to take time out, and thus a concession to the religious idiosyncrasies of this group? Or was the celebration of the festival ordered, as Sachau thought,[40] because the Jews at Elephantine had hitherto ignored it and because their coreligionists in Babylonia or Palestine wished to bring them into line and got the support of the Persian government to attain that objective? Or shall we go even further and assume that this decree actually marks the official introduction of the Mazzoth Festival as such? This is the view endorsed by Eduard Meyer.[41]

The Mazzoth Festival was probably a North Israelitic local observance, for it is first mentioned in Exod. 23:15, in the Elohistic Book of the Covenant, believed to have been of northern origin. The further references to the Mazzoth feast in Exod. 34:18 (J) and Deut. 16 are suspected of being late interpolations made after the festival was adopted by the Jews. Ezekiel (45:21) projected a seven-day Passover with the use of unleavened bread (thus in effect making Passover incorporate the Mazzoth feature). In the Priestly Document Mazzoth was originally missing and was inserted by later hands in Exod. 12:15 ff. and Num. 28:16 ff. In the Holiness code, Lev. 23:5 ff., it is likewise considered a later addition.[42] Passover, on the other hand, was a Judaean festival, not known to the Book of the Covenant. The law of Deut. 16:7 required that the Passover lamb be exclusively sacrificed at the temple at Jerusalem. As noted above this legislation originally took no notice of the Mazzoth Festival, for on the day after the Passover the participants could return to their homes. It also left the date of Passover open as "in the month of Abib" (leaving it to proper authority to set the day, perhaps according to the status of growth reached by the crop of young lambs). The Priestly Code, which also lacked the Mazzoth originally, did not require the Passover to be celebrated at Jerusalem and therein no doubt reverted to older Judaean custom. But it fixed the celebration according to a definite day by the Babylonian calendar as on the 14th of Nisan (Exod. 12:15 ff.; Lev. 23:6 ff.).

[39] Lidzbarski, *Ephemeris*, *3*, 243 f. Against this see Meyer, *Papyrusfund*, 92 n.

[40] Sach. 39. C. C. Torrey, "The Letters Prefixed to Second Maccabees," *JAOS*, *60*, 1940, 120 f., attempts to evade the inference that the celebration was ordered by the government. But the text restoration he offers is speculative. He is right, however, in denying that the Passover was mentioned.

[41] Meyer, *Papyrusfund*, 95 ff. (following Steuernagel; see n. 43, below).

[42] See, e. g., Immanuel Benzinger, *Hebräische Archäologie* (3d ed., Leipzig, 1927), 383 f. For recent discussions see H. G. May, "The Passover and the Unleavened Cakes," *JBL*, *55*, 1936, 68 ff.

When the Elephantine papyrus *A.P.* 21 was published Carl Steuernagel put forth the suggestion that those secondary references to the Mazzoth Festival, which had long been suspected of having been introduced harmonistically in the various Old Testament documents, were added around the time of this edict of Darius II.[43] It is not necessary, however, to be so precise about the date of the additions; it is enough to say that these additions flowed from the decision made at that time to adopt the Mazzoth Festival.

Did *A.P.* 21 mention the Passover in the lost part of the end of line 4 and of the beginning of line 5? Many scholars, from Sachau on, were persuaded that this was the case. They would restore the text thus: "You shall count four[teen days of the month of Nisan and then the Passover you shall ma]ke." That text restoration, however, is purely conjectural. In our opinion it is even unlikely. In the first place it does not fill the gap in the text, for as pointed out above 10 cm. of text are probably missing at the end of line 4, in addition to the loss of text at the beginning of line 5. This means that about 45 letter spaces are to be filled, and no guess as to what stood there is of much consequence. In the second place if line 4 says, "Thus shall you count: fourteen days," the thought need not have continued in a manner commanding the Passover; the reference might have been, e.g., to permission to have leaven in possession during fourteen days. In the third place a document which develops the taboos attending Mazzoth, as this text did in lines 6 ff., could certainly not have failed to develop the taboos of Passover at a length greater than can be taken care of in 45 letter spaces, especially when the directions were being given to such a community as the one at Elephantine. In the fourth place, if the Jewish leadership of the period went to the trouble of obtaining an edict from Darius II regulating Jewish festival observance, it stands to reason that an important innovation, difficult to achieve by other means, was being made. That innovation was in all probability the one that remained in force: to again restrict Passover to the Jerusalem temple in the Deuteronomic manner, thereby making it illegal for Jews in foreign lands, but at the same time to provide these foreign groups with an acceptable substitute in the form of the Mazzoth Festival. (Therein a bid for the allegiance of Northern Israelites to the community may have been a factor.)

Passover, of course, was an old Jewish rural festival, and so it is possible and even likely that the Jews of the Elephantine colony had previously observed it. A word that can be translated "Passover" (*psḥ*) occurs twice in earlier Elephantine ostraca. On the one[44] it occurs on the reverse in a broken connection: "on the Passover, and do thou rise up . . ." But it is not clear that a festival or holiday was

[43] See Carl Steuernagel, "Zum Passah-Maṣṣothfest," *ZAW*, *31*, 1911, 310; also his "Die jüdisch-aramäischen Papyri und Ostraka aus Elephantine . . .," *ZDPV*, *35*, 1912, 101 f.

[44] Lidzbarski, *Ephemeris*, *2*, 229 f.; *3*, 257, n. 1.

referred to, and so the rendering is not beyond doubt. On the other ostracon,[45] there is a sentence in lines 8–9 which Dupont-Sommer renders, "Send me (word) when you would celebrate the Passover."[46] He finds that the message exhibits uncertainty as to the date of the festival and points out that this is in accord with the Deuteronomic legislation in which, as already stated, the exact date of the Passover was left open.

Unfortunately the translations in these passages remain somewhat uncertain. But it is attractive to suppose that the Jews of Elephantine had a Passover. However, one can hardly read back into their situation the Passover ritual that we find in the Old Testament documents, as was done by Clermont-Ganneau to explain the origin of anti-Jewish outbreaks by the Khnum priesthood (Chapter 9). The Passover of old Jewish custom may have been quite different from anything we find described in the biblical sources. Killing of lambs would have constituted an unthinkable provocation to the followers of the god Khnum and would have been frowned upon by Persian officers. Elephantine was not in a grazing area and lambs (or kids if one wish to use the evasion suggested by Clermont-Ganneau) were not easily procurable. Furthermore, the Old Testament Passover ritual from Deuteronomy on is tinged with an anti-Egyptian coloring that would have been inappropriate for a group in Egypt desirous of living at peace with its neighbors. It is quite conceivable that this festival prior to the Deuteronomic law was observed by non-sheep and goat-raising persons with sacrifice of first fruits (cf. Gen. 4:3–4). In such a more primitive manner it would have been practicable to celebrate it at Elephantine.

We may, in passing, raise the question here whether a Cairo ostracon from Elephantine published in 1926[47] refers to a ritual practice, as suggested by Dupont-Sommer.[48] The writer, who addresses a certain Uriah, has left his tunic in "the house of the house of Yahoh." However, it would seem that for such a translation a preposition would be desirable. I would prefer to consider the first "house" as *construct* before the compound "house-of-Yahoh." The latter was the designation of the temple as a whole, while the first is "the house" in the narrower sense of the adyton, or "Holy of Holies." It may be assumed that the writer was a temple servant, so that he could have access to the adyton. But what was Uriah to do

[45] Sayce, "An Aramaic Ostracon from Elephantine," *PSBA*, *33*, 1911, 183 ff.

[46] Dupont-Sommer, *RÉJ*, 7, 1946–47, 43 ff., gives text translation and discussion of these ostraca, with reference to previous discussions. E. L. Sukenik and J. Kutsher, "A Passover Ostracon from Elephantine," *Kedem*, *1*, 1942, 53 ff. (in Hebrew), previously translated ll. 3–4 in the same way. They would date the ostracon ca. 80 years earlier than the Mazzoth letter on palaeographical grounds.

[47] Aimé-Giron, *ASAE*, *26*, 1926, 27 ff.

[48] A. Dupont-Sommer, "Maison de Yaho et vêtements sacrés à Éléphantine," *JA*, 1946–47, 74 ff.

about the tunic? Aimé-Giron held that he was "to return (?) it" to the custody of Salluah. Dupont-Sommer, however, taking "To Salluah" as the address of the missive, ingeniously reads the doubtful verb as [*ḥ*]*rm*, thus obtaining the directive that he was to "consecrate" it. Whether Uriah is the important personage mentioned in *A.P.* 37 and how or why he was to consecrate the tunic are questions that cannot be answered.[49]

In conclusion, the question whether the Jews of Elephantine had any knowledge of the religious literature of their people naturally suggests itself. The use of the Hebrew phrase "male and female" (*A.P.* 15:20, Brooklyn No. 3:20b), so characteristic of the Priestly writer of Gen. 1, hardly permits any inference as to the familiarity of the scribe with that work. The affinity of the phraseology in the Bagoas letter, *A.P.* 30:27 ("it shall be righteousness to you before Yahu"), with Deut. 24:13 ("it shall be righteousness unto thee before Yahweh thy god"), suggests contact with the Deuteronomic tradition but not necessarily knowledge of the Book of Deuteronomy.[50] Indeed, the only book with which the Aramaic-speaking people of the town had any demonstrable acquaintance was the Book of Aḥiḳar, which was of non-Israelitic origin. Some account of this book may not be out of place, for it reveals the moral pabulum that nurtured the community.

A Book of Aḥiḳar has long been known from sources of the Christian Era in a number of languages.[51] The Book of Tobit gave scholars reason to believe that all these versions were descended from an earlier Book of Aḥiḳar, which already existed at the time when Tobit was written — say the 2nd century B.C. — for "Achiacharus" is described as attending the wedding of Tobias at Nineveh (Tob. 11:17), and Tobit in parting gives his son an admonition based on a tale about that worthy (14:10). No one, however, was quite prepared for the surprise provided by the discovery by the Germans at Elephantine of fragments of an Aramaic Book of Aḥiḳar dating from the 5th century B.C.[52] Had the whole text been preserved

[49] The ostracon found at Elephantine by Adolf Erman, *CIS*, *2*, 137, was long believed to be of religious interest. But cf. the new study of this text by Dupont-Sommer, "Ostraca araméens d'Éléphantine," *ASAE*, *48*, 1948, 120 ff., who takes the word *ḥlm*, which scholars had linked with *ḥălōm*, "dream," as a plant name, so that the text seemingly loses any mystical import.

[50] *Twrh* in *A.P.* 82:10, a text of the Greek era, can hardly mean "the law."

[51] The versions are conveniently collected in F. C. Conybeare, J. R. Harris, and A. S. Lewis, *The Story of Ahikar from the Syriac, Arabic, Armenian, Ethiopic, Greek, and Slavonic Versions* (London, 1898; 2d ed., 1913). Cf. also the same editors in R. H. Charles, *Apocrypha and Pseudepigrapha of the Old Testament*, *2*, 715 f. For a good general account see Bruno Meissner, "Das Märchen vom weisen Achikar," in *Der Alte Orient* (Leipzig, 1917), *16*, No. 2. Important, too, is Rudolf Smend, "Alter und Herkunft des Ahikarromans und sein Verhältnis zu Äsop," *ZAW*, Beiheft *13*, 1908.

[52] Published and deciphered in Sach. 147 ff. Cowley in *A.P.* 212 ff. has given a revised text and translation, and in his introductory remarks on pp. 204 ff. gives references to the philological contributions made by others. A fresh translation was offered by Gressmann in his *Altorientalische Texte zum Alten Testament*, 454–462.

it would have provided a unique opportunity to study the vicissitudes of an ancient book and to see what was preserved, what dropped or altered, in the later versions. Even in its surviving fragmentary state, the Aramaic book permits interesting conclusions in this direction.[53]

The opening line of the Aramaic work is, "These are the words of a man named Aḥiḳar,[54] a scribe wise and ready, which he taught his son . . ." whereupon follow the utterances of the sage in the first person.

Aḥiḳar was a servant of Esarhaddon, King of Assyria, and had previously served that ruler's father, Sennacherib. Aḥiḳar had a son named Nadin,[55] who defamed his father before Esarhaddon. The king thereupon sent forth two men, one of whom was Nabu-sum-iskun,[56] the executioner (?), to kill Aḥiḳar. They traveled three days on horseback and then came upon Aḥiḳar as he was walking in his vineyards. This suggests that Aḥiḳar was not imagined as living in Assyria but rather in a more westerly wine-growing locality, where he presumably had an estate.

Aḥiḳar, informed of Nadin's treachery, reminds Nabu-sum-iskun that he had once saved him from the wrath of Sennacherib by hiding him away in his own house, though reporting to the king that he had executed him. Later he had presented Nabu-sum-iskun "before Sennacherib," after "removing his sin," and the king, far from being displeased, had "loved Aḥiḳar very much for keeping him alive and not executing him." Aḥiḳar suggests that Nabu-sum-iskun return the favor. It is known, he says, that King Esarhaddon is merciful; later on he will remember Aḥiḳar and ask for his counsel.

Nabu-sum-iskun reassures him and then consults with his companions:

"Hear me. This Aḥiḳar is a general and keeper of the seal of Esarhaddon king of Assyria, and all the army of Assyria were guided by his counsel and words. Let us not kill him. A eunuch of mine I will give you. Let him be killed between these two mountains instead of Aḥiḳar, and when it is reported the king will send other men after us to see the body of Aḥiḳar. Later, when the king thinks of Aḥiḳar he will give riches as the number of the sand to anyone who can bring him back."

[53] Cf. the excellent discussion of Meyer, *Papyrusfund*, 102 ff. For textual details see Friedrich Stummer, "Der kritische Wert der altaramäischen Achikartexte," *Alttestamentliche Abhandlungen* (Münster in W.) *5*, Heft 5, 1914.

[54] Cowley, *A.P.*, p. 206, falsely infers from this phraseology that the book was translated out of Persian into Aramaic. While "his name" after a person's name indicates a slave in legal texts, this is not always the case in literary texts.

[55] In Tobit the son is made a nephew whom the sage adopted. But the papyrus (ll. 1 and 139) implies that his own son was meant in the original story.

[56] He, too, is doubtless a historical personage and may be identical with the man of that name who had a high post under Sennacherib (C. H. W. Johns, *Assyrian Deeds and Documents . . .* (Cambridge, 1898–1924), *1*, No. 253, reverse l. 6). So Ungnad, 63; cf. Meissner (n. 51, above), 18.

The plan was thus carried out and Nabu-sum-iskun reported the death of Aḥiḳar to the ruler. Unfortunately the story breaks off at this point. Doubtless, however, everything went as foreseen.

The story serves only to provide a setting for a wisdom book — practical teachings on human conduct which were rendered attractive and impressive by being put into the mouth of a man of such celebrity and with so interesting a life history. It seems likely that after the teachings there may have followed a resumé of the later days and death of Aḥiḳar, just as is the case in such a wisdom book as the Book of Job.[57] The wisdom incorporated into the story is represented as instruction given by the wise man to his son, presumably after the latter's treachery, for passages in the text refer to it (*A.P.* Aḥ. 139 ff., 169 ff.).

While its popularity among Aramaic-speaking people, including the Jews, is attested both by this Elephantine text and by the allusions in Tobit, the ultimate origin of the Book of Aḥiḳar is held to be Assyrian.[58] Since the people inhabiting the old Assyrian territory had become Aramaic-speaking in the 5th century B.C., the translation of a popular Assyrian work into that tongue is understandable.[59]

[57] See E. G. Kraeling, *Book of the Ways of God* (London and New York, 1939), 22 f.

[58] Cf. Meissner (n. 51, above), 32. Albright observed the fact that a letter of Esarhaddon shows acquaintance with a proverb found in Aḥiḳar, thus demonstrating that Assyrian material is employed: "The Babylonian Sage Ut-Napishtim rūqu," *JAOS*, *38*, 1918, 64. See, further, Meissner, "Sprichwörter bei Essarhaddon," *AfO*, *10*, 1936, 361 ff.

[59] The statement of Strabo XVI, 2, 39, that "Achaikaros" was a lawgiver among the Bosporenes may be corrected to *Borsippenes* (see Meyer, *Papyrusfund*, 125). *Sipparenes* might be even better, in view of the fact that Shamash, god of Sippar, is Aḥiḳar's patron divinity. But though Greeks may have obtained knowledge of the book from Babylonia Aḥiḳar belongs in the Assyrian scene. When Clement of Alexandria (*Stromata* I, 15, 69) speaks of a stela of "Akikaros," a translation of which Democritus allegedly incorporated in his writings, he may very well have an actual stela in mind like that of Shamash-resh-uṣur in F. H. Weissbach, *Babylonische Miszellen*, WVDOG, Heft 4 (Leipzig, 1903), and not merely an inscribed clay prism or a tablet, as Cowley, *A.P.* 207, suggests. To the late echoes of Aḥiḳar should be added one in Egyptian: see Spiegelberg, "Aḥiḳar in einem demotischen Text der römischen Kaiserzeit," *OLZ*, *33*, 1930, 962 ff.

9. DESTRUCTION AND RESTORATION OF THE JEWISH TEMPLE

WE HAVE already mentioned the surprise experienced by students of the Old Testament when the Sayce-Cowley papyri first revealed the existence of a Jewish sanctuary on the Island of Elephantine. The word used to describe it was *'egōrā*. Many were reluctant to believe that the Jews at this time would have erected a real temple on foreign soil and argued that the word must refer to what was essentially a synagogue. But this possibility was dispelled by the publication of Sachau's first three papyri (*A.P.* 31–33), revealing the story of the destruction of the building. These papyri make it clear that the edifice was used for sacrifices. Sacrifices imply an altar and that there was an altar is shown by the use of the substitute expression "altar house" used in *A.P.* 32:3. The presence of an altar of sacrifice makes it certain that the building was a temple. Moreover, the word *'egōrā* is used in *A.P.* 30:14 in reference to the temples of the Egyptians. There can be little doubt that it is derived from the Assyrian word for temple, *ēkurru*,[1] and that it has the same meaning.

Whether the cult of the Jewish temple was subsidized by the Persian government, as it probably had been by the earlier native Egyptian rulers, is unknown. That the burden of support was borne by members of the community in the latter days of its existence is shown by the list of contributors to the temple discussed in the previous chapter; the men and some women made a standard contribution of two shekels of silver. One is immediately reminded of the annual temple tax of one-third shekel levied on the Jews of Palestine in the time of Nehemiah (Neh. 10:33–34). In Exod. 30:11 f., 38:25 f., which must be later than Nehemiah, the amount of this tax is raised to one-half shekel; and this was accepted as authoritative ever after.[2] It seems likely that the relatively larger contribution made by the Jews of Elephantine may also have been an annual tax. In addition to such fixed contri-

[1] Theodor Noeldeke, "Die Aramäischen Papyri von Assuan," *ZA*, *20*, 1907, 130 ff. Zimmern, *Akkadische Fremdwörter*, 68. The plural *ēkurrāti* is used for temples in general in a text from the time of Cyrus in Peiser, *Texte*, 268, No. 6, l. 13. This corresponds perfectly to the use of the Aramaic word in *A.P.* 30:14.

[2] Cf. Neh. 10:33–34. The passages in the laws, Exod. 30:11 f., 38:25 f., must therefore be later. Cf. Meyer, *Papyrusfund*, 55, E. Schürer, *Geschichte des Jüdischen Volkes im Zeitalter Jesu Christi* (Leipzig 1898), *2*, 258 f.

butions the temple must have had other revenue, such as that from sacrifices brought to it and from freewill offerings.

All this income was necessary, not only for the upkeep of the temple itself, but also for the support of the priests and other personnel. Two priests are mentioned by name in *A.P.* 38:1. Another functionary, "the *lḥn* of Yahu," appears prominently in the Brooklyn texts. Just what this title means remains obscure. We have rendered it "servitor of Yahu," but the man who bears it is obviously a freeman, not a temple slave and has a house of his own in the immediate vicinity of the temple.

Do we know anything about the external appearance of the Temple of Elephantine? Van Hoonacker went so far as to give several hypothetical restorations of it.[3] Vincent followed his example but with variations — cutting down on the Egyptianizing features used in Van Hoonacker's drawings and adding Clermont-Ganneau's supposition that it was built on an artificial elevation and had ramps leading up to it.[4] But the basis for such reconstructions is scant. The only certain facts that can be derived from the description given in the account of its destruction in *A.P.* 30:9 f. are the following: 1) it had pillars of stone; 2) it had five gateways built of carved stone[5]; 3) it had a roof of cedarwood.[6]

[3] Van Hoonacker, *Une communauté*, 52 f.

[4] Vincent, *Religion*, 351.

[5] The words in l. 10, which Cowley renders "and their doors they lifted off," could hardly mean that if one reads *qymw*; but I regard the reading itself as erroneous. The word is *qymn* and Brooklyn No. 3:4 gives an illustration of its use. The statement then means "their doors were standing," i. e., strong, in good condition.

[6] Of this roof l. 11 says, "All of it with the rest of the *'šrn'* and the other things which were there, all of it they burned with fire." Cowley renders 'šrn', "furniture," here, (in *A.P.* 27:6, "fittings"), while in the boat-repair order where the word also occurs (*A.P.* 26:9, 21) he vacillates between "specification" and "material." Kurt Galling, "Kyrusedikt und Tempelbau," *OLZ*, *40*, 1937, 473 f., would carry through the meaning "specification," "directions for construction," in all the payri passages (as well as in Ezra 5:3, 9 where the same word, but vocalized *uššarnā*, seems to occur). But that meaning does not seem probable in *A.P.* 30:11. Perhaps Brooklyn No. 3:23 sheds new light on the word by providing a noun *'šr*, plural *'šrn*, apparently meaning "poles" or "logs." A denominative *'ašrānā*, "woodwork," would then be the word meant in the papyri passages enumerated. In that case the Masoretic vocalization of the same consonants as uššarnā in Ezra 5:3, 9 would become doubtful. BL § 229 i[1] suggested vocalizing **ašrānā*, but mistakenly regarded the final syllable as pronominal suffix. It seems to me that the statement, "and timber is laid in the walls" (Ezra 5:8), explains what is meant by 'uššarnā in 5:3, i. e., the placement of joists or the reenforcement of the walls by insertion of logs, as at Elephantine (see Honroth and others, "Ausgrabungen," 41, and Tafel VIII; further information from other quarters on the use of wood is adduced in Sidney Smith, "Timber and Brick or Masonry Construction," *Palestine Exploration Quarterly*, *73*, 1941, 5 ff., but with no attempt to clarify the word 'uššarnā). Iranian explanations thus seem unnecessary; Schaeder, *Beiträge*, 263, doubted Iranian origin of the word, though H. S. Nyberg, in a review of Leander's book in *Monde Orientale*, *24*, 1929, 138 f., derived it from an Old Iranian (hypothetical) *uš-çarānā* that might mean "equipment."

The question is: was the temple a single building without a court corresponding to the Assyrian style[7] of temple edifices, or was it a walled enclosure, within which stood an altar and behind it a small chapel or Holy of Holies? The fact that an Assyrian word is used to designate the temple is indecisive, for that is used also for the Egyptian temples. But on general grounds it seems unlikely that the Jews would have been permitted to construct a walled enclosure of Egyptian type. That would require considerable space and would hardly have been permitted since such a temple could be turned into a fortress. An Assyrian-style temple, therefore, would appear most probable. How the gates or entrances were distributed, how many pillars there were and where they stood, are questions concerning which it is useless to speculate. The cedarwood roof obviously made a narrow building necessary — even the rooms of Assyrian palaces are limited in their width by the length of the available timbers.

What, one is moved to ask, was the reason for the destruction of the Temple of Yahu? Clermont-Ganneau argued that it was Jewish provocation in introducing the sacrifice of the paschal lamb.[8] This, he holds, must have been a horrible sacrilege to a priesthood that held the ram to be a sacred animal. But how is one to explain that the conflict did not arise sooner? How is it that the Pharaoh who authorized the Jews to establish themselves and their god in the city of Khnum, adjacent to his temple, had not foreseen this development? Clermont-Ganneau replies that the Jews must, until shortly before this time, have used the latitude which the law gave them of sacrificing a kid instead of a lamb,[9] but that at "a given moment" they went over to the sacrifice of lambs — hence the wrath of the Egyptians. The given moment is supposedly that of the reception of the Mazzoth Papyrus (*A.P.* 21, with suitable text restorations injecting mention of the Passover).[10]

[7] Cf. Walter Andrae, *Das Gotteshaus und die Urformen des Bauens im alten Orient* (Berlin, 1930).

[8] See J. B. Chabot, "Les fouilles de Clermont-Ganneau à Éléphantine, *Journal des Savants*, 1944, 137.

[9] He is thinking here of the report of Herodotus II, 42 and 46 that the inhabitants of the Theban nome did not slaughter sheep because these were sacred to Amon and instead offered up goats, while the people of Mendes, whose god (supposedly) was a goat, spared the goats and slaughtered sheep instead. (On this see Alexander Scharff, "Ein Besuch von Mendes," *Mitteilungen des Deutschen Instituts für ägyptische Altertumskunde in Kairo*, *1*, 1930, 132.) Since sheep were sacred to Khnum of Elephantine, Clermont-Ganneau infers that goats were used there and that the Jews accommodated themselves to this. For the "latitude" allowed by the Jewish law he must have the Mishnah tract, *Pesaḥim*, VIII, 2, in mind, which mentions lambs and kids as permissible. The only Old Testament justification for this is to be found in II Chron. 35:5–7, where Josiah distributes lambs, kids, and bullocks for the Passover. The law itself in Deut. 16:2 mentions sheep and bullocks but no kids. See N. M. Nicolsky, "Pascha im Kulte des Jerusalemischen Tempels," *ZAW*, *45*, 1927, 242 ff.

[10] See Vincent, *Religion*, 308 ff.

These are interesting speculations but they can hardly be upheld. We have seen in Chapter 8 that the Passover cannot have been mentioned in the Mazzoth Papyrus (*A.P.* 21) and that if the feast was celebrated at Elephantine a different ritual than is found in the biblical sources may have been followed. It is unthinkable that any ritual offensive to the Egyptian community would ever have been used. The religious modus vivendi was long established. The liberality of the Jews is evidenced by the bit of syncretism in which they indulged within the community of which they were a part. We must seek for a different explanation of the Egyptian outbreak against them.

The Strassburg papyrus (*A.P.* 27; see chapter 1) reveals enough about affairs at Elephantine to show in which area the explanation must be sought. While the beginning is lost it is clear that it must have been addressed to one of the highest officials in Egypt. It was written at a time closer to events than is the case with *A.P.* 30. The extant text begins with mention of a former rebellion of the Egyptians against Persian rule[11] and points out that the speakers (i. e., the Jews) at that time did not leave their posts and that no disloyalty was imputed to them. In the 14th year of Darius, when Arsham (the satrap of Egypt) went to the king (i. e., to Persia), the priests of Khnum did the following evil deed[12] in Yeb the fortress: They made a plot with Widrang, who was *prtrk* there, after giving him money and valuables, wrecked a part of a building of the king, constructed a (segregating?) wall in the middle (?) of the fortress and stopped up a well that provided the Jewish garrison with water. If the high personage addressed will check with the officials of the province of *Tšṭrs*, the writer says, he will find that these are the facts. On the reverse of the papyrus there is further reference to the Jews' having been prevented from carrying on their rites for Yahu and to the fact that their adversaries took away the "timber(?)" of the temple. Apparently their letter is an appeal for redress of this injury.

We can see from this document that the changed attitude of the Egyptians was rooted in politics. When the Jews first came to Elephantine they were in the service of native rulers and helped protect the Egyptian community at Assuan against inroads by the Ethiopians. Their religious needs had to be considered, as were those of Aramaeans, Phoenicians, and others. In the eyes of the Khnum worshipers the foreign gods were doubtless visiting satellites; such visits and temporary sojourns were not uncommon in the ancient East. But the Persian conquest changed the situation. The foreign soldiers entered Persian service and aided the oppressors of the Egyptians. There were many revolts against Persian rule. The one referred to in the Strassburg Papyrus may have taken place at the time of the accession of

[11] The Borchardt leather documents also look back on an Egyptian rebellion; cf. G. R. Driver, "New Aramaic Documents," *ZAW*, 67, 1949/50, 222. It seems likely that the one at the time of the accession of Darius II is meant.

[12] On the Iranian word *duškarta*, see Schaeder, *Beiträge*, 264.

Darius II (424 B.C). If the Jews, as they here affirm, remained loyal that means that they helped to put down rebellion in their area. That they thereby incurred the hatred of the Egyptians and that these should seek an opportunity to revenge themselves is understandable. The only obscure factor is the motive leading Widrang and his son, the local Persian chiefs, to cooperate with the Egyptians as described in *A.P.* 30 (see below). But personal ambition, greed for gain, or some more widespread plot in which they participated may be assumed.

A glimpse of happenings of a serious nature affecting the Jewish colony, perhaps from the year 410 when the Jewish temple was destroyed (hardly from the closing day of the colony, since the karsh is still in use), is given by the fragment of the end of a letter, *A.P.* 34.[13] It seems to have been written by a non-Jew, perhaps an Egyptian, who is reporting to someone in Yeb. It gives the names of six women and five men who were found at the gate in Thebes and "were taken as prisoners, Yedonia b. Gemariah, Hosha' b. Yathom, Hosha' b. Nathum, Haggai, his brother, and Aḥio b. . . ." It refers to their (?) having entered houses in Yeb and taken goods which, however, they had restored to their owners. Apparently they have mentioned money — 120 karsh — to a "lord," presumably for their liberation. The closing statement, which Cowley renders, "Moreover they will have no further authority here," may mean rather that no orders have as yet been issued with respect to them. The writer then expresses the wish that peace may be to the addressee and his family "till the gods let us (?) see our desire . . ." The latter statement may imply animus toward the Jews. Why Jewish men and women from Elephantine should be at Thebes is puzzling. Did they have to go there to appear before a higher court? The incident seems much more probable in the situation prior to the destruction of the Jewish temple than at a subsequent date. In any case it will be obvious that there is good reason to look for the causes of the trouble in the secular rather than the religious sphere.

The Bagoas letter, fortunately dated and complete, is preserved in two copies (Sach. 1 and 2, *A.P.* 30 and 31). It was written in the 17th year of Darius II, November 26, 407 B.C., more than three years after the events of which it speaks. It is addressed to the Persian governor of Judaea, Bagohi or Bagoas. It is not the first communication to people in Palestine on the subject, but a follow-up letter, for the writers refer to having written, when the events of which they complain first occurred, to Bagoas, to "the high priest Johanan and his colleagues, the priests who are in Jerusalem and to Ustan, the brother of Anani, and the nobles of the Jews" (ll. 18–19). None of these letters, they say, had received any reply. In this new letter of 407 B.C. the matter is presented to Bagoas once more.

The authorship of the letter is ascribed to "Yedoniah and his colleagues the

[13] Cf. below, p. 115. Meyer, *Papyrusfund*, 77, puts Sach. 10 (*A.P.* 37) in this situation, but that text must, in our opinion, be assigned to about 400 B.C. Cf. p. 114.

priests, who are in Yeb, the fortress."[14] Yedoniah is doubtless the Yedoniah b. Gemariah, who occurs in *A.P.* 22:121; 33:1; 34:5, and whose autograph as a witness appears in Brooklyn No. 10:20. Sachau, whom Meyer follows, would make him "ethnarch" of the Jewish colony. The letter states that in Tammuz (July 14—August 12) of the 14th year of Darius (410), when Arsham had gone to the king, the priests of Khnum plotted with Widrang the governor that the temple of the god Yahu, which was in the fortress of Yeb, should be destroyed. Widrang, "the evildoer," sent a letter to his son Nephayan, commander in Syene, ordering him to attend to the destruction. Nephayan led out the Egyptians with other forces. They came to Yeb with their implements and went into the temple and cast it to the ground. They destroyed and pilfered its contents. The Jewish complainants point out to Bagoas that the temple existed in the days of the native Egyptian rulers and that when the Persian Cambyses conquered Egypt he had overthrown all the Egyptian temples but had not harmed the sanctuary of Yahu. They describe their fasting and praying to Yahu, the long period in which their wives have been as widows. The God of Heaven had given them news of Widrang[15]; they (the Persians!) had removed the anklet from his feet (demoted him from the rank of *prtrk*?) and the riches he had gained (partly, no doubt, those referred to in *A.P.* 27:4) were taken from him. The other men who had sought to do evil to the temple were killed. This presumably refers to the archmovers in the plot — probably even to some priests of Khnum. Yedoniah and his colleagues and the (other) Jews, all of them inhabitants of Yeb, now appeal to Bagoas to bring about the rebuilding of the temple, "since they (the Egyptians?) do not allow us to build it." They request that a letter be sent giving them permission to do so. They promise to offer meal offering, incense, and sacrifice to Yahu and to pray for Bagoas, and they assure him that the merit he will store up before Yahu by his act will be greater than that of one who sacrificed to the value of a thousand talents. They hint at oral instructions about "gold" and also speak of having written to Delaiah and Shelemiah, the sons of Sanballat, governor of Samaria. They emphasize the fact that Arsham knew nothing of what had happened.

[14] For conveniently available translations see, e. g., Ginsberg in Pritchard, ed., *Ancient Near Eastern Texts*, 492, and Gressmann, in his *Altorientalische Texte*, 450. The question whether Yedoniah was a priest is raised by this formulation quoted above. Cowley, *A.P.* 111, makes that inference and is followed by Olmstead, *History of the Persian Empire*, 365. It is excluded by *A.P.* 38:1, where Mattan and Neriah are set apart as priests from Yedoniah and Uriah. The priests are "colleagues" of Yedoniah as fellow councilors.

[15] Cowley's rendering in *A.P.* 30:15, "the dogs tore off the anklet from his legs," is unsatisfactory. The verb used could not have dogs for subject. Brooklyn No. 13, furthermore, shows that Widrang was alive (but a prisoner?) in 399 B.C. I explain *klby*' as emphatic of singular **kalbāy*, a denominative of *kalbā*, "the son of a dog." It varies the other epithet "evildoer." He must have been out of favor politically that they can thus speak of him.

It would be difficult to exaggerate the importance of this document. The period of Jewish history after Nehemiah, down to the Maccabean uprising, is one of which next to nothing is known. And here a ray of light extending from Elephantine to Jerusalem gives us a momentary glimpse of the scene in the year 407 B.C. Certain things stand out with the utmost clarity. The governor of Judaea is Bagoas, while at Samaria Sanballat, well known from Neh. 2:10, etc., is carrying on as governor. The high priest of the Jews is Johanan. The Elephantine Jews have been trying to enlist support on the part of the Palestinian authorities for the restoration of their temple. The high priest has ignored their first appeal, as has another highly important personage, "Ustan, the brother of Anani." Apparently the representatives of the Elephantine community consider it useless to turn again to their coreligionists in the homeland. But they do not hesitate to approach the Persian political leaders, Bagoas and Sanballat, with hint of a largesse, for which such personages were ever receptive.

The message that the Jewish emissary brought back from his interview with Bagoas and one of the sons of Sanballat, Delaiah, is fortunately preserved in *A.P.* 32. Either he was able to consult both together or else both agreed on the formula of the answer. It is carefully worded:

1. Memorandum of what Bagohi and Delaiah said
2. to me. Memorandum. Let it be an instruction to you to say in Egypt
3. before Arsham concerning the altar house of the God
4. of Heaven which in Yeb the fortress was built
5. formerly before Cambyses,
6. which Widrang, the evildoer, did cast down
7. in the year 14 of Darius the king:
8. that it should be rebuilt in its place, as it was formerly,
9. and that meal offerings and frankincense should be brought upon
10. that altar corresponding to what formerly
11. was done.

The first important thing to notice is what the request of line 24 of the letter to Bagoas was and how it was dealt with. Yedoniah and his colleagues had asked that he send *them* a letter concerning the Temple of Yahu, the god, that it should be rebuilt, and that three kinds of offerings should be brought there in his name — the name of the governor of Judaea. This suggests that the Jewish colony and its temple in some way stood under the protectorate of the governor of Judaea and that the ruined edifice could not be restored until Bagoas issued the order. There is no mention in *A.P.* 30:17 of letters written to Arsham or any Egyptian official. The Elephantine colony had turned to Palestine for help from the beginning because permission from that quarter was necessary and had to be obtained before building. Bagoas, however, instead of sending them the requested letter (with which they could then go to Arsham) evidently considers it more correct to have

the Jews report his recommendation to Arsham orally. But the words were carefully weighed and the Jewish messenger must have taken them down on the spot. They provide Arsham with the essential legal information 1) that this altar house of the "God of Heaven" (the name Yahu is avoided) existed before Cambyses — wherefore the Egyptians could not claim that its existence there was due to Persian policy; 2) that in 410 Widrang destroyed it (thus putting the responsibility on a Persian official rather than on the Egyptians); 3) that it should be rebuilt *in its place* — a statement evidently intended to counteract certain Egyptian agitation to the effect that if it were to be rebuilt at all it should be moved away from the vicinity of the Temple of Khnum or perhaps even off the Island of Yeb; 4) that the restoration should be to its former completeness — a directive presumably suggesting that the rebuilding be done at government expense; 5) that offerings should be brought upon the altar as formerly (hint of government subsidy?). Here, however, only two classes of offerings are listed — meal offerings and frankincense. There is no mention of burnt offerings, the third class of offerings referred to in the petition of *A.P.* 30:25.

This memorandum doubtless represents the outcome of prolonged diplomatic activity. Bagoas and Delaiah had to consider carefully before they gave their recommendation, and that they consulted with the Jewish high priest and his colleagues and with Ustan, the brother of Anani, and the Jewish nobles (on whom confer below) before making it would seem obvious. The recommendation to disallow bloody sacrifice at Elephantine may represent a concession to the wish of the high priest and his colleagues to reserve such sacrifices for the Jerusalem Temple alone, and reflects some degree of allegiance to Deuteronomic principles. It is hardly due to the Persian religious inhibitions of Bagoas, as Meyer would have it,[16] or to a desire to avoid giving offense to the Egyptians; for there were so many cults of foreign gods in the Elephantine area that bloody sacrifice must have been common enough. The decision must therefore reflect a policy of lowering the importance of such foreign Jewish temples.

A few remarks concerning the personalities mentioned in *A.P.* 30 may be helpful here. Sanballat appears in the Book of Nehemiah as the latter's adversary and there has the "army of Samaria" at his disposal.[17] We now learn that he was

[16] Meyer, *Papyrusfund*, 89. Eugen Mittwoch, "Der Wiederaufbau des jüdischen Tempels in Elephantine," *Judaica* (Festschrift Hermann Cohen), (Berlin, 1912), 277 ff., sees a compromise between Jews and Samaritans in the decision arrived at here: the Samaritans conceding the forbidding of bloody sacrifice and the Jews conceding the right of a temple to exist outside of Jerusalem. But this view collapses if the Samaritan schism took place in the 4th century.

[17] The papyri write his name in a manner suggesting the correct Babylonian pronunciation, *Sinuballiṭ*. That he is called "the Horonite" is believed to mean that he came from Beth Horon, where his family may have had a fief. Cf. Neh. 2:10, 19; 3:33; 4:1; 6:1 f.; 13:28. Josephus, *Ant.*, XI, 302, makes him a "Cuthean" sent by Darius (III!) from Babylonia. Perhaps the vocalization

actually the governor of that province. Bagoas is known from Josephus,[18] though his status is inaccurately reported as that of "a general of the other Artaxerxes" (Artaxerxes II), whereas we now see that he actually was the governor of the province of Judaea under Darius II and probably the successor of Nehemiah, the first incumbent of that office. The high priest Johanan is mentioned several times in the Book of Nehemiah. Thus in Neh. 12:22 his name appears in a series of high priests: Eliashib, Joiada, Johanan, and Jaddua; the list allegedly extends to the time of "Darius the Persian," who, if Jaddua was the priest who went forth to greet Alexander the Great in 336, as Josephus claims,[19] must be Darius III, Codomannus. In the next sentence, however, allusion is made to a high priest "Johanan son of Eliashib." This may actually have been the way he spoke of himself; the Brooklyn texts happily provide us with instances in which a man drops the use of his father's name and uses that of his grandfather instead (see No. 15). Actually, then, Johanan was the son of Joiada.[20] In Neh. 12:10, furthermore, we get a list of the high priests from the time of Darius I on: Jeshua (the Joshua of Hag. 1:1, etc., Zech. 3:1 ff.), Eliashib, Joiada, Jonathan, and Jaddua. Jonathan is usually regarded as a corruption of Johanan, but it is is equally possible that Johanan's name has dropped out and that there was a high priest Jonathan. The length of time between Johanan's administration (he was in office in 407 B.C. at the time of *A.P.* 30) and Jaddua the contemporary of Alexander in 336 B.C. suggests that the list in Neh. 12:22 is not complete for that period any more than it can be complete for the period between Jeshua and Eliashib. At all events the Bagoas letter for the first time makes one of the 5th-century high priests tangible and datable. There is every reason to believe that Nehemiah means this same Johanan when he says, "And one of the sons of Joiada, the son of Eliashib the high priest, was son-in-law to Sanballat the Horonite: therefore I chased him from me" (Neh. 13:28). The presence of the sons of Sanballat at Jerusalem at the time of *A.P.* 30 and the amicable relations existing between them and the high priest Johanan suggest that Johanan was indeed the brother-in-law of these men. If Nehemiah drove him out of the city, the fact remains that he returned and subsequently became high priest after Nehemiah left Jerusalem.

Mysterious among the personalities mentioned in the Bagoas letter is solely the man called "Ustan[21] the brother of Anani." There can be little doubt that we must see in the Anani here referred to the leading figure of the aristocracy — probably

of MT is erroneous and the man was from the Hauran (Ezek. 47:16, 18), the erstwhile Assyrian province *Ḫaurēna*. This would make it more natural for him to be described with such a designation.

[18] *Ant.* XI, 297 f.

[19] *Ant.* XI, 326.

[20] In the received texts of Josephus the name Joiada is corrupted to Judas.

[21] On the Persian name Ustan (Uštanni in Babylonian texts, Ostanes in Greek reporting) see Schaeder, *Beiträge*, 70.

the head of the house of David. In I Chron. 3:24 is mentioned an Anani, a descendant of Zerubbabel, who is six generations removed from that ancestor and thus must have lived at about the time of *A.P.* 30.[22] That the Jews should have appealed to his brother Ustan (who may be referred to under another, Hebrew, name in I Chron. 3:24) rather than to him would be understandable — such a man could not afford to be compromised and so was approached indirectly.

Other information supplied by Josephus concerning the personalities of Bagoas and the high priests is partly applicable to later situations and partly garbled. According to that author the high priest Johanan murdered a brother, whom Bagoas sought to put in his place, whereupon Bagoas penalized the Jewish community.[23] That, if true, must have occurred some years later, at the beginning of the reign of Artaxerxes II. But when Josephus makes Sanballat the father-in-law of Manasseh,[24] founder of the Samaritan sect and brother of the high priest Jaddua, he has evidently confused times and men. It was Johanan who was the son-in-law of Sanballat and who was driven out, not Manasseh the brother of Jaddua. He certainly had nothing to do with founding the Samaritan sect, for the Bagoas letter shows him back in Jerusalem (whither he presumably returned after Nehemiah had quitted the scene) and as incumbent of the high priestly office. The presence of the sons of Sanballat at Jerusalem and their close cooperation with the Judaean governor show that the people of Samaria at this time were not separated from those of Judaea religiously speaking. The Samaritan schism must be of later date. Whatever its occasion and exact date it must have been a consequence of the racialism of Ezra. The picture of the Palestinian situation given by *A.P.* 30 provides strong support for the contention of recent scholarship that Ezra came to Jerusalem not under Artaxerxes I but rather under Artaxerxes II.[25] The Brooklyn papyri Nos. 9–12 show that "King Artaxerxes" in Ezra 7:8 could stand for Artaxerxes II just as well as for the earlier ruler of that name. If Ezra came on July 31, 398 B.C., the seeds of dissension between Jews and Samaritans had not yet been sown at the time of the Bagoas letter, and the whole handling of the Elephantine matter by the authorities there becomes far more understandable than if the rigoristic reformation of Ezra had preceded.

[22] See Meyer, *Papyrusfund*, 73; Rudolf Kittel, *Geschichte des Volkes Israel*, *3*, 675.

[23] *Ant.* XI, 297. He allegedly imposed a fine for every lamb slaughtered in the daily sacrifice.

[24] Charles C. Torrey, "Sanballat the Horonite," *JBL*, *47*, 1928, 380 ff., assumes that a Sanballat II, a descendant of the Sanballat of *A.P.* 30, is meant. But this Josephus material needs more drastic critical treatment than he gives it.

[25] See Harold H. Rowley's penetrating discussion, "The Chronological order of Ezra and Nehemiah," reprinted in his *The Servant of the Lord and Other Essays on the Old Testament* (London, 1952), 131 ff., also Norman H. Snaith, "The Date of Ezra's Arrival in Jerusalem," *ZAW*, *13*, 1951, 53 f. Albright, in Louis Finkelstein, *The Jews; Their History, Culture and Religion* (New York, 1949), 64, would correct the date in Ezra 7:7 to the 37th year and thus keep Ezra's arrival within the reign of Artaxerxes I (in 428 B.C.).

But did the message of Bagoas and Delaiah to Arsham have the desired effect? Was the temple in Elephantine actually restored? To obtain action from government has at all times been a slow process, nowhere more tedious than in the East. To get Arsham to act evidently required further petition and pressure. The letter *A.P.* 33 reflects further delays. In it five prominent men, Yedoniah, Shema'iah b. Haggai, and Ma'uzi(yah) b. Nathan (two scribes who wrote letters in the Brooklyn collection), Hosha' b. Yathom, and Hosha' b. Nathan, all of them Syenians who also held property in Yeb, abjectly (like slaves — hence "his name" is put after their names) offer to pay to the house of a certain unmentioned "lord" a sum of money and a thousand *ardab* of barley, on condition that the permission to restore their temple be forthcoming. They agree, however, that no sheep, oxen, or goats are to be sacrificed but that only incense and meal offerings are to be brought. It is interesting that the name of the person for whom this message was intended is not mentioned. The document is evidently to be communicated to the high personage in private, without passing through the regular channels.

It seems certain that the Jewish temple was reconstructed, if not on the former scale then at least to the extent required for practical purposes. The cult could easily be resumed on the old site once permission was given. The claim of Meyer that the temple could hardly have been restored, since there followed shortly a new rebellion of the Egyptians leading to temporary independence,[26] is proved by the Brooklyn texts to be erroneous (Chapter 10). Brooklyn No. 12, written some years after this, is the most explicit of all in localizing Yahu, the god, in Yeb the fortress, and so it seems clear that his cult must have been in existence.

The crisis into which the Elephantine colony had been plunged was thus successfully weathered. The persistence displayed by the Jews until their objecitve was won is, indeed, remarkable.

[26] Meyer, *Papyrusfund*, 90.

10. THE ECLIPSE OF PERSIAN POWER AND THE END OF THE JEWISH COLONY

IT HAS hitherto been regarded as certain that Egypt was lost to Artaxerxes II at the very inception of his reign. Thus Eduard Meyer could declare in 1915, "We know that Egypt liberated itself from Persian rule in 404. The first native ruler, according to Manetho, was Amyrtaeus of Saïs, who alone forms the Twenty-eighth Dynasty and reigned six years (404–399); the papyrus-find of Elephantine has for the first time provided us with a document from his reign, from his fifth year (400 B.C.)."[1] The fact that there was no dated Aramaic papyrus in the Sayce-Cowley or Sachau collections from the reign of Artaxerxes II seemed to confirm Meyer's date for the end of Persian rule in Egypt. When I began the study of the Brooklyn papyri and found that most of them were written under a "King Artaxerxes" (in years 1, 3, 4, 14, 16, 28, 31, 38), I naturally assumed that they were all from the time of Artaxerxes I. The family history involved, however, soon convinced me that those dated in the first, third, and fourth years of Artaxerxes were later than the others and that the "King Artaxerxes" to whom they refer was Artaxerxes II, who succeeded Darius II in the spring of 404. Thus, as has so often been the case, the dates of private documents shed unexpected light on historical matters. We learn from these new papyri that Persian rule was still recognized at Elephantine on December 12, 402 B.C. (according to S. H. Horn's and L. H. Wood's date of Brooklyn No. 12; but 401 according to Richard A. Parker's), and hence we must infer that the rule of Amyrtaeus, which allegedly began in December, 405 B.C., did not extend over a great part of Egypt during the first years of his reign, which must approximately have coincided with the first years of Artaxerxes II.

The year 401, which began a few weeks after No. 12 may have been written, is memorable in history as the one in which Artaxerxes' younger brother, Cyrus, made his attempt to overthrow him. The story of that revolt and of the odyssey of the Greeks who participated on the side of Cyrus was given immortality by Xenophon in his *Anabasis*. The Greek author refers to the situation in Egypt in two places.[2] Some of the Greek leaders, after the death of Cyrus, were quite willing

[1] Meyer, *SPAW*, *51*, 1915, 289.
[2] *Anabasis* II, 1, 14.

to become the allies of Artaxerxes and suggested that if he wished to employ them in an expedition against Egypt they would help him in reducing that country. Later Clearchus, in addressing the Persian leader Tissaphernes, speaks of the trouble caused to the latter by the Mysians and Pisidians and of his own readiness to be used against them and then adds, "As for the Egyptians, against whom I perceive you are most incensed, I do not see what auxiliary force you would use to chastise them better than that which I now have with me." This suggests that Egypt had only very recently passed out of Persian control. Had Tissaphernes availed himself of Clearchus' offer, it might have saved Egypt for Persia and have favorably affected the destinies of the Jewish colony at Elephantine. Amyrtaeus would probably have been crushed. In any case the words of Xenophon show that Amyrtaeus was obtaining control of the country in the spring of 401, though Persian forces may still have held the northern approaches.

It is easy to see how it was possible for Amyrtaeus to succeed, in spite of Artaxerxes' victory at Cunaxa. The Egyptian Tamos, governor of Cilicia under Cyrus, had fled with the fleet and the treasures of his province to "Psammetichus (error for Amyrtaeus), king of the Egyptians,"[3] and was slain by him. Amyrtaeus thus secured money and ships with which to establish his power. When *A.P.* 35 was written he was obviously the acknowledged sovereign at Elephantine. This document is dated the 21st of Pamenhotep in his fifth year. The years of Amyrtaeus were naturally reckoned from the time when he first seized power at Saïs, and once he was recognized at Elephantine that reckoning would be used there. According to recent chronology, his reign extended from December 2, 405, to November 11, 399.[4] The 21st of Pamenhotep of his fifth year thus must have been June 19, 400 B.C. He therefore became ruler of all Egypt some time after December 12, 402, presumably in the following spring or summer, the time of the *Anabasis* of Cyrus. If one prefers Parker's date for No. 12 the Elephantine garrison would have maintained its loyalty to the Persian crown until Dec. 401 at least.

The *Demotic Chronicle* speaks of Amyrtaeus in the following words: "The first ruler who came after the foreigners, which are the Medes [=Persians], Pharaoh Amyrtaeus. After one had found law at his time, one let him go the ways of yesterday (?). There is no rule by his son after him."[5] It would appear from this that

[3] Diodorus XIV, 35, Amyrtaeus must be meant. Since he was from Saïs, home of the famous founder of the 26th Dynasty, Psammetichus I, he may well have been a descendant of his. No doubt the Amyrtaeus who collaborated with Inaros in the revolt of 460 B.C. was one of his ancestors (grandfather?). See Meyer, *SPAW*, *51*, 1915, 289, n.

[4] Elias Bickermann, "Notes sur la chronologie du XXXe dynastie," *IFAO*, *Mémoires*, *66*, 1934, 77 ff. Some adjustments in the list are suggested by Etienne Drioton and Jacques Vandier, "L'Égypte," in *Les peuples de l'orient mediterranéen* (3rd ed., Paris, 1952), *2*, 623.

[5] See Meyer, *SPAW*, *51*, 1915, 297 ff.

Amyrtaeus sought to be a new Egyptian lawgiver.[6] But the statement need not mean more than that he restored the Egyptian law of pre-Persian times.

It is unlikely that the Elephantine colony ceased to exist at the time of this political change. Indeed, *A.P.* 35 would indicate that the Jews had made the transition to native Egyptian rule in the previous year without too much difficulty. The Saitic rulers, from whom Amyrtaeus was probably descended, had, we must recall, been the ones under whose aegis the Jews had been allowed to settle on the island and build a Temple of Yahu. The colony thus had a strong claim to favorable treatment by the new king.

Amyrtaeus' control of all Egypt was brief, for he (and with him the 28th Dynasty of which he was the sole ruler) was overthrown and a new dynasty, the 29th,[7] held a brief sway with King Nepherites I (399–393) as its first ruler. A papyrus published here (Brooklyn No. 13) reflects this important event of late Egyptian history. It is the fragmentary letter addressed "to my lord Yislaḥ" by Shewa b. Zekariah. The latter, absent on business, is evidently reporting the portentous news, from a place closer to the scene of events, to Yislaḥ (b. Nathan ?) who is in Elephantine. He mentions King Amyrtaeus (immediately after a reference to Memphis) and then alludes to the accession of Nepherites. The year date of the letter is not preserved, only the month date, the 5th of Epiphi, which fell on October 1 in the years 401–398. The letter must then have been written on October 1, 399 B.C., for the first regnal year of Nepherites began on December 1, 399 B.C.[8] Doubtless the slaying, arrest, or flight of Amyrtaeus was referred to in this papyrus. The garrison at Elephantine may thus have been under his orders for about two years. The mention of Widrang, the former Persian commander at Elephantine, in this papyrus is interesting; he may have been in the service of Amyrtaeus or one of that ruler's captives.

The new dynasty came from Mendes in the Delta. The ram-god worshiped at that city[9] no doubt took a great interest in his southern colleague, Khnum, the ram-headed god of Elephantine. It stands to reason that this circumstance gave new power and influence to the Khnum priesthood and at the same time boded ill for the Temple of Yahu and its adherents. With a new dynasty in power, the historic commitments of the Saitic rulers could easily be abrogated. We have no direct evidence that such was the case, but the fact that the Jewish documents cease at this point (for Brooklyn No. 13 is the last of the datable Elephantine texts)

[6] According to Diod. I, 95, Darius was the sixth and last Egyptian lawgiver.

[7] Cf., on this whole period, Walter Schur, "Zur Vorgeschichte des Ptolemäerreiches," *Klio*, n. s., *20*, 1926, 290 ff. For a concise summary, yet with references, see Meyer, *SPAW*, *51*, 1915, 289 ff.

[8] See Bickermann, *loc. cit.*

[9] See above, p. 102, n. 9.

suggests rather strongly that the colony came to an end in the reign of Nepherites I which lasted until December 1. If so the news sent by Shewa b. Zekariah sounded the death knell of the Elephantine colony.

It seems probable that two letters published by Sachau were written near the end of the period of Persian rule. The first, *A.P.* 38, was written by Ma'uziah b. Nathan, the writer of texts Nos. 4 and 7 of the Brooklyn collection. He addresses Yedoniah and Uriah, and the priests of the god Yahu, Mattan b. Yoshibiah and Neriah b. . . . and, as the postscript adds, the Jews of "the garrison." The letter refers to the fact that when "Widrang, the commander," came to Abydos (*'bwṭ*) he had imprisoned the writer on account of a stolen precious stone which was found in the hands of the dealers (who presumably claimed to have obtained it from Ma'uziah). Subsequently Ṣeho and Ḥor, the servants of Anani, used their influence with Widrang and Ḥornufi, doubtless an Egyptian official, with the protection of the "God of Heaven," until they delivered Ma'uziah. The latter writes that Ṣeho and Ḥor are coming to Elephantine and requests that they receive attention. In line 7 there is an interesting statement: "Khnum is against us ever since Hananiah is in Egypt until now." The Elephantine priesthood of Khnum thus became hostile after the arrival of this newcomer from Palestine or Babylonia. Apparently money is needed and the addressees are urged to "sell goods from our houses." The breaks in the connection and the faint legibility of some words make it difficult to arrive at a full understanding of what was involved. Whether Ma'uziah had suffered false arrest or not eludes us. No doubt it took money to effect his liberation and presumably the errand of the two slaves of Anani was concerned with that. Anani was evidently an important man, for it is stated that what the addressees do for his servants will not be hidden from him. Perhaps he is the Anani who appears as *be'ēl ṭe'ēm* in *A.P.* 26:23 of 412 B.C. Widrang's presence at Abydos may be linked with his mention in Brooklyn No. 13. Perhaps he was given a new post (after his punishment of *A.P.* 30:16) in a different area, involving a demotion from *prtrk* to *rab ḥailā*. His "coming" to Abydos could mark the beginning of this assignment and the arrest of Ma'uziah an act of revenge on his part for the punishment brought on him by the Jews.

To the time just before the seizure of power by Amyrtaeus must belong the other, fragmentary letter *A.P.* 37. It is undated, though reference is made in line 15 to letters arriving on the 6th of Paophi. The stater is referred to in line 12 as the monetary denomination in use. Since that coin first appears on the scene in Brooklyn No. 12 of December 12, 402 B.C., we must adjudge *A.P.* 37 to belong to this general time. The 6th of Paophi may therefore have been the summer of 401 (Parker, 400) B.C. The writer, whose name is not preserved, is reporting from Memphis, on behalf of a delegation or group, to Yedoniah, Ma'uziah, Uriah, and "the garrison." There is reference to rations, to bribery employed by the Egyptians — apparently in working against the Jews — and to the Egyptians doing

something "thievishly" before Arsham. An Egyptian slur on the "officer (*peḳīd*) of the province" is quoted: "He is a Mazdaean." The arrival of another Elephantine resident, Pasu b. Mannuki, at Memphis is mentioned. The contents of the papyrus mirror a situation of unrest.

The Jews expelled from Elephantine may well have joined their coreligionists in some other Egyptian community. If *A.P.* 34, which refers to the arrest and slaying of Jewish men and women, should mirror their final migration from the island,[10] one might infer that they had transferred their residence to Thebes. But all that one can say with certainty is that the Jewish colony of Elephantine, which bursts mysteriously into the historical picture with the coming of Cambyses, disappears from it equally mysteriously a few years after the eclipse of Persian rule.

It seems unlikely that any Jews were left at Yeb when, in the days of the 30th Dynasty, which came from Sebennytos, the rebuilding of the Temple of Khnum was begun by its last ruler, Nektanebos II (359–341). We have seen in our account of the excavations that the street which skirts the wall of the Khnum Temple seems to impinge on the houses of the Aramaean district in a manner suggesting that these were no longer occupied when it was laid (p. 67). The reconquest of Egypt by Artaxerxes III (Ochos) in 342 B.C. doubtless brought these building operations to a stop. The portal of Alexander II (315–311 B.C.), the outstanding landmark of Elephantine, marks the resumption of building in this area.

We may picture Nektanebos II as pausing in his southward flight before Artaxerxes III to inspect the work on the Temple of Khnum and pay homage to the god who was the patron of the southland. Probably his dynasty had had nothing to do with terminating the existence of the Temple of Yahu that once stood so close to that of Khnum, but if there were any survivors or descendants of the old Jewish colony living in Egypt who remembered that temple, they may well have regarded the royal fugitive's exile in darkest Africa as a punishment visited on the kingdom for what had been done to their ancient sanctuary. His fate stirred the imagination, as a Greek papyrus containing a tale of a dream in which he foresaw the fall of his kingdom vividly shows.[11]

Did the final destruction of the Yahu Temple of Elephantine and the end of the Jewish colony leave any echo in subsequent Old Testament prophecy? It has been suggested that when Joel says, "Egypt shall be a desolation, and Edom shall be a desolate wilderness, for the violence against the children of Judah, because they have shed innocent blood in their land" (3:19; M.T. 4:19), he is thinking in part

[10] Cf. Meyer, *Papyrusfund*, 90, and Vincent, *Religion*, 390 ff. We prefer an earlier date. See p. 104.

[11] Cf. Maspero, *Popular Stories of Ancient Egypt* (4th ed., London, 1915), 285 f., Ulrich Wilcken, *Urkunden der Ptolemäerzeit* (Berlin, 1923), No. 8. The astronomical date presupposed in this tale was July 5, 343 B.C. See the references given by Bickermann in his article, pp. 78 ff.

of the liquidation of the Elephantine colony.[12] However, an exact dating of this passage is impossible, and there were doubtless other occasions in the 4th and 3rd centuries when violence was done to Jews in Egypt.

More plausibility attaches to the thought of finding such an echo in Isa. 19:1–15. This oracle, entitled "The Burden of Egypt," describes the fate which is in store for that country. Poetically, the author pictures Yahweh as riding to Egypt on a swift cloud. The idols tremble, the heart of Egypt melts. Internecine strife breaks out, city against city, kingdom against kingdom, and within the cities there is civil war. The spirit of the Egyptians fails them. They are given into the hands of "a cruel lord and fierce king" who shall rule over them. The princes of Zoan (i. e., Sân = Tanis), now evidently important advisers of the Pharaoh and boasting of being sons of ancient kings, are become as fools, and the princes of Memphis are deceived. Influenced by a perverse spirit put into their midst by Yahweh, the Egyptians are led astray. Some scholars have thought that the author of this prophecy was angered by what the Egyptians had done to the Jews of Elephantine. Much depends, of course, on the dating of the passage. If the oracle is later than the time of the 29th Dynasty, the events at Elephantine would have receded into the past.

We may assume that the author of the prophecy had a contemporary foreign ruler in mind when he spoke of "the cruel lord and fierce king" into whose hands the Egyptians were to be given. He can hardly have thought of any other ruler than the king of Persia. It seems likely that he had in view Artaxerxes III (385–338), who had a reputation for cruelty.[13] It is less likely that he was thinking of Artaxerxes II (404–358), though that ruler, after losing control of Egypt in 401, undertook unsuccessful campaigns against Pharaoh Akhoris in the years 392–379 and against Nektanebos I, founder of the 30th Dynasty, in 373. There was more reason for a Judaean imitator of the old prophets to inveigh against Egypt after Pharaoh Teos had made his attempt to reestablish Egyptian imperial rule in Syria in 360 B.C. by means of a great campaign by land and sea. Palestine may well have suffered at this time under Egyptian exactions. The subsequent preparations of Artaxerxes III for the subjection of Egypt must have been apparent to Jewish observers. After a first unsuccessful attempt in 350 a decisive onslaught was

[12] Hermann Gunkel, "Der Yahutempel in Elephantine," *Deutsche Rundschau, 134,* 1908, 30 ff.

[13] Because of the allusion to "kingdom against kingdom," Steuernagel, *ZDPV, 35,* 1912, 98, would put this passage in the period of the "Dodekarchy," or division of Egypt into twelve kingdoms, and thus prior to the time when Psammetichus I (who then would be the "cruel and fierce king") united the land. But the title given the Pharaoh in Dupont-Sommer's papyrus (see Chapter 1, n. 69) should be noted. Apocalyptic texts, furthermore, often employ phraseology borrowed from older texts, so that one cannot rely on the idea that every statement faithfully mirrors a contemporary situation. — On the cruelty of Artaxerxes III, cf. the references in Olmstead, *History of the Persian Empire*, 424.

launched in November of 343. Nektanebos II was defeated and withdrew to Memphis. When his Greek mercenaries forsook him and went over to the Persian side his cause was lost. Either of the Egyptian campaigns of Artaxerxes III might well have elicited the prophecy. It was, we believe, the immediate experience of Egyptian oppression in Palestine, rather than any persecution of Jews in Egypt, that moved this Judaean prophet.

This poetic oracle against Egypt is followed by a series of supplementary prose predictions (Isa. 19:16 f.), one of which has been held to refer to the Elephantine sanctuary.[14] The passage states that "there shall be an altar to Yahweh in the midst of the land of Egypt and a pillar to Yahweh at the border thereof." Behind such predictions we must seek actualities: the author doubtless had an existing altar and pillar in view.

It would seem, however, that the statement has two separate localities in mind for the two objects, for the altar is "in the midst of the land," and "the midst" is scarcely the border but rather some point in the heart of Egypt. That would, of course, exclude Elephantine. In the 2nd century there seem to have been more Jewish temples in Egypt than this passage presupposes. When the Jewish high priest Onias came there, so Josephus relates, he found "that the greater part of our people had temples in an improper manner and that on this account they bare ill will one against another, which happens to the Egyptians also by reason of the multitude of their temples and the difference of opinions about divine worship."[15] There were thus a number of Jewish sanctuaries in existence, which Onias presumably closed with royal aid, carrying out a sort of Deuteronomic reformation. It hardly seems possible to date the prediction of Isa. 19:19 so late that it could be a reference to the temple that Onias then established at Leontopolis (ca. 162 B.C.). Indeed, if we can believe Josephus, this very prediction was used by Onias as a scriptural justification for its construction, and so an earlier temple must be meant by the Isaiah passage. Perhaps the Jews from Elephantine had set up their temple anew in a different locality after quitting the island. The passage certainly presupposes that there was only *one* Yahweh altar in all Egypt at the time when it was written.

But could not the "pillar at the border" be a reference to a sacred pillar at Elephantine? The worship of the god Bethel, whose name recalls the sacred pillars, was, as we have seen, carried on there. But this interpretation becomes altogether unlikely if one dismisses a connection of "the altar" with that place. True, Elephantine is on the border, but when a Palestinian author speaks of the border of Egypt, he certainly has in mind the *northern* border, not the remote southern border, which would, furthermore, be described as the border of Cush rather than of

[14] Steuernagel, *loc. cit.*

[15] *Ant.* XIII, 62–73.

Egypt. The passage is late but the object referred to may be old. The "pillar to Yahweh" (the sort of sacred stone more or less outlawed since the Deuteronomic reformation)[16] is obviously embarrassing to this Hebrew writer, for he tries to explain it as a mere symbol. It may have stood at Migdol (Pelusion), where there was also a Temple of Baal Zaphon (Zeus Kasios).[17] We may be sure that Jews of pre-Deuteronomic religious convictions, like those of Elephantine, regarded an ancient stone pillar like the one Jacob had called "Bethel" as a sacred object, and that their messengers (for example, the bearers of *A.P.* 30 and 32) paused to revere it when they traveled to and fro between Egypt and Palestine. The writer of Isa. 19:19 ff. predicts that this pillar shall be "a sign and a witness," unto Yahweh in the land of Egypt. It will testify to the deliverance of the Jews from their Egyptian oppressors by a "savior."[18] So impressive will this deliverance of the Jews be to the Egyptians, he asserts, that the latter will thereby be converted to Yahweh. Interesting as the passage is it sheds no light on Elephantine.

Aside from the Elephantine papyri, Aramaic-speaking Jews in Egypt have left few other traces of their existence. A fragmentary legal document of about 300 B.C., *A.P.* 82, alludes to Jewish persons and apparently mentions Abydos and the fortress of *Ṭbh.*[19] The long papyrus *A.P.* 81 gives many Jewish names, but with Greek names interspersed. It thus dates from after the time of the Macedonian conquest. Particularly interesting is its reference to a "Johanan the priest" (line 8), which suggests that there was a temple in the place where it was written. This might well have been the successor to the Temple of Elephantine and the very one

[16] Cf. Millar Burrows, "From Pillar to Post," *Journal of the Palestine Oriental Society*, *14*, 1934, 32 f.

[17] According to Herodotus III, 5, the Phoenician (Palestinian) border extended as far as Lake Serbonis where the mount (!) called the *Kasion* lies, but south of Lake Serbonis the country belonged to Egypt. Presumably, then, the Mons Casius (at best a tumulus) belonged to Egypt. In Strabo XVI, 2, 31, Egypt's boundary is just east of Pelusion — everything beyond that being reckoned as belonging to "Phoenicia." Midgol, the northernmost town of Egypt in Ezek. 29:10, 30:6 and center of a Jewish community according to Jer. 44:1, 46:14, is doubtless the Semitic name of Pelusion (Tell Farāma. See Alan H. Gardiner, "The Ancient Military Road from Egypt to Palestine," *JEA 6*, 1920, 99 ff.). Here in later times was a Temple of Zeus Kasios (see Jean Clédat, "Le temple de Zeus Casios à Peluse," *ASAE*, *13*, 1914, 79–85), doubtless a branch of the sanctuary at Lake Serbonis; the pillar revered by the Jews and given a spiritualizing reinterpretation by the biblical writer may well have stood there and have been an old Baitylion. Zeus Kasios is identical with Baal Zaphon, a deity of Phoenician origin. The real Mons Casius was near ancient Ugarit (Ras Shamra in Syria). See W. F. Albright, "Baal Zephon," *Festschrift für Alfred Bertholet* (Tübingen, 1950), 1 ff. Otto Eissfeldt, *Baal Ẓaphon, Ẓeus Kasios und der Durchzug der Israeliten durchs Meer* (Halle, 1932). Martin Noth, "Der Schauplatz des Meereswunders," *Festschrift Otto Eissfeldt* (Halle, 1947), 181 f.

[18] Perhaps he has Ptolemy II (Philadelphus) in mind, who freed many Jews; Josephus, *Against Apion*, II, 45.

[19] *A.P.* 83 is hardly of Jewish origin. On *Ṭbh* see Chapter 1, n. 48.

meant in Isa. 19:19.[20] A new influx of Hebrew-speaking Jews is presupposed in Isa. 19:18, where "the language of Canaan" is said to be spoken in five cities of Egypt. It is attractive to suppose that this verse mirrors the time of Ptolemy I or Ptolemy II, in which many Jews were brought to the land of the Nile.[21]

That Jews returned to the neighborhood of Elephantine in later times has been inferred from a statement of Philo Judaeus, who speaks of his people as spread abroad in Egypt, from the Libyan border to the confines of Ethiopia.[22] Those confines, as we have seen in Chapter 2, lay just above the Island of Elephantine. It is not likely, however, that the Jews who may have lived in Elephantine in the 1st century had any inkling that others from among their people had once dwelt there and even possessed their own "altar house."

[20] The papyrus is said to have come from Ḳūs near Luxor.

[21] "Assyria" in this prophecy is Seleucid Syria, in the opinion of most scholars.

[22] Philo, *Flaccus*, 43. See F. H. Colson, *Philo, with an English Translation*, Loeb Classical Library (Cambridge, Mass., 1941), *9*, 327. Cf. Staerk, "Die Anfänge der jüdischen Diaspora in Ägypten," *OLZ*, Beiheft *2*, 1908, 9.

II. TEXTS, TRANSLATIONS, AND COMMENTARIES

INTRODUCTION

The Papyri and Their Sealings, with a Brief Description of Their Unrolling

JOHN D. COONEY

FEW objects ever are so completely changed in appearance as is a papyrus between its transformation from a roll into a sheet, the final and essential stage to make it available for study. The physical aspect characteristic of the Brooklyn Aramaic papyri only a few years ago is now so changed that a brief history is desirable. While most of these Aramaic papyri were received segregated in three tin boxes, a few were mixed with hieratic papyri, the arrangement suggesting that they had been expertly packed in Egypt as purchased. Museum accession numbers were assigned to the papyri consecutively as the various boxes were opened and recorded; as Professor Kraeling has treated these papyri in chronological order, he has given them other, consecutive numbers for the purpose of publication.

All the papyrus rolls were originally tied and sealed, for without exception each intact roll retained either its mud seal or traces of one when received in the museum. Only five rolls still preserved seals with clear impressions. These have been drawn by Miss Suzanne E. Chapman of the Museum of Fine Arts, Boston, and are reproduced on Fig. 6.

Papyrus 9 was sealed with a hard stone gem of slightly convex surface, drawn in the lower right of Fig. 6. It reproduces an ancient Mesopotamian motif, a king grappling with a powerful beast, a subject which is common in Persian art. Both in design and workmanship obviously of Achaemenid origin and most probably of the 5th century B.C., the seal is of interest as one of the uncommon occurrences of Persian art in Egypt. The impression suggests that the workmanship was indifferent.

The seal impression on Papyrus 11, while at first glance suggesting the Egyptian uraeus, is certainly another example of a Persian gem used in this distant colony. Its form, similar to that of the one just described, leaves no doubt of its origin. Unfortunately the design, seemingly some conventionalized floral motif, is too incomplete to permit identification. The use of Persian gems in Elephantine is, in a minor way, somewhat remarkable, for not only did Persian art make a negligible impression on Egyptian art — the influence seems to have been almost entirely in

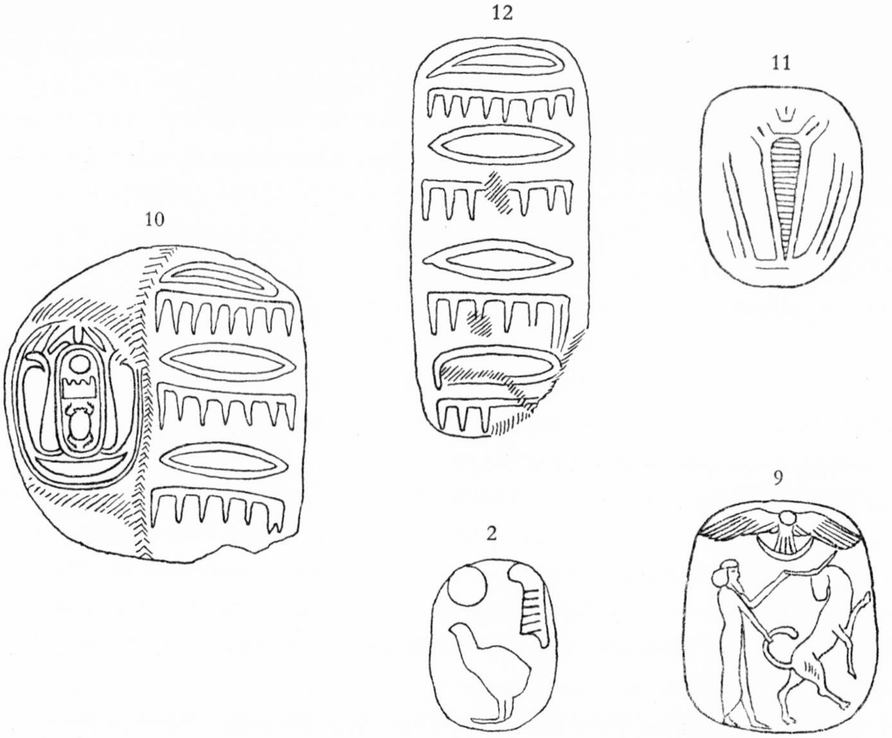

FIG. 6 Seals of Papyri 2, 9, 10, 11, 12. Drawn by Suzanne E. Chapman

the opposite direction — but so very few Persian objects have been found in Egypt that any evidence, however slight, of Persian influence there is of interest in reconstructing the shadowy art history of the period.

In the case of the impressions on Papyrus 10 we find purely Egyptian subjects and the only instance in this collection of a double sealing. On the left is a scarab impression with a cartouche enclosing the praenomen of Thutmose III of the 18th Dynasty, flanked by uraei representing the protective goddesses of Upper and Lower Egypt. The other impression is a hieroglyphic inscription (unreadable so far as I know) within a cartouche, made by a scarab or seal. It is of a well-known type frequently found on scarabs of the Hyksos period (ca. 1730–1580 B.C.), from which time the seal used to make this impression certainly dates. There is no evidence that this device was ever copied in later periods, and the rough style of the signs leaves no doubt of the Hyksos date. The period of the Thutmose III scarab cannot be determined with equal certainty. More than one king bore this praenomen, which was frequently associated with the names of later Egyptian rulers. Even on examining original scarabs with this inscription it is frequently impossible to determine the date with certainty, and clearly the difficulty is not less when only an impression survives. So great was the power of the very name of the great conqueror Thutmose III that scarabs inscribed to him were prized and even made

many centuries after his death. It is very likely that this Elephantine impression refers to him. Though the scarab used to make the impression was probably not contemporary with the conqueror — the use of crowns on the protective serpent goddesses suggests a post-New Kingdom date — the style of the inscription suggests that the scarab was centuries old when used to seal this papyrus.

The Hyksos scarab is even more striking evidence of the value placed on ancient seals by the Egyptians of this late period. Such objects could have been obtained only by looting ancient cemeteries or in chance finds — one wonders if there were antiquities dealers in those distant days. Doubtless the venerable age of the seals made them desirable, suggesting those amuletic powers which even today make scarabs and ancient tokens highly valued charms among the desert peoples of the Sudan and certain tribes in and around Assuan, a survival of a very ancient custom, as these Elephantine impressions prove.

Even if we did not know the connection of Papyrus 10 with Papyrus 12 it could be assumed, for on each document we find the impression of the same Hyksos seal. A careful examination of both impressions indicates clearly that they were made with the same ancient seal, which its owner treasured so greatly that he made it his personal seal. It would be interesting to know why in one case he added a supplementary impression.

The remaining impression, from Papyrus 2, was made from a scarab bearing an inscription apparently to be read Rēʿ-Shu, in reference to one of the innumerable compound manifestations of the sun-god. The form of the base and the relatively wide spacing of the signs leave little doubt of the approximate date of the original, about the 26th Dynasty. Similar inscriptions on scarabs and scaraboids of the Saïte kings are of fairly frequent occurrence. It is unlikely that its owner had any interest in the inscription, or indeed even knew what it signified, for as has been said such seals were valued for their magical powers and antiquity, though in the case of this scarab its antiquity was modest.

To judge by the slender evidence of these few seals, the Jewish colony at Elephantine produced no characteristic art or craft based on its own religion or culture. The few impressions mentioned in Sayce-Cowley and the one impression described by Erman in Sachau's publication tell the same story: a single Persian seal, the others, earlier Egyptian scarabs. If any sort of local art existed one would expect to find evidence of it in such intimate objects as seals. Instead there are two seals of probable contemporary date, both of Persian origin, while the remaining seals are of earlier Egyptian origin, indicating that this isolated colony had abandoned some of its traditions in succumbing to the influence of its Egyptian neighbors, at least to the extent of using as seals symbols which their fathers would certainly have condemned as idolatrous.

Pl. XXI shows the condition of some rolls when first examined in 1948. They duplicate exactly the forms of the Sayce-Cowley and Sachau papyri, having been

first rolled and then folded in on the center from each end, after which they were tied and sealed.

The successful opening of these rolls is due entirely to Mr. Anthony Giambalvo, the technician of the Department of Egyptian Art. He had frequently and with great success opened the conventional type of rolled papyrus, but these rolled and tightly folded papyri, flattened and completely dessicated, presented another problem.

The illustrations on pl. XXII show the simple but delicate method devised by Mr. Giambalvo. The roll was placed on a small stand covered with blotting paper to absorb excess moisture, the wooden board under the paper being pierced to allow for drainage; under the stand was a dish of water. After a glass bell jar had covered the group for about five hours, enough moisture had penetrated the outer layer of the papyrus to separate the mud seal from the surface of the papyrus without the loss of any of the fabric. The next and most important stage was the opening of the two main folds. The bell jar was replaced for a period of several hours to humidify the outer layers of the roll. With a little experience it was possible to decide when it was sufficiently relaxed to permit handling. With the roll placed on its side a spatula was inserted against the inner edge of the outer fold which was very gradually and gently pushed outward until it formed a right angle to the center. The process was repeated on the inner fold, after which the roll was placed on its back forming an upright letter U. As soon as the two arms were pushed slightly beyond the perpendicular, their weight, increased by the absorption of water, made them fall slowly into their original position, reconverting the document into a conventional papyrus roll.

It proved impractical to keep the unfolded papyrus within a humidified container, for the interior of the roll remained dry while its outer layers became too moist, risking buckling. The process adopted was to unroll the outer layers and then to apply water with a small brush to the inner layers. Papyrus becomes remarkably flexible when moistened and will withstand much handling. With the last fold exposed, the excess water was removed and the opened papyrus placed between sheets of white blotting paper changed at very frequent intervals for forty-eight hours and once a day for another five days. This skillful treatment has preserved each papyrus in a state which can differ very little, if at all, from its appearance on the day the ancient scribe finished his work.

The restoration of the broken rolls was a far more difficult task; that it was ever undertaken and completed is again due to Mr. Giambalvo's patience and skill. Of the damaged rolls, Papyrus 7 was by far the largest and most completely broken. Its condition when received in Brooklyn, broken into hundreds of fragments, is recorded on pl. XXIII. There is no doubt that in 1893 this papyrus was intact, but at an unknown date an unskilled attempt had been made to open it, apparently by cutting the folds and bends. Most of the resulting fragments had been kept

together but numerous pieces were found in 1948 packed with other Aramaic and hieratic papyri. The identification of these fragments scattered among hundreds, perhaps thousands, of unrelated pieces was a major task, one that had to be undertaken for each of the broken rolls.

One piece of good luck which greatly facilitated the assembling of Papyrus 7 was the discovery of the greater portion of the left bend, tightly curled and carbonized in a single mass. Its successful opening was a technical triumph which gave the clue to the final arrangement of this important text. After this the joining of fragments was largely accomplished by matching fibers — the final test of any join. The necessary equipment is very simple: a piece of frosted glass supported on a light frame with cold, movable lights under the glass. Nine months were devoted to the treating and assembling of Papyrus 7.

Technically these Aramaic papyri differ only slightly from their Egyptian predecessors. Their fabric is heavier than is usual in earlier periods, and their color a darker brown. Egyptian papyri were usually manufactured in sheets about sixteen inches long but a roll of almost any length was available by attaching to the left end another sheet of the same size, a process that was continued until the necessary length was obtained. The narrow areas where additional sheets are attached are called overlaps or joins. In using these sheets the Egyptians usually wrote only on the recto, that side of a papyrus on which the main fibers are horizontal, the texts running parallel with these lines. In these Aramaic papyri it is not always easy to distinguish recto from verso, a difficulty that is complicated by the occasional carelessness of the papyrus maker in joining sheets. Frequently the grain of an added sheet runs in a direction different from that in the balance of the roll. Contrary to the practice of their Egyptian neighbors, the scribes of these Aramaic papyri wrote their texts in most cases on the verso, leaving the recto unused except for the customary one-line endorsement. Again differing with Egyptian practice, which was to write texts in columns along the length of a payrus, our Aramaic papyri are inscribed in a single column running across the width of the papyrus. Possibly the scribes were forced to use this arrangement because of the surprisingly short lengths of papyrus which formed the separate sheets of these rolls. They run from five and a half to six and a half inches in length, necessitating constant joins, which would be a nuisance to any scribe attempting to write along the length of the document. Perhaps these short pieces of papyri were an inexpensive job lot from a local manufacturer, the best that the Elephantine colony could afford.

PAPYRUS 1

PAPYRUS 1

(*Brooklyn* 47.218.152) 32.7 *cm.* x 26.1 *cm.*

THIS papyrus, which has been reconstructed from numerous fragments, is the oldest in the collection herewith published. It is dated July 6, 451 B.C. and is virtually a complete text, for nearly all the missing words can be guessed and the damaged ones restored.

The document is made out by Mika, son of . . ., to a man whose full name and title can readily be restored on the basis of the documents that follow — Anani, son of Azariah, "*lḥn* (servitor ?) of Yahu in Yeb." The latter had apparently brought a suit against Mika about a piece of property described by the otherwise unknown word *hīrā* (or *hīdā* ?). If l. 6 is correct, Mika had obtained the property by a suit against Anani. The latter must thus have appealed the case. Mika here acknowledges the receipt of 5 shekels as the price of "this *hīrā* of thine," thereby implying that its ownership has already passed to Anani. It would seem that Anani had successfully established his right to obtain this property and that Mika was forced to cede it to him for the amount mentioned. (But see also note on l. 9 of commentary.) Mika gives assurance that he will not bring a return suit in the matter of this *hīrā* and concedes the obligation to pay a penalty of 5 karsh if he violates this pledge. He will also protect Anani against a suit by any of his own relations, singling out brother and sister for chief mention. The scribe was a very terse writer with a bold hand, and there are only two Jews among the seven witnesses, Micaiah b. Aḥio (mentioned in Brooklyn No. 5:17) and Maḥseiah b. Yedoniah, well-known from the previously published Elephantine documents as the father of Mibṭaḥiah.

ב 25 לפמנ[ח]ת̇ף הו יום 20 לסיון [ב]שנת 14 לארתחשסש מלכא
אמר מיכא בר .... [ל]ענני בר עז[ריה ל]חן ליהו ביב
לאמר יהבת לי כסף שקלן 5 בדמי הירא זילך זי
קבלת עלי בגו [וטי]ב לבבי בדמוה[י ולא] אכהל אגרנך
דן ודבב בשם [הי]רא זנה זי ק[ב]לת עלי בגו הן קבלת
עליך דין ומר[א] בשם הירא [זנה] זי קבלת עליך
בגו ויהבת ל[י] דמוהי כסף שקלן [5 ו]ר̇חק̇ת מנך
אנתן לך כסף כרשן 5 הן גרך א̇[ח לי] ואחה
קרב ורק בשם הירא זנה אנה [אפצ]ל ואנתן לך
כתב בתי בר מ̇נכי כפם מיכא בר א ... [שה]דיא בגו
זבדי נבוזיר   שפ̇אל בר כ̇ב̇ר̇ כ̇.ת̇ר
מכיה בר אחיו אחושן בר דנונוכי
מחסיה בר ידניה מנכי בר בגין עתרמלכי בר פ̇סמי
זבוד בר זבעדרי

1. On the 25th of Phamenoth, that is the 20th day of Siwan, [in] the 14th year of Artaxerxes, the king,
2. said Mika son of [. . . to] Anani son of Az[ariah, *l*]*ḥn* of Yahu in Yeb,
3. saying: "Thou hast given me silver, 5 shekels, as the price of the *hīrā* of thine about which
4. thou didst bring complaint against me, and my heart [is satis]fied with its price. [And] I shall [not] be able to institute against thee
5. suit or process with mention of this [*hī*]*rā*, about which thou didst bring c[om]plaint against me. If I bring complaint
6. against thee (before) judge and lor[d] with mention of [this] *hīrā* about which I complained against thee (error for "thou didst complain against me?")
7. and whose price, silver, [5] shekels, thou didst give [to me, and] I removed from thee,
8. I shall give thee silver, 5 karsh. If there should institute suit against thee a brother [of mine] or sister,
9. close or distant relative, with mention of this *hīrā*, I [shall reco]ver(?) and shall give to thee.
10. There wrote (this) Bty b. Mannuki at the dictation of Mika b. '[. . . Wit]nesses thereto:
11. Zabdai, Nabuzēr, Šapi-ili b. K̇ḃṙ k̇-ṫr,
12. Micaiah b. Aḥio, Aḫušunu b. Danunuki,
13. Maḥseiah b. Yedoniah, Mannuki b. Baga'in, ʿAtarmalki b. Pasmi,
14. Zabud b. Zabʿidri.

1. The fragment on the right is doubtlessly correctly placed. The head of the initial ב is still visible, as well as the top of the numeral 20. The month name, begun in this fragment, can only be *Pamenḥotep (Phamenoth); the ה and part of the ת are missing in the gap between this fragment and the next, which has the rest of the ת and the ף. In הו יום the waw's are damaged. Before שנת, which is also damaged, the ב is lost. In the gap after שנת only part of the sign for 10 is missing. The fourth unit sign was joined rather closely to the preposition preceding the king's name. Artaxerxes can only be Artaxerxes I. And so the year was 451 B.C. The 20th of Siwan was July 7, the 25th of *Pamenḥotep, July 6 in that year. The word מלכא was superimposed at the end of the line instead of being put in the following line; the writer wanted to begin there with his subject matter.

2. The man making out the document is Mika b. . . . The father's name is missing here as well as in l. 10. The hitherto published papyri do not help, as the Mika of *A.P.* 22:64 is known only by his son's name, Haggai b. Mika. Cf. further discussion in comments on l. 10. The fact that the other party referred to was Anani b. Azariah, so prominent a figure in the texts that are to follow (see notes on No. 2:2), is obvious, and hence the clue was given to place the fragment with the letter ע before the three surviving letters of his name; the feet of the מ in the line above are visible on the upper rim. A ל must be supplied before the name. Of his father's name, Azariah, only the first two letters and part of the third appear. The first letter of Anani's title לחן (on which see notes to No. 2:2) is broken away, save for a slight trace of it on the rim of the next piece.

ליהו. The preposition is used here, as also in 3:3, 25; 9:2. Elsewhere we have לחן זי יהו or less formally, in the course of a document, ענני לחנא. On the divine name see above, Chapter 8.

ביב. On Yeb as Elephantine see Chapter 2.

3. לאמר is believed by many to be a Hebraism. The usual Aramaic infinitive is למאמר (cf. Ezra 5:11, לממר). B.A. prefers the participle in such cases; cf. BL, § 81v. But לאמר occurs also in the letter from Ashur (Mark Lidzbarski, *Altaramäische Urkunden aus Assur*, WVDOG, *38* [Leipzig 1921], Tafel I, l. 8) and hence may not be a Hebraism. See Franz Rosenthal, "Die Sprache der palmyrenischen Inschriften," *MVAÄG*, *41*, 1936, 60.

Owing to the break in the papyrus, the ס in כסף looks a bit disjointed.

After the numerals the word must be בדמי (note the ב of price, GK, § 119p.). The ד in this case is written very much like a waw, but that is also the case in l. 7. The final י straddles the break, but the small fragment put there makes no perfect join, for something has crumbled away. That this piece is properly placed is evident from the heavy smudge (presumably due to erasure of something first written by the scribe) found on it and on the rest of the line, as well as from the fact that the letters on it fill out the word required here, which is vindicated both here and in l. 6 by its perfect occurrence in l. 9.

הירא or הידא (?). This word is only seemingly a new one. It is found on Sachau's Tafel 61, obv., l. 6, but was misread by him (p. 225) as well as by Cowley (*A.P.* 68, No. 6, rev.), who has יהיבא. It is not clear whether it means a building or an object of some sort. Rosenthal suggests linking it with the Syriac root *hrr*, "to litigate, dispute," but the next words would seem to require something concrete. W. Erichsen compares demotic *ḫjr* which usually means "street," but which also occurs in an Elephantine papyrus with the meaning "house."

זילך זי. The reading is certain.

4. קבלת עלי. The verb is found in the sense "to lodge complaint" in No. 10:12 and in the previously known texts; cf. *A.P.* 6:5, 16; 8:13; 10:12, 18; 47:7. This meaning, however, must be a derived one; that it evolved out of the basic sense of the root קבל is suggested by the way the word is used with a direct object in ll. 5 (end)–6 and in *A.P.* 8:13. In other comparable passages קדם is used after the verb.

בגו, as frequently in the previous papyri. See note on l. 10.

In the break the letters וטי are missing. They may be supplied to fill out the fixed phrase וטיב לבבי.

After בדמוה a final yodh is missing, as well as the negative particle לא. Traces of the ל of the latter remain.

אכהל. This verb is usually followed by another impf., instead of the inf. with ל; cf. BL § 107J.

אגרנך from גרי with nun energic before the suffix; cf. L § 40 f. Akkadian legal texts use a related verb *girū*, "carry on a suit"; cf. Schorr, *Urkunden*, No. 296, 4. The terminology is thus of Babylonian origin. Cf. Friedrich Schulthess, *GGA*, 1907, 193.

5. דן ודבב. This phrase was frequent in the previously published papyri. The first word is usually written דין. The phrase is of Babylonian origin. Cf. *tuāru dini u dabābu la-aš-šu*, "reopening the case and litigation are not to be"; *ša dini u dabābu* . . "whoever (seeks) suit or process (with N. N.)," in a text from Sennacherib's time; Peiser, *Texte*, 116. In Clay, BEUP, *10*, 34, No. 94:11, the phrase used is *dīnu u ragāmu*.

בשם, literally, "in the name of." Probably weakened here to "the mention of." In bringing suit a specific property had to be named, "house of N. N." or the like. Nothing seems to be missing in the break except the first two letters of the word [הי]רא.

קבלת. Enough of the word remains to put it beyond doubt.

הן קבלת. Here the word appears in the first person. Cf. further below.

6. דין here is *dayyān*, "judge," and the next word was undoubtedly מרא, "lord," as below in Nos. 9:19; 10:13; 12:28, the title given to some high personage such as the prefect. In *A.P.* 47:7 the word seems to have followed סגן. The phraseology there is קבל-על-קדם. Here, however, there is no קדם; "judge and lord" are the objects of קבל, as in *A.P.* 8:13, where, however, there is an על. This suggests that the verb

means "invoke (cf. Targ. Exod. 22:22 where it renders Hebrew צעק). In *A.P.* 6:16 the object is זי which refers back to דין "suit"; the reading *dayyān*, "judge," would seem possible but less likely.

בשם can be restored with certainty.

The final א of הירא is damaged and זנה may be supplied in the break. The feet of the last two letters of the latter word are still visible.

זי קבלת עליך is puzzling. If one takes זי in the sense of "so that," the connection becomes unduly complicated. Is עליך an error for עלי? The sense then would be as in ll. 3–4. The apodosis continuing the protasis (beginning with הן in l. 5) starts with אנתן in l. 8.

7. Shekels [5]. The numerals can be supplied from l. 3.

[ו]רׄחקׄת? —The verb gives good sense, but neither רׄ nor קׄ seem certain. On the word cf. *A.P.* 25:4 and the comments on Brooklyn No. 3:11, below. A waw is necessary before the word because there is no conjunction before the verb at the beginning of l. 8.

8. The penalty of 5 karsh is a tenfold multiplication of the 5 shekels originally received.

גרך, 3d pers. sing. perf., as in *A.P.* 14:9 (where the obj. suff. is fem.).

[אׄ]חת לי ו] can be confidently restored in the gap; part of the aleph is visible on the right rim.

9. ורק is a scribal error for ורחק. I take the phrase (familiar from *A.P.*1:5, etc.) to mean "close or distant relative," not "relative or unrelated person." Peiser, *OLZ*, *11*, 1908, 24, already took this view and compared the Assyrian phrase *kimtu nisūti u sallāti*. The general sense of the final statement of the line must have been: "I myself shall assume the liability and shall give (the money) to thee." The usual word for liable would be אחוב, but the word in the gap cannot have been that, for its last letter was ל; a portion of the upper stroke still remains. [אפצל] should be restored here, following the clue given by No. 3:20. See comments on that passage.

The tail of the final kaph at the end of the line was extended down by an unusually bold stroke to below the space for the next line.

Jacob Rabinowitz suggests that the sale referred to in this text is a fictitious one for the purpose of obtaining judicial sanction for the transfer of property and thinks that is also true of *A.P.* 6. I find support for such a view in Ulrich Wilcken's remarks on W. Spiegelberg's No. 12 in *Demotische Papyri von der Insel Elephantine* (Leipzig 1908). He rejects the idea that this is a "Traditionsurkunde," (see *Archiv für Papyrusforschung*, *5*, 1913, 216). In that text, too, a man speaks of a complaint he has brought.

10. With unusual brevity the writer of this text passes on to his conclusion.

בתי בר מׄנכי the scribe. On the first name cf. *Bi-ti-ia*, Clay, *Documents from the Temple Archives of Nippur*, BEUP, *14* (Philadelphia, 1906), 42; a Palmyrene name בתי is listed in Lidzbarski, *Epigraphik*, 246. The name Mannuki occurs again in

l. 13. It is found quite a number of times and of different persons in the previously known texts: thus a Luḥi b. Mannuki, *A.P.* 14:13, a Pasu b. Mannuki in *A.P.* 37:11; 53:10. It is an abridgement of such names as *Mannuki-Adad*, "who is like Adad?" Tallqvist, *APN*, 124.

כפם is the regular expression, but cf. על פם in *A.P.* 2:18; 11:16; Bauer-Meissner, l. 18.

The name of Mika's father must have begun with א, judging from the remains of that letter. At the edge of the break there is a trace of a letter, perhaps a gimel. אגור? He could be Agur b. Aḥio of *A.P.* 10:22 (456 B.C.), and a brother of Micaiah b. Aḥio, who signs as witness for Mika.

[שה]דיא is a certain restoration. The ש may survive in a fragment shown on the plate above the text.

בגו, literally, "in the inner part," "within," but probably just loosely "thereto." The expression is probably of Babylonian origin, *ina libbi*; cf. Ungnad, 34. The term could, at times, be taken more precisely, as the Mishnaic passage *Baba Bathra* 10, 1 clearly shows: גט פשוט עדיו מתוכו ומקושר עדיו מאחוריו, "A plain document has its witnesses within (on the recto); a tied up document has its witnesses on its back (verso)" (as pointed out to me by Jacob Rabinowitz). See also Chapter 5, n. 4.

11. The first name is clearly זבדי Cf. the fragment *A.P.* 65:7 and זבדיה *A.P.* 22:13, etc. Also *Zabdī*, Tallqvist, *APN*, 245, and *Zabdīa*, *NBN*, 216. It is odd that there is no בר after it. In the word that follows one may be in doubt whether the third and fourth strokes are two separate letters (וו) or just one (ח). The temptation is to connect it with Nabu or Nebo, written נבו. The next three letters then must be זיר (even though the last is written much like ב) and the name is Babylonian *Nabu-zēr*. This very form appears in the Babylonian texts; see Tallqvist, *NBN*, 265. It is doubtlessly a shortened form of such a name as *Nabu-zēr-iddina* or *Nabu-zēr-ibni*. Cf. נבוזראבן *A.P.* 9:16 and נבוזראדן, *A.P.* 8:28, 28:14 (where אדן seems to me to be the required reading rather than Cowley's אבן) and II Kings 25:8 f. After זיר there is a smudge and a break. On the left is a remnant of a ג that may not have been fully erased.

שפאל. I first read שכאל, for the second letter is similar to the כ in כתב in l. 10. This suggested comparison with such a name as שכיה, I Chron. 8:10 or שכיבל (hypocoristic שכיו) in Palmyrene. See Lidzbarski, *Epigraphik*, 375. Albright suggests reading שנאל which would be *Sin-ilī* (Tallqvist, *APN*, 199: *Sin-iliya*) and compares the שנדן of *A.P.* 22:19 — *Sin-iddin* ? (Cowley). However, I doubt that the second letter is a nun. It is like the פ on the Aramaic dockets on Babylonian tablets. See Clay, BEUP, *10*, 72. Reading it thus one gets the name *Šapī-iliya* (cf. Erich Ebeling, "Neubabylonische Briefe," *ABAW*, n. f., Heft 30, 1949, 94, No. 174:29). The man may be a native of Babylonia. The ר of בר is still legible though damaged. The lower portions of most of the letters in the father's name are visible: כבר כ־הר. On the element *khr* see W. W. Baudissin, *Kyrios*, *3*, 75 f. כבד is of course equally possible;

cf. the Punic name כבד עשתרת, Lidzbarski, *Ephemeris*, *1*, 162. Lidzbarski, *Epigraphik*, 300, lists a Phoenician personal name כתרא. If the father's name was West Semitic the reading שכאל would seem preferable.

12. The large unpracticed hand of מכיה בר אחיו begins the line. The א is partly broken away. The final waw in אחיו is exaggerated. This is the man's autograph. In No. 5:17 the scribe wrote his name and gave it as מיכיה.

אחושן בר דנונוכי. The first letter looks much like the א on the Babylonian dockets. A name אחושן with cuneiform equivalent *Aḫušunu* occurs in Clay, BEUP, *10*, 71. In the patronymic the waw's look like peh's. The next to the last letter is a kaph, as appears from the long downward stroke; the name is thus Danunuki. Tallqvist, *APN*, 69–71, gives *Dan(n)ānu–*, *Dinanu–*, *Dunanu/ni–*, but no *Danunuki*. Perhaps one should transcribe *Dunnunuki*.

13. Maḥseiah b. (Yed)oniah. The first two letters of the patronymic are only partly visible but may be confidently restored. This is the Maḥseiah (not to be confused with his grandson of the same name in *A.P.* 25:18) who appeared so prominently in the previously published papyri; cf. *A.P.* 5:2; 6:3; 8:1 f.; 9:1 f.; 13:1 f.; 14:2; 15:2, and who had a daughter named Mibṭaḥiah. He was a witness in *A.P.* 11:14, the first papyrus brought from Elephantine by Sayce (a document the date of which is lost but which must also come from about 450 B.C.; cf. Cowley, *A.P.*, p. 32).

מנכי בר בגין. The signature of Mannuki b. *Bgyn* is finely written. On Mannuki see l. 10; בגין possibly is the Persian name *Ba-ga-'-in*, Clay, BEUP, *8*, Pt. 1, No. 107:19 (cf. also *-bigīn* in the name cited below on No. 3:4); a בגבגן is found in Aimé-Giron, *Textes*, No. 87.

עתרמלכי בר פסמי. A different ʿAtarmalki in Brooklyn No. 8:10; an עתרשורי in *A.P.* 8:27; 9:16. On the divinity עתר see above Chapter 8.

פּסמי. The kaph from the line above creates an uncertainty in the first letter. It could be a nun or a waw.

זבוד בר זבעדרי. The first name is probably זבוד, for a זבור seems unlikely. The names *Za-bu-da-a* and *Za-bu-du* in Clay, BEUP, *10*, 66, may be compared. The patronymic זבעדרי is unusual. The element עדרי is typically Aramaic; cf. Noth, *IP*, 63. One expects a divine name to precede, as in *Adad-idri*, "Adad is my help," or אתעדרי (*A.P.* 2:20 for עתי as explained by Lidzbarski, *Ephemeris*, *3*, 249), or נשכעדרי (*A.P.* 65:15). זב then must stand for the Babylonian god *Zababa* (also written *Zamama*). This deity occurs frequently in neo-Babylonian names; cf. *Zababa-iddina*, Ebeling, *ABAW*, n. f., Heft 30, 1949, No. 73, l. 6.

A few fragments that look as though they belonged to this papyrus and were put under glass with it do not seem to fit anywhere in this text.

The "endorsement" is not preserved.

PAPYRUS 2

PAPYRUS 2

(*Brooklyn* 47.218.89) 26.5 *cm.* x 32.2 *cm.*

OUR text opens the history of a family. The founding event takes place in the 16th year of Artaxerxes. For reasons arising from the family history, this can only be Artaxerxes I. The Julian date is July 3, 449 B.C.

The man who receives leading mention here is Ananiah (also Anani for short in the first and subsequent lines) b. Azariah, *lḥn* (servitor?) of Yahu the god in Yeb the fortress. On the Yahu Temple at Yeb, see the account above in the introduction (Ch. 9). Since we find him living close to the temple and subsequently possessed of quite some property, one would like to consider him a prominent official. The man's father and his title, *lḥn*, already appear in a papyrus fragment published in 1912, but there the continuation "of Yahu the god in Yeb the fortress," which, as we can now see, must have followed, had been broken away (cf. notes for further details). Since Ananiah's father's name is given, he must have been a freeborn man himself, for in the case of persons of bound status the mother's name is used.

The papyrus here published provides us with another marriage document to place beside the longer and more elaborate one of Sayce-Cowley "G" (*A.P.* 15) and the even longer but only partially preserved Brooklyn No. 7 of this collection. It was written by the same scribe, Nathan b. Ananiah, who wrote papyrus "G" on October 15, 435 B.C. (cf. Chapter 5, n. 11). Short as this new text is, it is of significance for the history of law, for here a man marries another man's handmaiden named Tamut, who seems already to have a child, a boy named Palṭi (l. 13). The new legal status of Tamut is not entirely clear from this text alone and will have to be considered in the light of other texts yet to follow. It seems that marriage did not imply liberation, as Schorr, *Urkunden*, 59 (in comments on No. 36), assumes. Tamut is, however, a lawful wife, able to divorce her husband and to be divorced, and like him is subject to the same payment of "divorce money" of 7 shekels and 2 *R.* (see above, Ch. 3) in the event of taking the initiative. No matter who divorces, she takes her possessions that she brought in, which were valued at a slightly smaller amount than the "divorce money" — 7 shekels and 7½ *ḥallur* (see Ch. 3), a figure which is corrected, however, on the endorsement to 1 karsh and 5 shekels. In the event of the death of either of the partners the survivor has power over the property. Meshullam, whose handmaiden Tamut had been,

pledges that he will not take the child Palṭi away from Ananiah. If he does so (tries to do so ?), he will have to give Ananiah 5 karsh. Since the amount is larger than the money value of a slave child, this is evidently a fine. A condition, however, is attached: "If thou dost not drive out his mother Tamut!" Such a driving out is not identical with the divorce situation regulated above but involved a disregard of the law. Abraham's driving out of Hagar and her child (Gen. 21:10 f.) differs in that she was not his lawful wife (though the later Priestly source in Gen. 16:3 does give her the status of a second wife). Meshullam thus retains a legal hold on Palṭi in the event of Anani's driving out the mother.

There is no mention in this text of a *mohar*; in Schorr, *Urkunden*, 59, No. 36, a *terḫatu* (i. e., mohar) is given in the nominal amount of one shekel for the specified reason that no one should touch the slave girl given in marriage. Without such payment she evidently was not so well protected.

[ב] 18 [תמוז הו יום 3 ל]ירח פרמותי שנת 16 ארתחש מלכא אמר
ענניה בר עזריה לחן זי יהו אלהא זי ביב בירתא למשלם בר זכור ארמי זי סון
לדגל וריזת לאמר אנה אתית [ע]ליך למנתן לי לתמת שׄמׄהׄ זׄיׄ אׄמׄתׄךׄ לאנתו הי אנתתי
ואנה בעלה מן יומא זנה ועד עלם הנעלת לי תמת בידה לבש 1 זי עמר שוה כסף
שקלן 7 מחזי 1 שויה כסף חלרן 7 פלג שנן משאן 1 משח בשם
פלג חפנא תקם חפנן 6 פיק 1 כל כספא ודמי נכסיא כסף שקלן 7
חלרן 7 פלג מחר או יום אחרן יקום ענני בעדה ויאמר שנאת לתמת אנתתי
כסף שנא בראשה ינתן לתמת כסף תקלן 7 ר 2 וכל זי הנעלת בידה תהנפק מן חם
עד חוט מחר או יום אחרן תקם תמת ותאמר שנאת לבעלי ענני כסף שוה בראשה
תנתן לענני כסף שקלן 7 ר 2 וכל זי הנעלת בידה תהנפק מן חם עד חוט מחר או יום
אחרן ימות ענניה תמת הי שליטה בכל נכסן זי יהוון בין ענני ותמת
מחר או יום אחרן תמות תמת ענני הו שליט הו [...] בכל נכסן זי יהוון בין
תמת ובין ענני ואנה משלם מחר או יום אחרן לא אכל אנצל לפלטי מן תחת
והן הנצלתה מנך אנתן לענני כסף כרשן 5
לבבך בר מן זי אנת תתרך לאמה תמת כתב נתן בר ענניה ספרא זנה ושהדיא
בגו שהד נתן בר גדול מנחם בר זכור גמריה בר מחסיה
הנעלת תמת לענני בידה כסף כרש 1 שקלן 5

(Plate XIX, 1)

1. On the 18th [of Tammuz, that is the 3d day of the] month of Pharmouthi, the 16th year of Artaxerxes the king, said
2. Ananiah son of Azariah, *lḥn* of Yahu the god who is in Yeb the fortress, to Meshullam son of Zakkur, Aramaean of Syene,
3. of the *degel* of Warizath, saying: I have come unto thee that thou mightest give to me Tamut by name, who (is) thy handmaiden, in marriage. She is my wife
4. and I her husband from this day for ever. Tamut has brought in to me in her hand one garment of wool worth 7
5. shekels of silver; one mirror worth 7½ ḥallur; one *šnn mšʾn*; balsam ointment,
6. half a handful; a jar (?) of 6 handfuls; one *pyḳ*. All the money and the value of the goods in money is silver 7 shekels
7. and 7½ ḥallur. If tomorrow or another day Anani rises up on account of her(?) and says, "I divorce Tamut my wife," the
8. divorce money is on his head. He shall give to Tamut in silver 7 shekels, 2 *R.*, and all that she brought in in her hand she shall take out, from straw
9. to thread. If tomorrow or another day, Tamut rises up and says, "I divorce my husband Anani," a like sum shall be on her head.
10. She shall give to Anani in silver 7 shekels, 2 *R.*, and all which she brought in in her hand she shall take out, from straw to thread. If tomorrow or another day
11. Ananiah should die, Tamut shall have power over all the goods which there may be between Anani and Tamut.
12. If tomorrow or another day, Tamut should die, Anani — he — shall have power over all the goods which there may be between
13. Tamut and Anani. And I Meshullam, tomorrow or another day, will not be able to take away Palṭi from under
14. thy heart except if thou dost drive out his mother Tamut. And if I take him away from thee, I shall give to Anani 5 karsh of silver. There wrote Nathan b. Ananiah this document, and the witnesses
15. thereto (were) Nathan b. Gaddūl, Menaḥem b. Zakkur, Gemariah b. Maḥseiah.
16. (Endorsement:) Tamut brought in to Anani in her hand silver, 1 karsh, 5 shekels.

1. The Babylonian month name is missing, though the number 18 is preserved. Before it ב may be supplied. The day of the Egyptian month is also lost. According to Richard A. Parker, the Babylonian month name may be restored as Tammuz and the Egyptian day as the 3d of Pharmouthi. Pharmouthi was previously found in *A.P.* 35:6 where, however, it is not written *plene* as here.

ארתחש. The writing is unusual and possibly a scribal error. In the other texts we have ארתחשסש. The name was discussed by Andreas in Lidzbarski, *Ephemeris*, *2*, 221; cf. Schaeder, *Beiträge*, 268. The 16th year of that ruler began in Nisan of 449 B.C. The Julian date of our text is thus July 13 of that year.

2. The man who speaks here is Ananiah b. Azariah. Below in ll. 7 f. he is called Anani, as was the case in No. 1:2, and will be found the regular thing in some later texts. The tendency to use a shorter form appears prominently with many names ending in *-yahu*. His name doubtlessly stood also in the fragment of Aimé-Giron, *Textes*, No. 78, l. 1. This man's father, Azariah, was also *lḥn* before him and is mentioned in *A.P.* 63:9, 12. In the first of these passages the reading seems none too certain. The words appearing there are followed by נגרא, from which Driver, "Problems in Aramaic and Hebrew Texts," *Analecta Orientalia*, *12*, 1935, 59, would infer that the man was a carpenter, a maker of wooden bowls or dishes (connecting לחן with Akkadian *laḫanu*, on which word see Otto Schroeder, "Assyrische Gefässnamen," *AfO*, *6*, 1930, 111). But נגרא seems to have a different meaning in the papyrus from Saqqāra published by Dupont-Sommer (see *Semitica*, *1*, 1948, 52). The editor would connect it with Assyrian *nāgiru*, which according to Ebeling, *ABAW*, n. f., Heft 30, 1950, 139, means "herald, crier," or else read נגדא and connect with נגודא, "leader" (J. A.). A שרה לחנא (fem.?) occurs in the *dipinto* from Saqqāra published by Aimé-Giron, *Textes*, 102; the editor wrongly took the ל of לחנא as a preposition before a personal name חנא. The title is thus not restricted to the Elephantine scene or to Jews. In the light of the new papyri we can see that לחן is a functionary of the temple. In 12:2 Ananiah's wife Tamut gets the title לחנה (fem. of לחן). The לחנת of *A.P.* Aḥ. 83 is to be explained as this very word, with haplological ellipse of the first syllable after the preposition. The connection in Aḥiḳar requires the meaning "maid servant:" "a blow for a young manservant (עלים), a re[buke for] a maidservant (ל[לחנת]) and for all thy slaves dis[cipline]." There is doubtless a connection between this word and the לחנה of Dan. 5:2 f., 23. The traditional vocalization suggests an original **laḫinatu*. (This in turn suggests to Landsberger the possibility of the derivation of לחן from Assyrian (*a*)*laḫḫinu*, "grinder of flour." Cf. Landsberger, *AfO*, *10*, 1935–36, 150). For the word in Daniel, *laḫanatu* in the sense of "maid" or "damsel," Ebeling, *Ein Hymnenkatalog aus Assur* (Berlin, 1923), 23, was adduced by Baumgartner, *ZAW*, *45*, 1927, 81 f. The meaning in Daniel, where לחנה usually is rendered "concubine," may actually represent a nuance *in malam partem* of a word per se merely meaning "maidservant," as in

Aḥiḳar. Certainly the Aḥiḳar text must govern our understanding of the word in the papyri. The masculine לחן, then, must mean "minister, servitor." But Ananiah is a freeman by birth, as his name shows. His wife, indeed, has slave status, but that has nothing to do with her title לחנה, which is derived from his, as Hebrew נביאה is from the husband's in Isa. 8:3.

יהו (on the name cf. above Chapter 8) is described here as the "god who is in Yeb the fortress" (cf. "the god Khnum who is in Yeb the fortress," *A.P.* 30:5). The relative זי removes any ambiguity such as exists in *A.P.* 6:4.

בירתא in effect is "city." סון gets the same title as does ספרד, Sardis, in the inscription from there; see Lidzbarski, "Die lydisch-aramäische Inschrift von Sardis," *ZA*, *31*, 1917–18, 122. Original publication by Enno Littmann, "Lydian Inscriptions," *Sardis*, *6* (Leyden, 1916).

משלם בר זכור. See l. 13 and Nos. 5:2, 3; 12:11, 24. He was already known from *A.P.* 13:3 of 447 B.C. as the previous owner of a house which Maḥseiah b. Yedoniah had acquired, and from *A.P.* 10:2 of 456 B.C., where he lent money to Yauḥan, daughter of Meshullak. In the first passage his grandfather's name is added, Ater, on which Sayce-Cowley compared Ezra 2:16, etc. Meshullam b. Zakkur is described here as an "Aramaean of Syene"; he is called a Jew in No. 5:2.

3. Meshullam belongs to the *degel* of Warizath (*A.P.* 5:2, 3; 6:4; 6:10; 13:2; 14:3; 15:3; 28:2). On this term see Chapter 3. Does this *degel* have any connection with the man mentioned in No. 8:11?

The broken part in the first part of l. 3 can be filled in confidently because the tops of the letters are visible. Cf. the phraseology in *A.P.* 15:3, אנה אתית ביתך. Before למנתן one must mentally supply "to ask you." The one who "comes to someone" starts the negotiations; cf. *A.P.* 5:3.

לתמת. The accusative indicated by ל as in *A.P.* 13:2; 15:3. As for the name תמת itself, we must look for an Egyptian equivalent, since the bearer of it is a slave woman, and these were usually Egyptians at Elephantine. Albright would connect this name with Egyptian **Tamūt*, *T3*(*-n.t.*)*-Mwt* (Ranke, *ÄP*, 360:10), "the one belonging to the goddess Mut;" Erichsen would prefer to connect it with *t3-mwt*, "mother." The former view accords well with the considerations advanced in 5:3, where the same person is called תפמת — a name she thereafter bears (except in No. 6). Her father's name is given in No. 12:3. Spiegelberg, *Sprachgut*, 40 cites אסמת and פמת as names containing the name of the goddess Mut.

The break in the text after the name contained at least two words. A slave's name is usally followed by שמה, literally "his (or her) name," as in Babylonian texts (*šumšu*), and the remnants of the letters fit this. Cf. Schorr, *Urkunden*, 47; also BL § 108q. The last word is certainly אמתך. There must have been a letter or two between these words; זי would fit the indications.

לאנתו, "in marriage," as in *A.P.* 14:4; 15:3; 48:3; cf. Lidzbarski, *Ephemeris*, *3*, 80.

Targum Onkelos uses this word for Hebrew לאשה in Gen. 16:3. The phrase נתן לאנתו is obviously a translation of Assyrian *nadānu ana aššūti* (*u mutūti*); see Schorr, *Urkunden*, 540e, f, for references.

4. The marriage declaration is stated just as in *A.P.* 15:4: "She is my wife and I her husband from this day for ever." An element of sentiment is present in the declaration. For tenacious survival of basic forms, cf. the Syriac ordinance, Sachau, *Syrische Rechtsbücher* (Berlin, 1907), *1*, 75; there the groom declares before priest and congregation, "This woman is my wife," and therewith the marriage is legal.

Without transition of any sort the text proceeds to enumerate what articles the wife brought into the man's house. הנעלת is 3d pers. and not 1st; Cowley in *A.P.* 15:6–7 persisted in misunderstanding this, in spite of the convincing comments on the subject by others, notably Lidzbarski, *Ephemeris*, *3*, 129, 131, and L. Freund, "Bemerkungen zu Pap. G des Fundes von Assuan," *WZKM*, *14*, 1907, 169 f. One must, therefore, restore לי twice in *A.P.* 15:6–7. The articles are now enumerated and their value given just as in *A.P.* 15:6 f., but here everything is on a more simple scale — Tamut being a poor handmaiden.

"A woolen dress worth 7 shekels." In *A.P.* 15:6 the woolen dress of the newly-wed widow or divorcee is described as "new, striped, dyed on both sides" and even its length and breadth in cubits are given. Its worth was 2 karsh, 8 shekels. According to Herodotus II, 36 a man has two garments, a woman only one. This suits Tamut's case, but not No. 7 or *A.P.* 15.

5. מחזי, cf. No. 7:13, *A.P.* 15:11, and Hebrew (late) מחזית "mirror." שויה is the participle feminine of שוה, "be equal to," as in *A.P.* 15:12. It is worth 7½ ḥallur (the פלג goes with the preceding as in l. 7). In the Babylonian scale the ḥallur is one-tenth of a shekel. Mibṭaḥiah had a better mirror of copper worth one shekel, 2 *R*.

1 שנן משאן. The א is none too clear but is supported by this same phrase in *A.P.* 15:15, where the words are rendered by Cowley as "1 *mšʾn* knife (?)"; in his notes he states that this is a guess, based on J.A. שננא, "blade." In that passage the phrase is written between the lines and the connection likewise does not help. שנן occurs again below in 7:20 in the phrase שנן זי על פרסין. The absence of a זי before משאן should be noted. It is used after this word in *A.P.* 55:8. One may try to connect משאן with Assyrian *mešēnu*, "anklet."

משח בשם. It does not seem that these two words should be linked with the preceding. They apparently constitute a fresh item, though there is no numeral. The phrase means "oil (or ointment) of fragrance." In Isa. 3:24 it is predicted that there is to be a מק instead of בשם, in a connection where the stylish and luxury-loving women of Jerusalem are being spoken of. The Palmyrene tariff (Cooke, *NSI*, 325, l. 6) refers to the seller of משחא בשימא, and so בשם may be an adjective and mean "scented." In the Hermopolis letters (Kamil, *BIE*, *28*, 1947, 253 f.) משח בשם and משח זית are said to occur as objects of purchase or as gifts.

A measure of quantity presumably followed.

There are traces of the letters חפן after בשם. The scribe rubbed them out and corrected himself in the next line.

6. פלג, "half," must certainly be construed with חפנא as "half a *ḥupnā*." The latter appears in the plural in the interlinear material in *A.P.* 15:15 where Cowley retained his erroneous "8 ח," which Lidzbarski, *Ephemeris*, *3*, 131, had rightly corrected to 5 חפנן. We meet it again in 7:20. On this word cf. Heb. חפן, used in the dual (Exod. 9:8 etc.) for the hollow hands or what they can enclose. חפנן could be dual, but since the sing. חפנא, which then must mean "handful," is used here too, it seems better to take it as plural. The word then represents a small measure.

The meaning and explanation of the word תקם in *A.P.* 15 left scholars pretty much helpless. According to Murad Kamil, *BIE*, *28*, 1947, 256, תקם has the meaning "jar" in the Hermopolis papyri. If that be true, the word might be a derivative of קום, with ת prefixed, like B.A. תדירא, if from דור; cf. BL, p. 195. In *A.P.* 37:10 a phrase דבש תקם occurs. Does this mean "honey of the jar," i. e., a jar of honey? An inscription in Aimé-Giron, *Textes*, No. 99, mentions a priest of the god Nabu יתב תקמא בסון; the editor takes that to mean "ordinarily residing in Syene."

These items apparently are "no-value" items. The same is true of the last item: 1 פיק, where a numeral is again used (cf. again in 7:18). In *A.P.* 15:16 we have פק 1 זי סלק — the same word defectively written. This spelling rules out Scheftelowitz's attempt to connect the word with Old Persian *pāka*, "cooking pot," "Die Bewertung der aramäischen Urkunden von Assuan und Elephantine," *Scripta Universitatis atque Bibliothecae Hierosolymitanarum*, *1*, 1923, 15. In No. 7:18 סלק seems to be a metal or coin. Cf. the note on that passage.

כל כספא is not to be connected with the preceding but with what follows. The same phraseology appears as in *A.P.* 15:13–14, where Cowley rightly renders these and the next words "total (cash) money and value of goods in money is silver 7 shekels, etc." נכסיא is a Babylonian loanword *nikasu*; Zimmern, *Akkadische Fremdwörter*, 20. Cf. Peiser, *Texte*, 322, col. IV, 22 for its use. Deprivation of goods ענש נכסן is referred to in Ezra 7:26.

7. Note that as in l. 5 no conjunction is placed before פלג. The meaning is 7½ ḥallur.

A new sentence starts with מחר. It is a conditional sentence without the usual conditional particle הן (BL § 111) but with the imperfect. Does יום אחרן mean "another day" or "the next day?" The latter interpretation is favored by Rashi in commenting on the words למחר וליומא אחרא in *Baba Mezia* 17a, as Jacob Rabinowitz points out. Cf. also the Hebrew idiom תמול שלשום with reference to previous days.

יקום בעדה, the same phraseology as in *A.P.* 15:26. "Rises up in the congregation" was Cowley's rendering. Since the preposition בעד is vindicated by No. 11:10, it is quite possible that one should rather render "on his own (or her) behalf" (Rosen-

thal). Or is the nuance here "on her account"? Cf. Hebrew Prov. 6:26 בעד אשה זונה, where "on account of" would fit.

שנאת: "I divorce (literally "hate, take a dislike to") my wife" is evidently fixed phraseology that must be used to make the thing legal. It is Babylonian, however, and not found in demotic or Greek marriage contracts. On this see San Nicolò, *OLZ*, *30*, 1927, 217 f. and Paul Koschaker, "Beiträge zum altbabylonischen Recht," *ZA*, *35*, 1924, 200, according to whom the term originally refers to refusal of intercourse.

8. The first words of this line are similar to those in *A.P.* 15:23 which Cowley renders: "the price of divorce is on his head." There, as in No. 7:22, 25, the word שנאה appears, whereas here we have שנא — error or participle? In the Babylonian legal texts the corresponding technical term is *uzubbū* or *kasap uzubbī*; cf. Schorr, *Urkunden*, 2:21, 7:3; Ungnad, *Babylonische Briefe aus der Zeit der Hammurapidynastie* (Leipzig, 1914), 92, No. 109:16. Driver would render *A.P.* 15:23: "The divorce money in its full amount" on the basis of a phrase in Neo-Babylonian contracts (*kaspu ina ḳaḳḳadišu*), *Analecta Orientalia*, *12*, 1935, 55, but that translation will not do in 7:22, 25, and so one must return to Cowley's rendering. The amount is to be paid in silver, 7 shekels, 2 *R*. Shekels is spelled תקלן here (as in *A.P.* 10:5) instead of שקלן; see L § 2b. Note that such a variation is possible in one and the same text! Between the lines is added "2 *R*.," or two quarter-shekels. The personal property she brought into Anani's house she may take out; this too is stereotype (cf. *A.P.* 15:28). On חם in the alliterative phrase מן חם עד חוט cf. G. R. Driver, *JRAS*, 1932, 78. Cowley rendered "from shred to thread." Driver takes חם as "broom."

9. But Tamut, too, can divorce her "lord." Note that בעדה (cf. l. 7) is omitted here. In that case she must pay "like money," כסף שוה. שאה (then a scribal error) could be read instead of שוה; the line going off at an angle is ink but very faint. The stroke I take to be waw is very heavy and so it looks to me as though the scribe corrected himself. Tamut may take out what she brought into the marriage. It is interesting to note that in *A.P.* 15 Mibṭaḥiah ranks first in the matter of the possibility of divorcing a mate.

10. *R*. 2 is superimposed and *R*. did not come out well.

11. Again there is no conditional particle. The full name Ananiah reappears here, as in l. 2. For the pronoun see BL § 72d. There is an erasure of a word בפלג after הי. Tamut shall be שליטה, i. e., "have power (cf. *A.P.* 15:18)." Some take this to be an Egyptianism (cf. J. Leibovitch, "Quelques egyptianismes contenus dans les textes araméens d'Égypte," *BIE*, *18*, 1936, 19 f.), but it is Babylonian. Cf. such a statement as "another creditor shall not have power (*ul išallat*) over it," Clay, BEUP, *10*, 33, No. 62:9. An interesting formulation appears in "the goods which may be between Tamut and Anani" — evidently the joint possessions acquired after marriage, hardly just those now existing. Note בין---ו, while in ll. 12–13 בין----ובין is used.

12. The reverse situation obtains in the event of the death of Tamut. The pronoun הו is written a second time above the line, showing that the single occurrence might merely be the equivalent of our "shall have." The scribe wants Anani emphasized — "Anani, *he* shall have." There is another erasure after שליט; the scribe apparently wrote בכלה, rubbed the word out and started afresh on dry surface with בכל.

13. Meshullam b. Zakkur as grantor now states his reservation. A stroke in the margin on the right calls attention to the new speaker. We have not been told what, if anything, Anani had to give Meshullam to obtain his handmaiden as wife. There may or may not have been a document about it. אכל instead of אכהל was already found in *A.P.* 10:11, 12; 13:8; 15:31, 35; 47:7, 8; Aḥ. 26. The imperfect is continued by another imperfect אנצל and not by an infinitive. See BL § 107j. נצל haphel already appeared in *A.P.* 8:18; 9:10; 18:3. Here, however, there is a syncopation of the ה; the usual form would be אהנצל. See L § 35h.

לפלטי. This would be difficult if it were not for 4:18, 21, where we learn that Tamut has a child named Palṭi (i. e., Pelaṭiah; cf. No. 6, frag.). Various personages have this name in the Elphantine papyri (cf. below 9:25 and Cowley's index). He shall not be able to take Palṭi away "from under thy heart." (Cf. Prov. 22:27.)

14. The interlinear material (13b) really follows logically on "thy heart." הנצלתה is 1st pers. sing. with 3d pers. masc. sing. suff. Meshullam must pay 5 karsh as a fine; there seems to be no doubt of his right to reclaim the boy. The fine covers the injury to Anani, who has fed and clothed him and become attached to him. The cost of raising a child in Egypt in later times is given as 20 drachmas (Diodorus I, 80).

בר מן זי: the בר must be "except," as in Targumic (cf. Gen. 14:24 בר מן) and the זי in connection with מן is like the conditional מן די in B.A.; cf. BL § 109k.

תתרך. The verb is used in the pael in the Targum, Gen. 3:24, and is used in the pael here as well, as 6:16 and 7:30 show. Expulsion and legal divorce are two different things. The former is an illegal action. Cf. the introduction to this papyrus.

לאמה תמת is best rendered, with Rosenthal, as "his mother Tamut" rather than "the handmaiden Tamut." Cf. also 6:3. On ל as introducing the object, see BL § 100q.

The scribe Nathan b. Ananiah who wrote this is the same man who wrote the documents *A.P.* 10, 13, 15 and appears as witness in *A.P.* 8:32; 9:20. The pedigree in *A.P.* 18:3 shows that the scribe Ma'uziah b. Nathan was his son.

15. Witnesses are only three in number. Nathan b. Gaddūl is apparently not known from the previously published papyri. *Gaddūl*, as H. L. Ginsberg would read this name, instead of Cowley's *Gadol*, is a hypocoristicon for Gedaliah. Ginsberg compares names like Zakkūr, Yaddū', and Shammū'.

Menaḥem b. Zakkur was a witness of the marriage document of Mibṭaḥiah, *A.P.* 15:38.

Gemariah b. Maḥseiah is mentioned as a witness in 4:23, and in *A.P.* 8:29; 9:18; 22:2. His daughter Meshullemeth is mentioned first on the list of contributors to the temple funds in *A.P.* 22:2.

16. The "endorsement" appearing on the outside of the roll is usually a memorandum enabling the owner of a number of sealed rolls to know what each is about. Sometimes, however, it has a supplementary recording function, as here. The total of one karsh, 5 shekels is here given for what Tamut brought in. In the text we heard the value of the goods was 7 shekels and 7½ ḥallur. In the itemization no value was placed on the last items listed. The preceding items amounted to only 6 shekels, 7½ ḥallur. One shekel was evidently allowed to cover the value of the rest. Here in the endorsement her assets are doubled. She may thus have brought in some cash money, disclosed belatedly, or received wedding presents. The increase was taken into account in this way. The expression for total (cash) money was used in the summary remark of l. 6, but no cash item had preceded.

PAPYRUS 3

PAPYRUS 3

(*Brooklyn* 47.218.95) 80.8 *cm.* x 30.1 *cm.*

THIS document is dated September 14, 437 B.C. The married couple Bagazušt and Ūbīl have sold a house to Ananiah b. Azariah, the *lḥn* of the god Yahu. The previous owner from whom they had obtained it, *'pwly* b. Misdai, is mentioned, but it is pointed out that they had made improvements on it. In the further description of the property we learn that it had a court that was unencumbered, windows, etc. Directly addressing the vendee, the vendors state that they have sold it to him and have received its price, 1 karsh and 4 shekels. A typical Egyptian phrase, "our heart is satisfied," occurs in connection with the receipt acknowledgment. They then describe the location of the house by what we would call the four points of the compass. The boundaries are the neighboring properties, which include the Temple of Yahu (cf. above in Chapter 7). Once more Bagazušt and Ūbīl affirm that they have sold and handed over and that they henceforth are "removed" from it forever. Here Semitic idiom takes over some interesting Egyptian terminology. The Egyptians regarded the final act in the transfer of property bought and paid for as one in which the previous owner "removes himself" from it. The emphasis is not on the *taking* possession but on the *giving* possession. Some papyri even bear an Aramaic rendering of the Egyptian legal term, "document of removal," on the endorsement written on the outside of the rolled up and sealed papyrus (see *A.P.* 6:22; 25:20; cf. *A.P.* 8:23 f.). It speaks volumes for the persistence of native custom, no matter what conquering caste reigned over the land, that in the Greek papyri the very same usage persists. The Egyptian idiom is merely translated once more into another tongue.

Addressing Ananiah b. Azariah, Bagazušt and his wife affirm that he is "to have power" over this house. The right passes to his children or to whom he wills to give it (which includes permission to sell). In the matter of the house which they have sold, handed over, and "removed themselves from" Bagazušt and Ūbīl will not be able to start "suit or process" — Babylonian legal verbiage that persists not only here but likewise passes over into the Greek papyri in new dress — against Ananiah or his son or daughter (the wife is not mentioned because children would inherit the house) or to whomever he gives it. If Bagazušt and Ūbīl themselves do not keep their pledge and sue him or his legal successors for recovery of the prop-

erty, they must pay him a fine of 10 karsh, 2 *R.*, while if their children sue, they must pay 20 karsh. In either case final acknowledgement that the house belongs to him and his heirs must be made by the litigants.

The eventuality is foreseen, however, that some "other man" might sue (one might think, e. g., of a creditor). Bagazušt and Ūbīl pledge themselves to fight the case and restore the impounded property within 30 days, and if they fail to recover it in that time they or their children (evidently presupposing death of the vendors) must give Ananiah another house like this one. However, an exception is parenthetically made to this warranty clause: if it is a son (or daughter, as is added by an afterthought) of the former owner *'pwly* who sues to recover the property, they are not thus liable. This escape clause shows that there is no such thing as a search of title and consequent guarantee of title. That eventuality excepted, however, they continue their pledge to the effect that if they are unable to restore the property, they will refund to Ananiah the purchase price of 1 karsh, 4 shekels, and (the value of ?) any building improvements made on it. The *lḥn* of the god Yahu thus acquired a property directly across the street from the Yahu sanctuary.

On the endorsement of this papyrus the name "Yahu" is written "Yah," as in the Hebrew of Exod. 15:2, etc. Cf. Ps. 68:5, "His name is Jah."

ב 7 לאלול הו יום 9 לירח פאוני שנת 28 ארתחשסש מלכא אמר
בגושת בר בזו כספי לדגל נמסו ונשן ו[א]בל ברת שתבר כספיה זי סון לדגל נמסו
כל [גבר 1] נשן 1 לעניניה בר עזריה לחן ליהו אלהא לאמר אנחן זבן ויהבן
לך ביתה זי אפולי בר מסדי זי ביב ברתא זי אגרוה קימן ותרבצה
ארע הי ולא בניה וכוין בה וגשרן לא אחד אנחן זבנהי לך ויהבת
לן דמוהי כסף כרש 1 שקלן 4 באבני מלכא כסף 1ר1 לכרש 1 וטיב לבבן
בדמיא זי יהבת לן והא אלה תחמי ביתא זך זי אנחן זבן לך לעליה
לה בית שתבר לתחתיה לה תמי זי חנום אלהא ושוק מלכא ביניהם
מועה שמש לה אוצרא זי מלכא דבק לה למערב שמש [לה] אגור
[אלהא] יהו ושוק מלכא ביניהם אנה בגושת ואובל כל 2 אנחן זבן ויהבן
לך ורחקן מנה מן יומא זנה ועד עלמן אנת ענניה בר עזריה שליט
בביתא [זך] ובניך מן אחריך ולמן די צבית למנתן אנחן לא נכל נגרנך דין
ודבב בשם ביתא זנה זי אנחן זבן ויהבן לך ורחקן מנה ולא נכהל
נגרה לבר לך וברה ולמן זי צבית למנתן הן גרינך דין ודבב וגרין
לבר ב(!)ברה לך ולמן זי צבית למנתן אנחן ננתן לך כסף כרשן 20 כסף 1ר1
לעשרתא וביתא זילך אם וזי בניך מן אחריך ולמן זי צבית למנתן ולא
יכהל בר וברה לן יגרנך זין וזבב בשם ביתא זנה זי תחמוהי כתבן
מנעל הן גרוך וגרו לבר וברה לך ינתנון לך כסף כרשן 20 כסף 1ר 1 ל 10
וביתא זילך אם וזי בניך מן אחריך והן גבר אחרן יגרנך ויגרה
לבר וברה לך אנחן נקום ונפצל וננתן לך בין יומן 30 והן לא פצלן
אנחן ובנין ננתן לך בית לדמות ביתך ומשחתה בר מן [זכר ונקבה] בר זי אפולי

1. On the 7th of Elul, that is the 9th day of the month of Paoni, the 28th year of Artaxerxes the king, said
2. Bagazušt son of *Bzw*, "silverman" of the *degel* of *Nmsw*, and the woman Ūbīl daughter of Satibar, "silverwoman" of Syene of the *degel* of *Nmsw*,
3. together 1 man, 1 woman, to Ananiah son of Azariah, *lḥn* of Yahu the god, saying: We have sold and given (over)
4. to thee the house of *'pwly* son of Misdai which is in Yeb the fortress (and) the walls of which are standing (?) and a court
5. is below, and it is not built (upon), and windows are in it, and beams it does not have. We have sold it to thee and thou didst give
6. to us its value in money, 1 karsh, 4 shekels, in royal weight, silver 2 *R.* to the karsh, and our heart is satisfied
7. at the price which thou didst give to us. And behold, these are the boundaries of that house which we sold to thee: Above it
8. is the house of Satibar; below it is the *tmy* of Khnum the god, and the street of the king is between them;
9. east of it the treasury of the king adjoins it; on the west of it is the Temple
10. of Yahu the god, and the street of the king is between them. I, Bagazušt, and Ūbīl, both of us, we have sold and given (over)
11. to thee and have removed from it from this day unto forever. Thou Ananiah, son of Azariah, shalt have power over
12. that house and thy children after thee, and he to whom thou pleasest to give it. We shall not be able to start against thee suit
13. or process with mention of this house which we sold and gave (over) to thee, and from which we removed. We shall not be able
14. to sue son of thine or daughter, or whomever thou pleasest to give it to. If we start against thee suit or process or sue
15. son or daughter of thine, or whomever thou pleasest to give it to, we shall give thee in money 20 karsh silver, 2 *R.*
16. to the 10, and the house is thine in addition, and thy children's after thee, or his to whom thou pleasest to give it. Nor
17. shall son or daughter of ours be able to start against thee suit or process with mention of this house, the boundaries of which are recorded
18. above. If they start action against thee or bring action against son or daughter of thine, they shall give thee in money 20 karsh silver, 2 *R.* to the 10,
19. and the house is thine in addition, and thy children's after thee. And if another man sue thee or sue
20. son or daughter of thine, we will rise up and will recover(?) and will give (it) to thee within 30 days, and if we do not recover(?),
21. we or our children will give to thee a house in the likeness of thy house and its measurements, except from a son of *'pwly* (above line: male or female)

22a או ברה ולא כהלן פצלן נ‍‍תן לך כספך כרש 1 שקלן 4 ובנינא זי תבנה בה (above the line: לה יתה)

22b כתב חגי בר שמעיה כפם בגזשת ואבל ושהדי בגו

23a וכל אשרן זי יהכן על ביתא זך

23b מתרדת בר מתריזן שהד חיח בר אתרלי כספי

24 בית אׄובל כספי שהד איסך בר זמסף

25 ספר זי זבן בגׄושת ויׄבל לעניהׄ לחן ליׄה ביב (Plate XIX, 2)

22a. or daughter; and (above line: him, her) (if) we are not able to recover (?), we will give to thee thy money, 1 karsh, 4 shekels, and the (value of the) building (improvements) which thou didst build in it,
23a. and all the lumber (?) which may go upon that house.
22b. There wrote (this) Haggai, son of Shema'iah, at the dictation of Bagazušt and Ūbīl. And the witnesses thereto (were)
23b. Mithradata b. Mithrayazna; witness: *Ḥyḥ* b. Atarili, "silverman";
24. Beth Ūbīl, "silverman"; witness: *'ysk* b. *Zmsp*.
25. (Endorsement:) Document (concerning that) which Bagazušt and Ybl sold to Ananiah, *lḥn* of Yah in Yeb.

1. The name of the Egyptian month Paoni is here written out. In *A.P.* 20:1 and 76:3 letters are missing, though in the former instance a waw is visible that Cowley did not copy (see Lidzbarski, *Ephemeris*, *3*, 131), while in the latter instance he tacitly accepts Lidzbarski's reading in place of *CIS*, *2*, 151 [פאפי], but comments that the name does not occur for certain elsewhere in Semitic writing. Our papyrus settles the matter. In Babylonia the 7th of Elul in the 28th year of Artaxerxes was September 15; in Egypt the 9th of Paoni was September 14.

2. The name of the individual making out the deed is Persian (or rather Median), Bagazušt b. *Bzw*. The former name is spelled בגזושת in No. 4:3. It is Median and means "liked by the gods"; it appeared in Hilprecht and Clay, BEUP, *9*, 51, and in Clay BEUP, *10*, 41, *Ba-ga-zu-uš-tum*, *Ba-ga-ʾ-zu-uš-tum*. Geiger does not believe that *Bzw* is Iranian. The Median tribe, Bousoi, mentioned in Herodotus I, 101, invites comparison, but the Greek transcription permits no certainty as to the sibilant. Babylonian *bazū* does not seem a likely name for a man, though the fem. *Bazitu* occurs; see Ungnad's *Glossar*, *Beiheft zu* Mariano San Nicolò and Arthur Ungnad, *Neubabylonische Rechts und Verwaltungsurkunden*, Bd. I (Leipzig, 1937), s. v.

כספי, which occurred in *A.P.* 13:18, 19, was rendered "silversmith" by Cowley (cf. also L § 43q[4]). He rejects Lagrange's rendering "Caspian" (*A.P.* 41), but G. R. Driver, JRAS, 1932, 77, prefers it and thinks that "silversmith," though possible, would be *kassāp*. But "Caspian," though used by Herodotus VII, 67, is not a familiar geographical concept of the Old Persian inscriptions, and it is questionable whether it would not have been spelled differently in Aramaic (קצפי? Cf. Gustav Dalman, *Aramäisch-Neuhebräisches Handwörterbuch*, [2d ed. Frankfurt, 1922], s. v. קציא). The fem. form used here certainly supports the idea of a title. It seems possible that a כספי was one who had something to do with the control of money. At a frontier place like Elephantine duties and imposts were levied, and that would require a staff of officials with that concern. In the demotic text from Elephantine published by Spiegelberg, *SPAW*, *64*, 1928 (cf. Chapter 5, n. 9), 610, a certain *ʾIebr* is called *pꜣ rḫ ḥd* which Spiegelberg translates "Silberkenner (=Kontrolleur?)." He seems to be in the service of the goddess Neith, and this recalls to Spiegelberg the recorder of the moneys of "Athena" at Saïs mentioned in Herodotus II, 28, from whom Herodotus heard about the sources of the Nile. כספי may mean the same official. In our translation we have used "silverman," which leaves open just what function is meant. כספי זי אתרא in *A.P.* 13:19 is doubtlessly "local silverman." On נשן, "woman," see below on 12:1, where the plene writing appears.

אבל's name was first miswritten as ובל and then an א was written in above the line. It appears in l. 10 as אובל and as יבל on the outside of the roll. In 4:3 it is אוביל. It can therefore hardly be a hypocoristic ending with the god Bel, for that name is regularly written בל. Perhaps one should vocalize Ūbīl and compare the name *Ubil-Ištar*, J. J. Stamm, "Die Akkadische Namengebung," *MVAÄG*, *44*, 1939, 106 (vowel lengthening would naturally take place in the shortened form). Ūbīl is the

daughter of Satibar, whose house was next door (l. 8). This latter name is shortened from שתברזן, *A.P.* 5:16; 13:18; cf. also the *Šatabarzanu* in Clay, *Business Documents of Murashū Sons Dated in the Reign of Darius II*, UMBS, *2*, No. 1 (Philadelphia, 1912), 37. Greek sources transcribe it as Satibarzanes; according to Justi, *IN*, 291 the name means "happiness bringing."

The woman Ūbīl gets the husband's title in the fem.; he is a כספי and she is a כספיה (cf. on 12:2). It is odd that the woman too is assigned to a *degel*. While the man is of the *degel* of נמסו, he is not said to be of Syene, but the woman is so localized. I can shed no light on נמסו. For the ending cf. בזו 3:2, ארפחו 5:2.

3. כל is used adverbially. "Altogether 1 man, 1 woman," the "1 man" being written above the "1 woman." Ananiah's full name is used here, and he is "לחן to (=of) Yahu the god." See on 1:2.

זבן "to buy" means "to sell" in the pael. The latter meaning is the one required here. The form must be a 1st pers. pl. perf. like the peal form יהבן that follows, but with an assimilated nun, suggesting that there was a vowel after the suffixed nun: *Zabbénna*? see L § 28b. יהב means "to give," but the text as a whole shows that no gift was involved, so here it must mean "to transfer, give possession."

4. ביתה, status emphaticus, as often in B.A., with ה rather than א or the noun with anticipating suff. 3d pers. sing. masc.? That the former is possible is shown by 12:9. The name of the original owner of the house is given: אפולי בר מסדי. The same individual is called ינבולי בר מסדי in 12:4. This is suprisingly different. For מסדי Geiger rejects connection with Mazda (cf. מזדיזן *A.P.* 37:6). The name *Mi-is-da-bi-gi-in*, Clay BEUP, *10*, 55 is comparable here, however, for the first element, as the second is for the name בגין in 1:13. See on it Eilers, "Iranische Beamtennamen," *Abhandlungen für die Kunde des Morgenlandes*, *25*, No. 5, 1940, 122. But cf. also Elamitic *Mi-iš-da-aš-ba* (Vištašpa) cited *ibid.*, 34. Another *Mi-is-da* name in Hilprecht and Clay, BEUP, *9*, 63.

אגרוה. A verb seems unlikely here, especially since the word אגר appears to be a loan word. It is accordingly advisable to read אגרוהי[י] (Rosenthal, Albright).

The question is whether אגר is J.A. איגרא, "roof," or rather means "wall," like Akkadian *igaru*. For the former interpretation one might adduce the fact that the roof receives explicit mention in demotic conveyances of houses. Thus in S. R. K. Glanville, *Catalogue of the Demotic Papyri in the British Museum*, *1*, 4 f., we read, "I have ceded to thee the (documentary) claim to my house, which has been built and is (still) roofed," and a few lines further, "The boundaries of this house which has been built and is roofed, are." Over against Cowley's reading אגד (rendered "portico") in *A.P.* 5:4 f. G. R. Driver, *JRAS*, 1932, 77, urged אגר and the meaning "wall." This was supported by the occurrence of the word in that sense in the Aramaic cuneiform text from Warka, as noted by B. Landsberger, *AfO*, *12*, 1938, 251. The meaning "wall" seems to suit the following word better and is recommended by No. 9:8 and by *A.P.* 5.

קימן then is act. part. pl. and means "standing," i. e., strong, in good condition. The form appears as קמן in Beh. 59. The same word is also to be read in *A.P.* 30:10, where Cowley reads קימו. In our present connection one might take קימן as pael perf. 1st pers. pl. and render, "whose walls we raised up."

תרבצה is well known from J.A. and is ultimately derived from Assyrian *tarbaṣu*; it appears also in the Borchardt leather documents and in the Sardis inscription.

5. ארע הי: ארע is a substantive in the adverbial accusative. This should be added to L § 61i. Hitherto it was known only in combination with the preposition מן; cf. *A.P.* 5:5.

בניה is the fem. part. pass. (here modifying תרבצה), postulated by Cowley in his comment on *A.P.* 27:6, where the masc. בנה occurs.

כוין, "windows," as in *A.P.* 25:6, where the adjective "open" modifies the word. בה, sc. "the house."

וגשרן. It seems impossible to dissociate this word, which occurs also in the Hermopolis letters, from the J.A. גשורא<Akkadian *gušūru*, "beam." It is a plural as the writing גשורן in 4:8 shows. It probably precedes לא אחד for emphasis here, for it follows that word in the other passages.

לא אחד (see 4:8 f.; 9:12 f.; 10:2 f.); a reading אחר seems less likely. The form is most naturally taken as a verb, either 3d pers. sing. masc. perf. (unlikely here) or else a participle. But the subject cannot be גשרן, which is plural, but would have to be "house": "beams it does not hold (i. e., have)." לא אחד could, perhaps, be לא אחיד "with beams it is not held," i. e., "reenforced" (cf. Ch. 6) but in 4:8, 10:2 this does not fit so well. Furthermore, one would like to see a preposition used before גשרן. The use of אחז in I Kings 6:6, 10, Ezek. 41:6 needs renewed examination in the light of cognate אחד in these papyri. Demotic papyri speak of houses being "filled (*mḥ.*) with beams"; see Spiegelberg, *Die demotischen Papyri der Strassburger Bibliothek*, 19, 20, 25, 33. But *mḥ* also means "take, seize" (Erman-Grapow, *Wörterbuch der ägyptischen Sprache*, 2, 119) and so could be synonymous with אחד.

7. דמיא. This is the first occurrence of this word in the st. emph. in Elephantine texts.

The adjoining properties are now listed. תחמי is written תחומי in *A.P.* 6:7; 13:13. The word is a loan from Assyrian *taḫūmu*, "boundary."

לעליה לה, literally, at the upper side of it, above. Cf. *A.P.* 6:11; L § 62e[1]. On "above" and "below" see Chapter 7.

8. שתבר. The wife's father of l. 2 had the house "above."

לתחתיה לה, "at the lower side of it, below." Cf. *A.P.* 6:10 and L § 62f[1].

תמי. In 4:10 תמא. Erichsen would connect it with demotic *ṭme*, *ṭmy*, "town" (a possibility also mentioned by Albright), and H. J. Polotsky cites F. L. Griffith, *Catalogue of the Demotic Papyri in the John Rylands Library* (Manchester, 1909), *3*, 404, where a similar phrase, *ṭmy n Sbk* or *ṭme Sbk*, "town of the god Sobk," on "the Island of Sobk" is cited. Albright's alternative explanation *tꜣ-'m-yt*, "that which

belongs (to Khnum)," is thus unnecessary. See further the discussion above in Chapter 7.

On the god חנום, Khnum, see A. M. Badawi, *Der Gott Chnum* (Glückstadt, 1937), 22 f. In the previously known papyri the name is written חנוב except in proper names. The statement of Meyer that חנום is restricted to names, *Papyrusfund*, 8, thus needs to be modified.

The precincts were on the other side of the "street (שוק) of the king." Cf. 4:10; 6:6; 10:4, 5. In *A.P.* 25:6 we hear of the ארח מלכא. See above, chapter 7.

9. "East of it"; *A.P.* 6:8. See L § 62h[1]. אוצר: "treasury" or "storehouse" of the king. Cf. *A.P.* 2:12 where the "treasury" is linked with the "house of the king," i. e., government house (see Cowley on *A.P.* 2:12), and *A.P.* 11:6, where salary payments come from it. West (the "of it" was written above the line) is the Temple of Yahu.

אגור in the construct here — more commonly emph. plus זי. On this word see above, Chapter 9.

10. After Yahu, "the god" was omitted and then was written above the line.

Bagazušt und Ūbīl repeat part of their statement of l. 2 and declare:

11. "We have removed from it." רחק is an Aramaic reproduction of an Egyptian legal expression. Spiegelberg, *Die demotischen Papyri der Strassburger Bibliothek*, 7, points out that two kinds of documents were made out with respect to sales or gifts: 1) a receipt of sale in which receipt of money is acknowledged and the buyer gives assurance of possession and 2) a formal conveyance in which the previous owner relinquishes and hands over the property. The latter is called *sh3 n wi'*, "document of being far away." On some of the memoranda ("endorsements") on the exterior of sealed papyri we have ספר מרחק, which renders that term exactly (*A.P.* 6:22; 14:14; 25:20; cf. also *A.P.* 8:23, 25). The verb רחק here hints at the same thought. The Egyptian pattern, we may add, persists into the Greek papyri, where the second variety is called *apostasiou* (sc. *syngraphē*); see Ludwig M. Mitteis and Ulrich W. Wilcken, *Grundzüge und Chrestomathie der Papyruskunde* (Leipzig, 1912), *2*, 167. On the rabbinic equivalent שטר סלוק see L. Blau, "Zur demotischen und griechischen Papyruskunde," *Judaica, Festschrift zu H. Cohens 70. Geburtstag* (Berlin, 1912), 215. (שטר for ספר, exactly as in the Aramaic endorsements of BEUP, *9* and *10*.)

12. צבית: the 2d pers. in a sense similar to that of *A.P.* 28:7, 12.

לא נכל as in *A.P.* 1:4 from יכל; L § 38e. The verb כהל has the same meaning and is used frequently (so in the very next line), but the two are to be kept distinct (against Cowley *ad A.P.* 1:4).

נגרנך √גרה. The "energicus" almost always appears before the suffixes (an exception with the same verb in *A.P.* 1:4, נגרכי). See L § 31c, 40 f.

דין ודבב. See on 1:5.

13. בשם. See on 1:5.

15. בברה is a scribal error for וברה.

ננתן. The nun is not assimilated in the papyri, except in *A.P.* 81:24, 64, a text written a century or more later.

16. לעשרתא, "to the 10(-shekel-piece)," i.e., the karsh of l. 6.

אם as below in l. 19 and in *A.P.* 13:11; 34:6. It is thus a distinct particle and the theory that it is a mistake for אפם (Cowley ad *A.P.* 13:11) must be abandoned, as Cowley himself felt when he wrote his comment ad *A.P.* 34:6. L § 61q stresses the obscurity of the origin of this adverb, which he renders "certainly." Jacob Rabinowitz thinks אם and אפם mean "in addition, moreover," and that seems to fit.

17. The writing זין וזבב for דין ודבב (so above in ll. 12–13) is anomalous. It should be added to L § 2 f.

זי תחמוהי. See BL § 108c.

כתבן, written defectively here; כתיבן in *A.P.* 2:11, 13; 18:2; 25:8.

18. גרוך, a form not previously found: 3d pers. pl. perf. with the 2d masc. sing. suff. The numeral 10 is used at the end of the line instead of עשרתא or 1 karsh.

19. אם again, as in l. 16.

It is not enough to be protected against relatives of the seller! The possibility is entertained that "another man" might sue the buyer's son or daughter. The sellers pledge themselves to defend the case.

20. נקום is a newly attested form for the papyri. This is legal phraseology; קום in effect means to take legal action; cf. Bauer-Meissner, 415, l. 10: אקם ואקנה ואנתן.

נפצל. I first read ננצל, but נפצל is inescapable. Perhaps the verb is found also in *A.P.* 9:5 in the haphel 3d sing. impf. "if he separates from thee" (Cowley: נצל, 2d sing.!). Furthermore נצל means "take away"; cf. 2:13; 4:20; 6:15; 10:10. But "split" or "divide (costs?)" will hardly do for the peal form (especially in l. 22a). The required meaning there seems to be "recover something taken away." The same verb must be supplied in 1:9. Perhaps פצל means "to remove an adverse claim" in connection with the seller's duty to remove such claims from the property sold. Jacob Rabinowitz (who attributed that meaning to the supposed נצל in 1:9) noted that the same thing occurs in the Talmud, where פצי pael of פצא, "to deliver," is used. Cf. the example in Levy, s. v. Did פצא replace the verb פצל in this meaning?

וננתן has here the sense of restoring the impounded property to Anani.

בין יומן, a new idiom. "Between" applies because the thought is "between day 1 and 30." Solar rather than lunar reckoning!

הן לא פצלן: the perfect in the sense of a future. The only B.A. example is Dan. 6:6. See BL § 79n.

21. They give a pledge, binding on their children, in the event of not recovering the property within that time.

לדמות ביתך. The word דמות is new for the papyri; on the formation see BL § 51g.[4] This is construct; the absolute form should be *דמו. Hebrew דמות may represent Aramaic influence; cf. Julius Wellhausen, *Prolegomena zur Geschichte Israels* (2d ed.,

1883), 396. Syriac also has this word. The preposition ל is used in the sense of "according to," as in Hebrew למספר, Deut. 32:8.

משחתה. The size of the property has to be equivalent. The word appeared in *A.P.* 8:4; 9:4; cf. J.A. משחא. In the light of No. 4:12 it may be translated as plural here, but cf. No. 9:5. Since משחא is masc. this must be a fem. type pl. Cf. רבתא, No. 4:3. Or is it borrowed from Babylonian *mešiḫtu*? An exception, however, is added, "Except from a son of *'pwly*." בר מן, "except," is new in these papyri. Above the line is put "male or female," the former word written זכר instead of דכר. In *A.P.* 15:17 we already have בר דכר ונקבה showing that בר was often understood colorlessly as "child"; when the scribe put "male or female" above the line, he was thinking of the word in that sense and did not intend to continue, as he does in the next line, with "daughter" (whereby the preceding בר gets its stricter meaning "son" back again). In the distraction of the situation he evidently changed his line of thought and forgot to erase "male or female."

22a. The superimposed לה יתה is puzzling. לה could be inserted after ברה but יתה apparently is the sign of the accusative (found in Dan. 3:12) with the 3d pers. fem. sing. suff. (as Deut. 18:18 in the Targum) and thus means "her."

Hence לה is also an object: "him-her." It seems unlikely that יתה could be "it" (object of פצלן), for then it would have been written above that word. One should note that this is the earliest occurrence of ית in an Aramaic text. The condition is introduced here by waw and perfects, "If we cannot deliver, we will give," i. e., if a son or daughter of *'pwly* puts in a claim.

כספך, "thy money," the original payment.

בניגא, a new word in these papyri, though in *A.P.* 9:12 there is a בנויא, "the improvements which thou hast made (בנית) on this house." The sense is doubtlessly similar here, as the בה shows, for that precludes another independent structure. The word is already in Ezra 5:4.

23a. אשרן is a plural as the verb יהכן, of which it is the subject, shows. Its singular, then, is אשר. It can hardly be the אשר of old Aramaic inscriptions <Akkadian *ašru*, "place," but must have another meaning. Jacob Rabinowitz suggests "improvements" and reminds me of שבחיהון in the portion of a warranty clause quoted in *Bab. Mez.* 15a. I look for a more concrete meaning such as "post, board, lumber," or the like, for it evidently was attached to the top or to the outer surface of the walls of the house to warrant an על. Perhaps O.T. אשרה, "post (Deut. 16:21)" is the same word in the feminine. On the use of logs to reenforce walls of houses cf. Honroth and others, "Ausgrabungen," 19. Another related word may be אשרנא of Ezra 5:3, 9; *A.P.* 26:5, 9, 21; 27:18; 30:11, if that be Semitic; it could then mean "lumber" or the like. See chapter 9, n. 7.

יהכן is impf. of הלך in the masc. pl.: "All the אשרן which may go upon this house." In Hebrew הלך, when used of inanimate things, means "extend," "spread"; cf. Jer. 12:2; Hos. 14:3.

22b. The concluding remark is written between the lines, Apparently it had been forgotten in the haste of letting the witnesses sign. In the word "witnesses" the final aleph was omitted. Haggai b. Shema'iah was the scribe of this papyrus as of Nos. 9, 10, 12. He was a witness in 7:43. A ration of barley for him was listed in *A.P.* 24:3.

23b. מתרדת, the name Mithridates, borne by so many kings of Persian descent in Asia Minor in Hellenistic Roman times. Cf. *A.P.* 26:2, 7; 80:7.

חיח בר אתרלי. The first name is found in Tallqvist, *APN*, 88, as *Ḫi-ḫi-e*. Albright suggests that it is Egyptian, perhaps short for *ḥ3y-ḥr* (Ranke, ÄP, 262:8), and may have been pronounced **Ḥayḥe*. אתרלי was already known from *A.P.* 5:16; 13:18; cf. Tallqvist, *APN*, 47, *Atar-ili*, or was the name **Atar-lī*'? Cf. *Mannu-ki-Ištar-lī*', *ibid.*, 126, or *Nabū-lī*', *ibid.*, 153, and the like.

24. The בית at the beginning of the line is puzzling. The next word, אובל, identical with the name in l. 2, is an autograph of an individual, while בית was written by the scribe. Are the two to be joined, perhaps as בית אובל? The form אובל hardly recommends that; cf. names like *Bitum-šemi*, *Bitum-magir* in Stamm, *Akkadische Namengebung*, 91. In אובל we have an archaic aleph, somewhat like that in the Bauer-Meissner text. This man, too, is a כספי. For another name borne by either sex cf. הצול in *A.P.* 22:26, etc., with *A.P.* 22:112. See also the remarks on 10:19.

איסך בר זמסף, a most unusual name. איסך occurred in *A.P.* 51:8 and was taken as Iranian by Scheftelowitz, but Schaeder, *Beiträge*, 263, n., rejects his explanation. Cowley compared the names אסכישו (*A.P.* 2:19), אסכשית (*A.P.* 53:7). Albright and Geiger link זמסף with Iranian Jāmāspa, Zamasphes; see Justi, *IN*, 109.

25. The endorsement. The mark before זי is not a letter but a dark spot in the papyrus. ספר זי is "document (concerning that) which." Cf. the endorsement on the cuneiform tablet in Clay, BEUP, *10*, 26, No. 106, שטר זבדננא די קנא, "the document of Zabid-Nana concerning that which he acquired."

זבן, "sell," in pael.

ויבל. The waw is only partly preserved. Is Yod a scribal error for Aleph?

לחן ליה, with prep. as in No. 1:2, but with waw in the name of the deity omitted. G. R. Driver, "The Original Form of the Name Yahweh," *ZAW*, *46*, 1928, 21 ff., held that Yah is the original name.

PAPYRUS 4

PAPYRUS 4

(*Brooklyn* 47.218.91) 57.1 *cm.* x 28.4 *cm.*

THIS document was written on October 30, 434 B.C., fifteen years after the marriage of Tamut to Ananiah, the *lḥn* of the god Yahu of Elephantine, and three years after the purchase by him of the house owned by Bagazušt and Ūbīl. Here Ananiah gives his wife half of the house (apparently keeping in his own name the adjacent half) but with certain strings attached. Sales or gifts of parts of a house were not unusual in antiquity — strange as such a thing may seem to us today.

The property is described as "half of the two *rbt'* and the chamber." The length by width is given here as 11 cubits by 7 cubits *k* 1. In the description of the property the boundaries are given in terms of the adjoining properties. A comparison with the previous texts dealing with this house reveals some peculiar discrepancies. It is said here to be bounded "above" by the portion of Ananiah, "below" by the street and the Yahu Temple across the way, west by the house of Satibar, and east by the town of Khnum. In No. 3 the house of Satibar was "above" and the town of Khnum "below," the treasury of the king east, and the Yahu Temple west. Presumably, the portion of Ananiah lay between the part of the property here specified and the treasury of the king, which in No. 3 was on the east.

Ananiah pledges that no son or daughter, brother or sister can recapture this portion and guarantees it with 5 karsh against any attempt; an outsider, "another man," would have to pay 20 karsh as a penalty. After her death, the children Tamut bore him are to have power over it, and after his own death they are to have power over his portion too, so that nobody else, not even his mother or father, brother or sister, or anybody, will have power over any part of the house except the two children of Tamut. The man who attempts to take it from them will have to pay 10 karsh, which, since it is twice the 5 karsh specified for an attempt on her half ownership in l. 15, shows that the whole house will then be at stake.

On the scribe and witnesses see the notes. The last is clearly a man of Iranian stock.

ב 25 לתשרי הו יום 25 לירח אפף שנת 31 ארתחשסש מלכא אמר ענניה בר עזריה לחן זי יהו אלהא ביב בירתא לנשן תמת אנתתה לאמר אנה יהבת לכי פלג תרי רבתא ותונה זי ביתא זי זבנת מן אוביל ברת שתיבר ומן בגזושת כספין זי יב בירתא אנה ענניה יהבתה לכי ברחמן זילכי הו מן יומא זנה עד עלם וזי בניכי זי ילדתי לי מן אחריכי והא משחת ביתא זך זי אנה ענניה יהבת לכי תמת מן פלג תרי רבתא ותונה הוה מן עליה עד תחתיה אמן בעשתא 11 בפתי אמן מן מועה עד מערב אמן בעשתא 7 כ 1 לאברת אמן 81 בנה בי תחתי חדת אחד גשורן וכון והא זנה תחומי ביתא זך זי אנה יהבת לכי עליה לה חלקא זי לי אנה ענניה דבק לה תחתיה לה אגורא זי יהו אלהא ושוק מלכא בניהם מועה שמש לה תמא זי חנום אלהא ושוק מלכא בניהם מערב שמש לה ביתה זי שתיבר כספי דבק לה זנה חלק ביתא זי משחת כתיבן ותחומוהי אנה ענניה יהבתה לכי ברחמן לא אכהל אנה ענניה ארשנכי עלדברה דין אף לא יכהל בר לי וברה אח ואחה יגרנכי בשם ביתא זך והן אנה גריתכי דין בשם ביתא זך אנה אחוב ואנתן לכי כסף כרשן 5 הו חמשה באבני מלכא כסף ר 2 לכרש 1 ולא דין והן גבר אחרן יגרנך דין ינתן לכי כסף כרשן 20 וביתא אפם זילכי להן הן מיתתי ברת שנן 100 בני זי ילדתי לי המו שליטן בה אחר מותכי ואף הן אנה ענני אמות בר שנן 100 פלטי ויהוישמע כל 2 בני המו שליטן בחלקי אחרנא אנה ענני גבר אחרן אמי ואבי אח ואחה ואיש אחרן לא ישלט בביתה כלה להן בני זי ילדתי לי וגברא זי יהנצל

1. On the 25th of Tishri, that is the 25th of the month of Epiphi, of the 31st year of Artaxerxes the king, said Ananiah,
2. son of Azariah, *lḥn* of the god Yahu in Yeb the fortress, to the woman Tamut, his wife, saying: I give
3. to thee half of the two compartments (?) and the chamber of the house which I bought from Ūbīl the daughter of Satibar and from Bagazušt,
4. "silvermen" of Yeb the fortress. I, Ananiah, have given it to thee in affection. Thine it is from this day
5. unto forever and thy children's whom thou didst bear me after thee. And these are the measurements of that house which I,
6. Ananiah, have given to thee, Tamut. From half of the two compartments (?) and the chamber it is, from above to below, cubits
7. by the one(-cubit-measure) 11. In the width of cubits from east to west it is cubits by the one(-cubit-measure) 7 *k* 1; to the outside (?)
8. cubits 81. Built is the lower (part of the?) house, new, having (?) beams and windows. And lo, these are the boundaries of that house
9. which I have given to thee. Above it the portion which belongs to me — myself, Ananiah — adjoins it. Below it
10. is the Temple of Yahu the god, and the street of the king is between them. East of it is the *tm'* of Khnum the god,
11. and the street of the king is between them. On the west of it the house of Satibar, the "silverman," adjoins it. This is the portion of
12. the house, the measurements and boundaries of which are recorded (above). I, Ananiah, have given it to thee in affection. Not am I,
13. Ananiah, able to start a suit against thee on account of it. Nor shall a son of mine or daughter, or brother or sister, be able
14. to start a suit against thee with mention of that house. And if I start a suit against thee with mention of that house, I myself shall be liable
15. and shall (have to) give thee silver, 5 karsh — that is five — by royal weight, silver 2 *R.* to 1 karsh, and there shall be no suit.
16. And if another man stirs up proceedings against thee, he shall give to thee silver, 20 karsh, and the house in addition is thine. But
17. if thou shalt die at the age of 100 (?) years, my children whom thou didst bear me, shall have power over it after
18. thy death. And moreover, if I, Anani, shall die at the age of 100 (?) years, Palṭi and Yehoyishma, both of them, my children,
19. shall have power over my portion afterwards. I, Anani, or another man, my mother or my father, my brother or sister, or another
20. person shall not have power over this house — any (part) of it — but my children which thou didst bear me. And a man who would snatch away

21 ביתי אחרי מותי מן פלטי ויהוישמע ינתן להם כסף כרשן 10 באבני

22 מלכא ר 2 לכרש 1 וביתי זילהם אפם ולא דין כתב מעוזיה בר נתן כפם

23 ענניה בר עזריה לחנא ושהדיא בגו גמריה בר מחסיה

24 הושעיה בר יתום מתרסרה מגשיא תת מגשיא

25 ספר בי זי כתב ענניה לתות אנתתה (Plate XIX, 3)

21. my house after my death from Palṭi and Yehoyishma shall (have to) give them silver, 10 karsh, by royal weight,
22. 2 *R.* to 1 karsh, and my house is theirs in addition, and there shall be no suit. There wrote (this) Ma'uziyah b. Nathan at the dictation
23. of Ananiah b. Azariah, the *lḥn.* And the witnesses thereto (are) Gemariah b. Maḥseiah,
24. Hosha'yah b. Yathom, Mithrasarah the Magian, Tatt the Magian.
25. (Endorsement:) "Document of a house" which Ananiah wrote for Tamut, his wife.

1. The days of Tishri in the Babylonian calendar coincided exactly with those of the Egyptian month of Epiphi in this 31st year of Artaxerxes I or 434 B.C. The date is October 30.

2. The phrase "in Yeb the fortress" localizes Yahu the god. Cf. below on 12:2.

נשן. See below on 12:1.

תמת. On the name see above 2:3.

אנה. To avoid ambiguity the pronoun is used before the verb. יהבת evidently means "giving possession" in a legal sense, for while in this case a gift is involved, this is not so in 12:3 where the same verb is used in connection with a sale.

3. פלג means "half" in its occurrences with weights and measures, and this is presumably its meaning here.

תרי רבתא ותונה: תונה already in *A.P.* 21:9, תוניכם; here a st. emph. in ה. Cf. the word found in the Targum, Deut. 32:25, תוונא, *tawwānā*, "chamber, room"; cf. L § 43n.[4] Ananiah thus gives Tamut "half of the תרי רבתא and the chamber." The meaning of רבתא (or דבתא?), cf. l. 6 and 9:4, 11; 10:6; 12:13, 21, is obscure. If רבתא were feminine תרתי would be the required form. It must thus be a masculine but with a feminine ending in the plural. Of such nouns there are quite a number in B.A. I connect רבתא with J.A. ארבא, "row," "stratum," which is a masculine word, while ארובא, "lattice," "opening," is feminine. The demotic sale of a house from Roman times cited in F. L. Griffith, *Catalogue of the Demotic Papyri in the John Rylands Library, 3,* 169 f. (No. 44) speaks of a house "which is built furnished with beams and doors and repeated *in two stages,* with its courtyard making its eastern side, having a chamber built in it," and a similar reference to two "two stages" is also found in No. 45. Perhaps רבתא, "rows," means "stages" (if that meaning can itself be regarded as assured for the word *ẖ.t*). Provisionally I am rendering רבתא, "compartments" (?), since the word evidently applies to a part of the house here, and in 9:4, 10:5 that is further confirmed. For the loss of the initial aleph the close fusion with the numeral תרי may be responsible, as in לף for אלף after numerals, *A.P.* 30:28, etc., L § 60r.

זבנת, here in the sense of "buying" rather than "selling," and hence peal.

The names אוביל, שתיבר, and בגזושת are written out more fully than in No. 2. The woman's name here precedes that of the husband; contrast 2:2.

4. כספין. The two are "silvermen." See above 3:2. כספין זי instead of the expected כספיא זי; cf. Dan. 7:9 שבבין, 5:5 אצבען. BL § 90c explain this as due to the fading of the original demonstrative meaning of זי.

ברחמן, literally, "in affection," but in this connection it merely means that this was a case of a gift with no recompense. The word appeared in *A.P.* 18:2 and 25:11, 14. It is plural; cf. Hebrew in I Kings 3:26, where it also means "affection" rather than "mercy."

בניכי, "thy children." She has a son and a daughter. Cf. 9:19 f.; 10:9 f., below and *A.P.* 15:20.

5. והא begins a new sentence with a description of the location. משחת, pl.; see on l. 12 and 3:21.

6. A fresh statement seems to begin with מן. One may imagine a colon preceding that word.

הוה is the active participle.

7. בעשתא. It is possible to connect עשתא with the Aramaic word for "lump" or else to make it a derivative of עשת, "to think" (especially in view of that verb's occurrence in 5:3) as "reckoning" (Nöldeke, *ZA*, *20*, 1907, 145). It seems more likely, however, that this is an Assyrianism, as first suggested by Peiser, *OLZ*, 1907, 625, and means "by the one(-cubit-measure)." For such abbreviated terminology cf. the use of "ten" (עשרתא) in the weights. In the Assyrian building inscriptions the phrase *ina ištēn ammati* (with *ištēn* given as the numeral 1) is frequently found and may be rendered "measured by a 1 cubit (rule)." Cf. Streck, *Assurbanipal*, Teil II, 295 n. Friedrich Delitzsch (*Assyrisches Handwörterbuch*, 85) compared the Hebrew idiom מאה באמה "100 by the cubit," i. e., 100 cubits. If this interpretation is correct for עשתא, we certainly have an Aramaic representative of the Semitic etymon already attested by Hebrew עשתי (in עשתי עשר) and Akkadian *ištēnu.*

בפתי אמן goes with the following; one must imagine a comma before it.

מועה. See L § 10c.

כ, followed by a numeral 1 is puzzling. See again in 12:7 f. It must be an abbreviation for a measure, *kaph,* "hand?" In other texts פשכן, "handbreadth," goes with אמה. Perhaps כ is stenographic for כף and that word used for a "span" (זרת in Hebrew). In hollow measures the כ is a "handful."

לאברת (or אבדת?). This word, which occurs again in 9:7; 12:16, is puzzling. I take it to mean "to an exterior (total) of", regarding it as equivalent to J.A. לבר. From בר words like אברי "outside," and אבריתא, "outer area," "village" are derived. We must here posit a noun אברה (fem.) with constr. pl. אברת. The prep. ל as in לבר in the local sense of "direction toward." The measurement presumably refers to the ground area on which the house stands. Note that in Babylonian texts of the sale of houses the area on which a house stands is specified rather than the size of the building. Cf. Schorr, *Urkunden*, 130 f. It would seem less likely that the measurement was to some outside point like a "square." ברא occurs in Brooklyn No. 6:5 and Aḥ. 109.

8. בנה is the pass. part., as in *A.P.* 27:6, 30:14, 25; 31:13; 32:4, and here starts a new sentence.

תחתי is an adj. (suffix āi, L § 43r[4]) modifying בי, while חדת is an adj. used adverbially. אחד would seem to be an act. part., "having beams." See on 3:5 where we had לא אחד, and below 9:12; 10:2, 12:13.

גשורן וכון. On these words, see above 3:4–5.

A new sentence starts with והא. The boundaries of this house (i. e., the adjoining properties) are now listed.

זנה in substantive use; see L § 14c. Singular and plural (אלה) are both used when the next noun is plural.

9. Literally: "the portion which is upon me, I, Ananiah," i.e., "my own portion." It is odd that the adjoining properties are differently described in both deeds, yet both pertain to the same house.

10.–11. בניהם for ביניהם twice, and hence not a scribal error but defective writing.

12. On the names and details see comments on No. 3.

משחת כתיבן. In view of this passage it seems desirable to take the word as plural in all cases (3:21; 4:5; 9:5). See on 3:21.

13. ארשנכי √רשה; the nun energic before the suffix, L § 31c. and BL § 38. Cf. this form in *A.P.* 8:20.

עלדברה, compound preposition with suffix. See L § 62x and *A.P.* 6:6 etc.

14. יגרנכי, with nun energic, √גרה. Farther along the same verb occurs in the 1st pers. sing. with the same suffix.

אחוב. This verb is already attested in *A.P.* 2:15; 18:3. Ungnad, p. 43, compares the piel (declarative), Dan. 1:10.

15. ולא דין. This phrase echoes Babylonian terminology. Cf. "he shall pay 10 mina silver without legal process (*ša lā dīnu inamdin*)." Clay, BEUP, *10*, 34, No. 94:12–13.

16. The גבר אחרן has to pay a fine of 20 karsh.

אפם. See above on 3:16.

17. מיתתי, the 2d pers. fem. sing. perf., not hitherto found. The first pers. sing. perf. in *A.P.* 10:14.

"Daughter of . . . years," "son of . . . years." On this phrase cf. Gen. 5:32, etc.

The numeral here is one that appears in the Papyrus Vaticanus, *CIS*, *2*, No. 147 A, l. 5, with the meaning 100 (cf. Lidzbarski, *Epigraphik*, Teil II, Tafel XLVI). Here it is without the extra stroke ordinarily found with the sign for 100 in other Egyptian Aramaic papyri. Cf. Sach. 198, Aimé-Giron, *Textes*, 81, who explains it as a stylized ק (100). The unusual form of Sach., Tafel 25:15 (*A.P.* 2) is closer to the form found in the Brooklyn text. Other unusual numeral forms in 10:7.

18. Was Palṭi begotten by him? Cf. W. Erichsen, *APAW*, 1939, 8, p. 6, n. 2, for a similar case.

19. He fixes it that the portion given to Tamut can be inherited only after her death by her two children and furthermore pledges that these two children are to inherit his portion too.

אחרנא, "afterwards." None of his relatives, parents, brother, or sister are to have it. אחרן followed by על in Aḥ. 53; 64.

גבר אחרן and איש אחרן, "another man" and "another person."

20. כלה, "all of it (i.e., any part of it)," not merely Tamut's portion. He thus establishes a right for her children over his own portion.

21. יהנצל, "who attempts to snatch it." This form not previously evidenced, but the verb is used (*A.P.* 8:18; 18:3; 9:10; Aḥ. 81).

22. The person has to pay a fine of 10 karsh and the suit will be dismissed. אפם. See on 3:16.

Ma'uziah b. Nathan is doubtlessly identical with Ma'uziah b. Nathan b. Ananiah in *A.P.* 18:3; 20:16; 25:17; the shortened form Ma'uzi b. Nathan in *A.P.* 33:2.

23. Gemariah b. Maḥseiah: *A.P.* 8:29; 9:18; 22:2.

24. Hosha'yah b. Yathom: in *A.P.* 33:4; 34:5, but shortened to Hosha'.

מתרסרה. The mark before the מ is perhaps only accidental. In S.-C. "E," written twelve years before the Brooklyn text, there is a Mithrasarah b. Mithrasarah (so Lidzbarski, *Ephemeris, 3,* 129, which Cowley adopted). The ס and ר are similarly run together in both cases. Allowing for the interval of time, ours could be the writing of the same man. Lidzbarski compared the name *Mitr-sari,* Justi, *IN,* 216b. In our present text a title is added instead of a paternal name. It would appear to be מגשיא. In the Behistun text (*A.P.*, p. 254, l. 60) we have מגוש as equivalent of a cuneiform *magušu,* "magian." A מגיש in a bilingual inscription from Asia Minor is a verb form, "he acted as Magian"; see Lidzbarski, *Ephemeris, 3,* 67. A plural form, however, seems impossible and so we must take this as a gentilic; cf. Syriac מגושיא, *magicus,* מגושא, *magus.* The magi were a Median priestly caste or tribe, but the word is also used for an oracle priest. Compare also the use of *kspy'* in No. 12:4 and 12.

תת מגשיא. Is this a separate signature or a continuation written by the same hand? At all events we have here another name and the same title. The various *Tat* or *Tattan* names are shortened forms of Babylonian names like *Bel-tat-tan-nu-bul-lit-su,* "Bel keep alive him whom thou gavest." See Eilers, "Iranische Beamtennamen," 35, 121, and previously Clay BEUP, *10,* 11. The word read מגשיא is poorly written. It seems likely that the last letter is an aleph (like that in the Bauer-Meissner Papyrus), with the preceding yodh closely joined.

25. The endorsement is somewhat faded. The document is earmarked ספר בי, "a document concerning a house," with names of grantor and grantee. The spelling of Tamut's name as תות provides an interesting example of the use of waw for mem. There are numerous cases of this in the endorsements on Babylonian tablets published by Clay. Thus the gods Shamash, Amurrū, Nimurta appear in proper names containing them as שוש, אור, אנושת (in the last of these with the further change of *r* to *š* as in Uštagu <Urtagu; cf. Eilers, *ZDMG, 94,* 1940, 205). The same writing of Shamash as שוש, I believe, underlies the name Sheshbazzar of Ezra 1:11; the name was ש(ו)ש(א)בצר, i. e., *Shamash-abu-uṣur.* Cf. בלאבצר for *Bel-abu-uṣur* in Clay, BEUP, *10,* 42. Dropping of the waw in שוש prevented the completely wrong vocalization *shush* or *shosh.* Shesh remained close to *Shemesh.*

PAPYRUS 5

PAPYRUS 5

(*Brooklyn* 47.218.90) 38.2 *cm.* x 30.7 *cm.*

THIS document of June 12, 427 B.C., is a deed of manumission made out directly to the female slave *Tpmt* and including with her her daughter Yehoyishma. The man drawing the deed is Meshullam b. Zakkur. *Tpmt* is identified by the legend tattooed on her hand (wrist): "(belonging) to Meshullam." In Nos. 2 and 4 her name was Tamut.

Meshullam gives this woman and her child their freedom, legally speaking, but at the same time binds them by agreement to service for his lifetime and that of his son Zakkur, the arrangement known as *paramone* in the Hellenistic world. They are to support him "as a son supports his father." They may not be marked again with a slave marking or sold for money by the heirs and assigns of Meshullam, and anyone who attempts it will have to pay the woman a fine of 50 karsh. But the eventuality that she or her daughter might some day refuse to do further service to Meshullam or his son Zakkur is also considered. They would then become liable for an amount of 50 karsh of refined silver and would, furthermore, be unable to carry on legal proceedings. Meshullam and his son Zakkur are thus well protected.

There are echoes of Babylonian legal language here to which attention will be given in the notes. They bear witness to the persistence of the Babylonian legal tradition. But the most interesting statements of this text are several in ll. 9–10, referring to a liberation to the sun-god. It is not clear, however, whether this is part of a regular ritual of liberation, or applies only after an action by others to invalidate this document.

The same Meshullam who executed this manumission had in No. 2 given his handmaiden Tamut to Ananiah b. Azariah, *lḥn* of Yahu the god, as a wife. In No. 3 of 437 B.C. Ananiah b. Azariah bought a house in Yeb which in No. 4 of 434 B.C. he gave to his wife, referring to "the children that thou didst bear me" and "Palṭi and Yehoyishma, who are both my children." If Meshullam b. Zakkur here speaks of *Tpmt's* having borne *him* Yehoyishma, that raises interesting questions. It may be, however, that he is thinking not in terms of paternity but of ownership; the child of the handmaiden is *his property* — not that of the freeborn actual father. But it is odd that in No. 7 Zakkur b. Meshullam is called Yehoyishma's *brother*.

The name Yehoyishma, meaning "Yahu hears," was evidently very suitable

for a girl of bound status. One is reminded of the fact that the son of the freeman Abram and of the slave woman Hagar bears the name "Ishmael." Yehoyishma is a Yahwistic form of the same name, with the theophorous element put first for emphasis. Such a name makes the child that bears it look forward to liberation with divine help. It is noteworthy that a number of Elephantine women bear the name Yehoshema ("Yahu has heard"). Five of them are mentioned in *A.P.* 22, among them a daughter of Meshullam. One wonders if, after their freedom became actual, women named Yehoyishma changed their names to Yehoshema. Whether this is the Yehoyishma to whom greetings were sent in *A.P.* 39:2, or the one that appears as the (unfree) mother of a Micaiah in *A.P.* 22:126, is uncertain. It is quite possible that the Yehoyishma of our text is identical with the Yehoshema in *A.P.* 22:87, for Zakkur is not mentioned in that late text and so may have been dead.

ב 20 סיון הו יום 7 לפמנחתף שנת 38 ארתחשסש מלכא אדן
אמר משלם בר זכור יהודי זי יב ברתא לדגל ארפחו לנשן תפמת שמה
אמתה זי שניתה על ידה בימן כדנה למשלם לאמר אנה עשתת לכי
בחיי אזת שבקתכי במותי ושבקת ליהישמע שמה ברתכי זי
ילתי לי בר לי \וברה/ ואח לי ואחה קריב ורחיק הנגית והנבג
לא שליט בכי וביהישמע ברתכי זי לידתי לי לא שליט בך
למשנתכי ולמזלכי מנדת כסף זי יקום עליכי ועל יהישמע ברתך
זי ילתי לי ינתן לך אבגדן כסף כרשן 50 באבני מלכא ואנתי
שביקה מן טלא לסמשא ויהישמע ברתכי וגבר אחרן לא שליט
עליכי ועל יהישמע ברתכי ואנתי שביקה לאלהא
ואמרת תפמת ויהישמע ברתה אנחן יפלחנך זי יסבל בר וברה לאבוהי
בחייך ועד מותך נסבל לזכור ברך כבר זי יסבל לאבוהי כזי הוין עבדן
לך בחייך (...) אנחן הן קמן לאמר לא נסבלנך כזי יסבל בר
לאבוהי ולזכור ברך אחרי מותך אנחן נחוב לך ולזכור ברך אבגדן
כסף כרשן 50 באבני מלכא כסף צריף ולא דין ולא דבב כתב חגי
ספרא זנה ביב כפם משלם בר זכור ושהדיא בגו אתרפרן בר ניסי
מדי שהד מיכיה בר אחיו שהד ברכיה בר מפטח דלה בר גדול
מרחק̇ זי כתב משלם בר זכור לתפמת ויהישמ[ע]

(Plate XIX, 4)

1. On the 20th of Siwan, that is the 7th day of Phamenoth, the 38th year of Artaxerxes the king, at that time
2. said Meshullam, son of Zakkur, the Jew of Yeb the fortress of the *degel* of *Arpaḥu* to the woman *Tpmt* by name,
3. his handmaiden, upon whose hand is a mark, on the right, thus: "(belonging) to Meshullam" saying: I have taken thought for thee
4. in my life. I have gone and released thee (effective) at my death, and I have released Yehoyishma by name, thy daughter, whom
5. thou didst bear to me. Son of mine or daughter, or brother of mine or sister, close or distant (kin), *hngyt* or *hnbg*,
6. shall not have power over thee and Yehoyishma, thy daughter, whom thou didst bear to me. (Such a one) shall not have power over thee
7. to mark thee and to sell thee for payment of silver. Whoever shall rise up against thee and against Yehoyishma, thy daughter,
8. whom thou didst bear to me, shall give to thee a fine of silver, 50 karsh by royal weight, and thou
9. art freed before (?) the Sun, as well as Yehoyishma, thy daughter, and another man shall not have power
10. over thee and over Yehoyishma, thy daughter, but thou art freed to the god.
11. *Tpmt* and Yehoyishma, her daughter, say: We will serve thee as a son or daughter provides for his (or her) father
12. in thy lifetime and unto thy death, (and after thy death) we will provide for Zakkur as the son provides for his father, just as we were serving
13. thee in thy life. We, if we rise up saying, "we will not provide for thee as a son provides
14. for his father, or for Zakkur, thy son, after thy death," we are liable to thee and to Zakkur, thy son, for a fine
15. of silver, 50 karsh by royal weight, refined silver, and no suit or process (shall obtain). There wrote Haggai
16. this document in Yeb at the dictation of Meshullam b. Zakkur, and the witnesses thereto (are) Atarparan b. Nīsai,
17. the Mede; witness, Micaiah b. Aḥio; witness, Berechiah b. Miptaḥ, Delah b. Gaddūl.
18. (Endorsement:) Removal (document) which Meshullam b. Zakkur wrote to *Tpmt* and Yehoyishm[a].

1. The name of the Egyptian month Phamenoth (Pamenḥotep) appears in *A.P.* 22:1; 22:121; 35:1; 50:3. The date according to both calendars is June 12. The 38th year of Artaxerxes (427 B.C) brings this document down rather near the end of his reign. Sachau published a letter to Aršam from the 37th year of Artaxerxes (*A.P.* 17). Our text, therefore, is the youngest known Aramaic text from this ruler's reign.

אדן, defective for the usual **אדין**.

2. Meshullam b. Zakkur (cf. above), here described as a Jew, as in *A.P.* 10:3, is called an Aramaean in *A.P.* 13:3, where his grandfather's name Ater (cf. Ezra 2:16, etc.) is added. Is the name of the *degel* to be read **ארפחו** or **ארוחו**? For the former cf. the name *Ar-rap-ḫa-ai-ú* in Clay, BEUP, *14*, 40, which, however, is a nisbeh.

נשן. See 12:1.

תפמת. The name of the woman in question here is written **תפמת**, as also in No. 12. That she is identical with the Tamut of Nos. 2 and 4 is already obvious from the fact that the house sold by Anani and **תפמת** in No. 12 is there referred to as the one purchased from Bagazušt (see No. 3 for this purchase) — rights for which were assigned to **תמת** in No. 4. Under the assumption of a plene writing, I at first favored reading *Twmt* in Nos. 5 and 12, but though this is perhaps possible here in 5:2, it is hardly possible in l. 11 or anywhere in No. 12. If the name were spelled *Twmt*, an etymology suggested for such a form by Ranke and Edel, namely *t3 wmt*, "the fat one" (though the name itself is not attested) would be tempting. This name, according to Albright, would have been pronounced approximately *Tĕwṓmtĕ*. But as he points out such an interpretation would make a spelling *Tmt* impossible, since the waw is consonantal and must always be represented (cf. *Pwnš*, *A.P.* 71:11, 12, i. e., *Pĕwṓnĕš*, "the wolf"). The name *Tpmt* is explained by Albright, as *T3-pr-Mwt (for *T3-n.t-pr-Mwt), "the one belonging to the house (temple) of Mut," and pronounced *Tapimūt*, but Erichsen holds it more probable that the name is *t3-p-mty* "belonging to the true one" (Khnum). The general certainty that the woman in question is the same one who married Ananiah b. Azariah in No. 2 can scarcely be shaken. When Meshullam gave her in marriage, that did not free her. That the daughter Yehoyishma, who is liberated along with the mother here, was not mentioned in No. 2 suggests that she was born after the marriage.

How, then, are we to account for the use of two different (although related) names for the same person? Could it be that Tamut (from this text on), because of her new status, takes on a new name? If **תפמת** is explained with Erichsen (cf. above) the name could be expressive of the declaration in l. 9 and the fact of a new name would become understandable, since Mut can no longer be her patron divinity. (See further on l. 10) Subsequent occasional use of her original name would not be surprising and is apparently illustrated in 6:3. The name of the slave woman is followed by **שמה** as in 2:3.

3. The term שנית, "marking, tattooing" (pass. part. of שנת), appeared in *A.P.* 28:6 along with the abstract noun שניתת: "A *yodh* is marked upon his hand on the right of the marking of the Aramaic legend '(belonging) to Mibṭaḥiah.' " Other forms of the verb appear below in our text. It would also seem possible, however, to take שניתא as a noun and render "on whose hand is a mark." The Borchardt documents have a noun שנתא. If one could posit a masculine form שנית, one could even take שניתה as "his mark" (Rosenthal). The word is certainly to be connected with Babylonian *šintu*; cf. M. San Nicolò and A. Ungnad, *Neubabylonische Rechts u. Verwaltungsurkunden*, 100 f. and A. L. Oppenheim, "Assyriological Gleanings II," *BASOR*, No. 93, 1944, 14 f. According to the Neo-Babylonian texts cited by Oppenheim, *op. cit.*, 15, privately owned slaves had the name of their owner branded on their hand, while temple slaves and oblates were branded with symbols of the deity. "On the right" in our text is more vague than in *A.P.* 28:6.

כדנה, as in Dan. 3:29; Jer. 10:11. Cf. כזנה in *A.P.* 28:4, 6; 30:15; 37:8. The form דנה appears once in *A.P.* 16:9.

עשתת, with a separate personal pronoun preceding for emphasis and clarity. The verb is found in Hebrew, Jonah 1:6, with ל as here, and in Sirach 3:24, but is an Aramaism. It was used in *A.P.* Aḥ. 25; 68; and in *A.P.* 30:23; 31:[22]. Cf. L § 32.

4. אזת; meaning obscure. The word may specify in what respect he has taken thought of her and could be a noun meaning something like "maintenance." It could be a conjunction with the meaning "henceforth," or may be the 1st pers. sing. perf. of אזל with elision of the ל as in Syriac. Rosenthal suggests a euphemism for "to die," or an auxiliary use "I am going to"; the former would be difficult to fit in here but the latter seems possible (see BL § 107j on the omission of conjunction).

שבקתכי. This verb ordinarily means "to leave," as in *A.P.* 27:1, "We did not leave our posts," but in legal texts it must have a special nuance, as our papyrus shows. Apparently it refers here to setting a slave free. In the Syriac the related noun שבוקיא means "manumission," Carl Brockelmann, *Lexicon Syriacum* (2d ed., Halle, 1928), s. v. The freedom is peculiar, however, taking effect only at the time of the owner's death, as already explained in the introduction. See the literature cited in the note on l. 10.

יהישמע (cf. 6:2, etc.). This is an interesting variation (probably only orthographic) of the writing יהוישמע found in other texts — both ours and those previously known (*A.P.* 22:126; 39:2; 63:6; 68:10). But cf. already יהנתן instead of יהונתן, *A.P.* 2:21, on such a spelling. The O.T. use of Yah as a short form of Yahweh is well known (and is confirmed by No. 3:25 above) but is restricted in personal names in the O.T. to occurrence as final element; cf. Noth, *IP*, 105.

5. ילתי for ילדתי occurs again in l. 8 and hence is probably no scribal error but a phonetic spelling: *yelattī* (Rosenthal). A different spelling appears in l. 6.

וברה is put above the line; it had been forgotten by the scribe. The phraseology is familiar from the previously known texts. On קריב ורחיק see above on 1:9. הנגית והנבג occurs once in *A.P.* 43:9. Sachau misread the second word as הנבקא and was followed in this by Ungnad, but the correct reading הנבגא is found in Cowley, *A.P.*, p. 147 (q.v.). הנגית was correctly explained by Scheftelowitz, *Scripta Univ. atque Bibl. Hierosol.*, *1*, 12, as Old Persian **hangaitha*, "belonging to the family." For הנבג J. N. Epstein, "Weitere Glossen zu den Aramäischen Papyrus und Ostraca," *ZAW*, *33*, 1913, 225, had cited Mandaic האמבאגא. Scheftelowitz, in following Sachau's (and Ungnad's) הנבקא, connected the word with Old Persian **hanābaka*, "kinsman," (from *hannāba-ka*); Schaeder, *Beiträge*, 264 f., adds that the reading with ג simplifies the matter further. The word corresponds to Middle Persian *ham-bāga*, "having a common share," from which the above-mentioned Mandaic word and Syriac *habbāgā* are probably derived, and in effect means "comrade"; see H. S. Nyberg, *Hilfsbuch des Pehlevi* (Uppsala, 1931), *2*, Glossary, 94. Since progressively wider circles are described in the series of phrases, הנגית והנבג can hardly apply to kinsmen, as has been held by others, for that was exhausted with the terms "close and distant." It must refer to possible claimants not covered by the kinship phrase. No. 9:18, etc., add another word to the series, אדרנג.

6. לידתי is an error for ילדתי; cf. above, l. 5.

7. Here we have the first occurrence of the inf. of שנת.

ולמזלכי. Since this is an inf. constr., it must be peal, where there alone is a מ prefix and hence cannot well be from אזל, only a haphel of which would make sense here. It is best taken from זול, though J.A. would lead one to expect a haphel form for the meaning "to sell cheaply." In *A.P.* 38:8 we read זולו, "sell from our houses goods and according to your ability to pay what he assesses." The translation "sell" was suggested by Seidel and Barth; cf. Isa. 46:6. See L § 39g. Cowley, *A.P.* 137, weighs "remove"; cf. Arabian *zāla*, which would not fit our passage.

מנדת. The word appears in B.A. as "tribute" only. This is the first occurrence in another sense. It is originally Babylonian *mandattu*, which means "tribute" in the historical texts but has other meanings in the juridical texts. *Mandattu*, according to Koschaker, is the normal wage earned by a slave and paid to a master who rents him out. One might be tempted to see in the phrase ולמזלכי מנדת כסף a reference to such hiring out of *Tpmt* for money. However, in the light of the use of זול in *A.P.* 38:8, direct sale seems more likely and מנדת must simply mean "measuring out" of money. In that case מזלכי would mean "to let out." On *mandattu* see the text in Raymond P. Dougherty, "The Babylonian Principle of Suretyship," *AJSL*, *46*, 1930, 76 and the further elucidation of the term in Paul Koschaker, "Über einige Griechische Rechtsurkunden aus den östlichen Randgebieten des Hellenismus," *ASAW*, *42*, No. 1, 1931, 2.

זי starts a new sentence: "Whoever . . ."

8. ילתי again as in l. 5.

אבגדן, oftener אביגדן (6:17, etc.). Cowley, in whose texts it was first found (*A.P.* 20:14; 25:15; 28:10) rendered "fine," which, whatever the etymology, must be the general meaning. Scheftelowitz, *op. cit.*, 10, connects it with Avestan *aibigad*, "have a counter request." Lidzbarski, *Ephemeris*, *3*, 80, compared Mandaic אבוגדאנא, which, however, is the name of a demon. The reading אבגרן is equally possible and an etymology on that basis was offered by C. Bartholomae in Staerk, *Die jüdisch-aramäischen Papyri von Assuan*, 31; so also Schaeder, *Beiträge*, 264, and E. Benveniste, "Termes et noms en araméen," *JA*, *225*, 1934, 178. Bernhard Geiger considers all explanations offered as unsatisfactory. A shorter form *abigda* or *abigra* is found in the ostraca, according to Dupont-Sommer.

50 karsh; since the karsh is 1/6th of a Babylonian mina, or 10 shekels, the sum is a large one.

9. ואנתי שביקה, "thou art left (i. e., set free)"; cf. on l. 4.

מן טלא לסמשא. It seems certain that סמשא here is the sun. To connect with שמש pael, "serve," would produce a strained rendering. The writing סמשא is very interesting. Elsewhere in these papyri it is always שמש (in *A.P.* 21:8 שמשא). On the dissimilation involved here see Rudolf Růčička, "Konsonantische Dissimilation in den Semitischen Sprachen," *BA*, *6*, No. 4, 1909, 179. The *ᵈIl-tam-mesh* of the cuneiform texts, was correctly combined by Hilprecht in Clay, BEUP, *10*, xiii f., with Shamash (except that he wrongly took the first syllable as article, whereas it really is the west-Semitic word for god) according to Julius Lewy, "The Late Assyro-Babylonian Cult of the Moon and its Culmination in the Time of Nabonidus," *Hebrew Union College Annual*, *19*, 1945/46, 428; it illustrates a further variation in the first letter.

One may conclude from the parallelism between the statement of this line and that of l. 10 that סמשא is Shamash. It is interesting to note in this connection that in Babylonian slave names the god Shamash is particularly frequent; see J. J. Stamm, *MVAÄG*, *44*, 1939 307 f. The god Shamash, with the name written with final aleph, occurs in the Aramaic inscriptions found recently at Hatra in Mesopotamia. See Oluf Krückmann, "Die neuen Inschriften von Hatra," *AfO*, *16*, 1952, 141.

מן טלא ל. Hardly to be connected with the טלה √טלל in Beh̩. 5, etc. "shadow," "protection"; cf. טלל in *A.P.* 38:5. Rosenthal would take מן טלא as an adverb meaning "therefore," "consequently," and compares the preposition *meṭṭūl* in Syriac, noting that כות (No. 7:33) is also written כותא (Ah̩. 20). As a general guidepost for the interpretation I think that we should bear in mind the statement of such a slave-manumission text as Schorr, *Urkunden*, 51, No. 27:5–6, where the mistress frees her slave woman in a ritual act: *u-ul-li-il-ši pa-ni-ša a-na ṣīt ilu Šamši iš-ku-un*," "she cleansed her face and set it toward the sunrise." Cf. Paul Koschaker, *ASAW*, *42*, 1, 1931, 72. In the light of this ritual it seems to me that מן טלא ל means

"before." It is equivalent to Hebrew מנגד ל. Cf. Judg. 20:34, Prov. 14:7. In older language נגד alone appears. The same type of ritual in a different situation is presupposed in Num. 25:4, "Take all the heads of the people and hang them up before Yahweh against the sun (נגד השמש)." (It seems likely that the same phrase "against the sun" once stood in II Sam. 21:6 or 9). The word טלא may, therefore, be regarded as derived from the root נטל (similar in meaning to the Hebrew root נגד). If Rosenthal's explanation of מן טלא as adverb is preferred the nuance may be "thereupon" rather than "therefore"; the liberation to the god would then take place only if an attempt should be made to nullify this manumission document.

10. The statement, "and thou art freed to the god" apparently means that her freedom is divinely recognized and protected. In the Delphic manumission texts the method of liberating a slave is that of an "entrustment sale" by the owners to the god Apollo. See especially William L. Westermann, "The Paramone as General Service Contract," *Journal of Juristic Papyrology*, *2*, 1948, 9 f., and Koschaker, *ASAW*, *42*, 1, 1931, 39 f.

A mark in the right margin between ll. 10 and 11, as in No. 2, calls attention to a change of speaker.

11. ואמרת is 3d pers. sing. fem. Yehoyishma's joining in the dictum is added as an afterthought. The force of the verb is "T. has (herewith) declared."

יפלחנך, an error for נפלחנך. The verb פלח occurred in *A.P.* Aḥ. [15] 17.

זי here equals כזי, or perhaps an error for it; cf. l. 13.

יסבל, literally, "carry," then "provide for." The noun סבול means "support" in *A.P.* 43:4. The verb occurs a number of times in the Aḥiḳar and Behistun texts. Our form is with suff. and nun energic in Aḥ. 90. See G. R. Driver, *JRAS*, 1932, 89, on this verb and its Akkadian equivalents. The מסובלין in Ezra 6:3 is perhaps a J.A. poel, but the text may originally have intended a pass. part. pael מסבלין with the thought that the old foundations should be solicitously preserved.

The Babylonian text in Paul Koschaker and Arthur Ungnad, *Hammurabis Gesetz* (Leipzig, 1923) *6*, 5, No. 1427, provides service to former master and mistress by the manumitted slave for the rest of their lives, but their children are declared not entitled to it.

12. After ועד מותך the scribe evidently left out the words ואחרי מותך, "and after thy death," an interesting instance of haplography. A new sentence begins with נסבל.

הוין, 1st pers. pl. perf. of הוא before the part. expressing duration in the past. Cf. BL § 81 and *A.P.* 30:15 (31:14).

13. קמן, a perf. (1st pers. pl.) in the protasis, as in other instances in the papyri; BL § 111c. In B.A. the impf. is regular.

נסבלנך, the first occurrence of the 1st pers. pl. impf.; cf. the 1st pers. sing. impf. in Aḥ. 204.

14. נחוב, as in *A.P.* 2:15. Liability to a fine is here directly stated.

15. These items have already been explained except for כסף צריף; cf. Nos. 9:20; 10:11; 11:6; 12:30; *A.P.* 2:15; 5:7; 28:11. This may refer to Aryandes' coins (see above, p. 29). Herodotus IV, 166, states that his silver money was the purest "even now." In Assyrian *ṣarpu* has the meaning of refined silver; in Clay, BEUP, *10*, 21, No. 54:7, the equivalent phrase is *kaspu ḳalū*.

16. The scribe חגי does not give his full name. He is not identical with Haggai b. Shema'iah who wrote Nos. 3, 9, 10, 12. The place of execution is Yeb, as is the case with Nos. 9:23; 10:17.

Witnesses: אתרפרן בר ניסי מדי, Atarparan b. Nīsai, the Mede. His Median birth and ancestry evidently set him apart. There is a *degel* of אתרופרן in *A.P.* 6:9; this latter name Scheftelowitz, *op. cit.*, 12, identifies with *Athrava-farna*, "den Glanz des Priesters habend." Geiger, for אתרפרן, compares Old Persian **Ātar-farna(h)*, "having the splendor of fire," and the Sassanian name *Atur-farn-bag*; cf. Justi, *IN*, 48 f. ניסי is hardly a true personal name, but rather a gentilic. *Nīsāia*, mentioned as a region in Media in Darius, *Bis.* § 13, was doubtless his home.

17. Micaiah b. Aḥio, mentioned in 1:12, but written מכיה.

Berechiah b. Miptaḥ, seemingly a new personage. The name מפטח is short for מפטחיה, a feminine name (see *A.P.* 22:135 and 15:3, 32). Use of the mother's name shows that the man's mother was not of free status. In *A.P.* 13:2, 4 and in *A.P.* 15 מפטחיה is used for a woman otherwise called מבטחיה (*A.P.* 8:2, etc.). The writing suggests that the writers did not know Hebrew (though the scribe Haggai in this instance is probably Jewish), and that the root בטח did not exist in Aramaic (here Syriac is true to the tradition, while בטח in J.A. probably came in from Hebrew). The abbreviated name מפטח is not found in the S.-C. or Sachau papyri, however (contrary to the index in *A.P.*, for the names given there as מפטח are מפתח in the text).

Delah b. Gaddūl; on the latter name see 2:14. A Delah in *A.P.* 41:4, concerning which Cowley queries, "A name?" The existence of such a name need therefore no longer be doubted. It is short for Delaiah (cf. *A.P.* 30:29, etc.). The same element is found in names like *Bīt-ili-dala'*, Clay, UMBS, *2*, 17; *Nabu-dala'*, BEUP, *9*, 64; *Dalatani*, *ibid.*, 57.

18. The endorsement: the first word seems to be מרחק, "removal." If so, this provides an interesting extension of its use: the owner "removes" himself from his chattels (slaves are such) as from his real property.

יהישמ[ע]: it is a question whether the final letter of the name was left out or has disappeared.

PAPYRUS 6

PAPYRUS 6

(*Brooklyn* 47.218.32) 37.0 *cm.* x 31.9 *cm.*

THIS text has come down in a fragmentary condition. It is probably to be dated July 11, 420 B.C. (see the notes). Here Anani, son of Azariah, gives to Yehoyishma, his daughter, (part of?) a house adjoining that in which he himself is living. This gift is no doubt the one that is subsequently referred to in No. 12:9, 18 as given by Anani and his wife to Yehoyishma in connection with her marriage (cf. No. 7), which took place in October, 420 B.C. Years later he gave her the part of the house he had reserved (No. 9). The property is described in terms of its measurements and its location. Permission to use a staircase for entry and exit is given. In ll. 14 and 16 there is reference to houses, in the plural. We must assume either that the property was composed of several buildings, or that the writer is including a previously given house with this newly given one in his guarantee against gift recovery. The text breaks off at an interesting point where there is reference to the possible death of Yehoyishma at a certain age (cf. No. 4:17). Quite a number of lines are missing, and a few small fragments which seem to belong to this text cannot be placed because of that circumstance.

ב 8 פרמותי הו יום 8 לתמוז שנת 3 דריהוש מלכא אדין
[בסון] ב[י]רתא אמר [ע]נני בר עזריה לחן זי יהו אלהא ליהישמע
שמה ברי אמה תמ[ת שמה א]נתתי לאמר אנה ענני [יהב]ת לכי [...
אחד גשורן הוה [פתיה] אמן בעשתא שבע הו 3 [+4 וארכה אמן ...
אמרן לה מצדית [תחתי]א לה [ ] ביתי כתחת
בית ענני בר עזריה [ושו]ק ביניהם [על]י לה
אוצר מלכא מערב [שמש לה] מדנח שמש [ל]ה
בית חור עבד זי ח[נום אלהא]י אנת יהוישמע ברתי
שליט בבית [ ] תח[ו]מ[ו]ה כתיבן בספרא מן תחת ומ[נעל]
וש[ל]יטה אנת [למ]נסק [ולמ]נחת בדרגא [ב]יתי ותחות [...
בינ[י]הם תחתיתא ו[...
לפלגה ופלגא ל[ ] ברת [ ]בית
ופלג תחית ופלג דר[גא...]למנסק עלא ולמנחת
ולמנפק ברא אנה ענני יהבת לך בתיא אלה ברחמה לא אכהל
אנה ענני אהנצל מ[נ]כי ולא אכהל אמר נפש אחרית אהנצל מנכי
זי יקום עליכי לתרכתכי מן בתיא זי כתבת ויה[בת לכי ...
ברתי אביגדן כ[ס]ף כרשן 10 [...
הן תמות יהוי[ש]מע ברת ש[נן 100...
...יהוי]שמע ברתי
.ת ל..

a.]מלה
]הו

b. ...]בר]...ן פלטיה

c.]יתי[
]תמ[

d.]...ה בר [

e.]בית יהוה ל[
]הושעיה[

1. On the 8th of Pharmuthi, that is the 8th day of Tammuz, the 3d (read: 4th) year of Darius the king, at that time
2. [in Syene the for]tress said [A]nani son of Azariah, *lḥn* of Yahu the god, to Yehoyishma
3. by name, my child, whose mother is Ta[mut by name,] my wife, saying: I, Anani, [have giv]en thee [a house?]
4. having (?) beams. [Its width] is cubits by the one(-cubit-measure) seven, that is 7; [its length in cubits . . .]
5. We said (?) to her: "The empty space (?) . . . [belo]w it (there is) my house . . .
6. the house of Anani b. Azariah [. . . and the str]eet is between them. [Abo]ve it is
7. the treasury of the king. West [of it is the house of *Ḳnḥnty*]. East of it
8. is the house of Ḥor, servant of Kh[num, the god.] [None but ?] thee, Yehoyishma, my daughter,
9. shall have power over [this] house, the boundaries of which are written in [this] document from below and a[bove (?)].
10. And thou shalt have power [to as]cend [and des]cend by the stairs . . . my [ho]use and under . . .
11. be[twe]en them, the lower one and . . .
12. to its ha[lf] and the half . . . . daughter (?) . . . . house (?).
13. and half the lower part and half the st[airs . . .] to ascend above and to descend
14. and to go forth outside. I, Anani, have given thee these houses as a gift. I shall not be able
15. — I, Anani — to take it from thee, and I shall not be able to say, "Through (?) another soul will I take (it) away from thee."
16. Whoever rises up against thee to drive thee out from the houses which I wrote and ga[ve to thee, he shall pay to Yehoyishma,]
17. my daughter, a fine of silver, 10 karsh . . .
18. If Yehoyishma should die at the a[ge of a hundred years ?] . . .
19. . . . [Yehoyi]shma, my daughter . . .
20. . . . to . . .

1. The text of this line could be reconstructed. The small fragment containing the part of the word "day" was difficult to recognize because of the faded nature of the letter מ. The name Darius could be guessed from the first and last letters, and the fragment completing it happily turned up. Darius can only be Darius II, and the 3d year (421 B.C.) is clearly mentioned. However, Tammuz 8 was July 22, Pharmuthi 8 was July 11 in that year. There must thus be an error in a month name or the year. It is possible that a 20 stood in the gap before the 8 preceding Tammuz. Parker points out that if one read Tammuz 28 and assumed that the scribe erroneously wrote Pharmuthi instead of Paḥons, a synchronism would result (Tammuz 28, August 11; Paḥons 8, August 10). In 420 B.C. Tammuz 8 and Pharmuthi 8 both fell on July 11; it would seem easiest to assume an error in the year (correcting 3 to 4). This agrees with the gift of a house in that year referred to in 12:9, 18. S. H. Horn and L. H. Wood believe that the year date is according to a fall-to-fall calendar (3d year then is 4th by a spring-to-spring calendar). See their article in *JNES*, *12*, 1953.

דריהוש. The spelling stands midway between the still shorter דריוש of *A.P.* 1:1 and the longer form דריוהוש that appears in 7:1, *A.P.* 20:1, and in numerous other papyri (cf. Cowley's index). More archaic yet is the דרוש of the Bauer-Meissner text.

2. The first legible word in this line, it seems, must be read בׄ[י]רׄתא. The preceding word then must have been ביב or בסון, preferably the latter; allowing even for the indentation of the second line, the available space seems a bit wide for the former word.

The ע of [ע]נני is missing, but the lower portions of the other letters are visible.

לחן זי יהו. Cf. 2:2, etc. Contrast לחן ליהו in 1:2.

ליהישמע. We have here the shortened form instead of יהוישמע, as in 5:4, etc.

3. [שמה], used especially after the names of bondsmen or bondwomen (see above, p. 145), would fill the empty space.

ברי אמה, "my child, whose mother is Tamut"; cf. אמה in the Memphis stela, *CIS*, *2*, 122:2. Cf. also on 2:14.

תמׄ[ות]: the name is partly broken away, but enough remains of the second letter to show that it was מ. Since Anani's wife's name was Tamut, it may be restored here. The space is too wide for a direct connection between the name and the next fragment, and so there was doubtlessly a [שמה] in the gap. The following word is [א]נתתי, "my wife." The balance of the line can be restored in part with the help of the narrow strip probably belonging there.

יהבׄ[ת] לכי. The remains of the following letters scarcely permit a reconstruction, and 9:3–4 do not seem to help.

4. אחד גשורן. Cf. above on 3:5; 4:8; and below 9:13; 10:2.

הוה starts a new connection. In the gap between it and אמן stood the subject, which was probably "its width" (cf. 9:7). The "seven" was repeated with numerals.

As only three strokes have survived, another four strokes must be supplied. This would leave about ten letters missing to complete the line. There is barely room for וארכה, "its length"+"cubits"+numeral signs.

5. The third word is מצדית (less probably מצרית), as in 9:4 (cf. on that). If אמרן is "we said," Tamut must be imagined as concurring in the matter. לה, "to her" (Yehoyishma)? or "with respect to it" (the house)?

All that remains of the rest of the line is a few tops of letters. א and לה are definitely discernible. Perhaps the א is a remnant of [תחתי]א לה; for this spelling cf. *A.P.* 13:13. The top of a ח with an uncertain letter before it is next visible. A narrow strip has been placed here which provides ביתי and then כתחת.

6. Since the house of Ḥor (cf. on 9:10) lay to the east according to ll. 7–8, Anani's house lies on the "lower" side (cf. 9:8 f.; 10:3 f., adjusting the directions). What stood in the gap after "the house of Anani b. Azariah" is uncertain. After the gap there is the letter ק, which doubtlessly is the end of the word שוק, "street": "the street between them," as in *A.P.* 13:14: ושקא ביניהם. The words force us to suppose some other building (the Temple of Yahu?) had been mentioned. At the end of the line one would expect "above it," עליה לה. This would put the "treasury" in the proper place when the directions are viewed as in 4:9 f. The piece seemingly belonging here has לה, but the remains of the last letter of the previous word are not those of ה, but of י. Evidently the absolute עלי, found in B.A., was used in this instance.

7. After מערב the words שמש לה may be supplied. In the remaining part of the gap there must have stood "the house of *ḳnḥnty*" (9:9).

מדנח שמש instead of the usual מועה. This word is common in Aramaic (including Syriac) for the rising of the sun. Cf. *A.P.* Aḥ. 138, and *CIS*, *2*, 213:5 in Nabataean. The word שמש must have been followed by לה. Since the ל was written high, no portion of its base is visible.

8.–9. After עבד זי must have stood [חנום אלהא]ח. The top of the ח is still visible. But these words do not fill out the gap. In 9:10 Ḥor's function is given more precisely. There may be a loss of about eight letters. On the edge of the piece at the left is a yodh. A masculine subject is necessary in view of the שליט of l. 9 (cf. שליטה in l. 10). One might expect something like "No one except thee, Y., my daughter, shall have power"; cf. the שטר מן of *A.P.* 25:13. But this does not explain the yodh. After a gap we get several fragments whose placement was suggested by the papyrus overlap. The seemingly hopeless fragment with the מ could be put in l. 9 between תח and ה and give the word תח[ו]מ[ו]ה, with final yodh missing (cf. 3:4). This was followed by כתיבן בספרא. Of the word after מן תחת we have only two letters, ומ (with the מ not absolutely certain). The tip of a ל is visible at the end in the piece above. One would like to read ומ[נעל], "and from above."

10. The papyrus is stripped, but the first words surely were ושל[ל]יטה אנת[י]. The gap that follows is small. In fact, nothing may be missing except the bracketed

letters, On the adjoining fragment נסק suggests an infinitive [למ]נסק (cf. 9:15: למסלק). Cf. BL § 43a.

The placement of this piece here is dictated by the papyrus overlap and by the logical consideration that מנסק must have preceded ול[מ]נחת, the next word. The top of the מ is still visible, and the top of the ל appears in the small fragment put in the line above. Through the proper placement of the adjoining fragment, בדרגא was regained. This word, which appears again in 9:4 f.; 10:3, was not found in previous papyri, though the verb דרג, "bend the bow," occurs in Aḥ. 128. It doubtlessly means "stairs," as in J.A.; see 9:10; *durgu* in Assyrian means "way, path." In the gap after דרגא there may have been a three- or four-letter word.

[ב]יתי. After ותחות a word is broken away.

11. The first word would seem to be בי[ניה]ם (as in l. 6); the letter before the final one was plainly a ה.

תחתיתא. The א was forgotten and then written in above the line. Cf. Hebrew תחתית. The conjunction waw follows and part of another letter is still visible. There is then a gap for the rest of the line, for the remains of the letters on the piece at the left belong with l. 12.

12. לפלג[ה]. While parts of the letters are broken away, the reading is certain. Part of a ל is visible on the left of the fragment. After a 7.5 cm. gap the feet of a word, probably ב̇ר̇ת, are discernible. After a break that must have contained a short word there is a ב̇י̇ת followed by a short word.

13. On תחית cf. on 9:4. After the second פלג a small fragment דר[גא] has been placed which seems to fit. After a break of 6 cm. the infinitives "ascend" and "descend" follow (cf. l. 10).

14. ברא, "outside," was found in *A.P.* Aḥ. 109.

A new sentence begins with אנה. Instead of ברחמה one might also have ברחמן (pl.); cf. 9:12; *A.P.* 18:2; 25:11, 14. ברחמה should be translated "as a gift"; cf. *A.P.* 9:7, where this is best. Cowley takes ברחמן as "in friendship" in the note on *A.P.* 9:7. Cf. also Cowley's note on *A.P.* 25:11, which differs from the translation, where we find "gift."

He refers to houses in the plural here (ביתא as in *A.P.* 34:6, Beh. 23). This would seem to indicate that more than one building was mentioned above in l. 3. Was the document concerned with the תרי רבתא of Nos. 4:3; 9:4; 10:6; 12:13?

ב[ר]חמה. The word made possible the proper placement of the entire left-hand fragment. In 12:26 רחמת appears as in *A.P.* 9:7; 43:3. The more usual phrase is ברחמן (see just above). רחמה must be רחמא and thus provides an instance of the masc. word "womb" used in the sense of "love." See Levy, s. v.

לא was superimposed after being forgotten.

15. Gifts were by nature revocable unless specified as otherwise.

אהנצל. Cf. L § 35 h.

In מ[נ]כי the foot of the נ is visible alongside that of the previous letter. The word

is repeated more clearly at the end of the line. A direct quotation is introduced by the following words.

נפש was followed by אחרית; a piece of every letter of that word is discernible. B.A. אחרי is used as fem. of אחרון. Cf. J.A. אוחרי.

One would like to read the next word as תהנצל, but the first letter can only be an א, hence אהנצל. It is then necessary to construe the connection "through another soul will I take (it) away."

16. זי, here "whoever," must start a new sentence. It is written out into the margin, as is the ב in l. 1.

לתרכתכי; apparently inf. pael with ת ending before the suffix. This shows that the verb תרך is not only in use for the ejection of a wife, as in Nos. 2 and 7. Some one pretending to legal rights could evidently eject Yehoyishma.

בתיא. The plural is intended, as in l. 14. The yodh was forgotten and superimposed.

ויה[בת לכי]: the act of giving possession. [ינתן ליהישמע] must be supplied at the end in all probability.

17. The first word seems to be ברתי. Part of the ב appears on the piece put below it, which, however, has been put too close.

אביגדן. Cf. above 5:8.

כ[ס]ף: the restoration is certain. The penalty of 10 karsh is not as stiff as in other cases.

18. הן could have been guessed, but the fragment providing it turned up.

The eventuality of Yehoyishma's death is now taken up.

ברת שנ[ן]. The phrase must be as in 4:17, 18.

19. Only [יהוי]שמע ברתי remains.

20. Some tops of letters remain: – – – ל ת – – –

On the fragments put at the bottom of the plate and from all indications belonging to this text we may add the following:

a) This piece, according to the fibers, belongs below the end of l. 18, but it cannot be from l. 19.

b) From fibers and appearance belongs close to c) – – –ן פלטיה בר; the first letter, a part of which remains, is uncertain. End of a previous name?

c) This was the bottom piece of the papyrus on the left, but the name must have run over into another line on the right of the sheet.

d) This piece is an "overlap piece," from a place where the two sheets of papyrus were glued. It cannot come from ll. 9–10, where there is no room, and so must belong below l. 20. "the house (?) shall be to . . ." In the second line there is the name Hosha'ia[h].

e) The lines are close together, and so יתי could be a superimposed word. It could be a remnant of [ב]יתי. תמ may be a remnant of תמ[ת] or תמ[י] (less probably).

PAPYRUS 7

PAPYRUS 7

(*Brooklyn* 47.218.150) 68.7 *cm.* x 30.5 *cm.*

THIS is the most elaborate of the known Aramaic marriage documents. It was almost completely broken up, but it has been possible to restore it to a considerable degree. If the dating in the 4th year of Darius is correct (see the notes) it was written on October 2, 420 B.C. The groom Ananiah, son of Haggai, has asked the bride Yehoyishma in marriage from her "brother" Zakkur son of Meshullam. The by-passing of Ananiah, son of Azariah, who always speaks of her as his daughter, is very curious. The seemingly conflicting claims of Nos. 5:6 f. and 4:18 concerning the parentage of Yehoyishma have already been noted above. Since Zakkur is called her "brother," it seems possible that her father actually was Meshullam, son of Zakkur. *A.P.* 22:87 mentions a Yehoyishma, daughter of Meshullam, who might conceivably be identical with the woman in question. She was evidently not born yet at the time of No. 2, for some stipulation concerning her would then have been in order, but was born subsequently. In any case it is understandable in view of No. 5 that after the death of Meshullam, son of Zakkur, his son Zakkur, son of Meshullam, should give the bride away and receive the mohar or price, the present made by the groom, for her freedom was complete only at Zakkur's death. It is conceivable that the title "brother" was traditional for the role he played and conveyed no actual kinship in this case.

Yehoyishma's possessions are listed in detail. The purpose of this is that in the event of divorce proof can be adduced of what she brought into marriage, for she is entitled to take it all out with her if she goes forth from her husband's house. One might suppose that Yehoyishma was previously married, for she is already mentioned in No. 4 of 434 B.C. and so would be at least twenty-four and perhaps much older since her parents were married in 449 B.C., and that one or more divorces account for the quantity of her possessions. But the size of the mohar (cf. on l. 5) suggests that this was her first marriage, and her age might account for her possessions. Meshullam b. Zakkur may not have wanted to give her in marriage during his lifetime. Papyrus No. 5 may have a bearing on the matter. The articles of wool and linen clothing are listed first and their number is summed up in l. 13. A fresh rubric, "vessels of bronze," is then introduced. Probably their number was also summed up in l. 14b. A summary statement gives the total value of her

assets, including the mohar or gift of the groom, which was thus regarded as her possession, even if given *pro forma* to her brother. The list is then supplemented by some additional items which are not given any monetary value (or is the item at the end of l. 18 an exception?) and which do not fall under the two rubrics previouly named — notably cosmetics.

In ll. 21 f. the document stipulates what is to happen in the event of divorce. The declaration of the party seeking the divorce is given more fully than in the comparable document Sayce-Cowley "G" (*A.P.* 15). The husband says, "I divorce my wife Yehoyishma. She shall not be a wife to me (any longer)," while the woman seeking divorce says, "I divorce [thee]. I will not be to thee a wife (any longer)." The "divorce money" (see below) is "on the head" of the party seeking the divorce. In the event the husband seeks the divorce he must restore to her all the possessions she brought in with her "on one day, at one time," and she may go forth whither she desires. In the event of the woman's seeking the divorce she receives all her original possessions in the same way and even keeps the mohar (this would seem to be the meaning of the statement: "his mohar is lost"). However, she must pay her husband 7 shekels, 2 *R*. This cannot be a return of the mohar, for the latter must have been at least one karsh (cf. the notes). The figure, furthermore, is exactly the same as in *A.P.* 15:24, where it was larger than the mohar (which in *A.P.* 15:5 is given as 5 shekels, while here it is one karsh). It seems likely that it is "the divorce money." It is hardly a fine, but rather to be regarded as defraying costs of the action. If there is no mention in either document of the man's paying it to the woman, that may have been because it was customary for the man to deliver it to the court; if the woman divorces, she presumably has to give the man the money wherewith to pay the costs.

The agreement thereupon (ll. 28 f.) takes up the contingency of the mortality of the husband. If he has no child, male or female, by her, she is to inherit his house, his goods, his possessions, and all he has. One would expect the reverse situation to be considered immediately, as is done in *A.P.* 15:20 f., but that is not the case. From the point of view of "form criticism" the latter document has the more original pattern in this particular. In l. 30 the contingency of the husband's ejecting the wife from his house and possessions is brought up instead. A fine of 20 karsh royal weight is imposed. A qualification, however, is added in ll. 33–34; the connection is broken here but the meaning seems clear. In the middle of l. 34 the reverse contingency of the wife's death, which one would have expected to be mentioned in l. 30, is taken up.

A highly interesting point is raised in l. 33. The connection is a bit broken, but the sense can hardly be in doubt: Yehoyishma is prohibited from having extramarital intercourse after being ejected from Anani's house. Her violation of this stipulation means divorce. This passage confirms the idea that the Elephantine community followed other laws and customs than those which were imposed on

the Palestinian community by Ezra and his circle, or the earlier ones of Deuteronomy or of the Book of the Covenant (Exod. 20:23–23:19).

In the middle of l. 34 the contingency of the wife's death, which one would have expected to be taken up in l. 30, is brought in. If she has no child by her husband he shall "inherit her" and all her goods and possessions.

In the broken connection of ll. 36–37 there followed the counterpart to l. 33. There was, however, no allusion to extramarital intercourse on the husband's part. Instead he is prohibited from taking any other woman in marriage. The consequence of a violation of this was likewise divorce.

In the following lines (38–39) the husband is forbidden to join with one or two of the wives of his colleagues in taking legal action against his wife, and the wife from similar cooperation of one or two men against the husband, another surprising new feature of this document.

At the end of l. 40 a new stipulation which concerns the bride's brother Zakkur begins. He is not to be allowed to reclaim the goods she took along on the grounds that they were a gift (gifts were evidently revocable).

The scribe signs his name as Maʿuziyah, son of Nathan. He is the writer of several previously published texts, one a fragment of a marriage document (*A.P.* 18) which helps to clarify some statements in this one. Owing to the peculiar circumstances obtaining here the two parties and not merely one, as in *A.P.* 15:37, have instructed the scribe as to what to write.

The witnesses did not sign personally but are only listed and include very prominent people. One name is broken away, except for the trace of one letter, *l*.

1 בירח תשרי הו אפף [ש]נת [3+]1 דריוהוש [מלכא אדין] ביב בירתא אמר ענניה בר
חגי

2 ארמי זי יב בירתא [ל]דגל [אדנ]נבו לזכור בר מ[שלם ארמ]י זי סון לדכם דגלא לאמר

3 אנה אתית על [בי]תך ושאלת מנך לנשן יהוישמע שמה אחתך לאנתו ויהבתה

4 לי הי אנתתי ואנה בעל[ה] מניומא זנה עד עלם ויהבת לך מהר אחתך יהוישמע

5 כסף כר[ש 1] על עליך [וטיב לבבך בג]ו הנעלת לי יהוישמע אחתך לביתי תכונה

6 זי כסף כרשן תרין ש[קל]ן 2 חלרן 5 לבש 1 זי קמר [ח]דת לאמן 7 פשכן 3 פתי

7 אמן 4 ר 2 שוה כסף כרש [1] שקלן 2 גמירה 1 זי קמר חדת לאמן 6 ב 4 חטיב

8 צבע ידין פשך 1 לפם 1 שוה כסף כרש 1 לבש 1 מעדר חדת [א]מן 6 ב 4 דמי כסף

9 שקלן 7 שביט [1] חדת לאמן 6 ב 3 + [..] ר 2

10 צבען 2 לפם 1 שוה כסף ש[קל]ן 8 לב[ש 1 ב..]שו[ה...

11 שנטא 1 זי כתן חדת ארך [ ] שוה כסף שק[לן...

12 ארך אמן 6 ב 3 שוה [ ] כתן 1 בליה ו[ד]מי כסף שקל 1

13 כל לבשן זי קמר וכתן [4] 8 מאני נחש מחזי 1 [דמי] כס[ף שקל] 1 תמסא 1 זי נחש

14 דמי כסף שקל 1 ח 10 כס 1 זי נחש דמי כסף [שק]ל [1] כס [1 דמי] כסף חלרן 20

15 זלוע 1 דמי כסף ח 20 [...] [כ]ל [מ]אנ[י נחש] נ]חש ותכ[ו]נתא ומהרא

16 כסף כרשן שבעה ה[ו 7 ש]ק[ל]ן תמניה הו 8 חלרן 5 באבני

17 מלכא כסף 2ר לעשרתא קוף 1 זי חוצן תחת לבשיה ת[וי] זי גמא 1 חדת בה

18 נעבצן זי אבן שש [ ]מין זלוען 2 פיק [זי סלק] 2 בגו [...]י[ד]ה 1 דמן זי סלק 1

19 כפן למנשא משח זי [2+] 1 זי עק 2 אבן בכל 5 ת[ז]י עק 1 תחת חמדיה

20 שנן זי צל פרסין מש[ח חפנן] 2 משח זית חפנן 4 משח מ[ב]שים חפן 1 תקם

21 חפנן 5 מחר או יום אחרן יקום ענניה בעדה וי[א]מר שני[ת] לאנתתי יהוישמע

22 לא תהוה לי אנתת כסף ש[נא]ה בראשה כל זי הנעלת בביתה ינתן לה תכונתה

23 ולבשיה דמי כסף כ[רש]ן שבעה ש[קלן תמניה חלרן 5] וש[א]רת נכסיא זי כתיבן

1. In the month of Tishri, that is Epiphi, in the 4th year of Darius [the king, at that time] in Yeb the fortress said Ananiah b. Haggai,
2. Aramaean of Yeb the fortress, [of] the *degel* of [Iddin]- Nabu, to Zakkur b. Me[shullam, Aramae]an of Syene, of the same *degel*, saying:
3. I have come to thy house and asked of thee the woman Yehoyishma (by name), thy sister, for marriage. And thou didst give her
4. to me. She is my wife and I am her husband from this day forth unto forever. And I have given thee as the *mohar* of thy sister Yehoyishma
5. silver [1 karsh]. It has gone in to thee [and thy heart is satisfied there]with. There brought in to me Yehoyishma, thy sister, to my house, "substance"
6. of silver (amounting to) karsh 2, sh[ekels] 2, ḥallur 5; garment of wool 1, new, (length) cubits 7, handbreadths 3, width
7. cubits 4, *R.* 2, worth silver karsh [1], shekels 2; full-cloth (?) garment of wool 1, new, cubits 6 by 4, striped,
8. dyed on both sides, handbreadth 1 on edge 1, wor[th] silver karsh 1. Garment 1, flounced (?), new, [cu]bits 6 by 4, value in silver
9. shekels 7. Shawl (?) [1 . . .], new, cubits 6 by 3 . . . *R.* 2 . . .
10. fingerbreadths 2 on edge 1, worth silver sh[eke]ls 8. Garment (1) . . . wor[th] . . .
11. Dress (?) of linen 1, new, length . . . worth in silver shek[el]s . . .
12. length cubits 6 by 3, worth . . ., . . . of linen, 1, worn and . . . in the value of silver, shekel 1.
13. All the garments of wool and linen were 8 (above the line: 4). The vessels of bronze: mirror 1 [worth] in sil[ver shekel] 1. Dish of bronze 1
14. worth silver shekel 1 Ḥ. 10. Cup of bronze 1, worth silver [shek]el [1]. Cup [1, worth] silver 20 ḥallur . . .
15. Bowl 1 worth silver Ḥ. 20 . . . (above the line: [al]l the [ve]sse[ls of bronze]) . . . [of br]onze, and the substance and the bridal gift were
16. silver karsh seven, that is 7, shekels eight, that is 8, and ḥallur 5 by royal
17. weight, silver 2 *R.* to the ten . . . Basket, 1, of palm leaves (?) for her garments. Box (?) of reeds 1, new, on it . .
18. inlays (?) of stone six; . . . bowls 2; *pyḳ* [of *slḳ*] 2, thereon . . ., 1, value of 1 *slq.*
19. Ladles (?) for carrying ointment of . . . (2+)1 of wood; 2 of stone; in all 5. . . ., 1, of wood for (?) her jewelry (?)
20. A *šnn* of *ṣl*, two (?) peras. Oil [handfuls] 2; olive oil handfuls 4; balsam oil handful 1; *tqm*
21. handfuls 5. If tomorrow or another day Anani shall rise up on her account (?) and say: "I divorce my wife Yehoyishma,
22. she shall not be to me a wife," the di[vorc]e money is on his head. All that she brought into his house he shall give to her, her substance
23. and her garments in the value of silver karsh seven, sh[ekels eight, ḥallur 5] and the rest of the goods which are written (above)

24 ינתן לה ביום 1 בכף 1 [ו]תהך [לה]אן [זי צבית] והן יה[וי]ש[מע] תשנא לבעלה
25 ענניה ותאמר לה שני[ת]ך לא אהוה לך אנתת כסף שנאה בראשה מהרה יאבד
26 תתב על מוזנא ותנתן ל[ב]עלה ענניה כסף שקלן 7 ר [2] ותנפק מנה עם שארת
27 תכונתה ונכסיה וקנ[ינה בדמי כרשן 7 שקלן 5 +] 3 ח 5 ושארת נכסיה
28 זי כתיבן ינתן לה ביו[ם 1] בכף 1 ותהך לבית אבוה וה[ן מחר] ימות ענניה ובר זכר
29 ונקבה לאיתי לה מן [יהוי]שמע אנתתה יהוישמע הי[בא]חדתה בביתה ונכסוהי
30 וקנינה... י]קום ע[נניה] לתרכותה מן ביתה
31 [ומן נכסוהי וקנינ]ה וכל זי אית [לה... ינ]תן ל[ה אבי]גדנא זי כסף
32 כרשן עשרן באבני [מלכא] כסף ר 2 ל 10 ויעבד [לה] דין ספרא זנה ולא דין
33 להן לא שליטה יה[וישמע ל]הבעלה בעל אחרן בר [מן] ענני והן תעבד כות
34 שנאה הי יעבדון ל[ה דין שנאה] תמות [יהוישמע] ובר [זכר] ונקבה לא
35 איתי לה מן ענני בע[לה ענני] הו ירתנה [תכונת]ה ונכסיה וקנינה וכל
36 זי אית[י] לה אף ל[א יכהל ענני יל]קח אנתה [...
37 לה לאנתו הן יעבד [כות ... ש]נאהי ואף לא יכהל
38 ענניה ולא יעבד דין [חדה] ותרתין מן נשי כנותה לי[ה]וישמע אנתתה והן
39 לא יעבד כות שנאה [הי ו]יעבד לה דין שנאה ואף [ל]א תכהל יהוישמע
40 ולא תעבד דין חד ו[ת]רין לענניה בעלה והן לא תע[ב]ד לה שנאהי אף לא
41 יכהל זכור יאמר לאח[תה נכ]סיא אלה ברחמן יהבת לי[ה]וישמע כען צבית
42 אהנצל המו הן יאמר [כות] לא ישתמע לה חיב הו כתב מעוזיה בר נתן ספרא
43 זנה כפם ענניה בר חגי [ו]זכור בר משלם ושהדיא בגו חגי בר שמעיה יסלח בר
44 גדול [...] בר אצול מנחם בר עזריה ידניה בר גמריה

24. he shall give to her on one day at one time [and] she shall go [where]ver [she will] . . . And if Yehoyishma divorces her husband
25. Ananiah and says to him, "I divorce [thee]. I will not be to thee a wife," the divorce money is on her head; his mohar is lost.
26. She shall sit by the scales and shall give to Ananiah her husband silver shekels 7, [2] *R.*, and she shall go forth from him with the rest of
27. her "substance" and her goods and possess[ions in the value of karsh 7, shekels 5+]3, ḥ(allur) 5, and the rest of her goods
28. which are written (above) he shall give to her on [one d]ay, at one time, and she shall go to the house of her father. And if Ananiah dies [tomorrow], and a child, male
29. or female, there is not to him from [Yeho]yishma his wife, Yehoyishma [shall have power (?)] over his property (?), his house, his goods
30. and his possessions . . . [If] . . . A[nani] rises up to drive her out from his house
31. [and his goods and possessions] and all which is [to him] . . . [he shall] give to [her a fi]ne of silver,
32. karsh 20 by [royal] weight, silver 2 *R.* to the 10, and he shall do [to her] the law of this document and no suit (shall obtain).
33. But Yeho[yishma] shall not have power to cohabit with (?) another man beside Anani, and if she does thus,
34. she is divorced; they shall do to [her the law of divorce (?)]. [If Yehoyishma] dies, and a child, [male] or female, there is not
35. to her from Anani, her hus[band, Anani] — he — shall inherit her [her sub]stance, and her goods and her possessions and all
36. which was to her. Moreover, [Anani shall] not [be able to] take [another] woman (beside Yehoyishma)
37. to him for marriage. If he does [thus] . . . he has divorced her. And moreover Ananiah shall not be able
38. to go to law in cooperation with (?) [one] or two of the wives of his companions with respect to Yehoyishma his wife. And if
39. he does not act thus, divorced [she is]. He shall do to her the law of divorce. And moreover, Yehoyishma shall not be able
40. to go to law in cooperation with (?) one or [t]wo (men) . . . with respect to Ananiah her husband. And if she does not act (thus) toward him, he has divorced her. Moreover, Zakkur
41. shall not be able to say with respect to his si[ster], "These goods I gave in affection to Yehoyishma. Now I want
42. to recover them." If he speaks [thus], no attention shall be paid to him; he is incurring guilt. There wrote Ma'uziyah b. Nathan this document
43. at the dictation of Ananiah b. Haggai [and] Zakkur b. Meshullam. And the witnesses thereto (are) Haggai b. Shema'iah, Yislaḥ b.
44. Gaddūl [. . .] b. Aṣṣūl, Menaḥem b. Azariah, Yedoniah b. Gemariah.

1. At first glance there seems to have been no day specified, but merely the month Tishri (October), which is equated with the Egyptian month Epiphi. But it seems likely that the first day is meant in such cases (cf. also 11:1). The ש of [ש]נת is missing, but there can be no doubt about the word. The fragment happily fell into place here, giving connection elements in ll. 2 and 3 as well. The exact year date is missing, but the numeral stroke set at an angle suggests that three other strokes are missing before it. In *A.P.* 20 we have another document from the 4th year of Darius, written by the same scribe with the strokes thus arranged, though in *A.P.* 20 the third stroke is written with a slant. In 420 B.C. Tishri began on October 1 (Parker; Horn and Wood say October 2) and Epiphi on October 2, so that this close synchronism confirms the suggested year date. In 421 Tishri began on October 12 and Epiphi on October 2, which would seem to rule out that year.

דריוהוש. The long form is used here, in contrast to 6:1. The last two letters of the name were on a separate fragment that fits perfectly here. After the ruler's name must have stood the word **מלכא**, "king," and the word **אדין**.

[ב]יב. A trace of the preposition is still visible before the name.

ענניה בר חגי. The groom is called that plus **בר משלם** in 10:8, etc.; in the endorsement of a lost papyrus, No. 15, he is Ananiah b. Meshullam. 12:2 adds **בסס** to his pedigree.

2. He is an "Aramaean of Yeb," not of Syene, which proves that the term is not restricted to the latter place. He thus had a house there and was Aramaic-speaking or attached to that ethnic group (see above, Ch. 4). Before **דגל** the preposition **ל** must be supplied. Since the word **נבו** . . . appears on the adjoining piece, one may readily fill in [אדין] on the basis of *A.P.* 20:2 (cf. *A.P.* 67:1).

מ[שלם]. The name can be filled in with certainty; cf. l. 44. He is the son of **משלם בר זכור**; cf. Nos. 2 and 5.

[ארמ]י can be supplied. His father was so described in *A.P.* 13:3.

זי סון. This man and his father are described as of Syene rather than Yeb. After Meshullam sold his house in Yeb (*A.P.* 13), he must have resided on the east shore rather than at Yeb.

דכם (**זכם** in *A.P.* 9:2; 20:4; 65:3); cf. L § 14k, r. This is a strengthened form of the demonstrative, used as an adjective. One could thus live either in Yeb or in Syene and yet belong to the same *degel*.

3. The fragments placed here restore the connection with only a few letters missing. [א]תית is followed by [בית] עֲל. In *A.P.* 15:3 and above in No. 2:3 no preposition was used; but cf. *A.P.* 5:2. See also the fuller phraseology of No. 11:2.

ושאלת. A different phraseology is used in this case than in *A.P.* 15:3 or above in 2:3.

לנשן. See below on 12:1. The preposition here indicates the object.

שמה after her name reveals that she does not have "free" status. On this see on 2:3.

אחתך. See the remarks in the introduction above.

לאנתו. Cf. on 2:3.

ויהבתה is here the 2d pers. sing. with suffix.

4. The familiar formula, as in *A.P.* 15:4 and above, 2:3–4. A fragment with the required בעל[ה] was successfully placed here.

מניומא. The two words have been closely joined with others, as is the case a number of times in these papyri; cf. מנעל, עלדבר.

ויהבת, here 1st pers. sing. perf.

5. The mohar, "price" (really a present), was also mentioned in *A.P.* 15:4, but is not found in 2:3. The amount paid is not preserved. From *A.P.* 15, where it was 5 shekels, one would look for a shekel figure, but on the edge of the broken piece there are traces of the bottoms of two letters which could not have been those in 1 שקל but could only have been כרש. Probably a numeral 1 followed the word; there is no room for more numeral strokes. Yehoyishma's mohar was thus twice that of Mibṭaḥiah. The mohar was naturally higher for virgins than for widows or divorcees. According to Kethub. 10b, 200 *zuz* were the mohar for a virgin, while 100 were given for the widow (in Roman times). This may be the explanation in Yehoyishma's case. Cf. the introductory remarks.

על עליך, sc. "the mohar." It must have been followed, as in *A.P.* 15:5, by וטב לבבך בגו. The last letter of [בג]ו still remains on the edge of the break.

הנעלת לי. Cf. on 2:4.

The property the bride brings into the marriage is now itemized.

תכונה is already in *A.P.* 15:6, not in J.A. or Syriac. In Nah. 2:10 it means the stock or supply of silver and gold. We have rendered "substance," but *assets* might be more correct. It is not clear whether the word includes the items subsequently listed. From l. 15 we can see that תכונה did not include the mohar or the bronze vessels; in l. 23 the clothes are separate from it and are apparently to be grouped with the נכסיא. In l. 27 קנין, נכסיא, תכונה are the three varieties of her possessions.

In general consult Millar Burrows, *The Basis of Israelite Marriage* (New Haven, 1938) on the *mohar* and related matters.

6. In the gap between תרין and the next piece stood ש[קל]ן, part of the first letter still being visible. The two numeral strokes and ן are on the fragment put there.

חלרן. The first two letters are faint.

The itemization of other possessions now follows without any transitional phrase. לבש, "garment," is put first, as in *A.P.* 15:7. The numerals indicating the quantity follow the words and are put before any elucidating phrase; so here: "garment 1 of wool."

קמר, Hebrew צמר (on ק for the Primitive Semitic dental spirant, see L § 2m), was found in *A.P.* 20:5, 36:3; 42:9. In *A.P.* 15:7, 10, it appeared as עמר, the alternate and younger development.

חד[ת]. The ת is missing, but may be confidently supplied.

The cubit specification is introduced by the preposition ל. Length is mentioned first.

פשכן, pl. "handbreadths," already in *A.P.* 26:10 f.; 36:2; 79:2. The word פשכא, *puškā*, is known from J.A.; cf. L § 43t[1].

פתי is introductory to the width figures.

7. The ר must be a different subdivision of the cubit than the פשכא, handbreadth. The cubit was six handbreadths. ר may stand for "foot," i. e., 1/3 of the large cubit.

שוה, as in *A.P.* 15:8 f. Participle of שוה, "to be equal to, worth." This stands for estimated value, the goods evidently being home-woven. Where an object has been bought for money the word דמן is used.

The garment had a karsh figure — the word was successfully placed here — doubtlessly followed by a 1 and then "two shekels."

גמירה (st. emph.?; note masc. adjectives that follow), is also a term for a garment, etymologically from גמר, "to be complete." (Cf. the coat without seam, "woven from the top throughout," John 19:23.) The word is a new one for the papyri. The word "width" is not employed in giving the dimensions of this item, but instead the preposition ב is used.

8. חטיב צבע ידין. The phrase modifies גמירה, as it did in *A.P.* 15:7 (where חטב was written; our passage shows the correct vocalization as a pass. part.). On חטב Cowley already adduced Prov. 7:16, where חטבות is taken as "striped cloths," and referred to J.A. חטב "to embroider." צבע in J.A. is "wet, immerse, dye"; cf. Assyrian *ṣibū*, "dye." But this is probably the noun צבעא in the accusative of specification after חט(י)ב, "stained with dye." Dan. 4:12, etc., uses צבע for "wet with the dew of heaven."

ידין. Cowley took this to mean "on both sides." Left and right? Or obverse and reverse? If it were not for the next word one could take צבע ידין as "finger of the hands"; cf. II Sam. 21:20.

פשך 1 לפם 1. This is a specification not previously found. I take it to mean that it was dyed to the width of one handbreadth on one edge (literally, mouth). A fragment belonging here and giving the word could be supplied.

לבש 1 מעדר (מעדדר?). The second word is probably from עדר. It could be pael or aphel part. "hacked?" i. e., "flounced?" or "damaged?"

The א of [א]מן has to be supplied, though a piece of it is still visible. In the difficult job of joining the fragments, the line got down a bit too low. The words that follow are legible, though the bottoms are broken off. This was evidently not a homemade dress but a bought one, since its "price" rather than its "worth" is specified. Compared to the preceding ones, it is less expensive. (They run 12 shekels, 10 shekels, 7 shekels)

9. שביט. The word was already known from *A.P.* 15:9. Cowley took it as signifying a "closely woven stuff" etymologically, but as being a trade term for a

"shawl" of some kind. The small piece with חדת placed here must belong here, judging from the texture, but there was a gap of about six letters before it. The texture of the papyrus governed the placement; perhaps שביט [1 זי קמר]. In *A.P.* 15:19 this particular article is 8 x 5 cubits and worth 8 shekels. The fragments with the dimensions, which were placed here from the texture of the papyrus, provide a size of 6 x 3(+ – –) cubits. *R.* 2 on the narrow strip on the left presumably is the end of the width measurement.

10. צבען 2 means "two finger(breadths)," as in *A.P.* 26:16 f. The colored edging thus was narrower on this than on the other garment. Fragments that could be placed here show the value of 8 shekels. There followed mention of a garment לב[ש], succeeded, no doubt, by the numeral 1 and a word of which traces are still visible on the fragment at the left. The first letter was ב; one is tempted to guess it was בוץ, "byssus." The word in the strip is probably שוה (though the ה looks a bit unnatural).

11. שנטא. Note the use of the article in contrast to the other objects. This is seemingly a new word. Cf. Babylonian *šinṭu* (from *šamāṭu*), described in a word list as *šipatu*, which word, in turn, is used also of "fur," "wool," "dyed material," etc. It must have been a term for a dress; the material is specified as כתן, "linen." Is the כתון שטטן of *A.P.* 42:8 related? The word "length" could be placed here, but the dimensions are missing. The piece that has been joined to the thin strip gives שוה כסף, "worth silver," while the strip has שק[לן]. The rest of the line is missing. In addition to giving the number of shekels, the line must have introduced a new object, the dimensions of which continue in l. 12. Garments of linen were the regular thing in Egypt, Herodotus II, 36.

12. The ש at the edge of the break could be filled out with the help of the traces on the fragment above to make שוה. There are 4 cm. missing and traces of a word which was followed by כתן 1, "of linen, 1."

. . . בליה, *A.P.* 26:1, בלא[ה], perhaps "well worn," not necessarily "worn out." Another adjective seems to have followed, because of the ו in the narrow strip.

The first line of the fragment of four lines on the left which has been placed here continues l. 12. Before כסף one may guess that there was a [ד]מי; the lower parts of the last two letters remain. The top of the ל of שקל is cut off; the stroke following it is not ן but the numeral 1. This completes the 8 items required by l. 13.

13. The itemized articles of clothing are now summed up.

וכתן. The last two letters of the word were supplied by a fragment belonging here. This is followed by an 8 with a superimposed 4. Does this raise the 8 to 12?

מאני נחש, "vessels (i. e., objects) of bronze," is apparently introductory to the series of items that follow. The phrase also occurs in *A.P.* 20:5.

מחזי; apparently נחש was not repeated after this word. The fragment attached here by physical indications has bottoms of these letters, but the last could not be ש. Perhaps a numeral followed by דמי.

In the thin strip are the first two letters of כס[ף]. Presumably שקל and a numeral followed in the gap. A numeral stroke appears on the edge of the piece on the left.

תמסא starts the next item. This word should be read also in *A.P.* 15:12, where Cowley read תמ[חי] and Lidzbarski, *Ephemeris*, *3*, 131, תמ[ני]. The papyrus *A.P.* 15 was not smoothed out properly here when it was relaxed, and hence the last two letters are not clearly visible. In תמסא the א must be part of the word, which is evidently feminine, as *A.P.* 15:12 shows, where it is followed by שויה, part. fem. It is comparable to, though not identical with, Assyrian *namsītu*, "bowl," which can be of *siparri* (bronze). That is the requirement here. We have rendered "dish" to vary from זלוע.

14. כס, "cup." The singular is found also in *A.P.* 61:4, 14. The numerals and denomination (shekels and ḥallur) are missing. The top of the ל of "shekel" is visible on the lower edge of the piece. In the thin strip the two letters כס are probably not the remains of כסף, as in the line above, but mean "cup," for the word follows closely in the adjoining piece; there doubtlessly was a numeral, followed by דמי[. According to Herodotus II, 37 the Egyptians drank from cups of bronze.

15. זלוע, as in *A.P.* 15:13; 36:4, "bowl." The word is found in J.A. in the sense of "jar"; cf. Targ. Jer. 19:1. But that may be a late development. Above the line, after the price of the bowl are the letters –אנ–. Before them a trace of ל remains. [כל מ]אני נחש]? Perhaps the total number of bronze objects was given here.

At this point must have followed a general concluding statement. Something like כל כספא ודמי נכסיא ומאני (cf. *A.P.* 15:13 f.), which is needed to lead over to [נ]חש. The latter word is in the narrow vertical strip. It was followed by ותכ[ו]נתא (a piece completing the word could be placed) and מהרא. We thus are in an appraisal of the total assets, including the mohar, which evidently became part of the bride's capital — for Semitic custom an important point, not hitherto clarified.

16. The 7 karsh were no doubt followed by 7 הו. Part of [ש]ק[ל]ן. is preserved (see the nun in the next word); תמניה, "eight," is followed by הו and the numerals for 8, one of which is lost in the break between the narrow strip and the fragment with a single numeral stroke on the left. Since the cash portion of her תכונה is given in l. 6 as 2 karsh, 2 shekels, 5 ḥallur, 5 karsh and 6 shekels remain for the rest.

17. As in *A.P.* 15:15, a supplementary list of items follows — presumably those not fitting the previous twofold classification of apparel and bronze objects.

קוף suggests קופא, "needle's eye" (or eyed needle?), or Akkadian *ḳūpū* — a "stiletto" or the like. A different line of thought suggests itself if one links with קפה, "container," Akkadian *ḳuppu* (so Rosenthal).

חוצן. In *A.P.* 15:16 there is a חצן, in the phrase פרכס 1 זי חצן חדת, but in *A.P.* 20:6 a חוצן, as here, but in a connection where vessels or instruments of different substances are enumerated: מאני עק וחוצן. Cowley took the latter word to mean "ivory" (that would go well in the present case also with "needle"!) on the basis of Arabic *ḥiḍn*. The *ḍ* could only have become צ, if it passed into Aramaic via Babylonian

or Canaanite, as Rosenthal observes. Quite probably חוצן is plural (cf. L § 430). But Nöldeke's rendering "palm leaves" would fit only if one takes קוף as "container."

תחת לבשיה; the preposition תחת must mean "for" here, as perhaps also in l. 19. "Under" gives no sense here.

לבשיה was happily completed by the placement of a fragment belonging here. The ה is now spread apart too far.

In the narrow strip there is part of a ת. Since the next words are זי גמא, one is reminded of the phrase שוי זי גמא in *A.P.* 15:15, which here may have been written תוי. (Or was there reference to a תבת גמא, cf. Exod. 2:3, a box made of reeds? If it was written תבא, that would be possible.) Cowley linked שוי with the J.A. word for "bed," שויא, *šiwāyyā*.

18. It is described as "new" and בה "on it" are נעבצן זי אבן, exactly as in *A.P.* 15:15, where the guess is ventured that נעבצן means "feet" of the supposed "bed." Felix Perles, *OLZ*, *11*, 1908, 28, would connect the word with the Assyrian root *ḫabāṣu*, "to swell up," in the sense of "projections," but no such noun is known. The word must be from the root known from J.A. עבץ, "to grow pale," from which עבצא, "tin," is derived. Perhaps "inlays?"

שש. In *A.P.* 15:15 there were only four נעבצן. That passage shows that שש is a numeral and not "alabaster" or "byssus" (שיש). In the middle l. 18 a number of fragments were successfully placed on the basis of color, fiber, etc., but the connection remains obscure. . . . מין is only part of a word. Note how the letters continue into the piece below. זלועין, "bowls," as in l. 15. The numeral 2 follows.

פיק, already in 2:6; the phrase in *A.P.* 15:16 is פק 1 זי סלק; the space and the remains of the letters permit restoring זי סלק here, but the numeral 2 followed in the narrow strip. On the left edge of the strip and continuing into the adjoining piece was בגו, "thereon (was)". Then came ידה — or ירה. It has the numeral 1 after it. For פיק one thinks of the J.A. word for "lump." That would suggest a metal. Or may one connect with Assyrian *pāḳu*, "be firm," "be locked"? If "chest" were meant צירה, "hinge" (cf. *A.P.* 30:10) in the emph. or with suff. may be the word after בגו. For סלק words containing the root סלק in a variety of meanings do not help. "The value of 1 *slq* suggests it here is a denomination of money.

19. כפן. Cowley suggested *kappīn* (pl. of כף), "ladles," which also can mean "bowls." The word should not be connected with the preceding words, either here or in *A.P.* 15:16, but constitutes a fresh item. It is continued by למנשא, inf., "to lift up, carry."

The word after משח זי is lost. One would like to supply [זית]; cf. l. 20. The numeral 1 after the break goes with the following: "(2+)1" — for two strokes are lost, as the subsequent total shows — "of wood, 2 of stone, in all 5," the whole being an elaboration of כפן.

עק as in *A.P.* 20:5, etc. Hebrew עץ; cf. L § 21.

In אבן the second letter is faint. I read 5 בכל, though the letters are faint. This shows that two number strokes preceded the 1 before זי עק. There are traces of a letter in the narrow strip — probably ת. It was a short word, giving another item (cf. the one in l. 18 also beginning with ת). It was followed by a זי, still partly visible, before 1 עק.

תחת חמדיה. Perhaps the word is חמידין, "valuables," equivalent to Hebrew חמודות; cf. Dan. 9:23, Ezra 8:27. The preposition תחת may mean "for" as in l. 17, though "under" is possible if the word means "its adornment," or the like.

20. שנן זי צל פרסין would seem to start a new item. In *A.P.* 15:16 there is a שנן משאן 1, as also in 2:5 above. The word צל permits a connection with J.A. צלא, "skin," "leather." In *A.P.* 37:10 we hear of משכי צל, which Driver, *JRAS*, 1932, 80, connects with Assyrian *mašak ṣalli*, "leather wallet" (?). Is שנן then a container or vessel? Is פרסין the measure פרס (see on 11:3) and to be taken as a dual? "A leather container of 2 peras"?

משׁ[ח]. The word would seem to start a new item. Standing alone, as in Ezra 6:9; 7:22, it is evidently ordinary oil. The letters on the adjoining pieces successfully put here were followed by the numeral 2. Perhaps חפנן 2?

משח זית, the first of two special varieties of oil.

חפנן, the pl. of חפן. See on 2:6.

The next משח extends over the narrow strip. The fragment adjoining on the left has a letter מ. In the gap after it one whole letter and the greater part of another (probably a ש) are missing. I restore מ[בש]ים, and connect it with בשם, "balsam," which appeared in 2:5 and in the papyri from Ṭuna-el-Gebel (see Kamil, *BIE*, *28*, 1947, 256). Scented oil may be meant (cf. Palmyrene משח בשימא, referred to in the note on 2:5). Is מבשים an Assyrian loan word, *mubaššim* (*bšm*, II,1 part.)?

On תקם see the notes on 2:6. It is directly followed by the measure 5 חפנן, and thus seems to be an oil or ointment, or a container for such.

21. The added items terminate abruptly. The terms of the agreement start with מחר. The letter ם of יו[ם] is missing, and the ר of אח[ר]ן. The divorce problem is regulated here before the mortality contingency (in *A.P.* 15 the reverse is the case).

בעדה, to "rise up" is to initiate legal action, and seems to be said only of a man's role. See on 2:7.

וי[א]מר. Parts of the letters bracketed are still visible.

שני[ת]. Cf. l. 25. The form found in *A.P.* 15:23, 27, is שנאת. Cf. L. § 42b. On the implication see above on 2:7.

22. The form אנתת here is in the absolute, not in the construct as in *A.P.* 63:2 or the contracted form אתת of *A.P.* 34:4. Our text here is more vivid than *A.P.* 15:23, where the direct quotation used in divorce is not given.

ש[נא]ה must be restored here, the phrase being as in *A.P.* 15:23. On the rendering "the divorce money is on his head" see on 2:8.

As in No. 2:8 and *A.P.* 15:25, the wife gets back what she brought along when she entered the man's house. The preposition ב before "house" is unmistakable. One must imagine a comma after לה.

The phrases that follow specify two groups of things brought in and their total value. תכונה, "substance," here is evidently comprehensive for all assets, including the mohar, but excluding wearing apparel which is covered by לבשיה.

23. דמי is grammatically an accusative.

כלר[ש]ן parts of the bracketed letters are still visible.

It does not seem that numerals were used here, as the piece is too small, and the trace of the next letter remaining on the edge of the break suggests ש. We may fill in [5 ש]קלן תמניה חלרן.

ושא[א]רת; the א must be restored. The "rest of the goods," etc., covers the additions of ll. 17–21, where no monetary value was given. Those, too, are returnable.

24. Oddly the scribe does not use the phrase found in 2:10 and *A.P.* 15:25, מן חם עד חוט, but he has the other phrase found in *A.P.* 15:28, ביום 1 בכף 1. On בכף 1 Peiser, *OLZ*, *10*, 1907, 617, compared the Assyrian idiom *ina eštēnit retti*, "at one time." Before תהך a waw is missing.

אן was put in the gap here solely on the basis of the color and fibers of the papyrus on the reverse side. The stroke of the nun continuing to the edge of the piece below confirms the placement. One should restore after *A.P.* 15:29: אן [זי צבית]. But before אן more is missing than the לה offered by that passage, though there is not room enough for the phrase, "to her father's house," l. 28.

The eventuality of the husband's desiring a divorce is considered first here, whereas in *A.P.* 15:22 the woman preceded.

והן יה[וי]ש[מע]. The feet of the first three letters are visible. The name is readily restored.

25. שני[ת]ך. The formula here is very interesting. It is not the exact reverse of the one in l. 22, which would read: "Not shalt thou be to me a husband" but rather "Not will I be to thee a wife." The "patriarchal" position of the male is implied (cf. Hos. 2:4).

מהרה יאבד, "his (or her?) mohar is lost." In *A.P.* 15:23 f. nothing was said about the loss of the mohar if the woman divorces. It was mentioned in l. 27 only in connection with the man's divorcing, and there must certainly refer to its forfeiture by him. Presumably it also does so in this case.

26. תתב על מוזנא. The sentence differs only slightly from *A.P.* 15:23–4. We cannot agree with Cowley's rendering, "she shall return to the scales," for על in the sense of אל is not to be expected here. Nöldeke rendered "she shall sit *beside* the scales," which is probably correct. Personal presence is essential. Cf. this nuance in the case of Akkadian *ašābu*, M. San Nicolò and A. Ungnad, *Neubabylonische Rechts und Verwaltungsurkunden*, 737.

ותנתן. In *A.P.* 15:24 ותתקל, "and she shall weigh out," was used.

ל+[ב]עׄלׄה, the fragment with the word could be placed in the break before the husband's name.

The feet of the letters of שקלן and the numeral signs are missing but it cannot be in doubt that 7 shekels were specified. However, there are traces of the top of a letter ר after the seventh numeral stroke. It was no doubt followed by two numeral strokes. The figure thus is exactly that of *A.P.* 15:24: 7 shekels, 2 *R.* This cannot be the returned mohar, but is rather the כסף שנאה (see above in the general comments) and was evidently the customary figure.

שארת תכונתה is the balance of her cash assets after deduction of the 7 shekels, 2 *R.*

27. וקנ[ינה]. The word occured in *A.P.* 15:19 f. Perhaps בדמי followed in the gap.

In the gap there must have stood a repetition of what was given in l. 16: 7 karsh, 8 shekels, 5 ḥallur.

שארת, etc. This refers to the supplementary items of נכסיא of ll. 17–18.

28. ביו[ם 1]. Part of the word is on the small fragment placed here.

Does the בית אבוה on the central fragment mean the house of Meshullam b. Zakkur now presided over by Zakkur b. Meshullam, or the house of Ananiah b. Azariah? The scribe probably just repeated the familiar phraseology without reflecting on that problem.

Another fragment that was placed next to the central one, on the basis of texture and color when the papyrus was reversed before sealing, providing the rest of the last letter of אבוה and the beginning of the next word which may be reconstructed as וה[ן], "and if." The thin strip, which extended down from the top as a valuable guide for the number of lines and the anchoring of the fragments, was broken up here. A number of pieces seemingly belonging to it are preserved, but all efforts to place them proved fruitless, except perhaps, for the one put with ll. 31–32. The others will be found on pl. XVIII, Nos. 2, 10, 11, 22. But the space is not satisfactorily filled up by וה[ן], and so מחר may have followed. But fragment 22, which one would like to place here, does not fit.

ימות is conditional, even without הן. See 2:11, etc.

בר is used here in the sense of "child." The whole phrase is found in *A.P.* 15:17–18.

29. לאיתי for לא איתי (the latter spelling below in ll. 34–35, as in *A.P.* 15:18). The small fragment after לה provided the missing preposition מן.

[יהוי]שמע. The missing letters can be supplied with certainty. The small fragment put next has the missing final consonant of the next יהוישמע and the הי, required by the sense. The thought is that she will inherit him, or have power over what he leaves. One naturally looks for the same verb to express this that appears below in the fragment l. 35 and in *A.P.* 15:21 (ירת).

But the next word is חדתה – – or חרתה – –? Perhaps [בא]חדתה, "his possessions." The word would be new to the papyri but is known from J.A. A ב must have

preceded because there is one before "his house." In the gap [שליטה] can be supplied as a guess.

בביתה. While the first two letters are very faint on the bottom, they may still be discerned.

ונכסוהי. The word is very faint but unmistakable. The preposition is not repeated before it.

30. Only the tops of some letters of וקנ[ינה] are visible at the beginning of the line. No doubt זי אית לה or something like it rounded out the sentence. The fragment put in the middle contains for this line only [י]קום ע[נ]ניה; [על אנתתה] may have followed these words; there is hardly enough space for the woman's name, as in *A.P.* 15:29.

לתרכותה. This is a different situation than divorce, as already noted on 2:14. Ejection from his house is put under a stiff penalty. Before this word the fragment on pl. xviii, No. 23 was loosely attached, if I remember rightly, but I could not make it fit.

31. The first part of this line is missing. Traces of the bottoms of some letters appear on the piece below at the right. On the middle fragment we read ה וכל – – זי אית [לה]. *A.P.* 15:30 has, "If he rise up against M. to drive her out from the house of A. and his goods and possessions." It seems likely that the missing part of the text ran similarly here. We may thus restore the first part of the line [ומן נכסוהי וקנינ]ה. One piece of the narrow strip fragments seems to fit here, as well as with the following line. It makes possible the restoration [ינ]תן ל[ה].

In the left-hand "column" the first word is [אבי]גדנא, "fine"; cf. above on 5:8.

32. The penalty of 20 karsh is agreed on. After באבני the word [מלכא] must be supplied, and the requisite space for it gives us the width of the gap to the next piece.

ויעבד. Here we seemingly meet new phraseology. Yet we may assert with confidence that it is not completely new and that it is the word which stood in *A.P.* 15:31, where Cowley restored ויע[די]. Actually then, the statement in *A.P.* 15:31 was ויע[בד]דין ספרא זנה. It would seem that the fragment from the thin strip with דין which has been placed in the gap after ויעבד enables us to restore this phraseology here. [לה] is then missing between the two words. One must render "he shall do to her" or "one shall do to her the law (i. e., the terms) of this document." In addition to paying the fine he must carry out the stipulations for regular divorce. In Ezra 7:26 we have the same terminology in the passive: דינה להוא מתעבד מנה, "Let judgment be executed speedily upon him" (מן in the sense of "upon," Isa. 53:5). The phrase עבד דין occurs in the sense of "executing punishment" in the passage quoted in Levy, *1*, 398, from Ber. 5b: "Is it thinkable that God should execute punishment in an unjust manner? (דעביד דינא בלא דינא)" But that nuance does not fit here, where the meaning must be to carry out the terms previously set forth.

Jacob Rabinowitz calls my attention to the survival of this sort of thing in much later times; see *Sepher Haschtaroth, Dokumentenbuch von Rabbi Jehudah ben Barsillai aus Barcelona*, C. J. Halberstamm, ed. (Berlin, 1898), No. 72, though the verbiage differs.

ולא דין. This remark, missing in the *A.P.* parallel, is important; there is to be no court action.

33. The first word of this line was לְהֵן. It introduces a qualification in the above situation. Before the gap there is –יה. Hence, יה[וישמע] must be restored. One can only guess what may have stood in the lacuna after the name. The first problem is the width of the available space. The fragment of the continuation of l. 33 center has been placed in proper vertical position below the fragment of ll. 30–32. Most of this blank space is needed to fill out the name of "[Yeh]oyishma," thus leaving space for two letters. On the right side of the fragment put next, there appear the lower portions of the letters הבעלה. After שליטה one may expect an infinitive with ל (cf. *A.P.* 9:9) and so one would like to have לבעלה (pael inf.), but the ה before it seems certain so one must suppose that we have here the haphel inf., though the haphel of this verb is not found in the J.A. nor is the equivalent hiphil in Hebrew attested. The haphel is often identical in meaning with the pael (BL § 76n). In J.A. the word means "cohabit with," and that may be the nuance here. A prohibition of marriage does not fit at this point, since the mention of divorce follows. Bigamy in any legal sense seems outside the pale of the probable. להבעלה is continued by –בעל אח. A fragment with the missing –רן could be placed here at the last moment. It also provides another word בׄרׄ, which probably is בר [מן], "except," and was then possibly followed by a בעלה, which is then suitably continued on the left by ענני. This surprising stipulation seems to indicate that an ejected wife was not yet divorced when she had collected the penalty for ejection. Or is the statement to be taken as a new one, having no connection with ejection? In that case polyandry could be implied.

A new conditional clause starts with והן. Yehoyishma is still the subject. Here the verb עבד is followed by כות, "thus" (as in *A.P.* 18:3; cf. on l. 42), No. 7:33, etc., כותא in Aḥ. 20.

34. שנאה is apparently pass. part. fem., "divorced she is."

יעבדון לה, "they shall do (apply) to her." The tops of the last two letters of the sentence visible on the central fragment, could fit אה (the slanting stroke being part of ה, which often projects considerably). One should then restore דין שנאה (cf. l. 39).

A new conditional sentence starts with תמות.

[יהוישמע]. The name certainly followed תמות and will fill the empty space fairly well.

וׄבׄרׄ [זכר]. In the left-hand column only the bottoms of a few letters appear on the right, but the words can be restored with certainty.

35. In this text the mortality statements have not been kept apart in as clean-cut a manner as in *A.P.* 15.

בע[לה] at the end of the right-hand column can readily be restored and must have been followed by a repetition of the man's name, ענני.

ירתנה, impf. with suff. 3d pers. fem. as in *A.P.* 15:21. See L § 38d. Derivatives of ירת passed from Aramaic into Assyrian (*yaritu* and *yaritūtu*); see Meissner, "Ein neubabylonischer Erbschaftsprozess," *AfO*, *11*, 1937, 153 f.

In the left-hand column a ה is discernible. It seems likely that it is the final letter of [בתכונת]ה, which would fill in the gap after ירתנה.

36. זי איתי[י] לה cannot be in doubt.

Another statement starts with אף ל[א]. Nothing remains of it except the word אנתה, "woman," on the central fragment, before which word are visible the bottoms of the letters קח– –. The first two words of the next line suggest that Anani was prohibited from taking another wife. The comparable statement in *A.P.* 15:31 f. suggests that the missing words were [יכהל ענני יל]קח. The space allows that number of letters.

After אנתה may have stood [אחרה להן יהוישמע אנתתה], which would lead over suitably to the opening words of l. 37. Cf. *A.P.* 15:32.

37. לה לאנתו. In his case, bigamy is forbidden, not extramarital relations. A new condition starts with הן יעבד. There is not space enough for a financial penalty as in *A.P.* 15:34. Three or four words are missing, the first was doubtlessly כות. The tip of a ל is visible above on the central fragment and perhaps the bottom of an ע, and that of a ה on the piece below: [ב]עׄלׄהׄ? The line inclines downward; the next partly legible word seems to be [שנ]אׄהי and it ended a sentence. Whatever else may have stood here, divorce was certainly the final upshot of it. שנאהי again in l. 40; 3d pers. sing. perf. with suff.?

A new statement starts with ואף.

38. The two imperfects are to be closely joined (see BL § 107j): "Not shall Ananiah be able to do דין." The question is: what is missing before ותרתין? In the allowable space there would appear to be room for only a short word. The solution is supplied by l. 40 where the comparable situation for the wife is considered. The missing word was וחדה. The word דין is construct; "once or twice" would not fit well here, though it might in l. 40.

מׄן. The word after תרתין is written on the "overlap," where the surface is rough, and hence did not turn out well; but it can hardly be in doubt.

נשי כנותה. It is not said who his colleagues were. Anani must have enjoyed a position where he has such. The husband is thus forbidden from cooperating with one or two women in legal action against his wife. What the occasion for such action might be is not stated. The reverse of this is in l. 40.

ליׄ[ה]וישמע. The thin strip contains the first two letters and the top of the third is visible on the adjoining piece.

39. לא יעבד כות. On כות, "thus," cf. on l. 33. This, in effect, means: "if he does not act according to the aforesaid stipulation."

After שנאה there must have been a הי (cf. l. 34) and a conjunction and ויעבד לה דין שנאה. The verb is a jussive; see BL § 78s. He has to carry out the law of divorce with respect to her. In *A.P.* 18:1 דין שנאה appeared and before the name Meshullak one must put ויעבד לה.

The reader who is following the text with the facsimile of the original will be puzzled by the piece now placed in the gap after שנאת. This will be discussed below on l. 41.

ואף [ל]א; the ל is missing in the break. A new point is introduced as in l. 36.

40. Yehoyishma's corresponding legal action is envisaged here, as above in ll. 33–34. What stood in the gap after חד ו? The parallel in l. 38 suggests that it was תרין. The piece now placed in the gap provides [ת]רין. This piece was put here for reasons discussed below on l. 41. The phrase goes with דין as in l. 33: "the judgment of 1 and 2." The wife cannot join forces with one or two men (presumably colleagues) in legal action against Anani. In the Greek marriage contract published by Rubensohn, *Elephantine Papyri*, No. 1, ll. 7–9, three men on whom both parties agree function as judges before whom husband or wife must prove their accusations.

תע[ב]ד. The ב has crumbled away along with much of the ד, and so the letters have had to be drawn together too closely, while initial ת was spread too far apart. The meaning must be as in l. 32. There is a לה here, however, so that the matter is personalized, "If she does not act thus with reference to him."

שנאתי. Cf. l. 40. The perf. seems difficult here. Could this be a part. with object suff.? Cf. Aḥ. 167, L § 30b.

אף לא again introduces a new point, as in ll. 36, 39.

41. זכור, the brother of Yehoyishma, to whom Anani speaks in l. 3.

יאמ̇ר̇. The bottom of the last two letters has been chipped off.

לא[חתה]. The third letter, from its remnant, would appear to have been ח. The reference can only have been to his sister (l. 3). However, one must render ל "of" and not "to," for he does not address his sister in what follows.

The size of the gap is governed by the fragment placed in l. 43.

It would be possible to restore the text in l. 41 by conjecture based on the fragment of the marriage contract, Sach. 6 (*A. P.* 18). On the uniqueness of that text in another respect see Chapter 5. Here we need only note that in ll. 1–2 of that fragment the revocation of נכסיא וכספא given the bride is ruled out in exactly the same manner. The missing word in No. 7:41 is therefore in all probability [נכ]ס̇י̇א. The final א still remains, with a trace of י before it and the foot of the ס.

However, the actual piece belonging here still exists. A three-line fragment has been put in the gap opposite ll. 39–41. This fragment was tried countless times in every conceivable place, but nowhere do three lines line up with it. At the last moment, when the document was reversed before being sealed, some fragments

could be placed "blindly," purely on the basis of fiber and color, and among them was this. In l. 40 this surprisingly gave the convincing reading [ת]דין. (I had looked for a connection requiring דין for this fragment in the area higher up, but it would fit nowhere.) It is obvious, however, that something is wrong with the two lines above [ת]דין, which do not fall into place and cannot pertain to the lines they are nearest to. The technical counsel was that the top portion was not separable from the lower. And yet, in my final revision, I cut this upper part off (on a photograph) and tried it below, opposite ll. 41–42. It fits here exactly and provides the correct text. The first letter on the fragment turns out to be a nun (when one connects it with the trace of a letter extending down from above). To the left of the נ was a כ, the extension of which appears faintly on the edge of the adjoining piece, while the next downward stroke is the base of the ס. Allowing room for the latter's extension to the left, the word נכסיא is actually regained. The piece also gives decisive aid in the line below. But how explain the fact that the upper piece seemingly hangs together at one point with the lower piece, as may be seen on the photograph and is still more apparent under the microscope? That something unusual has happened here, however, seems certain, because the bottoms of the letters of the upper half have been cut off. As we shall see, the cut-off portions appear below in l. 42. A broken-out lower piece has evidently been jammed into connection with a fragment from above.

ברחמן. A gift made "in affection" (see on 4:4) was not a contract and hence was revocable if that were not insured against. Note that only the נכסיא are mentioned here. In *A.P.* 18 also כספא! Apparently a substantial part of the bride's assets are gifts of her family — in this case of her brother Zakkur.

ליה –. The edge of the yodh is visible on the thin strip and part of the ה on the adjoining piece. They are joined more closely than in the original letter spacing of the undamaged text.

42. צבית אהנצל, as in *A.P.* 18:2–3 (cf. No. 9:10), where this whole phraseology was already found. The attempt to recover a gift at a later date was evidently often made and had to be guarded against. On אהנצל cf. L § 35h.

יאמ[ר]. The ר is only partly visible but certain. One may guess the word for "thus." Cowley in *A.P.* 18:3 read כזת, remarking that the ז is badly formed and that זת (= זאת) does not appear elsewhere in these texts, but that it can hardly be anything else. His reading should be corrected to כות, "thus." See above on l. 33.

When the piece of which we spoke in detail in the note on l. 41 is transferred into the gap below [ת]דין, it will be found that we here have the appropriate word כות, and that the missing feet of the letters appear on the fragment beneath (except for the long stroke of the ת which would have fallen in the vacant space at the left). The text of ll. 38–42 can thus be fully reconstructed.

ישתמע. Cf. *A.P.* 18:3, where the לה, however, referred to a fem. antecedent, while here it refers to Zakkur. The form is ethpeel, of שמע; see L § 34d.

חיב הו. The הו is on the narrow strip. In *A.P.* 18:3 a woman was the subject and so the phrase was חיבה הי (fem. part. act.? So L § 39b). Perhaps חיב and חיבה are pass. part., for the act. part. in *'ayin waw* verbs in B.A. is קאם (BL § 46m). Cf. pael part. pass. in 9:22. It is not clear whether a penalty was customary or whether only moral opprobrium was the consequence.

The scribal attestation follows now.

Ma'uziyah b. Nathan was the author also of *A.P.* 18, 20, and 25. In the first of these texts his grandfather's name Ananiah is added. In *A.P.* 33:2 his name is shortened to Ma'uzi, and he there is second on a list of petitioners.

43. The fragment with זכור on it could be fitted to the adjoining center "column." The conjunction ו also has to be supplied before the name and a trace of it is still visible on the edge of the papyrus on the right after חגי. That gives us the full line and establishes the width of the gap. It is interesting to note that two persons here gave directions, exactly as in *A.P.* 18:4. In *A.P.* 15:37 it is dubious who gave the directions to the scribe. There would be room for two names if [ספרא זנה] were left out: (אסחור ומחסיה בר ידניה). In No. 2 the scribe wrote without dictation.

Witnesses are then listed. They did not have to sign personally.

Haggai b. Shema'iah. Part of the first letter of his name is broken away. He was the scribe of our documents Nos. 3, 9, 10, 12; cf. on 3:23.

Yislaḥ b. – – was continued on the next line.

44. The last line in the right-hand column is broken away. Only the first word can be guessed: גדול, Gaddūl (cf. 2:15). Yislaḥ b. Gaddūl was mentioned as a witness in *A.P.* 25:19 (9th year of Darius II) and was one of the contracting parties in *A.P.* 29:2 (16th [?] year of Darius II), and is perhaps the addressee of No. 13. The Clermont-Ganneau Ostracon No. 152 seems to provide a female named Yislaḥ; see Dupont-Sommer, *Semitica*, *2*, 1949, 29 f.

One name of a witness is completely lost except for traces of two or three letters, the last a ל.

בר אצול. His first name is lost, but a trace of its final letter, probably an aleph, remains. He does not appear in the earlier papyri. On אצול cf. Hebrew אציל, "noble." *Aṣṣūl* is probably a hypocoristicon for אצליה, II Kings 22:3. הצול and חצול are different names.

Menaḥem b. Azariah. He was a witness in *A.P.* 20:17.

Yedoniah b. Gemariah was the leading citizen, as evidenced by *A.P.* 30:1, the treasurer who received temple moneys in *A.P.* 22:121, and the first of the five petitioners on the list in *A.P.* 33:1. Sachau and Meyer consider him to be the ethnarch of the Jewish colony, an idea opposed by Cowley, *A.P.* 111.

Some fragments of this text which could not be placed will be found on pl. XVIII. All except 1; 4; 8; 9; 12 (?); 20; 25; 31 seem to belong to this text.

The endorsement of the papyrus is not preserved.

PAPYRUS 8

PAPYRUS 8

(*Brooklyn* 47.218.96) 36.3 *cm.* x 30.8 *cm.*

THE document is dated October 22, 416 B.C. by the Babylonian calendar and September 22 by the Egyptian (see the notes on this disagreement). The former date is probably correct.

Uriah b. Maḥseiah, who had this document written by a scribe in Syene, is described as an "Aramaean of Syene," and Zakkur b. Meshullam, to whom he made out the deed, is given the same designation. The declaration is made "before Widrang, commander at Syene," who thus had a magisterial function in such legal matters. A new title appears here after his name: *hptḥpt'*. The scribe's name is Dwḥšn b. Nergal-ušēzib.

Uriah b. Maḥseiah is clearly identical with Uri b. Maḥseh mentioned in the name list published by Sachau as father of Didi (*A.P.* 23:14). He was then perhaps a brother of Mibṭaḥiah, the woman of whom we hear in the Sayce-Cowley papyri. Zakkur b. Meshullam was encountered in 5:12 and in 7:2, 43. He is the son of the Meshullam b. Zakkur who figured in Nos. 2 and 5 and in the transactions of *A.P.* 10 and 13 of 456 and 447 B.C.

Zakkur here gives (or transfers) a slave named Yedoniah to Uriah and writes him a document about it. A condition of this transfer was the slave's liberation. We may perhaps assume that the young boy (for such he doubtlessly was, since he had not been "marked" yet) was Zakkur's own child, begotten of the slave woman *Tḥw'*, after whom the child is called. For the son of the handmaiden is not described as son of his begetter but rather as son of his slave mother and is himself a slave. Even when liberated and acknowledged by his father, he bears his mother's name. Quite a number of Jewish names from the Elephantine colony are of this sort. In this way society kept track of people's origin and one can see readily that to set up a pedigree of all-male ancestral names was not merely a matter of curiosity and interest, but a proof of descent from a line of freemen.

In this document Uriah pledges both for himself and his heirs that Yedoniah will not be reduced to slave status again — an outward sign of which would be marking him. What the latter means is quite vividly set forth in *A.P.* 28 of the year 409 B.C., where we hear of two slaves, Petosiri and Belo, on whose hands (wrists?) a yodh is tattooed to the right of the Aramaic legend "belonging to Mibṭaḥiah."

The liberation takes on the form of adoption. Uriah repeatedly says of Yedoniah, "My son he shall be." Nothing is said, however, about his having any right of inheritance. If that were contemplated, one would expect it to be specified, as in the Babylonian adoption texts.

The grantor, Zakkur b. Meshullam, receives a guarantee from Uriah's side that Yedoniah will never be pressed into slave status again. If anyone attempts to do so, a fine of 30 karsh of silver is to be imposed on such a one and paid to Zakkur. The former owner is evidently considered damaged if his ex-slave is treated contrary to his intentions. In Lev. 27:5 20 shekels is the price of a male slave from five to twenty years of age. This conforms well with the situation prior to the 6th century B.C. The Babylonian documents show that in Neo-Babylonian times (i. e., the 6th century B.C.) the price of slaves doubled (coming to 50 shekels) and redoubled in Persian times (the 5th–4th centuries B.C.), at which time it was from 90 to 120 shekels (see I. Mendelsohn, *Slavery in the Ancient Near East*, 117 f.). The 30 karsh or 300 shekels thus represent at least a double indemnity, even on the basis of Persian period economic standards.

1 בׄ 6 לתשרי הו יום 22 לפאוני שנת 8 דריוהוש מלכא אדין בסון בירתא אמר

2 אוריה בר מחסיה ארמי זי סון קדם וידרנג הפתחפתא רב חילא זי סון לזכור בר משלם

3 ארמי זי סון קדם וידרנג הפתחפתא רב חילא זי סון לאמר ידניה שמה בר תחוא

עׄלׄימׄ[א ל]ךׄ

4 זי יהׄבת לי וספר כתבת לי עלא לא אכהל אנה אוריה ובר וברה לי אח ואחה לי ואיש

5 לי יכבשנהי עבד ברי יהוה אנה ובר וברה לי ואיש לי ואנש אחרן לא שליטן

6 למשנתה לא אכהל אנה ובר וברה לי אח ואחה לי ואיש לי נקום למעבדה עׄ[בד]

7 ולמשנתה זי יקום על ידניה זך למשנתה ולמעבדה עבד ינתן לך אביגדן כסף

8 כרשן תלתין במתקלת מלכא כסף ור1 לעשרתא וידניה זך ברי יהוה אפם ואנש לא

9 שליט למשנתה ולמעבדה עבד להן ברי יהוה כתב דוחשן בר נרגלשזב כפם אוריה

10 שהדיא בגו עתרמלכי בר קלקלן סנכשׂר בר שבתי שהד עקב בר כפא

11 נבושלם בר ביתאלרעי אשמרם בר אשמשזב וריזת בר ביתאלזבד

12 חרמנתן בר פחא אשמזבד בר שוין

1. [On the] 6th of Tishri, that is the 22d day of Paoni (read: Mesore), the 8th year of Darius the king, at that time, in Syene the fortress, said
2. Uriah son of Maḥseiah, Aramaean of Syene, before Widrang, *hptḥpt'*, commander of Syene, to Zakkur son of Meshullam,
3. Aramaean of Syene, before Widrang, *hptḥpt'*, commander of Syene, saying: Yedoniah, by name, son of *Tḥw'*, [the servant of thine,]
4. whom thou didst give to me and a document thou didst write to me about it, I, Uriah — or a son or daughter of mine, or brother or sister of mine, or anyone
5. of mine — am not able to oppress him (again) as a slave. My son he shall be. I, or son or daughter of mine, or anyone of mine, or any other person, shall not have the power
6. to mark him. Nor shall I, or son or daughter of mine, or person of mine, be able to rise up to enslave him [as a slave]
7. and to mark him. Whoever shall rise up against that Yedoniah to mark him and enslave him as a slave shall give to thee a fine of silver,
8. thirty karsh by royal weight, silver 2 *R.* to the ten, and that Yedoniah shall still be my son, and no man
9. shall have power to mark him and enslave him as a slave; but my son he shall be. There has written this Dwḥšn (or Rwḥšn) b. Nergal-ušēzib at the dictation of Uriah.
10. Witnesses thereto: 'Atar-malki b. *Ḳlḳln*; Sin-kišir b. Šabbethai; witness: 'Aḳab b. *Kp'*;
11. Nabū-šallim b. Bethel-ro'i; Ešemram b. Ešem-šēzib; Warizath b. Bethel-zebed,
12. Ḥeremnathan b. *Pḥ'*; Ešemzebed b. *Šwyn*.

1. The stroke before the numerals is not a 10 but part of the prep. ב (cf. ב in רב, l. 3). The Aramaic form of the Egyptian month name Paoni was already known from *CIS*, *2*, No. 151 (*A.P.* 76:3), where, however, the first letter had to be restored by conjecture and where it was misread by the editor as Paophi. The reading was corrected by Lidzbarski, *Ephemeris*, *3*, 131, who also suggested reading the same word in the text now given in *A.P.* 20:1, where, however, there should be a waw in the bracket before [ני]. In our text we have the name fully and legibly written. Unfortunately the dates do not agree. The 6th of Tishri in 416 B.C. was October 22, while the 22d of Paoni was September 22. One must assume that the scribe erred in one of his month names. It seems more likely that he intended to write Epiphi for Paoni than that he confused Elul and Tishri. October 22 thus seems to be the correct date.

Darius can only be Darius II (424–404 B.C). The royal name is spelled in the regular manner — not as in an earlier papyrus from the reign of Darius I (dated 515 B.C.), where it appears as דרוש. Cf. Bauer-Meissner, 414 f.

2. Uriah b. Maḥseiah is doubtlessly identical with the Uri b. Maḥseh who is father of a man in a name list (*A.P.* 23:14).

In וידרנג we meet the same Persian leader who was so bitterly accused by the Jews in connection with the destruction of their temple. We shall meet him again in No. 13. The Persian name is explained by Andreas (see Lidzbarski, *Ephemeris*, *2*, 213) as equivalent to the *Vidarna* of the Behistun inscription, IX, 84, but as *vidranga* (Avestan *vi-drang*), "Entkräftiger," by Scheftelowitz, *Scripta Univ. atque Bibl. Hierosol.*, *1*, 13. Schaeder, *Beiträge*, 259, rejects all explanations offered. Bernhard Geiger holds *vidrang* to be the correct Iranian equivalent, but renders "having wide (far-reaching) firmness." Here he is described as commander of Syene, while in *A.P.* 27:4; 30:5, written some years later, he is *fratarak* at Yeb. Apparently Yeb was the real headquarters and so he had advanced to a higher post when these letters were written. A previous *fratarak* is mentioned in *A.P.* 20:4 (of 420 B.C.).

הפתחפתא is new, probably Persian. It seems likely to Geiger that it is a compound with Old Iranian *pati*, "lord" (cf. נופתא, "shipmaster," in *A.P.* 26:2 f.). But then, ‑הפתח can hardly be connected with *hapta*, "seven," on account of the guttural.

That Widrang was רב חילא was already known from *A.P.* 20:4; 25:2; 38:3. The first two of these texts were written in 420 and 415 B.C. The title is given as equivalent to *strategos* in a bilingual inscription from Asia Minor; see Lidzbarski, *Ephemeris*, *3*, 67 (if the text is correctly restored).

Zakkur b. Meshullam. Cf. the introduction to this papyrus. A Zakkur b. Shallum appears in *A.P.* 13:20, a Zachariah b. Meshullam in *A.P.* 8:30; 9:18, but they are probably different men.

Both Uriah and Zakkur are called Aramaeans of Syene.

3. ידניה. The name occurs frequently (cf. *A.P.* index). Note the fact that the boy has a Hebrew name. In Babylonian style the name of the slave is followed by the word "his name," i. e., "by name." The word is fully legible on the original but not so clear on the photograph. The mother's name תחויא is an Egyptian name; see Aimé-Giron, *Textes*, 73, No. 87:8, where it is given as תחא.

A piece is broken out of the margin of the papyrus at the end of l. 3, causing the loss of a word or two. The lower portions of three or four letters of the next word are visible and at the left the tail of a nun or kaph. Perhaps the last word was [ל]ך. Before it I restore עלימ[א]. The mark at the left of the ע belongs to the ל.

4. זי יהבת must be restored at the beginning. A sliver of papyrus running through these words is lost. Cf. L § 38d, g on the verb.

כתבת, 2d pers. sing.

עלא, "about it," as in *A.P.* 13:3, 10; 28:9; (43:5); cf. L § 61i.

לא אכהל begins a new clause. איש לי, "anyone of mine" — a person under his authority (as distinct from איש אחרן in l. 5).

5. יכבשנהי. The verb appears in Aḥ. 92, 152, in the participle. Here we have the impf. with nun energ. and the suffix. Cf. L § 31c. The verb is at home in the sphere of enslavement. Subduing of enemies for which כבש so often appears in the O.T. usually involved enslavement.

עבד, accusative of specification.

ברי יהוה, "my son he shall be." Cf. the adoption formula spoken directly: "My son art thou" (Ps. 2:6). In the Babylonian texts the formula is not quoted, but its reverse is given in the case of an annulment of the adoption: "Thou art not my son." Cf. Schorr, *Urkunden*, 21, No. 8:15, etc.

6. למשנתה. This is the first occurrence of the inf. with suff. of the verb שנת, "to mark, tattoo."

Neither Uriah nor any of those previously mentioned will be able to rise up; נקום, 1st pers. pl. impf. (cf. נחוב, *A.P.* 2:15).

למעבדה [עבד], inf. Peal with suff. The עבד supplied for the break in the papyrus seems certain in view of the repetition of the phrase in ll. 7 and 9. On an instance of reenslavement and renewed marking see Peiser, *Texte*, 245, No. 44, and the remarks of Mendelsohn, *Slavery in the Ancient Near East*, 83.

8. The violator of this shall have to pay Zakkur b. Meshullam a fine of 3 karsh.

מתקלת מלכא. This was already found in *A.P.* 28:11 (cf. with פרס, "Persia," *A.P.* 26:21). The more usual phrase is "by stones of the king." On the standard cf. above, Chapter 3.

After such an attempt *that* Yedoniah shall (still) be his son. The farther demonstrative serves to distinguish the slave boy as chattel.

אפם. Cf. on 4:16. "Still" seems to be the nuance here.

ואנש לא = "no man shall."

9. Once more emphatic reassurance: "but my son he shall be."

There follows the scribal attestation. The scribe is apparently a man of Babylonian origin.

דוחשן בר נרגלשזב. The first name is clearly written with ד (or ר) דוחשן or רוחשן. It seems likely that חשן -- is the Akkadian name element -- *aḫušunu*, "their brother"; *dū* or *rū* could be the final syllable of a verb. A deity Dū, the existence of which Clay, BEUP, *10*, 48 n., would infer from the parallelism of Du-u with Bel in the names *Du-u-iaḫabbe* and *Bēl iaḫabbi*, seems a bit uncertain. The father's name נרגלשזב may be *Nergal-(u)šēzib*, but it is also possible that it is shortened; see Tallqvist, *APN*, 172, *Nergal-suzib-a-ni* and *NBN*, 268, *Nergal-suzibanni*. In Dan. 3:15 etc. שיזב has become a common Aramaic word.

עתרמלכי בר קלקלן, a new individual. The first name was already found in 1:13. The name קלקלן is a formation with reduplication and suffix *-ān* (from קלל), and hence is Aramaic.

סנכשר בר שבתי. The first name, *Sin-kišir*, was already found in *A.P.* 6:19 (Peiser, *OLZ*, *10*, 1907, 625). Cowley read סנכשד, *Sin-kašid*, but *kišir* is a much more frequent element in the Babylonian names. See Tallqvist, *NBN*, 274, for both names. The father's name שבתי was found in *A.P.* 58:3. The same man? The name Shabbethai, Ezra 10:15, Neh. 8:7; 11:16, may be compared. The latter supposedly means "born on the Sabbath," Noth, *IP*, 222. Clay, BEUP, *10*, 62, lists a number of Babylonians with the name *Ša-ba-ta-ai* or *Šab-ba-ta-ai*.

עקב בר כפא. It is the perf. (or part.) of the same verb that appears in the impf. in יעקב, Jacob. In both cases we have hypocoristica — the full name must have been something like עקביה (on a 3d century B.C. inscription from Alexandria; see RÉS, *2*, No. 79) or עקבנבו, Aqab-Nebo, in *A.P.* 54:10. Tallqvist, *NBN*, 10, has an *Aḳabi-ia* and *Aḳabi-ilu*; others in BEUP, *10*, 39. The name כפא must also have a deity for a subject; J.A. כפא, "overthrows." Or may one compare *kf3*, Ranke, *ÄP*, 344:15?

נבושלם בר ביתאלרעי. The first, which is also found in *CIS*, *2*, 25, is either *Nabū-šallim(-aḫē)* or *Nabū-ušallim*, Tallqvist, *APN*, 158, 163. On ביתאלרעי cf. נבורעי, *A.P.* 14:12, 13, with which Peiser, *OLZ*, *10*, 1907, 626, compared the Assyrian name *Nabū-rēʾua*. Less certain is the explanation of *Nabū-ra-ḫi-i*, Clay, BEUP, *10*, 57. The Canaanitic רעי is used.

אשמרם בר אשמשזב; new אשם names! See Chapter 8. אשמרם, like אברם, contains the element רם, on which see Albright, "The Names Shaddai and Abram," *JBL*, *54*, 1935, 193 f., Noth, *IP*, 145, Baudissin, *Kyrios*, *3*, 77 f. On שזב see l. 9.

וריזת בר ביתאלזבד. The name וריזת was that of a *degel* in No. 2:3 and *A.P.* 5:2, 3, etc. It is Iranian; see Schaeder, *Beiträge*, 269. But his father has a Semitic name. On Bethel, see Chapter 8. The element זבד is typically Aramaic; see Noth, *IP*, 46 f. A ביתאלזבד בר אשמרם is found on a sarcophagus inscription from Saqqāra, Aimé-Giron, *Textes*, No. 110. Cf. such names as *Ilī-zabaddu*. Clay, BEUP, *10*, 52.

חרמנתן בר פחא. On Ḥerem, see above, chapter 9. The name חרמנתן was borne by another individual in *A.P.* 18:4, and Aimé-Giron, *Textes*, Nos. 97, 100, provides still two other men of that name from sarcophagi inscriptions. On the obviously Egyptian name פחא, which would appear to him masc., Ranke tentatively compares *ÄP* 115:9.

אשמזבד בר שוין, another new אשם name and a hitherto unknown name שוין. Probably hypocoristic — this being the predicate, pl. part. of שוה? Cf. also the name שוא in No. 13:1.

This list of witnesses, like that of No. 8, is illustrative of the "Aramaeans of Syene." Contrast such a Jewish list as that of No. 9.

The "endorsement" is not preserved.

PAPYRUS 9

PAPYRUS 9

(*Brooklyn* 47.218.92) 69.3 *cm.* x 30.9 *cm.*

THIS fine papyrus is dated in the first year of an Artaxerxes. Internal evidence makes it certain that this is not Artaxerxes I (464–425 B.C.) but Artaxerxes II (404–358 B.C.). The date must therefore be November 26, 404 B.C. In this document Anani — in the earlier texts usually called Ananiah, son of Azariah, *lḥn* of the god Yahu in Yeb — gives his daughter Yehoyishma a part of a house he had originally bought and paid for. Giving or selling part of a property to someone was not unusual, as has been pointed out in connection with No. 3. The portion is then described. The dimensions of the property are given as 8½ by 7 cubits and 98 cubits to the *'brt* (see the notes). After the measurements come the boundaries in terms of the adjacent properties. New and interesting is the reference to a structure on the east built by the Egyptians. The "house of *Ḳnḥnty*" is again referred to in No. 10:5, 6, as well as that of "the gardener of the god Khnum," Ḥor b. Petesi. The house of Ḥor was already mentioned in the fragmentary connection, 6:8. After assuring Yehoyishma that this house is hers and that she will have power over it, he describes some features of the building and specifies certain rights and privileges as to courtyard, gate, and stairs. The gift is to become entirely valid at Anani's death, and the reason for it is stated: she is taking care (or going to take care?) of her father in his old age. Once more he repeats that this gift shall become valid at his death. She is protected from lawsuits over the matter by a fine of 30 karsh, which anyone who brings action will have to pay. She and her children shall have power over it, or whoever she wills to give it. No other document is to be adduced. A battery of prominent witnesses follows. All except the last are mentioned in Elephantine papyri previously published.

1 ב 24 למרחשון הו יום 29 למסורע שנת 1 ארתחשס[ש] מלכא אדין אמר ענני בר עזריה

2 לחן ליהו אלהא ביב ברתא לנשן יהוישמע ברתה לאמר אנה עשתת לכי בחיי ויהבת

3 לכי קצת מן ביתי זי זבנת בכסף ודמוהי יהבתה לכי דרימיי הו מועה שמש מן

4 תרי רבתא זילי ופלג תרבצא הו פלג תחית מצדית ופלג דרגא ותחת מנה בית פרסא הו

5 זנה משחת ביתא זי אנה יהבת ליהוישמע ברתי ברחמן זנה משחת ביתא זי אנה ענני

6 יהבת ליהוישמע ברתי מן תחתיא לעליא אמן 8 ופלג בעשתא ומן מועה למערב

7 אמן 7 בעשתא לאברת אמן 98 בעשתא ופלג תרבצא ופלג דרגא ובית

8 פרסא פלגה והא תחומי ביתא זי אנה ענני יהבת ליהוישמע ברתי מועה שמש לה אגרא

9 זי הנפנא זי בנהו מצריא הו תמואנתי עליא לה בית קנחנתי דבק לה אגר באגר

10 תחתיא מנה אגר דרגא ובית חור בר פטאסי גנן זי חנום אלהא דבק לדרגא דך

11 מערב שמש לה אגר תרי רבתא זילך הי אנתי שליטה בה ביתא זנה זי משחת

12 ותחומוהי כתבן בספרא זנה אנה ענני בר עזריה יהבתה לך ברחמן מבני בי

13 תחתי אחד גשורן וכון בה 3 דש חד בה אחד ופתח אף שליטא אנתי בתחית

14 הו תרבצא שליטא למסמך דחה ומדשה בפלגא דילך אף שליטא אנת למנפק

15 בתרע זי תחית הו תרבצא אף שליטא אנתי בפלג דרגא למסלק ומנחת זנה

16 זנא ביתא זי תחומוהי ומשחתה כתיבן ומלוהי כתיבן בספרא זנה אנה ענני יהבתה
ליהוישמע

17 ברתי במותי ברחמן לקבל זי סבלתני ואנה ימין סב לא כהל הוית בידי וסבלתני אף אנה

18 יהבת לה במותי לא יכהל בר לי וברה לי הנגית זילי והנבג ואדרנג זילי ירשנכי דין

1. On the 24th of Marḥešwan, that is the 29th day of Mesore, the 1st year of Artaxerxes the king, at that time said Anani son of Azariah,
2. *lḥn* of Yahu, the god in Yeb the fortress, to the woman Yehoyishma, his daughter, saying: I have taken thought of thee in my life and I have given
3. to thee part of my house which I bought with silver and whose price I gave. I have given it to thee as my *drmy*. It is east of
4. the two compartments (?) of mine, and half the court, that is half the lower portion of the empty space (?) and half the stairs. And below it is the *beth parsa*.
5. These are the measurements of the house which I gave to Yehoyishma my daughter in affection. These are the measurements of the house which I Anani
6. gave to Yehoyishma my daughter. From the lower side to the upper it is 8 cubits and a half by the one(-cubit-measure), and from east to west
7. 7 cubits by the one(-cubit-measure), to the outside (?) 98 cubits by the one (-cubit-measure), and (in addition) half the court and half the stairs, and the
8. beth parsa, its half, And these are the boundaries of the house which I gave to Yehoyishma my daughter. East of it is the wall
9. of the *hnpn'* which the Egyptians built, that is the *tmw'nty*. Above it the house of *Ḳnḥnty* adjoins it wall to wall.
10. Below it is the wall of the staircase, and the house of Ḥor son of Petēsi, gardener of the god Khnum, adjoins that staircase.
11. West of it is the wall of the two compartments (?). Thine it is. Thou shalt have power over it. This house, of which the measurements
12. and its boundaries are written in this document, I, Anani son of Azariah, gave it to thee in affection. The construction of the lower
13. house has (?) beams, and there are 3 windows in it, one door is in it, shutting and opening. Moreover, thou shalt have power over the lower part —
14. that is the court — (thou shalt have) power to prop up what is knocked over and what is falling in thy half. Moreover, thou shalt have power to go forth
15. in the gate of the lower part, that is the court. Moreover, thou shalt have power over half the stairs to ascend and descend. This —
16. this (sic) — is the house whose boundaries and measurements are written and its words are written in this document. I, Anani, give it to Yehoyishma
17. my daughter at my death in affection, because she did maintain me when I was old in days and was not able (to work) with my hands, and she did maintain me. Moreover, I
18. give (it) to her at my death. Son of mine or daughter of mine, *hngyt* of mine or *hnbg* or *'drng* of mine, will not be able to start against thee suit

19 ודבב וירשה לבניכי אחריכי ויקבל עליכי לסגן ומרא ועל בניכי אחריכי זי ירשנכי דין

20 ודבב ויקבל עליכי ועל בניכי ינתן לכי אביגדן כסף כרשן 30 באבני מלכא כסף צריף
ואנתי

21 יהוישמע אם שליטה ובניכי שליטן אחריכי ולמן זי רחמתי תנתנן אף לא יכהילון ינפקון

22 עליכי ספר חדת ועטיק להן ספרא זנה זי אנה עבדת לכי הו מיחב כתב חגי בר שמעיה
ספרא

23 זנה ביב ברתא כפם ענני בר עזריה לחנא זי יהו אלהא שהדיא בגו שהד הושעיה בר

24 יתום זכור בר שלם שהד נתן בר יהואור שהד הושעיה בר נתן

25 שהד משלם בר מעוזי פלטי בר יאוש ישביה בר ידניה

26 שהד חגי בר מרדו

27 ספר בי זי כתב ענני בר עזריה לחנא ליהוישמע ברתה (Plate XIX, 5)

19. or action or start it against thy children after thee and bring complaint against thee before prefect or lord or against thy children after thee. Whoever shall start against thee suit
20. or action or bring complaint against thee or against thy children shall give thee a fine of 30 karsh of silver, royal weight, refined silver, and thou,
21. Yehoyishma, in addition shalt have power and thy children shall have power after thee and to whomsoever thou wilt thou shalt give it. Moreover, they shall not be able to bring forth
22. against thee a document, new or old, except this document which I made out to thee. Guilty he is. There wrote Haggai b. Shema'iah
23. this document in Yeb the fortress at the dictation of Anani b. Azariah, *lḥn* of Yahu the god. Witnesses thereto: witness, Hosha'iah b.
24. Yathom. Zakkur b. Shallum. Witness, Nathan b. Yeho'or. Witness, Hosha'iah b. Nathan.
25. Witness, Meshullam b. Ma'uzi. Palṭi b. Ye'ūsh. Yoshibiah b. Yedoniah.
26. Haggai b. Mardu.
27. Document concerning a house, which Anani b. Azariah the *lḥn* wrote to Yehoyishma his daughter.

1. Marḥešwan was already mentioned in *A.P.* 17:7; 30:30; 31:29; Mesore in *A.P.* 8:1; 9:1; 13:1; 29:1; 63:16. The 24th of Marḥešwan in the 1st year of Artaxerxes II (404 B.C.) was November 26; the 29th of Mesore was November 25.

In contrast to the earlier texts in which he generally used his full name Ananiah, the shorter form is now preferred. "Yahu, the god in Yeb the fortress"— not "the *lḥn* of Yahu, the god, (said) in Yeb the fortress." See above Chapter 8, n. 6.

2. נשן. Cf. below, 11:1.

עשתת. See on 5:3.

יהבת, 1st pers. sing. perf.

3. קצת, "part" (in *A.P.* 29:3, construct; cf. L § 55d and *A.P.* 27:4; 35:4). In *A.P.* 27:4 it is followed by מן as here.

יהבת was written a second time; the suffix had been forgotten and was added above the line.

There is an epigraphic difficulty in the word דדימיי. The fifth letter looks like a samekh, but if the fourth letter is מ, as seems probable (cf. e.g., the מ of שמש a few words later), the fifth cannot be ס but must be a yodh (it is impossible to read the suffix כי here). The word must be a foreign one, perhaps Iranian, and mean a kind of gift.

הו starts a sentence.

4. Here we meet the תרי רבתא of 4:3, 6; 10:6; 12:13, 21; cf. on 4:3.

הו פלג. The הו seems to be explanatory: "that is, half, etc."

תרבצא. Cf. above on 3:4.

תחית מצדית. The word תחית is distinct from תח(ו)ת, the preposition. It occurs again in ll. 13, 16; 6:13. מצדית (or מצרית) appeared already in the broken connection of 6:5. The formation suggests a derivative of a tert. inf. root or possibly an Akkadian loan word in *ītu*. In the latter sphere no exact equivalent of suitable meaning seems to be available. It would appear advisable, then, to abide by the Aramaic alternative. Could צדי (J.A., "be desolate") have had the nuance of "empty" and מצדית "space not built on"? From צרא (J.A., "tear") מצרית could suggest "cleft."

דרגא. See on 6:10 and cf. 10:3.

"Below is the בית פרסא." Since the property includes half of it (l. 8), it cannot be a major building. One might explain it also as connected with פרס, "portion," so that it could be a storage place for the ration of grain. Honroth and others, "Ausgrabungen," 20 give a photo of a barrel-like container, doubtless for grain, in the cellar of an early Ptolemaic house, but also mention an outbuilding in the corner of the court.

5. משחת. See above on 3:21; 4:12. זנה can be followed by a plural; see L § 14c.

ברחמן, i. e., as gratuitous gift; cf. on 4:4.

The writer makes a fresh start in זנה משחת, but the repetition omits the ברחמן.

6. One must imagine a colon before מן תחית.

7. אברת as in 4:7; 12:8, 16.

8. In addition there is half the court and half the stairs and the beth parsa, "its half." *Parsa* was left out and then written in the margin.

There now follows a description of the boundaries in terms of the adjoining properties. It begins with the east. אגרא here apparently means "wall" and clinches that meaning for the word, as a "roof" (J.A. איגרא) could not very well be an adjoining boundary. Cf. on No. 3:4.

9. "הנפנא which the Egyptians built, that is the תמואנתי." This is an interesting reference. The first word would be explained, according to Geiger, as an Iranian *han-pān(a)*, something like "shelter," a compound of *han-* and *pāna*, "protection." The second word would then presumably be the Egyptian equivalent, but no suggestion has been received concerning it. One wonders whether it has anything to do with a guardhouse. Its proximity to the treasury is referred to in 10:4.

בנוהו, error for בנוה (if הנפנא is fem.) or בנוהי? Defective spelling of the 3d pers. pl. without the suff. can hardly be assumed. Or a correction of בנה to בנו (so in 10:4!) with ה left in? (Rosenthal).

בית קנחנתי also in 10:5, where it would seem to be a personal name. Albright suggests interpreting this as **ḳn-ḫntj*, comparing the analogous *ḳn-'mn*, Ranke, *ÄP* 334:18, and the deity *ḫntj*, *ibid.*, 272. Ranke himself would adduce *ḳn-Ḥr(w)*, *ÄP*, 334:21, because it is a name found in late times.

10. Below is the wall of the staircase and another house adjoins those stairs.

חור בר פטאסי is a gardener of Khnum; cf. 6:8; 10:6. Both names are found in previous Aramaic papyri. See *A.P.* index and Aimé-Giron, *Textes*, index. The name Ḥor is doubtlessly shortened. See Spiegelberg, *Sprachgut*, 8 f. Petēsi, "the one whom Isis gives," *ibid.*, 11.

11. On the west there is the wall of the תרי רבתא; cf. l. 13. A new sentence begins with זילך (instead of זילכי; cf. ll. 12 and 14).

12. לך instead of the expected fem. לכי, as in 6:14.

A new sentence must begin with מבני, which would appear to mean "construction;" cf. Nos. 10:2, 3; 12:13, where this word must be a substantive. This usage of the infinitive confirms the hitherto unique instance of use without preceding preposition in Dan. 5:12 מפשר, משרא. See BL § 26i.

אחד seems to fit best here, as in 4:8, as an active participle: "holds (or has) beams." On כון see 3:5. The numerals go with this, though they follow בה.

13. דש here the singular — the plural דששן in 10:3; 12:13.

אחד ופתח, "holding (i. e., closing) and opening." On this meaning of אחד see Hebrew אחז in Neh. 7:3.

אף starts a new sentence.

14. The זה seems to introduce תרבצא (on final א as fem., see L § 44g) as explanatory of תחית.

שליטא (fem.) starts afresh, but without repetition of the אנתי.

למסמך, inf. of סמך, "support." A new verb for these texts.

דחה, presumably pass. part. of דחה, "to knock over"; the דחון of Dan. 6:19 may be related and is itself to be connected with late Hebrew דחוונות, "tables," an explanation already given by Rashi.

מדשה, doubtlessly from נדש, is a pass. part., intensive (or causative?); see L § 21k. The verb is found only as a peal in previous texts. Whether the final ה is the article or a suffix, "that of it which is thrown down," remains uncertain. A feminine seems unlikely in view of דחה. Explanations based on דשש or רשש are less likely. For a similar stipulation see Peiser, *Texte*, 223, No. 17:7.

דילך for דילכי; cf. above l. 11, זילך. Note the inconsistency of spelling.

אף again starts a new sentence.

שליטא אנת, regularly אנתי, as in the previous line.

15. תחית is again explained with הו תרבצה.

אף again starts a sentence.

16. Line 15 ends with זנה, l. 16 begins with זנא. It is a case of repetition, but oddly enough with different spelling.

זנא ביתא, "this (is) the house."

מלוהי, as in Aḥ. 43, 60, 114, but in the sense of "matters," as in Dan. 2:11, etc.

כתיבן is plural; cf. *A.P.* 2:11, 13; 18:2; 25:8.

17. במותי. The gift becomes fully realized only at his death.

לקבל is followed here by זי and initially means "because," as in Ezra 6:13. In previously published papyri the phrase means "according as"; cf. L § 63i.

סבלתני, a new form (3d pers. sing. fem. perf. with suff.) of a verb occurring in the Aḥiḳar text and Behistun inscription. See above, on 5:11. According to Herodotus II, 35 daughters in Egypt had a greater obligation than sons to take care of parents.

ואנה introduces a circumstantial clause; see BL § 107.

סב, a new spelling for the papyri, but סבא in Targum; cf. Gen. 24:2. *A.P.* Aḥ. 17 and B.A. spell it שב. On ש and ס see L § 2p, q. ואנה ימין סב, "when I am old in days." סב is peal participle. ימין is accusative of specification. Is סב ימין intentionally avoided? Cf. עתיק יומין, Dan. 7:9, etc. (עטיק here in l. 22!).

לא כהל is a new sentence; participle with auxiliary verb הוה, with the latter following in other persons than the third, BL § 81p. The second סבלתני concludes the short sentence, driving the matter home once more by a repetition.

אף אנה again starts a new sentence. The new declaration is not addressed to Yehoyishma but to others to whom this document may later be shown.

18. יהבת לה במותי, as in l. 17. The gift is fully validated only at his death. One misses a suffix after יהבת.

לא יכהל, new sentence. No son or daughter or other persons with conceivable

rights are to sue. Note the זילי after הנגית, which as usual is paired with הנבג; cf. 5:5; 10:12; 12:27. Here the latter word is continued by אדרנג or ארדנג, also followed by a זילי. The word אדרנג is new and is doubtlessly Iranian; it must have a meaning similar to that of הנבג and הנגית. Geiger explains it as *a-drang*, "with firm (close) association" connecting it with the root *drang–*, "to make firm," and compares Yasht 10:16, where a group called *supti-darenga*, which he renders approximately "(friends) having a firm shoulder association," occurs with two other groups, one of which is *haδōgaēϑa* (same word as הנגית). The name וידרנג is related. Cf. 10:12; 11:8, 9; 12:27.

ירשנכי. Cf. 10:12, *A.P.* 8:12. See L § 40 f.

דין ודבב. Cf. above, on 1:5.

ויקבל. This is not elaborated here as in 1:4 f.

אביגדן. Cf. above, on 5:8.

19. On יקבל עלי see on 1:4, here followed by ל.

סגן, originally "governor," "prefect" (Assyrian *šaknu*), retained in Persian use as shown by B.A. The Aramaic (or Hebrew?) form appears in a Neo-Babylonian letter as *saganu*. See Erich Ebeling, "Glossar zu den Neubabylonischen Briefen," *SBAW*, 1953, No. 1, 201. Apparently a district chief in charge of a foreign group, as shown by Eilers, *ZDMG*, *94*, 1940, 225 ff. The בנשיא of Clay, BEUP, *10*, No. 126, whose סגן *Bēl-uṣuršu* is mentioned, were Carians! On vocalizing *segēn* see L § 53b.

21. למן זי, "to whom"; cf. Dan. 4:14, etc., BL § 23a.

רחמתי, "thou pleasest," 2d pers. sing. fem. perf., BL § 33.

יכהילון. In *A.P.* 8:15; 20:11, etc., יכהלון. The verb is thus haphel and L § 33 needs correction.

ינפקון, haphel, with the *h* syncopated as in 10:15 and *A.P.* 13:12; contrast *A.P.* 8:17, יהנפקון.

22. עטיק also in 10:15; 12:29. In *A.P.* 8:16, עתיק; cf. 13:6, 12, as in B.A., Dan. 7:9, etc. In view of Arabic *'ataqa* the *ṭ* must be due to the influence of *ḳ*. But Carl Brockelmann, *Grundriss der Vergleichenden Grammatik der Semitischen Sprachen* (Berlin, 1908), *1*, 156 *d*, has no exact equivalent.

עבדת is unusual. A pael in the sense of "prepared"?

מיחב. Is this an error for מחב, the peal inf. of חוב? The inf. would then be a substantive, "guiltiness it is"; cf. Dan. 5:12. One prefers to render "guilty he is," but this would require a pass. part. (usually hithpaal). Rosenthal suggests a scribal error for מחיב. That might be the pael pass. part. See BL § 58g for examples.

On the scribe Haggai b. Shema'iah see 3:23.

23. Anani gets his full professional title, "*lḥn*," etc.

Hosha'iah b. Yathom, previously known from *A.P.* 33:4; 34:5.

24. Zakkur b. Shallum (or Shillem? See Noth, *IP*, 174), previously known from *A.P.* 13:20.

Nathan b. Yeho'or, previously known from *A.P.* 28:16.

Hosha'iah b. Nathan, previously known from *A.P.* 40:5.

25. Meshullam b. Ma'ūzi, previously known from *A.P.* 22:109.

Palṭi b. Ye'ūsh, previously known from *A.P.* 22:89 (40:5). On the name Ye'ūsh, "he bestows," see Noth, *IP*, 213. Driver, *ZAW*, *46*, 1928, 14 n.

Yoshibiah b. Yedoniah. The name Yoshibiah occurs in *A.P.* 7:2; 22:51, 59, 130; 38:1, but apparently does not refer to this man. On it see Noth, *IP*, *loc. cit.*

PAPYRUS 10

PAPYRUS 10

(*Brooklyn* 47.218.88) 43.4 *cm.* x 32.7 *cm.*

THIS finely preserved and well-written papyrus dates from the 3d year of Artaxerxes. The family history makes it apparent that this is Artaxerxes II (404–358 B.C.), so the date is March 9/10, 402 B.C. (Horn-Wood; Parker March 28, 401 B.C.). Anani (who in earlier texts usually calls himself Ananiah), the *lḥn* of Yahu, gives a house to his daughter Yehoyishma. There are some descriptive details in ll. 2 and 3 which are obscure, but we can discern that the property has three windows, one (outside) stairway, and a courtyard. Its location is described in terms of four points of the compass and the adjacent properties. The description is important for the location of the Yahu Temple (see Chapter 7). If Anani attempts to recover the property, he imposes a fine on himself of 30 karsh, refined silver. No other children or relatives shall be able to start suit or bring complaint before prefect or lord in order to deprive her of it while he lives or after his death. Those making such an attempt, whether against her or her children, will become liable to the same fine he had imposed on himself. He insists that she is to have power over his house and that whoever goes to law about it shall not succeed. They shall not be able to put forth a new or old document to sue for this house. Any document (other than this) that is produced will be a forgery. This document, however, which he, Anani, wrote is "valid" or "authoritative" (*yaṣṣib*) — a word found also in the Book of Daniel, where the A.V. renderings "certain" (2:45) and "true" (6:12) now appear inadequate.

The scribe Haggai b. Shemaʿiah, known to us from a previously published name list, is the writer of a number of our documents and is one of the best of the scribes.

A long list of witnesses follows. It is evident that Ananiah felt the need of protecting Yehoyishma's title with prominent names. It evidently could be assailed with some prospect of success. That may well be rooted in the fact that she and her mother had been slaves. The question of her status is vividly raised by her marriage document which has come down to us (No. 7).

1 ב 20 לאדר הו יום 8 לכיחך שנת 3 ארתחשסש מלכא אדין אמר ענני בר עזריה לחן זי

2 יהו אלהא ביב ברתא ליהוישמע ברתה לאמר יהבת לכי בי ח[ד] מבני בי תחתי אחד גשורן

3 ודששן 3 הו תרי דסי מבני דרגה ותרבצה הו ובה למנפק ודנה תחומוהי מועה שמש לה

4 אוצר מלכא דבק אגר באגר להנפנא זי בנו מצריא מערב שמש לה הו בבא זילך למנפק ושוק

5 מלכא בינים עליא לה בית קנחנתי דבק לה אגר באגר ואגר ביתא זילה דבק לה אגר באגר

6 הו תרי רבתא זילי תחתיא לה ביתה זי חור בר פטאסי גנן זי חנום אלהא דבק לה אגר באגר

7 זנה ביתא זי תחומוהי כתיבן בספרא זנה אנה ענני בר עזריה יהבתה לך פס שרת . . . זי לא כתב על ספר אנתתכי

8 עם ענני בר חגי בר משלם בר בסס אנתי יהוישמע ברתי שליטה בה מן יומא זנה זנה עד עלם

9 ובניכי שליטן אחריכי אנה ענני בר עזריה לחנא לא אכהל אמר יהבת לך ברחמן פס שרת על ספר

10 אנתותכי עד אחרן הן אמר אהנצל מנך אחוב ואנתן ליהוישמע אביגדן כסף כרשן 30 כסף

11 צרף באבני מלכא ואנתי אם שליטה בביתא זנה זי תחומוהי כתבן מנעל בחיי ובמותי אף

12 לא יכהל בר לי וברה לי אח ואחה הנגית והנבג ואדרנג זי ירשנכי דין ודבב ויקבל עליך

13 ועל בניכי לסגן ומרא להעדיה ביתא זנה מן קדמיכי בחיי ובמותי יחוב וינתן לכי

14 ועל בניכי אביגדן כסף כרשן 30 באבני מלכא ואנתי אם שליטה בביתא זנה זי תחומוהי

15 כתבן בספרא זנה ויהך בדן ולא יצדק אף לא יכלון ינפקון עליכי ספר חדת ועתיק בשם ביתא

16 זנה זי תחומוהי מנעל כתב בספרא זנה זי יהנפק כדב הו זנה ספרא זי אנה ענני כתבת לכי

1. On the 20th of Adar, that is the 8th day of Koiḥak, the 3d year of Artaxerxes the king, at that time said Anani the son of Azariah, the *lḥn* of
2. Yahu the god in Yeb the fortress, to Yehoyishma his daughter saying: I have given thee a (?) house. The construction of the lower (part of the?) house has (?) beams
3. and three doors there are. Two flights (?) of construction of stairs and a court there are, and by it (there is a way) to go forth. And these are its boundaries. East of it
4. the king's treasury adjoins wall to wall (up to?) the *hnpn'* which the Egyptians built. West of it is thy gate to go forth, and the street
5. of the king between them. Above it the house of *Ḳnḥnty* adjoins it wall to wall, and the wall of his house adjoins it wall to wall,
6. that is the two compartments (?) of mine. Below it the house of Ḥor b. Petēsi, the gardener of Khnum the god, adjoins it wall to wall.
7. This is the house of which the boundaries are written in this document. I, Anani son of Azariah, gave it to thee as remainder portion (?) which is not written in the document of thy marriage
8. with Anani son of Haggai son of Meshullam son of *Bss*. Ṭhou, Yehoyishma, my daughter, shalt have power over it from this (this!) day unto forever,
9. and thy children shall have power after thee. I, Anani son of Azariah, *lḥn*, shall not be able to say, "I gave (it) to thee in affection as remainder portion (?) on the document
10. of thy marriage until another (time)." If I say: "I will take it away from thee," I shall be liable and shall (have to) give Yehoyishma a fine of silver, 30 karsh,
11. refined silver, in royal weight, and thou in addition shalt have power over this house, the boundaries of which are written above, in my life and at my death. Moreover not will be able
12. son of mine or daughter of mine, brother or sister, *hngyt* or *hnbg* or *'drng*, who starts against thee suit or process and brings complaint against thee
13. and thy children to prefect or lord, to remove this house from (before) thee in my life, or at my death. Such a one shall be liable and shall give to thee
14. and to thy children a fine of silver 30 karsh by royal weight, and thou in addition shalt have power over this house, whose confines
15. are written in this document. If he goes into court, he shall not win. Moreover, they shall not be able to put forth against thee a document new or old in the name of this house
16. of which the boundaries were written above in this document. Whoever causes to go forth (a document), a lying (one) it is. This document which I, Anani, wrote to thee

17 הו יצב כתב חגי בר שמעיה ספרא זנה ביב כפם ענני בר עזריה לחנא זי יהו אלהא

18 שהדיא בגו שהד נתן בר יהואור שהד מנחם בר גדול שהד אחיו בר נתן

19 שהד רחום בר ביתא שהד נתן בר מעוזיה שהד שמוע בר פלפליה

20 שהד חגי בר מרדו שהד ידניה בר גמריה

21 ספר   בי זי כתב   ענני בר עזריה ליה[ו]ישמע ברתה   (Plate XIX, 6)

17. is valid. There wrote Haggai son of Shema'iah this document in Yeb at the dictation of Anani son of Azariah, the *lḥn* of Yahu the god.
18. Witnesses thereto: Witness, Nathan b. Yeho'or. Witness, Menahem b. Gaddūl. Witness, Aḥio b. Nathan.
19. Witness, Reḥum b. Beitha. Witness, Nathan b. Ma'uziyah. Witness, Šammū' b. Pilpeliah.
20. Witness, Haggai b. Mardu. Witness, Yedoniah b. Gemariah.
21. (Endorsement:) Document of the house which Anani b. Azariah wrote to Yehoyishma his daughter.

1. The month of אדר was previously mentioned in these papyri: *A.P.* 61:12; 67:4.

כיחך occurred in *A.P.* 72:18.

On the 3d year of Artaxerxes and the necessity of identifying him with Artaxerxes II, see Ch. 10. Again there is a discrepancy in the dates. The 20th of Adar in 401 B.C. was March 28, while the 8th of Koiḥak was March 8. Emendation to Koiḥak 28 is suggested by Parker as the easiest way of meeting the difficulty. Horn-Wood, holding that the third year of Artaxerxes was counted in the Egyptian manner, attain a near-synchronism on March 9/10 of 402 B.C.

ענני. The short form is used here. On לחן see on 2:2.

2. On the phrase "Yahu, the god in Yeb the fortress," cf. above, Chapter 8.

יהוישמע. If she was a child in the 31st year of Artaxerxes I, 434 B.C. (she is first mentioned in No. 4), she would have been whatever age she was then plus 33 years. Her parents had been married as far back as 449 B.C. (See No. 2 above). She was married in the 4th year of Darius (420 B.C.) according to No. 7. Her husband, Anani b. Haggai, is mentioned below in l. 8.

יהבת here means an actual gift, not as in 12:7, where it signifies a conveying of purchased property.

The balance of l. 2 and part of l. 3 to דרגה are difficult. After בי, "house," (as in *A.P.* 8:35, etc.) there is an epigraphic uncertainty. There is what looks like a letter ח with a smudge after it, as though it had been rubbed out. One may restore a ד, though the space seems cramped for it. On חד as indefinite ("a") cf. Dan. 2:31: צלם חד.

מבני, as in 9:12 and below in l. 3.

בי תחתי, as in 4:8; 9:12–13; 12:13.

אחד. See on 3:5, etc.

3. ודשנן. Cf. 12:13. This word, which occurs in the Targums (cf. Deut. 15:17) for "door," is found in the Bagoas letter (*A.P.* 30:10, 11: דששיא). The singular דש occured above in 9:13.

הו takes the place of the verb *to be* and usually comes at the end of the sentence. Cf. the next הו in the same line after ותרבצה. The הו after "three doors," therefore, concludes the statement. The plural number is disregarded.

תרי דסי מבני דרגה ותרבצה הו is evidently all one statement. מבני must be a noun here, since דסי is construct. We obviously have a series of constructs before דרגה, "stairs." See 6:10.

דסי is unknown. Cf. Assyrian *dassū*, "valley (?)," "depression (?)" One may hazard a guess that the reference is to "two flights of construction of stairs." מבני, "construction," must have a technical nuance: masonry?

תרבצה. Cf. above, the note on No. 3:4. הו goes not only with "court" but with the preceding words. Or should one render "There are two flights (?) of construction of stairs. And a court there is, etc."?

ובה, "and by it to go forth (sc. there is a way)"; her right of exit is by a different way mentioned below.

ודנה introduces a new sentence giving the description of the property.

4. The אוצר מלכא, see 3:9; 6:7; 11:4.

הנפנא זי בנו. See on 9:9.

בבא, "gate," had occurred in *A.P.* 34:3–4 and in Aḥ. 17, 23. The street is between the gate and the group of buildings composed of אוצר + הנפנא.

5. בינים, error for ביניהם; cf. *A.P.* 13:14; 25:7.

"Above," the house of קנחנתי adjoins. Owing to the subsequent זילה, this would appear to be personal name. Cf. on 9:9.

One wonders whether the scribe lost sight of the fact that he had written the words דבק לה אגר באגר when he continued with the rest of the line. If that element is removed, the connection gains in clarity.

6. הו תרי רבתא זילי. The הו here means "that is," and the statement is explanatory of לה. It hardly seems possible to begin the sentence with the preceding אגר באגר.

Below is the house of Ḥor b. Petēsi (cf. on 9:10).

7. Having made clear what house he is speaking of, Anani says, "I gave it to thee as פס שרת" (cf. l. 9 and 12:9, 18). I took this phrase as one word at first, seeking an Egyptian or Iranian expression, but there seems to be a slight gap between ס and ש. The first word is evidently פס and may mean "portion." Cf. J.A. פסא. The פס ידה, Dan. 5:5, 24, thus may mean "part of a hand" (so A.V.!) rather than "hollow of the hand." שרת may be from √שאר, cf. שירית *A.P.* 30:11, so that the phrase means "remainder portion," or be שרתא, "meal," from *שרו (L § 43t[4]), found in *CIS*, *2*, 158. Then פס שרת, "sustenance portion"?

The next two signs must represent numerals. The first is a ק but with a downward connecting stroke to the left, rather than up and to the right as when written for 100. The second is a ל written with a flourish. One suspects a fraction here, defining the portion, 30/100? Above the line are put words which were forgotten and which belong after זי לא.

כתב must be passive. Note the "defective" writing.

ספר אנתתכי, "the document of thy marriage." Below in l. 10, אנתותכי. That document is preserved in No. 7. For the phraseology cf. *A.P.* 35:4.

8. Anani b. Haggai b. Meshullam b. *Bss* is her husband, and this is evidenced by No. 7, where, however, his pedigree is not given as fully as here and in 12:2, 11. On בסס cf. the name *Bu-sa-sa*, in Ethel W. Moore, *Neo-Babylonian Business and Administrative Documents* (Ann Arbor, 1935), 337.

Why the פס שרת was not mentioned in that document is not clear. Perhaps it is because that text was not made out to her father Ananiah, but rather to Zakkur b. Meshullam, her "brother." There are peculiarities of ancient law here which will require further investigation.

Yehoyishma is to have power over the house. זנה has been repeated by error.

9. Her children are to have power after her. "I" was forgotten by the writer and has been put over the line after "Anani." He will not be able to claim that he had given it to her as a present, a פס שרת on her marriage document, until some future date — the same thought of a gift being revocable as in 7:41. Cf. also on 12:18.

אכהל אמר. The second verb is also 1st pers. sing. impf.; L § 37a, *A.P.* 5:6, and Cowley's comment, *A.P.*, p. 14.

10. עד אחרן, "until another (time)." The question here is whether these words end a sentence or begin a new one, in which case one would render "Later on." This very expression is found at the beginning of a sentence in Dan. 4:5 (the Kethib has אחרין, the Qere, *'oḥ^ŏrēn* and *'oḥ^ŏrān*; BL § 68w would prefer *'oḥ^ŏrān*). However, in *A.P.* 38:4, Aḥ. 53, 64, an על אחרן appears in the sense of "finally"; cf. Lidzbarski, *Ephemeris, 3,* 255. The עד in Dan. 4:5 is probably an error for על.

אהנצל. Cf. 2:13, אנצל.

אחוב begins the apodosis.

אביגדן. Cf. on 5:8.

11. צרף, so also in 12:30. See above in 5:5, צריף.

אם. See on 3:16.

Supply "shalt be" before שליטה.

כתבן, in *A.P.* 2:11, 13; 18:2; 25:8: כתיבן.

מנעל, already in *A.P.* 25:8; 35:8; 43:10. A prep. + noun (על; cf. B.A. עלא, Dan. 6:3; L § 61m).

בחיי goes with בביתא זנה; the intervening words are parenthetical.

אף begins a new sentence.

12. לא יכהל. It seems that this is continued by the infinitive in l. 13. In addition to children, brother, sister, the document lists

הנבג, הנגית. Cf. on 5:5.

אדרנג. Cf. on 9:18.

דין ודבב. See on 1:5.

ויקבל עליך, as in 1:4 and *A.P.* 8:13, "complain against thee." Cf. Cowley's note on its use in *A.P.*, p. 25.

13. סגן ומרא., so in 9:19; 12:28, and the fragment, *A.P.* 47:7.

להעדיה, inf. haphel, a new form of the verb עדה, which is found in previous papyri, *A.P.* 15:35; 30:6; 31:6; Aḥ. 50, 146. The verb occurs in B.A. (cf. Dan. 5:20) in the sense of "take away," "remove."

קדמיכי. In *A.P.* Aḥ. 203, קדמיך occurs. Other persons, cf. Cowley, index. The sentence apparently ends with במותי (cf. l. 11).

יחוב, "he shall be liable," i. e., the doer of what was described.

14. Yehoyishma and her children are protected by an אביגדן (see on 5:8) of 30 karsh against such a contingency. על is used in the sense of אל in על בניכי.

The text does not say, as in other instances, ולא דין, "case to be dismissed." A case could evidently be carried on.

15. On the formulation ויהך בדן ולא יצדק, "If he goes into court, he shall not win," see *A.P.* 8:22; 10:19, where we have the same thing in 1st pers. sing. and the 3d pl.

לא יכלון, as in *A.P.* 10:18, and similarly followed by an imperfect.

ינפקון is haphel impf. In *A.P.* 8:15, 17: יהנפקון. Cf. L § 35h. For the same verb with the same object, "document new or old," cf. *A.P.* 13:12.

בשם, "with the mention"; cf. above on 1:5. The writer of this document is verbose and repeats himself.

16. כתב is ungrammatical for כתיבין. Similarly in 12:22 (without מנעל), but probably not in 11:5.

A new sentence starts with זי יהנפק, "Whoever causes to go forth (a document), a lying (one) it is," i. e., forged. כדב, part., as in *A.P.* 8:17, a passage preventing one from translating, "he is lying."

זנה ספרא starts a new sentence.

17. הו יצב, "is firm," "valid." Not found in previous texts, but in B.A.; cf. Dan. 2:45; 6:13. In the latter passage the legal background of the term is discernible.

The scribe is Haggai b. Shema'iah; cf. on 3:23.

Anani's title is respectfully repeated.

18. The witnesses; the long list shows the need of much support.

Nathan b. Yeho'or, mentioned in *A.P.* 28:16 as a witness.

Menahem b. Gaddūl, mentioned in *A.P.* 20:17 as a witness.

Aḥio b. Nathan, mentioned in *A.P.* 23:1 and as the very first in the list *A.P.* 25:19.

19. רחום בר ביתא. This individual is new but occurs again in 11:14 and 12:34. The name Reḥum confirms the name in Ezra 2:2; 4:8 f.; Neh. 3:17; 10:26; 12:3. Cf. רחימאל, *Raḫim-ili*, Clay, BEUP, *10*, 61. Is בר ביתא to be connected with Babylonian *mār bīti*? When a man like Arsham, the satrap of Egypt, is called *mār bīti* in Babylonian texts (cf. Meissner, "Die Achaemenidenkönige und das Judentum," *SPAW*, 1938, 24 ff.), or בר ביתא in the Borchardt scrolls (Driver, *ZAW*, *62*, 1949–50, 223) this carries a different weight than in the case of the ordinary individual (member of the royal house?). For the ordinary citizen *mār bīti* required further specification, as Babylonian examples show: [m]*Bibanu mār bīti ša Šulum-Babili*, [m]*Ḫarrimaḫi mār bīti ša* [m]*Ḫarimunatu*, Clay, BEUP, *10*, 47, 51. In "Reḥum b. Beitha" the name of the head of the house to which Reḥum belongs is left out. On the other hand in בית אובל, 3:24, the first name and בר may be omitted. But what does the phrase *mār bīti* or בר ביתא signify? Perhaps a "house-born slave." Cf. such a name as *Nannar-mār-bīti-iddina*, "the god Nannar has given a *mār-bīti*," Clay,

BEUP, *14,* 48. The term also occurs in Hebrew; in Eccles. 2:7, "the sons of the house" are differentiated from slaves and handmaidens. Perhaps the added assumption is needed that the "son of the house" is *adopted*. For how could "the son of his house" inherit Abram, Gen. 15:3, unless he had legal rights such as a slave could only gain by adoption?

Nathan b. Maʿuziah, mentioned in *A.P.* 23:2.

Šammūʿ b. Pilpeliah, a new individual. Two other men named *Šammūʿ* are mentioned in *A.P.* 12:5; 22:41. The name Pilpeliah represents an interesting variation of Pelaliah, *A.P.* 8:30; 9:17; Neh. 11:12.

20. Haggai b. Mardu; this Haggai occurred in 9:26 and appears again in 11:14. For the name Mardu see Tallqvist, *APN*, 128, *Mar-du-u.*

Yedoniah b. Gemariah, a case of the first being last. See *A.P.* 31:1; 22:121; 34:5.

21. Endorsement: A large gap is left between ספר and בי.

In the name יה ישמע a space has been left between ה and the next letter, due to the string having been tied here, and showing that the endorsement was made after the sealing. Possibly there was reluctance to write the third letter of the divine name on the other side of the string and thus leave a hiatus in that name when the text was opened. Or is the short writing of the divine name in 3:25 to be compared? *A.P.* 2:21 provides a יהנתן — not a "mistake," as Cowley seems to think.

PAPYRUS 11

PAPYRUS 11

(*Brooklyn* 47.218.93) 34.8 *cm.* x 30.5 *cm.*

OUR text limits itself to a purely Egyptian dating (month of Thoth) and does not mention the calendar day; perhaps the suggestion made in the case of No. 7 that the new-moon day is meant is applicable here as well. It seems quite clear on the basis of general considerations that the king referred to is the second Artaxerxes and hence the year is 402 B.C. (Horn-Wood; Parker, 401 B.C.), and the first day of Thoth was December 1.

In the present text Anani b. Haggai, son-in-law of Anani b. Azariah, borrows spelt (the favorite Egyptian grain for flour, Herodotus II, 36) from Paḥnum b. *Bs'*. He agrees to pay back from the ration issued him from the king's storehouse (l. 6, in repeating, varies this with "from the house of the king"), no doubt on the next payday. For we must assume that payment in kind, rather than money, was practiced. This has always been the normal thing in the East. It simplified the regulation of affairs, since so much of what was paid the government by the Egyptian peasants was in the form of grain. Failure to pay the debt makes Anani liable to a fine of one karsh of refined silver (see Introduction, Chapter 3). He agrees to pay such a fine within twenty days and any suit over the matter is excluded. In the event of his death before paying, his children and *'drng* shall pay. If they fail to do so, Paḥnum shall have power to confiscate from his house enough to pay the above debt — he is given blanket authority over his slaves, his utensils, both of copper and of iron, clothing, and grain. An addition to the document specifies that he can take what he finds of Anani's in Yeb and in Syene — a curiously sweeping contract for such a small loan. One wonders, too, why a man like Anani, who in No. 12, eleven days later, can buy a house, has to make it. The text is comparable notably to *A.P.* 10 and 3.

This is the only document written by this particular scribe, Šewahram b. Ešemram b. Ešemzebed. It was written at Syene and witnessed by four men. One signed himself merely as Haggai without further identification.

Above the beginning of this text are discernible traces of previous writing which have been rubbed out.

1 ירח תחות שנת 4 ארתחשסש מלכא אדין בסון בירתא א[מר] ענני בר חגי בר משלם

2 יהודי לדגל נבוכדרי לפחנום בר בסא ארמי זי סון לדגלא זך [כ]נם לאמר אנה אתית עליך

3 בביתך בסון בירתא ויזפת מנך ויהבת לי כנתן פרסן 2 סאן 2 (+ 1 ?) אחר אנה ענני בר חגי

4 אשלם ואנתן לך כנתניא אלך כף 2 סאן 5 + 1 מן פתפא זי ית[נת]ן לי מן אוצר מלכא

5 והן לא שלמת ויהבת לך כנתיא אלך זי מנעל כתיב[ן כ]זי יתנתן לי פתפא

6 מן בית מלכא אחר אנה ענני אחוב ואנתן לך כסף א[בג]דן כרש חד (1) כסף צריף

7 אחר אנה ענני אשלם ואנתן לך אבגדנא זי מנעל כתי[ב] בין יומן 20 הו עשרן

8 ולא דן והן מיתת ולעד שלמת ויהבת לך כספא זילך זי מנעל כתיב אחר בני

9 ואדרנגי ישלמון לך כספך זי מנעל כתיב והן לא שלמו לך בני ואדרנגי

10 כספא זנה זי מנעל כתיב אחר אנת פחנום שליט בעד בני למחר ותלקח לך מן

זי תהשכח לי ביב ובסון ובמבנתא

11 בי זׄי לבנן עבד ואמה מאן נחש ופרזל לבוש ועבור עד תשלם בכספך זי מנעל

12 כתיב ולא דן כתב שוהרם בר אשמרם בר אשמשזב ספרא זנה בסון בירתא כפם

13 ענני בר חגי בר משלם שהדיא בגו שהד מנחם בר שלום שהד חגי

14 שהד רחום בר ביתא שהד חגי בר מרדו

15 ... עׄבוׄר... בר משלם לפחנום בר בסא (Plate XIX, 7)

1. Month of Thoth, year 4 of Artaxerxes the king, at that time in Syene the fortress s[aid] Anani son of Haggai son of Meshullam,
2. a Jew of the *degel* of Nabukudurri, to Paḥnum son of *Bs'*, an Aramaean of Syene of that *degel*, thus saying: I came to thee
3. in thy house in Syene, the fortress, and I borrowed from thee and thou didst give to me spelt 2 peras 2 (+1?) seah. Later on, I, Anani son of Haggai,
4. shall pay back and give to thee that spelt, two times 5+1 seah, from the ration which will be given to me from the storehouse of the king.
5. And if I do not pay back and give to thee that spelt which is written above, when the ration is given to me
6. from the house of the king, then I, Anani, shall become liable to pay thee a fine of one karsh (1), refined silver.
7. Thereafter, I, Anani, shall pay and give to thee the fine which is written above within 20 days — that is twenty —
8. and no lawsuit (shall obtain). And if I die and have not yet paid back and given thee the silver of thine which is written above, then my children
9. and my '*drng* shall pay thee thy silver which is written above. And if my children and my '*drng* do not pay thee
10. this silver which is written above, then thou, Paḥnum shalt have power over my children tomorrow and shalt take for thyself from
11. the house belonging to the children slave and handmaiden, vessels of copper and iron, clothing and produce, what thou shalt find of mine in Yeb and in Syene and even in buildings (?), until thou dost get back thy money which
12. is written above, and no lawsuit (shall obtain). There wrote this document Šewahram son of Ešemram son of Ešemzebed in Syene the fortress at the dictation of
13. Anani son of Haggai son of Meshullam. Witnesses thereto: Witness, Menahem b. Shallum. Witness, Haggai.
14. Witness, Reḥum b. Beitha. Witness, Haggai b. Mardu.
15. (Endorsement:) Corn (?) . . . b. Meshullam to Paḥnum b. *Bs'*.

1. Thoth appeared previously in the papyri *A.P.* 6:1; 10:1; 11:8; 25:1; 81:122. No day is given. Presumably the new-moon day is meant. Anani b. Haggai b. Meshullam, the man making out this document, here gives his name in full. We find him dropping his father's name in No. 15. He is the son-in-law of Anani b. Azariah and Tamut, and the husband of Yehoyishma (see No. 7).

2. Jew of the *degel* of Nabukudurri. The latter name is Babylonian and appears again in 12:3. Cf. the further references and comment given in the note on that passage. The man with whom he is doing business is described as Aramaean of Syene of the same *degel*. His name is פחנום בר בסא. A Paḥnum b. Zakkur appears in *A.P.* 23:12. Paḥnum is Egyptian, "the one belonging to Khnum." See Ranke, *ÄP*, 110:17. *Bs'* is also Egyptian and is found in Aimé-Giron, *Textes*, Nos. 100, 112; cf. also *Bi-i-sa*, Tallqvist, *APN*, 64. After the demonstrative זך and before "saying" there stood a word of three letters of which only ם is fully clear. It must be an adverb. אפם hardly fits here and the next to last letter seems to be nun. We restore כנם, which in B.A. appears as כנמא; cf. Ezra 5:4, where it precedes לאמר, exactly as is the case here. On כנמא as derived from כן, "so," plus the generalizing element מא see BL § 68d.

אתית, followed by על, as in *A.P.* 5:3.

3. יזף, "borrow," occurs in Aḥ. 129–130. On זפת, "loan," cf. Aḥ. 130 and *A.P.* 10:3.

כנתן, "spelt" (cf. masc. pl., *A.P.* 10:10: שערן כנתן). In l. 4 a pl. כנתניא is found. The J.A. form in the sing. is כנתא (*kunnātā*) <Akkadian *kunāšu.*

פרסן here is doubtlessly the pl. of פרס, Hebrew *peres*, but probably *peras* in Aramaic, and signifies a measure. In its previous occurrences in the Elephantine papyri it was taken to mean "share" (*A.P.* 2:16; 11:6; 45:8). However, in *A.P.* 45:8, "1 *qab* to 1 *peras*," it is doubtlessly a measure. It also occurs in that sense in the Bauer-Meissner papyrus, l. 5. The stroke following is a "one," while the next stroke could be a kaph but is probably just another corrected numeral 1. Is the peras a larger or a smaller measure than the seah? Ordinarily the larger precedes, but the opposite seems to be the case in the repayment clause in l. 4. Bauer-Meissner suggest it is one-half a homer. Since the homer is 30 seah, a peras would be 15 seah. But l. 4 below shows that this is erroneous. The peras, at least in the present connection, is probably one-half an ardab (cf. further on l. 4).

2(+1) סאן. Here we have the pl. of סאה, as in *A.P.* 63:3. If there had been only 2, the second numeral stroke would have been lengthened as in 2 כף (l. 4).

אחר begins a new sentence: "Afterward," "In the future," L § 61i.

4. שלם, pael, "to pay," as often in the other Elephantine papyri. This is the first occurrence of the form without the energic nun (cf. אשלמן in *A.P.* 35:5), for in *A.P.* 29:4 it is merely a conjectural reading.

כנתניא is probably an error for כנתיא (see l. 5). The expected form for the plural emphatic is כנתיא. In later Aramaic the pl. emph. is *kunnātayyā.*

2 כף, hardly a measure, but meaning "two times." Cf. 1 בכף in the meaning "at one time" in 7:24, etc. He must pay back double the original amount. If so, then the original amount loaned must be mentioned next. This need not take the exact form in which it was given, but must quantitatively amount to the same thing. The total to be returned is here given in seah. There is a seemingly new number after סאן and then a single stroke, so $x+1$. On the supposition that the peras is half a homer, the total of l. 2 in seah would be 33. But whatever $x+1$ may be, it cannot be $30+3$. If one will assume that a peras is half an ardab (already mentioned in *A.P.* 2), the ardab being one-tenth homer or 3 seah, we then have $1\frac{1}{2}+1\frac{1}{2}+3=6$ seah originally lent. In $x+1$ the unknown quantity then is *five*. And so in x we doubtlessly have another (older?) form of the numeral 5, which is given in Lidzbarski, *Epigraphik*, Zweiter Teil, Tafel XLVI, Zahlentafel, col. 3, under 7, on the basis of *CIS*, *2*, 17.

פתפא, "ration," as in *A.P.* 24:39; 43:8; in 24:42 probably פתף. On this Iranian word see Eilers, "Eine Mittelpersische Wortform aus frühachämenidischer Zeit," *ZDMG*, *90* 1936, 195.

ית--ן. There seems to be room for two letters. We restore ית[נת]ן as in l. 5, which would then be the first occurrence of this word in the papyri in the ethpeel.

אוצר, the one on Elephantine Island, referred to in 3:9; 6:7; 10:4 ?

5. The eventuality that he does not pay back his loan is now regulated.

כתיב[י]ן, nun has to be restored here, followed by [כ]זי.

יתנתן, as in l. 4. בית, "house," as the place where payments were made, is the common word. So also in the Borchardt documents Ch. 1, n. 64 we hear of the בית of Arsham.

6. אחר, here = "then," continuing the sentence, not starting a new one.

אחוב. Cf. 4:14.

ואנתן. The waw is practically subordinating; "liable to pay," actual payment is another step., l. 7.

אבג[ד]ן. See above on 5:8. Two letters have to be supplied. One karsh is 30 shekels, so quite a penalty is imposed.

כסף צריף. Cf. on 5:15.

7. אחר starts a new sentence.

בין, [within the] interval of 20 days.

8. דן without yodh; cf. 1:5; 10:15.

והן starts a new sentence.

מיתת, 1st pers. sing., as in *A.P.* 10:14; L § 39b.

ולעד must be ולא עד (cf. *A.P.* 28:13: לא עד, "not yet"). In B.A. עד is עוד; cf. L § 61i, BL § 68o. The words were evidently run together and the aleph elided, as after the article in Hebrew (see GK § 35d).

אחר, "then," introducing apodosis.

9. אדרנג (see on 9:18) here appears in close connection with "children."

10. בעד בני. The preposition is used as in Hebrew. This occurrence of בעד may be important for the interpretation of בעדה in 2:7, etc. See the note to that passage.

לך מן. This seems to be the reading of the end of l. 10. The ל is written with a flourish as in the last word of l. 11.

10b. The material written between the lines belongs logically after עבור in l. 11, above which it is written. Cf. below.

11. The first word is בי, "house." The following signs look like numerals, but are actually to be read זי ל, yodh and lamedh having been linked. We thus get the phrase found in *A.P.* 10:9, בי זי לבנן. Our context shows that the rendering which Cowley adopted in revising Sachau's incorrect reading and translation, לבן, "tiles," "counting house," had no basis. The ל is the prep. before בנן, "the house which belongs *to the children*," and then is followed by the series of objects. The occurrence of the same phrase in *A.P.* 3:18 shows that that fragmentary text was also concerned with a loan of grain (barley and lentils). Cowley, following the false assumption of "counting house" (developed on *A.P.* 3:18) also supplied the words in *A.P.* 2:16, where they are inappropriate. It should be noted that in *A.P.* 10:9 the house itself is pledged at the outset, which is not the case in this papyrus (though it is subsequently brought in below).

בנן must be the first in the series of objects of the verb ותלקח.

מאן is used collectively here (as in *A.P.* 65, No. 1). There is trace of an erased א after the word. The writer changed his mind and decided to specify further.

עבור, "corn," i. e., grain or produce in general.

A general statement is added above the line (hence numbered 10b) after לבוש, but in sense belonging after ועבור.

תהשכח, haphel, L § 34h, in *A.P.* 10:9, 10, 17.

ביב ובסון. He had possessions in both places.

ובמבנתא. One might think of reading ובמונתא, but the fourth letter must be a ב; it is written with a long, downward flourish and is bisected by the נ that follows. One would expect another place name, but the word looks like a derivative of בנה, "build," and may mean "buildings" (other peoples' houses? Cf. *A.P.* 20, where a decedent's property in the possession of another is the subject of litigation). Neither מונתא nor מבנתא are likely geographical names. The last letters are heavily written. The waw then would be augmentative "and even in the buildings."

תשלם. Cf. *A.P.* 10:7, etc., "pay back," but here "get back," the ב before the object.

12. This is the only preserved production of this scribe. His names with רם are interesting. In שוהרם we may have a fuller form of the name שוא of No. 13:1; רם is the subject and so must be the appellation of a God. For the two elements see Noth, *IP*, 145, 222. In אשמרם, however, רם is the predicate: "the god *'šm* is exalted."

Witnesses: Menahem b. Shallum in *A.P.* 25:18; 35:[2], 5; 44:1; 63:10.
Haggai, not further identified.
Reḥum b. Beitha; see on 10:19; 12:34.
Haggai b. Mardu; cf. on 10:20.

15. Endorsement. At the right edge of the fragment there appears a mark which looks like a remnant of a numeral 10. The next word probably is עבור, though the second letter looks more like a ז. After a gap of 4.50 cm., large enough to contain זי כתב ענני, but hardly בר חגי, follows the rest of the name of the borrower and that of the lender.

PAPYRUS 12

PAPYRUS 12

(*Brooklyn* 47.218.94) 61.4 *cm.* x 31.8 *cm.*

ON THE 12th of Thoth of the 4th year of Artaxerxes II or December 12, 402 B.C. (Horn-Wood; Parker, 401 B.C.) Anani, son of Azariah, the *lḥn* of the god Yahu, and his wife *Tpmt* sold to their son-in-law, Anani, son of Haggai, the house that they had bought from Bagazušt, son of *Plyn*, in No. 3, dated September 15, 437 B.C. Before Bagazušt had owned the house it had belonged to Yanbuli (called *'pwly* in 3:4), son of Misdai. The price of this new sale was 1 karsh and 3 shekels of silver. The amount is receipted as paid in full. The dimensions of the house are given. Thereupon the description of the boundaries begins but is suddenly broken off and a fresh start made with an entirely new document that has been glued to the unfinished one. This is an interesting and anomalous situation. Apparently the customers were dissatisfied about something the scribe had written, so that he had to begin with a new document, but after the new document — in which the scribe very naturally tended to go more briefly over the same ground — was completed, it was felt that some of the material first written was worth preserving, and so the new document was simply attached to the unfinished one and the whole thing was duly witnessed and sealed.

The boundaries, as set forth in the new document, show certain changes when compared with the earlier descriptions given in No. 3. The Temple of Yahu is still to the west, but instead of mention of the king's treasury in the east there is reference to the house of Anani and his wife Yehoyishma. This suggests that our deed concerns only the western half of the house in question; beyond the eastern half must have been the treasury. "Below" we now find mentioned the house of Peḥi and Pemeṭ, the boatmen. Above, where the home of Satibar had been, now is the house of Parnu b. Zili and his brother.

Anani b. Haggai is to have complete ownership, with power to give or sell to whom he wills and the right to pass to his children (without mention of any limitation as to their being children of Yehoyishma). Anani b. Azariah and his wife sign away any right to sue for recapture of this house and express themselves satisfied with the price received. They bind themselves not to sue Anani b. Haggai's sons or daughters or anyone he sells or gives it to and impose the same condition on other children, brothers, and sisters, etc. Whoever invokes prefect, "lord," or

judge in the matter of this house or brings forward any document new or old against Anani is liable to a fine of 20 karsh. The case is to be dismissed and Anani b. Haggai and his heirs and assigns are to have undisputed possession. They turn over to him also the original deed made out by Bagazušt. The witnesses are only three in number. One of them has an Egyptian name.

There are items of remarkable interest in this papyrus. Outstanding on the economic and historical side is the fact the selling price of 1 karsh and 3 shekels is equated with "silver of Yawan 6 staters and 1 shekel." Yawan (Biblical Javan) is the name for Greece. It is derived, of course, from "Ionia" and appears in Gen. 10:2, etc.; Isa. 66:19; Ezek. 27:13, 19; Zech. 9:13; Joel 4:6 — all passages from the 6th century or later. This is in all probability the oldest reference to a stater in the Aramaic papyri. The fact that the stater was current in Egypt in 402/1 B.C. reflects the ascendancy of Greece in Egyptian affairs and thus agrees well with what is known of the history of the time.

On the social side it is noteworthy that a wife who is an ex-handmaiden and probably still is under a paramone arrangement executes a deed together with her husband. The references to her having been *prypt* and *gw'* of Meshullam b. Zakkur take on a certain amount of color from the situation revealed by Nos. 5 and 7.

On the religious side it is noteworthy that Yahu the god is explicitly localized in Yeb with the same phraseology with which the Judaean official view had localized him at Jerusalem. Interesting also is the fact that whatever the office of *lḥn* may have been, Anani's wife shares the title and is called *lḥnh* of Yahu.

1 ב 12 לתחות שנת 4 ארתחשסש מלכא אדין אמר ענני בר עזריה לחן זי יהו ונשן תפמת
2 אנתתה לחנה זי יהו אלהא שכן יב ברתא לענני בר חגי בר משלם בר בסס ארמי זי
3 זי יב ברתא לדגל נבוכדרי לאמר אנה ותפמת ברת פתו כל 2 זבן ויהבן לך ביתן זי
4 זבן בכסף מן בגזשת בר פלין כספיא הו ביתה זי ינבולי בר מסדי כספי זי ביב הו
5 מהחסן ויהבת לן דמי ביתן כסף כרש חד הו 1 שקלן תלתה הו 3 כסף יון סתתרי 6
6 שקל 1 חד וטיב לבבן בגו זי לא אשתאר לן עליך מן דמיא זנה משחת ביתא זי זבן
7 ויהבן לך מן מועה למערב שמש ארך אמן 16 כ 2 בעשתא
8 ומן תחתיא לעליא פתי אמן 5 כ 2 בעשתא לאברת אמין 150 והא זנה
9 תחומי ביתא זי זבן ויהבן לך מועה שמש לה ביתה זי יהבת לך פס שרת

---

10 ב 12 לתחות שנת 4 ארתחשסש מלכא אדין אמר ענני בר עזריה לחן ליהו
11 אלהא ותפמת אנתתה פ(ר)יפת זי משלם בר זכור כל 2 כפם חד לענני בר חגי בר בסס
12 לאמר אנחנה זבן ויהבן לך ביתן זי זבן מן בגזשת בר פלין כספיא בי תחתי מבני
13 אחד גשורן כון ודשן 2 מבני בי תחתי הו תרי רבתא זילי ויהבת לן דמוהי
14 כסף כרש חד שקלן 3 כסף יון במנין סתתרי 6 שקל 1 וטיב לבבן בדמיא זי
15 יהבת לן זנה משחת ביתא זי זבן ויהבן לך מן מועה שמש למערב ארך אמין
16 16 כ 2 בעשתא ומן עליה לתחתיא פתי אמן 5 כ 2 (ל)אברת (אמן) 151 כ 1 זנה
17 תחומוהי ביתא זי זבן ויהבן לך מועה שמש לה ביתך אנת ענני בר חגי זי יהבן
18 ליהוישמע ברתן פס שרת על ספר אנתותה דבק אגר באגר מערב שמש לה אגורא
19 זי יהו ושוק מלכא ביניהן עליה לה בית פרנו בר זלי ומרדו אחוהי דבק לה

1. On the 12th of Thoth, the 4th year of Artaxerxes the king, at that time said Anani b. Azariah, the *lḥn* of Yahu, and the woman *Tpmt*
2. his wife, *lḥnh* of Yahu the god who dwells in Yeb the fortress, to Anani b. Haggai b. Meshullam b. *Bss*, Aramaean of
3. Yeb the fortress, of the *degel* of Nabukudurri, saying: I and *Tpmt*, daughter of Pethu, the two of us, have sold and given over to you our house which
4. we bought with silver from Bagazušt b. *Plyn*, "silverman," that is the house of Yanbuli b. Misdai, "silverman," which in Yeb
5. he possessed, and thou didst give to us the price of our house in money, one karsh, that is 1, three shekels, that is 3, in money of Yawan 6 staters (and)
6. 1 shekel, (that is) one, and our heart is satisfied therewith, that there is not outstanding to us against thee any part of the price. These are the measurements of the house which we sold
7. and gave over to thee. From the east to west (*ditt.*) a length of 16 cubits *k* 2 by the one(-cubit-measure),
8. and from below to above a width of 5 cubits *k* 2 by the one(-cubit-measure), to the outside (?) 150 cubits. And behold, these are
9. the boundaries of the house which we sold and gave over to thee. On the east of it is the house which I gave to thee as remainder portion (?)

- -

10. On the 12th of Thoth, the 4th year of Artaxerxes the king, at that time said Anani son of Azariah, *lḥn* of Yahu
11. the god, and *Tpmt* his wife, *pr(d?)ypt* of Meshullam b. Zakkur, both of them in full accord, to Anani b. Haggai b. *Bss*, saying:
12. We sold and gave over to thee our house which we bought from Bagazušt b. *Plyn*, "silverman." The lower house is a construction having beams, windows,
13. and 2 doors. The construction of the lower house consists of (?) the two compartments (?) of mine. And thou didst give us its price
14. in silver one karsh, 3 shekels, in money of Yawan in the number of staters 6 (and) one shekel, and our heart is satisfied at the price which
15. thou hast given to us. These are the measurements of the house which we sold and gave over to thee. From east to west the length of cubits is
16. 16 *k* 2 by the one(-cubit-measure) and from above to below the width is 5 cubits *k* 2, to the outside (?) 151 cubits *k* 1. These are
17. the boundaries of the house which we sold and gave over to thee. East of it thy house, O Anani b. Haggai, which we gave
18. to Yehoyishma our daughter as remainder portion (?) on the document of her marriage, adjoins it wall to wall. On the west of it is the Temple
19. of Yahu and the street of the king is between them. Above it the house of Parnu b. Zili and Mardu, his brother, adjoins it

אגר באגר תחתיא לה ביתה זי פחי ופמט אחוהי מלחן זי מיא בני תויא
ושוק מלכא ביניהן וכונה 1 פתיח לתרי רבתא ותרעא עלה פתיח לשוק מלכא
מן תמה תנפק ותנעל ביתא זנה זי משחתה ותחומוהי כתיב בספרא זנה אנת ענני
שליט בה מן יומא זנה ועד עלמן ובניך שליטן אחריך ולמן זי רחמת תנתן או זי
תזבן לה בכסף אנה ענני ותפמת אנתתי זי הות גוא למשלם בר זכור ויהבה לי
לאנתו לא נכהל נרשנך דין ודבב בשם ביתא זנה זי זבן ויהבן לך ויהבת לן דמוהי
לבבן בגו
כסף וטיב אף לא נכהל נרשה לבניך ובנתך וזי תנתן לה בכסף או רחמת אף לא
יכהל בר לן וברה אח ואחה לן הנגית והנבג ואדרנג זילן זי ירשנך דין וירשה
לבניך ולאיש זי תנתן לה וזי יקבל עליך לסגן ומרא ודין בשם ביתא זנה זי משחת
כתב מנעל וזי ינפק עליך ספר חדת ועתיק בשם ביתא זנה זי זבן ויהבן לך יחוב
וינתן לך ולבניך אביגדן כסף כרשן 20 באבני מלכא כסף צרף וביתא זילך ודי בניך
ודי תנתן לה רחמת אף יהבן לך ספרא עטיקא זי כתב לן בגזשת ספר זבנתא
זי זבן לן ויהבן לה דמוהי ... כסף כתב חגי בר שמעיה ספרא זנה ביב ברתא
כפם ענני לחנא זי יהו אלהא תפממת ברת פתו אנתתה כל 2 כפם חד שהד משלם
בר מעוזיה שהד רחום בר ביתא שהד נתן בר יהואור מגר
ספר בי זי זבן ענני בר עזריה ותפמת אנתתה (Plate XIX, 8)

20. wall to wall. Below it is the house of Peḥi and Pemeṭ, his brother, boatmen of the waters, sons of Tawi,
21. and the street of the king is between them, and its one window opens to the two compartments (?) and the gate above opens to the street of the king.
22. From there thou shalt go forth and go in to this house, of which the measurements and boundaries are recorded in this document. Thou, Anani,
23. shalt have power over it from this day unto forevermore, and thy children shall have power after thee, and to whomsoever thou wilt thou mayest give it and to whom
24. thou wilt sell it for money (thou mayest sell it). I, Anani, and *Tpmt*, my wife, who was handmaiden (?) to Meshullam b. Zakkur, who gave her to me in
25. marriage, we shall not be able to start against thee suit or process with mention of this house which we sold and gave over to thee and (for which) thou didst give to us its price
26. in silver, and our heart was satisfied therewith. Moreover, we shall not be able to start suit against thy sons and thy daughters or whomever thou mayest give it for money or as a gift. Moreover not shall
27. be able son of ours or daughter, brother or sister of ours, *hngyt* or *hnbg* or *'drng* of ours (to sue). Whoever shall start against thee a suit or sue
28. thy children or anyone to whom thou mayest have given it, and whoever brings complaint against thee to prefect or lord or judge with mention of this house, of which the measurements
29. are written above, or whoever causes to go forth against thee a document new or old with mention of this house which we sold and gave over to thee, shall be liable,
30. and shall give thee or thy children a fine of silver 20 karsh, royal weight, refined silver, and the house is thine and thy children's
31. or his to whom thou mayest give it as a gift. Moreover, we have given to thee the old document which Bagazušt wrote to us as document of sale
32. which he sold to us, and we gave him its price . . . in silver. There wrote Haggai b. Shema'iah this document in Yeb the fortress
33. at the dictation of Anani, *lḥn* of Yahu the god, (and) *Tpmmt*, daughter of Pethu, his wife, both of them in full accord. Witness: Meshullam
34. b. Ma'uziah; witness: Reḥum b. Beitha; witness: Nathan b. Yeho'or; *Magir*.
35. (Endorsement:) Document (concerning) the house which Anani b. Azariah and *Tpmt* his wife did sell.

1. This papyrus restricts itself to an Egyptian dating — the month of Thoth, which already appeared in previous papyri (*A.P.* 6:1; 10:1; 11:8; 25:1; 81:122). The month name is identical with the god name found in *A.P.* 69:10. That ארתחשסש is Artaxerxes II becomes evident from the fact that Anani (or Ananiah) married in the 16th year of an Artaxerxes, while here we find him husband of a *Tpmt* in the 4th year of an Artaxerxes, as well as from the fact that the house here, sold in the 4th year of an Artaxerxes, was bought in No. 3 in the 28th of an Artaxerxes. Parker dates this December 12, 401 B.C., Horn-Wood, 402 B.C., holding that in Egypt the accession year of Artaxerxes was counted in the Egyptian manner. The synchronism attained for No. 10 under this theory seems to recommend it. Adaptation to Egyptian reckoning may reflect the weakening of Persian control.

נשין. The spelling with yodh here is of decisive importance for the recognition of the form. Its occurrence in 5:2 above shows that the word does not mean "spinster," as Cowley thought, for it is given to married women too, nor "ladyship," for it is given to a slave woman. It apparently means merely "a female personage, a woman" and seems to be a plural form, in view of the plene writing. It is apparently used in emulation of the Egyptian word *(t3) s.t* found in demotic texts; cf. Spiegelberg, "Der Papyrus Libbey," *Schriften der Wissenschaftlichen Gesellschaft zu Strassburg, 1,* 7, n. 2. It deserves a place in L § 45j with other plurals having the meaning of a singular; cf. דמן, רחמן, etc.

2. לחנה. It is interesting that she, too, gets the title; cf. the inscription of Aimé-Giron (above, 2:2), and cf. כספיה, 3:2; in Hebrew נביאה, Isa. 8:3, and כהנת, "a priest's wife," or even his daughter; in Assyrian *šakintu* and *šaknu* (the former, then, wife of the šaknu or prefect). For examples see Kohler and Ungnad, *Assyrische Rechtsurkunden,* No. 40, 5 and No. 150, 3. The surprising thing is, however, that in our passage she, as לחנה, is also "of Yahu the god," and that the predicate given the deity follows her title rather than her husband's.

שכן יב, part., "who dwells in Yeb." This formulation is astonishingly like O.T. usage in such passages as Deut. 33:16, שכני סנה, Ps. 135:21, שכן ירושלים and probably reveals the impact of Palestinian theology. These Elephantine Jews did not worship a far-away god but one who was near. No doubt they had a cult object of some sort in which the divine presence was held concentrated. The pre-Deuteronomic character of this religion is made vivid for us by this statement.

Anani b. Haggai's pedigree of 10:8 is repeated.

3. The זי at the beginning of the line is repeated by mistake.

נבוכדרי is found as a proper name in *A.P.* 5:18 and as the name of a *degel* in *A.P.* [7:3, 4]; 29:2; 35:2. The name is Babylonian; cf. *Nabu-kudurri-*(*uṣur*?), Nebuchadre(zzar). Kudurru in names means "son" in effect; see J. J. Stamm, *MVAÄG, 44,* 1939, 43. While Anani b. Azariah speaks he does so also in his wife's name. *Tpmt* is the daughter of פתו. The latter appeared as a proper name in the much younger papyrus *A.P.* 81:103, 106, 113, 114. According to Ranke it should not be

compared with the name *Ptw* (Ranke, *ÄP*, 137:25), as I had thought of doing. Spiegelberg, *OLZ*, *15*, 1912, 10, explained it as *p3-t3w*. Ranke and Edel think that erroneous and regard it as a short form of *p3-(n)-t3wy*, "the one belonging to both lands," *ÄP*, 112:4. It appears also in Greek guise as *patou(s)*. On תו– they would compare the name סמתו in Cowley, *A.P.* 74:4, which goes back to *sm3 t3wy*. פתו is thus a masculine name. They regard it as an appellation for a god and hence as a hypocoristic personal name. Does this indicate that *Tpmt* was freeborn, but had gotten into slavery?

2 כל, "both of them."

זבן here means "sell" and יהבן, "give," in the sense of "giving possession" — not of a present.

ביתן (cf. ביתנא, *A.P.* 81:110, and בתנא, 81:115; also L § 59e). This is property which as No. 2 would say is "between Anani and Tamut," i. e., is jointly acquired since their marriage.

4. זבן, the 1st pers. pl. perf. form normally ends in ן, L § 25d. Here there has been assimilation of the 3d radical to the ending. The previous acquisition by purchase rather than any hereditary reception is important legally.

בגזשת, here and in No. 3; it is spelled בגזושת in No. 4:3. Instead of his father's name בזו that appeared in No. 3:2 he now uses that of his grandfather.

פלין. The name is a new one for the papyri. B. Geiger does not think it Iranian. Perhaps a form from the root פלא? Cf. שוין in 8:12. A theophorous element has perhaps been dropped.

כספיא. Cf. above, on 3:2. The st. emph. here and in l. 12.

הו, here: "that."

ביתה זי; typical Aramaic, with advance indication of the genitive by the suffix? BL § 90j. But cf. l. 9 where that cannot be the case.

ינבולי בר מסדי. The title of the property goes back to this individual, who was called אפולי in 3:4, 21. ינבולי reminds one of נבולי, *A.P.* 5:18. If not an error the name may be tribal, with a gentilic ending added. Cf. *Bagazuštum* the *šaknu* of the *In-du-ú-ba-ai*, Clay, BEUP, *10*, 41.

הו at the end of the line takes the place of the verb "to be"; it might even be an error for הוה, for an indication of the past would seem desirable. (Rosenthal)

5. מהחסן. This pass. part. already appeared in *A.P.* 7:2; 8:2; 16:2. On the form see L § 32g. In *A.P.* 28:14 the verb means "take possession of" one's share; in *A.P.* 20:7 it is used of holding another's property. The verb is already found in B.A.

ויהבת is 2d pers. and addressed to the buyer, son-in-law of the sellers.

Cf. 1 karsh, 3 shekels, with the price of 1 karsh, 4 shekels, paid to Bagazušt in 3:6. Each item is given first in cardinal numbers spelled out and then in numerals.

כסף יון (cf. l. 14). The need is now felt to give the equivalent in Greek money. This reflects in an interesting manner the impact of Greek political interference in Egypt at this time. See above, Chapter 3.

סתתרי, as in *A.P.* 35:4, 7; 67:9. According to Sethe, *NGGW*, 1916, 114, the seeming construct ending is due to Egyptian influence. Cf. Coptic *sateere* > **stater-ye*(*t*). Schaeder, *Beiträge*, 267, points out that סתריא זי כספא on the lion weight of Abydos, *CIS*, 2, 108, gives the form סתר, which passed also into Armenian, Pahlavi, and Sogdian. It can hardly be called "more correct," however. The abs. pl. סתתרין occurred in *A.P.* 37:12, a text which as we can now see must come from this same general time (see Chapter 10), and in *A.P.* 61:8 (?). Ours is now the earliest dated reference to the stater in Egypt. Since the stater is two shekels, the shekel is the "Median shekel." See above, Chapter 3.

6. וחד. Here the numeral precedes the cardinal. "Our heart is satisfied"; cf. 1:4, etc.

בגו, "therewith," here employed in the manner of 7:5; it is generally used as "thereto" before a list of witnesses. A more literal usage of גו, "midst," in Aḥ., ll. 9, 23.

זי here "that," as object; cf. BL § 109d.

אשתאר, as in *A.P.* 11:9, ישתאר, "be outstanding" (there of interest, here of payments). The initial א in the perf. instead of ה, as in Aḥ. 70, אשתמיע, BL § 34h. The metathesis of ת and ש (L § 8) is also illustrated by that word.

לן עליך is a fine example of the common Semitic ל for the creditor and על for the debtor.

דמיא (also below, l. 14). The first occurrence in the papyri of the emph. pl. (abs. pl. דמן in *A.P.* 30:28).

זנה משחת starts a new sentence. On this word see on 2:9.

7.–8. Length is 16 cubits *k* 2, width 5 cubits *k* 2 (cf. on l. 16). Is כ an abbreviation of the word for "handbreadth" or "span"? See on 4:7.

לאברת. See on 4:7.

והא starts a new sentence. The boundaries of the house sold to Anani b. Haggai by Anani b. Azariah and *Tpmt* are now to be described.

פס שרת. See on 10:7.

At this point the scribe interrupted his work. As noted in the introduction, his customers were evidently dissatisfied with something. For one thing, perhaps the other house had not been given (as פס שרת) to Anani but to Yehoyishma, his wife. Then, too, there was no description of the property such as is found in the new piece in ll. 12–13. Finally, the measurement to the *'brt* lacked 2 *k*. Instead of discarding this sheet of papyrus, however, the newly written document of l. 10 and following was subsequently attached to the unfinished one of ll. 1–9. The latter, perhaps, contained a few things which the other did not have and that one of the parties wanted to have on record. The allusions to Yeb and to the *degel* of Nabukudurri, to *Tpmt*'s being the daughter of Pethu, and to the house having originally belonged to Yanbuli b. Misdai who owned property in Yeb, the price having been fully paid with nothing left outstanding, are not found below. Or was there a

superstitious fear of destroying a document on which had been written "Yahu, the god dwelling in Yeb the fortress" — the same motive later leading to putting discarded religious texts in the Geniza?

Following l. 9 another was begun but was erased. The scribe had written: . . . [על]ספר אנתותה זה, ". . . on her document of marriage. This . . ." Cf. l. 18.

10. Here Anani is לחן ליהו, as in 1:2; his wife's title לחנה is not repeated.

11. It is new that *Tpmt* is called פריפת (or פדיפת) of Meshullam b. Zakkur. Erichsen suggests connecting the word with demotic *pr-íp.t*, "workhouse," and thinks it designates the slave as an inmate of it.

כל 2 כפם חד stresses the full concord of husband and wife in this sale; it must have been important that there was such agreement. The phrase is a new one for the papyri and may be influenced by Assyrian *ešten pū*, "concord." Did it occur in Aḥ. 204?

The name Meshullam is here omitted from the pedigree of Anani b. Haggai b. Meshullam b. *Bss*. Instead, Haggai was omitted in No. 15. This shows how easily such a series can lose a member and should make us cautious in accepting any Old Testament pedigree as complete.

12.–13. The specification of what is involved repeats the phraseology of 9:12; 10:2, above, to which we may refer.

Note that מבני here is after בי תחתי instead of before it. One must thus render "the lower house is a construction having . . ." A new statement starts with the next מבני. Its meaning is obscure and the verbiage redundant. "The construction of the lower house consists of (?) the two compartments of mine."

ויהבת לך is 2d pers. sing. and starts a new sentence. The scribe was evidently disgusted at having to do the job over again and so does not write out the numbers carefully as in l. 5.

15. The equivalent in Greek coins is given.

כסף יון is accusative of specification.

במנין. The same expression is in *A.P.* 2:14; 3:13. Cowley takes it to mean "in full," but this does not fit our passage. It here means "by number (equal to)," in Ezra 6:17 למנין, "according to the number of."

16. Above the first letter of אברת (cf. 4:7; 9:7) is a ל. The original ל in the line had been run too close to the numeral and was rubbed out. To the left of the ל is the אמן which was forgotten after אברת.

151: This is a corrected figure (cf. 150 above in l. 8).

זנה starts a new sentence.

17. One would expect a זי before ביתא. Scribal omission? "thy house . . . which we gave." While the property is legally the wife's, it is also considered the husband's as long as they are not divorced.

אנת עני. The sequence is interrupted by direct address.

18. פס שרת. See above, 10:7, 9.

ספר אנתותה. Cf. *A.P.* 35:5. Perhaps על here and in 10:9 means "beside," "apart from." But "on" seems better. In view of 10:7 it is probably an erroneous claim (cf. 10:9).

19. ביניהן, here and in l. 21 in place of the usual ביניהם.

פרנו (or פדנו) is a name not found in the other texts. B. Geiger thinks that it could be Iranian *farna*(*h*)-*vā*, "possessing splendor," if one assumes that ו stands for וא. One is certainly reminded of names ending in פרן - -, which are of such origin. בר זלי reminds one of the name Barzillai, Ezra 2:61, Neh. 7:63, which is (wrongly?) written as one word and hitherto held to be derived from ברזל, "iron"; cf. Noth, *IP*, 225. For a similar name, cf. Peiser, *Texte*, 293, *Zil-la-a*.

מרדו. A Haggai b. Mardu appeared in 9:26; 10:20; 11:14.

20. אגר באגר. Cf. above on 9:9.

תחתיא starts a new sentence.

פחי appears as a name in *A.P.* 14:2, 12; 51:4; 81:111, and Aimé-Giron, *Textes*, No. 105; cf. *Pa-ḫi-i* in Tallqvist, *APN*, 179. On it see Spiegelberg, *Sprachgut*, No. 98. פמט is not to be confused with פמת, "servant of Mut" (*A.P.* 72:4; 74:2; Spiegelberg, *Sprachgut*, No. 40), but according to Ranke and Edel is *pꜣ-mdw* and a hitherto unattested short form of אספמט, *A.P.* 4:7. For the Egyptian name see Ranke, *ÄP*, 175:1.

מלחן זי מיא. This is the first occurrence of the pl. abs. of מלח, "boatman," sing. in *A.P.* 6:11, 8:8; emph. *A.P.* 2:[2]; 5:13. But מיא קשיא, "rough waters," in the first two of these passages is more vivid. The taking up or down of boats through the cataract above Elephantine required such men. They are sons of תויא. The name appeared in *A.P.* 63:2 as the name of a woman and is found as *Thauēs* in Greek papyri; see Spiegelberg, *OLZ*, *15*, 1912, 10. Since these men were named after a woman, their mother was evidently a slave.

21. "street of the king," as in 3:10; 4:10; 10:4, 5.

וכונה 1. Cf. *A.P.* 25:6. כוין appeared as pl. of a fem. noun in Dan. 6:11. The sing. posited is *כוה. See BL § 510, L § 43t. But here we apparently have a sing. כונה, and פתיח suggests that כונה is a masc. (probably with suff.).

ל before תרי, indicating direction; in Dan. 6:11 נגד is used.

עלה presumably the word written עלא, "above," in 6:13 and *A.P.* 5:5, where it occurs alone (otherwise after a prep.).

22. אנת starts a new sentence.

23. עד עלמן, regularly עד עלם, but the same plural form is found in Aḥ. 95. In Dan. 7:18 עד is used, otherwise על.

24. בכסף. There is an anacoluthon here (supply: thou mayest sell it).

גוא (cf. פריפת in l. 11). This is a new word for the Old Aramaic vocabulary. J.A. *gawwā*, "belly"? A coarse expression for slave concubine or handmaiden? In the Palmyrene inscriptions, Jean Cantineau, *Inventaire des inscriptions de Palmyre*

(Beyrouth, 1930), *1*, No. 193, there is a גויא מהימנא, "a faithful eunuch"; and also see on this Rosenthal, *Die aramäistische Forschung*, 98, n. 2. Compare the J.A. adjective גואה, "inner one." For גוא one is reminded of the use of כלי "vessel" for a woman in Meg. 12b.

ויהבה, suff. 3d pers. sing. fem.

25. לאנתו. See above, 2:3, etc.

ולא נכל נרשנך. For the first verb, see on 3:12. The second gives a form not yet found in the papyri; see L § 40 f.

ויהבת, 2d pers. sing.

דמוהי. The מ is not fully preserved.

26. כסף, "in silver," accusative of specification.

After וטיב the scribe had forgotten לבבן בגו, and he subsequently wrote it above the line. לבבן, 1st pers. pl. suff., as in *A.P.* 2:9; 20:8, 9.

אף לא starts a new sentence.

נכהל. The 1st pers. pl. implies that either Ananiah or *Tpmt* could conceivably bring action to reclaim. Together they sign away such a right.

רחמת. Cf. *A.P.* 9:7 and L § 61i.

27. They rule out such action also for son or daughter (did they have any other daughter or is this just legal terminology?).

On הנגית, etc.; cf. above 9:18; 10:12.

זי ירשנך starts a new sentence: "whoever, etc."

וירשה, the form (without waw) in *A.P.* 8:26. Note that in l. 24 of that text the scope of רשה is clarified: bringing forward a claim to property before judges.

28. וזי יקבל, another "whoever" clause with זי. On קבל see 1:5 f.

דין, here *dayyān*, "judge," as in 1:6 and *A.P.* 8:13; 10:13, 19.

29. זי ינפק. A third "whoever" clause begins here. The אביגדן; cf. above, 5:8 etc.

30. זילך ודי, side by side, show a curious lack of conformity in spelling. The other texts have here אפם; see on 3:16.

31. אף starts a new sentence.

ספר זבנתא sounds like a "terminus technicus," but it does not occur on any of the endorsements where one might expect to find it. ספר מרחק is the regular expression used. See above, No. 5:18.

זבן, here: "sold" (pael).

כסף. There is a gap before this word, as though the amount paid were to be filled in later. Perhaps they could not recollect the price at the moment or did not wish to state it. Actually, the document handed over is preserved in No. 3, and the price paid Bagazušt and Ūbīl was 1 karsh, 4 shekels. Anani b. Haggai is thus getting the house for 1 shekel less than it had cost his father-in-law 36 years before. Real estate in Yeb was evidently not subject to much depreciation.

32. דמוהי, with masc. suff., can hardly be referring to ספר; it must rather refer

to זבנתא. It is curious, however, to speak of the price of a document, and so one should perhaps take זי זבן in the sense of "when he sold"; cf. Dan. 3:15 די ... תפלון, BL § 109e.

33. Haggai b. Shema'iah (cf. n. on 3:23) wrote this in Yeb at the dictation of Ananiah and *Tpmt*. The latter name is here written תפממת (note hiatus) by mistake.

כפם חד. Cf. l. 11. The usual "witnesses thereto" is omitted, but שהד precedes each name.

Meshullam b. Ma'uziah, in *A.P.* 22:109 b. Ma'uzi.

Reḥum b. Beitha; see on 11:14.

Nathan b. Yeho'or, mentioned a decade earlier in *A.P.* 28:16. Yeho'or is a fem. name in *A.P.* 1:2 (there written יההאור).

מגר. This is evidently another witness, who uses an abridged form of his (Babylonian) name and omits the paternal name. Compare in Stamm, *Akkadische Namengebung*, 222 such names as *Assur-magir* or *Sin-magir* (the god Assur or Sin "is favorably inclined"). The latter was the name of an officer of Nebuchadrezzar and appears as סמגר in Jer. 39:3. Cf. Samuel Feigin, "The Babylonian Officials in Jeremiah 39:3–13," *JBL*, *45*, 1926, 149 f.

35. The endorsement. זבן here is pael, as in l. 31. Note the use of the singular. The emphasis is on the man's action, but the woman had a legal right in the property and her consent was essential, hence she is named. Traces of erased writing are visible on the sheet, which thus is being reused.

PAPYRUS 13

PAPYRUS 13

(*Brooklyn* 47.218.151) 12.8 *cm.* x 24.2 *cm.*

THE letter here published is of historical interest because it refers to events about which little is known (Chapter 10). Brooklyn No. 12 showed that Artaxerxes II was still acknowledged as sovereign in Upper Egypt at the end of 402 B.C. (Horn and Wood's date but according to Parker 401 B.C.). The one Elephantine text explicitly dated under Amyrtaeus (*A.P.* 35, though we would assign *A.P.* 22 to this time) comes from the 21st (?) of Phamenoth in his 5th year (June 19, 400 B.C.). This new letter alludes to the death (?) of King Amyrtaeus and then reports the accession of "King *Nf'wrt*," i. e., Nepherites I, founder of the 29th Dynasty, in Epiphi. While the latter ruler's name is found in a few brief hieroglyphic inscriptions (see Gauthier, "Le livre des rois d'Égypte," *IFAO*, *Mémoires*, *20*, Pts. 1–2, 1915–16, 161 f.) in the form *nȝf-ʿȝrd* (cf. Ranke, *ÄP*, 170:18), this text provides the first occurrence of the name in Semitic transcription. His reign began officially December 1, 399 B.C. See Bickermann, *IFAO*, *Mémoires*, *66*, 1934, 79. The date of his actual seizure of regnal power was doubtlessly the 1st of Epiphi, for this letter was written under the fresh impression of that event, on the 5th of Epiphi, October 1, 399 B.C.

The letter may have been written at Thebes, Abydos, or even at Memphis. Its writer, however, is an Elephantine resident, Shewa b. Zekariah, who is reporting to "my lord Yislaḥ" the significant political change that has taken place, while at the same time referring also to business matters. Personal regards are conveyed to other people, including Anani b. Neriah.

It is surprising to find allusion to Widrang in l. 8. If he is the same man who was fratarak at Yeb in the summer of 410 B.C., and whom not only the Bagoas letter but the reply of Delaiah calls "the evildoer," he was evidently alive and a factor in the situation in the year 399. The statement in the Bagoas letter (*A.P.* 30:16), referred to in Chapter 9, therefore, cannot mean that he was executed for his role in the matter of the destruction of the Jewish temple. If fragment *d* is properly placed and interpreted, he may even have held the post of military commander. That makes possible the assignment of *A.P.* 38, which refers to him with this same title and as acting at Abydos, to a date later than 410 (cf. Chapter 10).

1 [אל מראי יסלח בר ... עבדך] שוא שלם מראי אלהיא כלאׄ [ישאלו] שגיא בכל עדן
וׄ[כעת].................

2 ....[ע]ל דבר אפוחס וׄא..ה .. ל .. [מט]אני כזי
תמטנך אגׄ[רתי]..........

3 ....[יהי]תׄון מנפי מלכא אמורטי [ס...] מלכא נפעורת יתב
[בא]פף הׄ.........

4 ....אנפיך בשלם בירת. פ..[יר]חק מלכא
נפעוׄ[רת] כספא זי הושרת לי ביד

5 ....וון מליא אלה זבנה מנחם וׄ....... [ל]עליא
הקׄ............רׄ נחשא זי

6 ....שלם ענני בר נריה שלם כל בני........קׄנה אל...
[ע]לׄ דבר.....מלה מלה

7 ....[מ]טאת ספינתא תנה עלין יפטרו[ן]....םׄ וידרנג [רב]
חיל גׄ..... תׄרדי על

8 ....ב 5 לאפף כתיב אגרתי ז[א]

9 אׄ[ל] מראי יסלח בר ... עבדך שוא בר זכריה

1. [To my lord Yislaḥ b. . . . thy servant] Shewa. The peace of my lord may the gods all [desire] greatly at all times. And [now?]
2. . . . in the matter of the *'pwḥs* . . . [reach]ed me. When [my] let[ter] reaches thee . . .
3. . . . [they brou]ght to (?) Memphis the king, Amyrtae[us ? . . .]; the king Nepherites sat (upon the throne) [in E]piphi . . .
4. . . . thy face in peace. The fortress (?) . . . . the king Neph[erites depar]ts. The silver which thou didst send to me by the hand of . . .
5. . . . [they will make kn]own (?) these things. There bought (it?) Menahem and . . . above . . . . of copper which . . .
6. . . . Greetings, Anani b. Neriah. Greetings, all the sons of . . . to . . . in the matter of . . . each thing . . .
7. . . . The ship has [re]ached here unto us. They loosed . . . . Widrang [the com]mander (?) . . . . concerning . . .
8. . . . On the 5th of Epiphi was written th[is] my letter.

9. Address: T[o] my lord Yislaḥ b. . . . thy servant Shewa b. Zekariah.

This letter is broken away at the right, in the center, and on the left. Epistolary papyri were usually written on sheets wider than those used for legal texts, but often, when the communication was brief, they were not as long. Taking such a letter as Sach. 1 (*A.P.* 30) as an example, we find that its width measures 32 cm. The total width indicated for the preserved parts of No. 13 is about 22 cm. How much is missing on the right can be gauged from the rather certain reconstruction of the opening words, namely, about 7 cm. of the text plus a margin of 1 cm. That would leave a loss of only 2 cm. between fragment *b* and *c*+*d* to bring it up to the width of Sach. 1. The loss thus was chiefly on the right.

In the reconstruction of this papyrus the reverse, with the address, is of great aid in properly placing the fragments. A different arrangement of *c*, *d*, *e*, *g* (between *a* and *b*) was first projected before *c* was joined to *d*, but the present arrangement is probably correct.

1. Mention of the addressee and of the writer comes first in letters. In the light of the address as given on the reverse, the missing words must be [אל מראי יסלח בר . . . עבדך] ["to my lord Yislaḥ son of . . . thy servant"]. It seems possible that he is Yislaḥ b. Nathan, author of the interesting letter fragment *A.P.* 56, or Yislaḥ b. Gaddūl of No. 7:44; *A.P.* 25:19; 29:2.

שוא is the name of the writer. The name is found in I Chron. 2:49, where it is now vocalized "Shewā." Noth, *IP*, 223, thinks it refers to a child being *like* someone (Arabic *sawā'un*). But one suspects a shortened form, with a god as subject; perhaps the full name was שוהרם (cf. 11:12). The endorsement gives בר זכריה, so we here have a man already known from *A.P.* 23:15 (and perhaps *A.P.* 40:1, "Shewa and his children"). Cowley dates the former text about 420 B.C., but that is too early; sons of men of that time appear in this list.

שלם begins a new sentence. The word doubtlessly was the object of a verb [ישאלו] as in various letters published by Sachau.

אלהיא כלא, in *A.P.* 41:1, כלא, 39:1, כל; on כלא see BL § 25 f. Shewa wishes that the gods may show favor to Yislaḥ. Both are evidently religious "liberals." In *A.P.* 40:1, Hosha'iah b. Nathan, who sends Shewa greetings, uses the monotheistic formula of *A.P.* 30:2 and was evidently less liberally inclined. Is the שלמא כלא of Ezra 5:7 an abridgement of such paganizing phraseology?

[ישאלו]. This verb must be restored, as stated above; cf. *A.P.* (17:1); 37:2; 39:1; 41:1; 56:1. It is probably the only word missing in the gap and thus helps determine the width of the latter. The idiom is not quite the same as "greet" in Gen. 43:27 (שאל ל לשלום) or שאל בשלום in post-biblical Hebrew (so Harris Birkeland, "Drei Bemerkungen zu den Papyrus aus Elephantine," *Acta Orientalia*, *13*, 1934, 81 f.), which is equivalent to Assyrian *šulum N. N. ša'ālu*. Cowley, in his note on *A.P.* 17:1, renders "inquire after the health of someone," i. e., "be careful of it," but this is too weak. In the Neo-Babylonian letters (cf., e. g., Ebeling, *ABAW*, n. f., Heft 30, 1949, No. 8, etc.) the introductory wish often is "May the gods command

the welfare of N. N." (*šulum ša N. N. liḳbū*). שאל, while not as strong as *ḳibū*, "command," has the same thing in mind: the efficacious bringing about of the desired result. The rendering "may the gods desire the welfare of N. N." would seem best, since this meaning of שאל is found in J.A. and fits best with שגיא. The idiom imagines the gods as desiring favorable omina for their devotee.

שגיא, adverbial; cf. *A.P.* 30:2, etc. In these instances it follows ישאלו directly, and the probability is that that was the case here. That provides a strong argument in favor of putting *c*+*d* to the left of *b* rather than between *a* and *b*, whereby a large gap of about 7 cm. would be created. Polite phrases should be shorter here than in *A.P.* 30, for Yislaḥ is no Bagoas!

בכל עדן ו. Cf. *A.P.* 30:2, etc. The last letter looks like nun, but must be waw, for a conjunction is in order. A trace of a letter is visible on the left; a kaph? Then ו[כען] (Rosenthal) or ו[כעת] cf. *A.P.* 56:1.

In the Hermopolis papyri, according to Kamil, *BIE*, *28*, 1947, the latter is regularly used to begin a new sequence "and now." He finds this illuminating for the understanding of the וכעת in Ezra 4:17. Obviously in that passage the excerpted document has been cut off at the very point where its message began.

2. The line now begins with [על] דבר. The matter in hand was directly taken up. Something like [שלחת עלי] "you sent to me" may have preceded (Rosenthal).

אפוחס. This word is certainly not Aramaic. A personal name seems unlikely after the preceding phrase. Unfortunately, the broken connection gives little clue as to what to look for in Iranian or demotic. A Greek word seems unlikely.

The next two words are only partly legible. The variability of this scribe's letters makes it difficult to guess what letter stood first. I think it was a ו. The letters after א look more like זי than a ד or ר. The long letter could be ך, ן, ף; the last is a ה (or דו). Could one read ואזיפה from יזף, "I borrowed it?"

The first preserved letter of the next word is ל, but there would seem to be room for a letter before it. The remains of the next word permit of no certain identification. Rosenthal would read לאמר. But the gap between this word and the next is so narrow (when the missing letters are restored) that there is hardly room for another word. The subject of the next word (a verb) ought then to have stood here.

--- אני This is certainly to be filled out י[מט]אני, "reached me." The subject could be something sent or even a person. The subject of תמטנך (fem. sing. 3d pers. impf. energ. of מטא with suffix, L § 40 f.) began with א. H. L. Ginsberg rightly suggested א[גרתי]. Traces of another letter that may well have been ג are visible. Rosenthal would construe the connection "It (he?) shall come to me when my letter comes to you." In *A.P.* 42:7 על is used after מטא.

3. Several words are missing. Only the last two letters of a word ending in --- ון appear on the right, but the tops of the three preceding letters are visible. The last of these letters had a long downward stroke, which is still discernible on the

edge of the fragment. Rosenthal thinks it is a ת and looks for a form of נחת, such as [יהנ]תון, "they brought," and would have them bring the king mentioned in the following to the city named. But the remains of the letters scarcely permit reading a form of נחת. It would agree better with the indications to restore [יהי]תון, (אתא haphel). מנפי is Memphis, as in *A.P.* 37:11; 42:7; 42:11; 83:2, and Aimé-Giron, *Textes*, No. 10, verso 3. Is Memphis direct object and did the verb end in סֹן?

מלכא here precedes the name, instead of following it, as so frequently occurs in the date formulas: not "King A." but "the king, A."

אמורט[יס]. There can be no doubt that the name of the native ruler found in *A.P.* 35:1, 6, appears here. If the restoration [יהי]תֹון is correct a short word like חיא, "alive," might have stood here; cf. אחד חין, Beh. 1:6, etc., and the similar situation with Apries, Herodotus II, 169. In the fragment *b* we have מלכא נפעורת יתב. The title "king" precedes a king name, as was the case with מלכא אמורט[יס]. The name נפעורת is evidently that of the founder of the 29th Dynasty, Nepherites I (*nʒf-ʿʒrd*; Ranke, *ÄP*, 170:18). ו and ר are run together (Rosenthal).

יתב. Impf.? Cf. Dan. 7:26. Here used in abridged manner of accession.

On fragment *c* we have פף – –, doubtlessly [בא]פף, "in Epiphi," i. e., the 1st of Epiphi (cf. on 7:1). The initial letter of another word – – – ה (or ג?) is visible on the left. Amyrtaeus' execution could have been mentioned here: ה[תקטל], cf. Aḥ. 62, or ה[קטל]?

4. אנפיך בשלם. Perhaps a wish like "may I see" was expressed at the beginning of l. 4 and is concluded in "thy face in peace." This phraseology appears in the Hermopolis papyri; cf. Kamil, *BIE*, *28*, 1947, 256.

בירת[א]? Rosenthal would read ביד and a name. The next word began with a פ, and there is trace of an additional letter. There is no room for an additional word.

The word חק – – – could be from רחק (or דחק). The sentence presumably ended with the next two words. If a בירתא was mentioned ידחק would have to be supplied; but [יר]חק or [הר]חק would seem more likely.

נפעו[רת]. The name of Nepherites occurs again. He hopes to see him when Nepherites departs? Or is he reporting that he has departed?

כספא זי joins perfectly with the following and helped in putting together *c* and *d*. A new sentence must have begun here. The horizontal stroke under the final aleph is peculiar.

הושרת, 2d pers. sing. perf. haphel. The fem. הושרתי, *A.P.* 39:3, where Cowley's translation needs correction. In the ostraca the verb means "send." So already in the Assur ostracon, Lidzbarski, *Altaramäische Urkunden aus Assur*, p. 8; cf. also הושרו לי מלח in the Clermont-Ganneau Ostracon No. 16, published by Dupont-Sommer, *ASAE*, *48*, 1948, 112. It is probably an Assyrianism, for (*w*)*ašāru*, "to be let loose," gets the derived meaning "send." In J.A. ישר does not have this meaning.

5. [יח]וון, "they will make known" or [יש]וון, "they will do"? (Suggestions of Rosenthal.)

מליא, "words" or "things," already in the Assur ostracon (l. 12) and *A.P.* 30:29, etc.

זבנה. This must be 3d pers. masc. sing. with an obj. suff.: "there bought it" (or "sold it," if pael). Apparently the word starts a new sentence.

מנחם. There are a number of men of this name in the Elephantine colony of this period (cf. *A.P.* 22), and as his father's name is not given he cannot be further identified. After the name there are traces of two letters, the first probably ו. Two short words would fill the gap.

[ל]עליא, the first word in this line of *b*. The top of the preposition is visible above the break.

--- הק must remain uncertain; cf. הקשט, *A.P.* 4:3, "made ready"?

Traces of the tops of the letters of two words appear on the *c-d* fragments, followed by נחשא זי. Rosenthal would read the second סיר "pot." Better yet וסר?

6. שלם. One might take this as a verb and see in it a statement that the persons mentioned are with the writer at Memphis and are all well (cf. *A.P.* 37:2) in spite of the political troubles. But the analogy of other letters, notably those from Hermopolis, suggests that it is a noun and that greetings to people in Elephantine are meant (cf. *A.P.* 39:2 f.). Probably greetings to one individual preceded in the lost material on the right. The recipients of the preserved greetings are "Anani b. Neriah and all the sons of . . ." The named individual may have been a son of the priest Neriah of *A.P.* 38:1.

קנה --. I first read תנה, "here," as in l. 7, but this writer's ת shows no tendency to close (Rosenthal). ק is thus preferable, but it is not so easy to find a suitable form. If final ה represented a feminine suffix, the נ could be energic and then ק the only remaining radical (one might think of a haphel of סלק). If the נ is a radical letter, the verb might be קנה. Is אל "to" or "not" here?

The fragment *e* (and *g*, which must have stood below it) has been placed to the left of *b* because of the word in the next line.

[ע]ל דבר, as in l. 2. The piece cannot be placed higher up because it would then extend into the "wavy-line" area. The fibers, particularly in the verso, recommend its placement here. The identical shape of *e* and *g* is due to their having been above each other in the rolled-up papyrus when a worm ate into it.

On the piece *f*, which obviously is the left bottom piece, there followed מלה מלה. The words are evidently distributive, "each thing." Cf. *GK* § 123c.

7. את -- at the beginning of the line is perhaps to be restored to [מט]את, as Rosenthal suggests. Traces of ט are still visible.

ספינתא, "ship," occurs in *A.P.* 26:3 f., a text concerned with the repair of a boat used in government service. ספינה, the absolute form, is an Aramaism in Jonah 1:5.

יפטרו[ן]. "They loosed" *sc.* "their prisoners" or "their bonds?"

Before וידרגג there is visible the final letter of a word, possibly a מ. Suffix הם?

וידרנג, the name of the commander (רב חיל) (see Brooklyn No. 8 and *A.P.* 20:4; 25:2) and later *prtrk* at Yeb, in *A.P.* 27:4; 30:5.

חיל seems to be the word on the fragment *e* and suggested the placement of it here as part of [רב] חיל (cf. *A.P.* 30:7) or else as object of a verb of which Widrang is the subject. On the left edge are the remains of a letter נ that extends down rather far to the right.

On the left bottom piece *f* there seems to be תרדי על (or תודי?). The sentence must have continued to the next line, as the preposition requires a continuation.

8. The date evidently followed directly on the end of the sentence. On it cf. the introduction.

אגרתי, the first example in the papyri of the word "letter" with suffix. The remains of a letter ז appear on the edge of the piece. Perhaps ז[א]?

9. The endorsement. On such papyri as *A.P.* 37–38 (see Sach. Tafeln XI and XII) אל, "to," is put far out to the right before the name of the addressee. While the remains of a letter on the reverse of *d* do not primarily suggest an א as written in most cases by this scribe, the א at the end of the word "ship" in l. 7 has a similar inward flourish of the right foot. There is, furthermore, a trace of the base of a ל to the left, which would correspond well to the spread out אל illustrated in the above-mentioned papyri. If this were no אֹל, then the piece *c-d* would have to be put between *a* and *b* (where the technician first put it), and the letter in question be considered part of the name of Yislaḥ's father (then not Nathan but Gaddūl!). On the difficulty caused by that arrangement cf. above on l. 1.

The ligature of yod and samekh in Yislaḥ (Rosenthal) should be noted.

PAPYRUS 14

PAPYRUS 14

(*Brooklyn* 47.218.12) 9.8 *cm.* x 14.9 *cm.*

BESIDE the two important marriage documents, Nos. 2 and 7, which so excellently supplement *A.P.* 15, we have here a fragment of a marriage document which thus may be grouped with the fragmentary ones, *A.P.* 18, 36, 48. Neither the name of the bride nor that of the groom is preserved, but the groom belonged to the *degel* of Iddin-Nabū (cf. *A.P.* 20:2; 67:1).

Even though the year date and name of the sovereign in whose reign the marriage took place are lost, its date can, perhaps, be inferred from the synchronisms of month and day, on the basis of the general considerations which limit the origin of the document to the 5th century. There is a slight uncertainty as to the Iyyar date owing to the fact that there is a gap in the numerals. The question is whether to reconstruct Iyyar 15 or Iyyar 8. The latter possibility seems more likely. Under that assumption, according to Richard A. Parker, there are only two possibilities between 464 B.C. and 400 B.C. — the 8th and 19th years of Artaxerxes I.

	Iyyar 8	Tybi 20
457 B.C.	May 3	May 3
446 B.C.	May 1	April 30

For a synchronism of Iyyar 15, Tybi 20, the only 5th-century date would fall on May 14, 498 B.C., according to S. H. Horn and L. H. Wood, which seems too early for general as well as paleographic reasons. The date May 1, 446 B.C., is probably the correct one. *A.P.* 13 was written in that same year.

One may ask whether this can be a contract of a previous marriage on the part of Yehoyishma? Hardly! She was probably not born until after 449 B.C., for the marriage of her parents took place in that year and she is not mentioned in the contract. It could, however, have been a previous marriage of Anani b. Haggai or a marriage of Meshullam b. Zakkur, who both belonged to that *degel*.

ב 8 לאיר הו יום 20 לתעבי ב[שנת]...

ארמי זי יב בירתא לדגל אדננב̇ו ל...

לאמר אנה אתית עליך בבית[ך] ו[ש]א[לת]

ואנה בעלה מן יומא זנה [ו]עד [עלם]

(a 1 לפם 1 שוה כ[סף]

[חט]ב צבע יד[ין]

(b א כסף ר 2

(c ...ס...

(d מלכ[א]

כסף 2

1. On the 8th (?) of Iyyar, that is the 20th day of Tybi, in the . . . [year of Artaxerxes the king] . . .
2. Aramaean of Yeb the fortress of the *degel* of Iddin-Nabū to . . .
3. saying: I have come unto thee in [thy] house and have asked . . . [she is my wife]
4. and I am her husband from this day forth unto [forever] . . .

a) . . . on one edge, worth silver . . .
. . . striped, dyed on both sides . . .

b) . . . silver 2 R. . . .

c) . . . 1 letter . . .

d) . . . the king . . .
. . . silver 2 . . .

1. The fragment placed at the right of the first and second lines has been put too close; the gap must have been a little wider. The mark on the left of the fragment is probably the remnant of a 1, rather than of a 10; there must, therefore, have been two more single strokes, so that the full number was 8. On the date see the introductory remarks.

תעבי, as in *A.P.* 83:1. In *A.P.* 42:14; 67:1; 68:11.

בשׁנת. The letters are only faintly legible.

2. ארמי. There can hardly be any doubt about the reading. As noted above, the gap between the fragment and the main piece should be a little wider. This would allow for the proper formation of the מ.

אדננבו. (*A.P.* 20:2; 67:1). The next to the last letter does not look like ב, but some ink has evidently been flaked off. It seems impossible to read ארפחו, since the third letter is clearly a נ.

The final ל of the line must have been followed by the name of the bride's father or whoever acted on her behalf in receiving the mohar.

3. The text can be restored here on the basis of the parallels.

4. The groom's promise to make this marriage permanent is preserved. The faded or missing letters can easily be restored.

a) is from the list of objects brought in by the bride.

b) is likewise from that list, giving the value of some object.

c) a single ס and probably to be put at the end of the first line of fragment *a*.

d) The word "king" presumably comes from a connection where "stones of the king" were referred to. In the second line כסף is the most likely reading.

PAPYRUS 15

PAPYRUS 15

(*Brooklyn* 47.218.97) 11.2 *cm.* x 25.1 *cm.*

THIS is an endorsement of a lost papyrus. The handwriting seems to be the same as that of No. 14, but it cannot belong to that document. The papyrus is different in texture and color. Furthermore, this document cannot have been a marriage contract, but was doubtlessly a conveyance.

There is every reason to suppose that Yehoyishma is the same person about whom we have heard so much in these texts. It seems equally probable that Ananiah b. Meshullam is none other than her husband Anani b. Haggai b. Meshullam. It is natural for the husband to convey property to the wife, especially after she has borne a child. Presumably Ananiah gave Yehoyishma a house as Anani b. Azariah did Tamut in No. 4. The omission of a name in the pedigree is extremely interesting; cf. 12:4 (3:2); 11:15. It suggests that in many an Old Testament pedigree similar abridgement has occurred. The natural inference here is that Ananiah had more reason, since the time of No. 7, to stress the name of his grandfather than of his father. The latter may meanwhile have died.

ספר   זי כתב ענניה בר משלם ליהוישמע

"Document which Ananiah son of Meshullam wrote to Yehoyishma."

PAPYRUS 16

PAPYRUS 16

(*Brooklyn* 47.218.13) 6.5 *cm.* x 4.6 *cm.*

THIS text is the most perplexing in the collection, for it does not fall into a recognizable category with the aid of which its fragments might be arranged. The papyrus is so dark that it is not translucent when held against the light and so fragile that it does not permit of much handling. To complicate matters it is written on both sides — on the verso with the sheet turned upside down. It was no longer possible, when I finally tried to do something with it, to expect the technical aide to devote much time to so discouraging a proposition, and so the fragments were sealed in the manner shown on the plate.

The initial word of the text, "the corn," is preserved. The text would seem to have had a topical title, e. g., the corn which was supplied to the garrison (cf. *A.P.* 2–4). There seem to be several first person singular words or phrases. The most certain and most interesting thing about it is that the two pieces containing reference to "Khnum, the god," H2 and I3, belong together. Whether the word "sacrifices" in G3 belongs before "Khnum" is less certain. Perhaps this papyrus was not of Jewish origin but came from the house of a priest of Khnum.

RECTO

A

1 עבורא
2 ב 15 ...
3 אדׄיׄן

B

1 ן כרש 1
2 בׄרת אׄ...
3 —

C

1 ...2 לכסף ש
2 .כזי לא
3 כען א...
4 ל...

D

1 ה...
2 אמרת
3 ...דתׄ
4 10 ש

E

1 שׄ לׄ
2 ואמׄר אנהׄ
3 שאל אנה ש
4 לך [כס]ף כנה
5 לׄ

F

1 חׄ
2 על בזי
3 ...

G

1 עשיׄ
2 [ע]שרתה
3 ...דבחי

H

1 ך למ...
2 ... חנום

I

1 ו לחרׄ
2 עׄרק בא...
3 [א]להא

J

1 רה
2 נׄיהׄ

K

....

L

...
לת

M

ה

N

...
דןׄ

O

...ך

P

ל

Q

ה...
ל

R

...ם כ...

VERSO

k

תה

l

...ה...

כס

ן ל...

m

...

...

n

ת

תׄא

o

מׄת לד

p

...

q

לכי

ל...

...

r

נׄ

מו

נׄ

j

...ה...

יל

g

1 ...

2 דלן ...

3 ...כזי כנ...

4 ...סבל...

h

1 [...]ל[...] וחש

2 ום ירׄה (לא above the line)

3 ל תז

i

1 ...ש

2 אוני

3 מן איש

4 ...נׄוׄ

d

1 ב...

2 לי מת

3 זבנו

4 הב ל...

e

1 בעד –נת זפׄ...

2 זי מׄתת כען... (י above the line)

3 כסף ש 3

4 ביום ...

5 .ל.

f

1 ... ש...

2 ...י כנׄש...

a

(blank)

b

1 .כף

2 לעלי

3 שׄיתת

4 מן שא ל

c

1 א...

2 יהוה

3 ינת לכי כסׄף (זה above the line)

4 ...זי נחש

5 ם סחפ[ו]ם

PAPYRUS 17

PAPYRUS 17

(*Brooklyn* 47.218.153) 10.1 *cm.* x 3.9 *cm.*

THIS fragment is much lighter in color than any other of the collection. It was written by a scribe who had a facility with the pen, like the "ready writer" of Ps. 45:2. But since it is only a small piece it is difficult to say much about it. There are allusions to a man's "bringing" something and to measures, one called the *šp* and one that is abbreviated to *s*. One would like to consider the latter as the seah, but the *šp* is a linear measure in *A.P.* 26:11, 19. Line 8 evidently referred to the person who was to do the delivering and whose name may have been Ma'u-[ziah]. The line of blank space between ll. 6 and 7 further confirms the thought that this was a letter; compare the Mazzoth Letter, *Sach.*, Plate 6.

1 ....מפחת

2 ..מהיתה

3 שף 1 ס 3

4 .ז]נ̇א שף 1 ס 2

5 זנא ש ף

6 תו פ

7 ..ת 5 יהי

8 ..ביד מעו[זיה]

INDEX OF PROPER NAMES

חור בר פטאסי 9:10; 10:6.
חיח בר אתרלי 3:23.
חנום 3:8; 4:10; 6:8; 9:10; 10:6; 16:H.
חרמנתן בר פחא 8:12.

יאוש f. of פלטי. 9:25.
יב 1:2; 2:2; 3:4, 25; 4:2, 4, 10; 5:2, 16; 6:2; 7:2; 9:2, 23; 10:3, 17; 11:10 b; 12:2, 3, 4, 32; 13:4(?); 14:2.
יבל for אובל. 3:25.
ידניה f. of ישביה. 9:25.
ידניה f. of מחסיה. 1:13.
ידניה בר גמריה 10:20.
ידניה בר מחסיה 7:44.
ידניה בר תחא 8:3, 7, 8.
יה 3:25.
יהו 1:2; 2:2; 3:3, 10; 4:2, 4, 10; 6:2; 9:2, 23; 10:2, 17; 12:1, 2, 10, 19, 33.
יהואור m. of נתן. 9:24; 10:18: 12:34.
יהוישמע 4:18, 21; 7:3, 4, 5, 21, 24, 29, 33, (34), 38, 39, 41; 8:18, 19; 9:2, 5, 6, 8, 16, 21, 27; 10:2, 8, 10; 12:18, 34; 15:1.
יהישמע 5:4, 7, 9, 10, 11; 6:2; 10:21.
יהישם 5:18.
יון 12:5, 14.
ינבולי בר מסדי 12:4. See אפולי.
יסלח 13:(1), 9.
יסלח בר גדול 7:43.
ישביה בר ידניה 9:25.
יתום f. of הושעיה 4:24; 9:24.

כפא f. of עקב. 8:10.

מגר 12:34.
מחסיה f. of אוריה. 8:2.
מחסיה f. of גמריה. 2:15; 4:23.
מחסיה f. of ידניה. 7:44.
מחסיה בר ידניה 1:13.
מיכא בר א . . . 1:2, 10.
מיכיה בר אחיו 5:17.
מכיה 1:12.
מנחם 13:5.
מנחם בר גדול 10:18.
מנחם בר זכור 2:15.
מנחם בר עזריה 7:44.
מנחם בר שלום 11:13.
מנכי f. of בתי. 1:10.
מנכי בר בגין 1:13.
מנפי 13:3.
מסדי f. of אפולי, ינבולי. 3:4; 12:4.
מעוזי f. of משלם. 9:25; 12:34.
מעוזיה f. of נתן. 10:19.
מעוזיה בר נתן 4:22; 7:42.
מפטח m. of ברכיה. 5:17.
מרדו f. of חגי. 9:26; 10:20; 11:14.
מרדו br. of פרנו. 12:19.
משלם grandfather of ענני. 10:8; 11:1, 13, 15; 12:2.
משלם f. of זכור. 7:2, 43; 8:2.
משלם בר זכור 2:2, 13; 5:2, 3, 16, 18; 12:11, 24.
משלם בר מעוזי(ה) 9:25; 12:33.
מתרדת בר מתריזן 3:23.
מתריזן f. of מתרדת. 3:23.
מתרסרה 4:24.

נבוזיר 1:11.
נבוכדרי 11:2; 12:3.
נבושלם בר ביתאלרעי 8:11.
ניסי f. of אתרפרן. 5:16.
נסמו 3:2.
נפעורת 13:3, 4.
נרגלשזב f. of דוחשן. 8:9.
נריה f. of ענני. 13:6.
נתן f. of אחיו. 10:18.
נתן f. of הושעיה. 9:24.
נתן בר גדול 2:15.
נתן בר יהואור 9:24; 10:18; 12:34.
נתן בר מעוזיה 10:19.
נתן בר ענני 2:14.

סון 2:2; 3:2; (6:2 ?); 7:2; 8:1, 2, 3; 11:1, 2, 3, 10 b, 12.
סנכשר בר שבתי 8:10.

INDEX OF WORDS

אב *father.*
אבי 4:19.
אבוהי 5:11, 12, 14; 7:24.
אבוה 7:28.
אביגדן *a fine.* 6:17; 8:7; 9:20; 10:10, 14; 12:30.
אבגדן 5:8, 14; 11:6.
אבגדנא 11:7.
אביגדנא 7:31; 11:7.
אבד *to perish, be lost.*
יאבד 7:25.
אבן *stone.* 7:18, 19.
אבני 3:6; 4:15, 21; 5:8, 15; 7:16, 32; 9:20; 10:11, 14; 12:30.
אברת 4:7; 9:7; 12:8, 16.
אגור *temple.* 3:9.
אגורא 4:10; 12:18.
אגר *wall.* 9:9, 10, 11; 10:4, 5, 6; 12:18, 20.
אגרא 9:8.
אגרוה[י] 3:4.
אגרה *a letter.*
אגרתי 13:8.
אדין adv., *at that time.* 6:1; 7:1; 8:1; 9:1; 10:1; 11:1; 12:1, 10; 16A?
אדן 5:1.
אדר pr. n., Babylonian month *Adar.* 10:2.
אדרנג 9:18; 10:12; 12:27.
אדרנגי 11:8, 9.
או conj., *or.* 2:7, 9, 10, 12, 13; 3:22; 7:21; 12:23, 26.
אוצר *treasury.* 6:7; 10:4; 11:4.
אוצרא 3:9.
אזת 5:4.
אח *brother.* 1:(8); 4:13, 19; 5:5; 8:4, 6; 10:12; 12:27.
אחוהי 12:19, 20.
אחד *to hold.* ptc.? 3:5; 4:8; 6:4; 9:13; 10:2; 12:13.
אחדה ? *possession.*
[א]חדתה ? 7:29.
אחה *sister.* 1:8; 4:13, 19; 5:5; 8:4, 6; 10:12; 12:27.
אחתה 7:41.
אחתך 7:3, 4, 5.
אחר adv., *afterwards.* 11:3, 6, 7, 8, 10.
אחר prep., *after.* 4:17.
אחרי 4:21; 5:14.
אחריך 3:12, 16, 19; 12:23.
אחריכי 4:5; 9:19, 21; 10:9.
אחרית *other?* 6:15.
אחרן *other.* 2:7, 9, 11, 12, 13; 3:19; 4:16, 19, 20; 5:9; 7:21, 33; 8:5; 10:10.
אחרנא adv., *afterwards.* 4:19.
איר pr. n., Babylonian month *Iyyar.* 14:1.
איש *man.* 4:19; 8:4, 5, 6; 12:28.
אית *there is.* 7:31.
איתי 7:29, 35, 36.
אל 13:(1), 6.
אלה *these.* 3:7; 6:14; 7:41; 12:2, 11, 33; 13:5.
אלהא *god.* 2:2; 3:3, 8, 10; 4:2, 10; 5:10; 6:2, (8); 9:2, 10, 23; 10:2, 6, 17; 12:2, 11, 33; 16:I.
אלהיא 13:1.
אלול pr. n., Babylonian month *Elul.* 3:1.
אלך *these.* 11:4, 5.
אם adv., *moreover?* 3:16, 19; 9:21; 10:11, 14. See also **אפם**.
אם *mother.*
אמי 4:19.
אמה 2:14; 6:3.
אמה *handmaiden.* 11:11.
אמתך 2:3.
אמתה 5:3; 12:9a, 18.
אמין *cubits.* 12:8, 15.
אמן 4:6, 7, 8; 6:4; 7:6, 7, 8, (9), 12; 9:6, 7; 12:7, 16.
אמר *to say.* 3 p. s. pf. 1:2; 2:1; 3:1; 4:1; 5:2; 6:2; 7:1; 8:1, 3; 9:1; 10:1; 11:1; 12:1, 10.

אמרת 3 s. f. pf. 5:11; 16:D?
אמרן 1 pl. pf. 6:5 (?).
יאמר 3 s. impf. 2:7; 7:21, 41, 42.
תאמר 3 f. s. impf. 2:9; 7:25.
אמר 1 s. impf. 6:15; 10:9, 10.
לאמר inf. 1:3; 2:3, 4, 13; 3:3; 4:2; 5:3, 13; 6:3; 7:2; 8:3; 9:2; 10:2; 11:2; 12:3, 12; 14:3.
אן *where*. 7:24.
אנה pron., *I*. 1:9; 2:3; 3:10; 4:2, 4, 5, 9, 12, 13, 14, 18, 19; 5:3; 6:3, 14, 15; 7:3, 4; 8:4, 5, 6; 9:2, 5, 8, 12, 16, 17, 22; 10:7, 9, 16; 11:2, 3, 6, 7; 12:3, 24; 14:3, 4; 16:E.
אנחנה pron., *we*.
אנחן 3:3, 5, 7, 10, 12, 13, 15, 20, 21; 5:11, 13, 14; 12:12.
אנף pl. *face*.
אנפיך 13:4.
אנש *man*. 8:5, 8.
אנת pron., *thou*, m. 2:14; 3:11; 11:10; 12:17, 22. For f., 6:8, 10; 9:14.
אנתי pron., *thou*, f. 5:8, 10; 9:11, 13, 15, 20; 10:8, 11, 14.
אנתה *woman*, *wife*. 7:36.
אנתת 7:22, 25.
אנתתי 2:3, 7; 6:3; 7:4, 21; 12:24.
אנתתה 4:2, 25; 7:29, 38; 12:2, 11, 33, 35.
אנתו *marriage*. 2:3; 7:3, 37; 12:25.
אנתותכי 10:10.
אנתתכי 10:7.
אנתותה 12:18.
אף conj., *moreover*. 4:13, 18; 7:36, 39, 40; 9:13, 14, 15, 17, 21; 10:11, 15; 12:26, 31.
אפוחס ? 13:2.
אפם adv., *moreover* (?). 4:16, 22; 8:8. See also אם.
אפף pr. n., Egyptian month *Epiphi*. 2:1; 7:1; 13:(3), 8.
ארך *length*. 7:(11), 12; 12:7, 15.
ארמי *Aramaean*. 2:2; 7:2; 8:2; 11:2; 12:2; 14:2.
ארע *earth*. Adv., *below*. 3:5.
אשר ?
אשרן 3:23.
אתה *to come*.
אתית 1 s. pf. 2:3; 7:3; 11:2; 14:3.
מהיתה ? 17:2.

ב prep., frequent, esp. before שנת, יום, and numerals in date formulas. For בגו see גו. Other uses: 3:4, 6, 7, 12, 13, 17, 23, 25; 4:2, 4, 7, 14, 15, 19, 20, 21; 5:3, 4, 6, 8, 12, 13, 15, 16; 6:2, 8, 9, 14; 7:16, 19, 21 ?, 22, 24, 25, 28, 29, 32, 41; 8:8, 10; 9:2, 3, 5, 6, 7, 9, 12, 13, 14, 15, 16, 17, 18, 20, 23; 10:4, 5, 6, 7, 9, 11, 13, 14, 15, 16, 17; 11:1, 3, 10b, 12; 12:4, 6, 7, 8, 14, 15, 16, 18, 20, 22, 24, 25, 26, 28, 29, 30, 32; 13:1, 4, 8; 14:3.
בך 5:6.
בכי 5:6.
בה 3:5, 22; 4:17; 5:3, 4; 7:17; 9:11, 13; 10:3, 8; 12:23.
בבא *gate*. 10:4.
בין prep., *between*. 2:11, 12, 13; 3:20; 11:17.
ביניהם 3:8, 10; 6:6, 11.
בניהם 4:10, 11.
בינים 10:5 (error?)
ביניהן 12:19, 21.
בירתא *fortress*. 2:2; 4:2, 4; 6:2; 7:1, 2; 8:1; 11:1, 3, 12; 14:2.
ברתא 3:4; 5:2; 7:1, 2; 9:2, 23; 10:2; 12:2, 3, 32.
בית *house*. 3:8, 21; 6:6, 8, 9, 11 ?, 12, d; 7:28; 9:4, 7, 9, 10; 10:5; 11:6; 12:19.
בי (=בית) 4:8, 25; 6:11; 9:12, 27; 10:2, 21; 11:11; 12:12, 13, 35.
ביתא 3:7, 12, 13, 16, 17, 19, 23; 4:5, 8, 12, 14, 16, 20; 6:14, 16; 9:5, 8, 11, 16; 10:5, 7, 11, 13, 14, 15; 12:6, 8, 15, 17, 22, 25, 28, 29, 30.
ביתה emph. 3:4; 4:11, 20; 10:6; 12:4, 9, 20.
ביתי 4:21, 22; 6:10 ?; 7:5; 9:3.
ביתך 2:3; 7:3; 11:3; 12:17; 14:3.
ביתה 7:22, 29, 39.
ביתן 12:3, 5, 12.

בליה *worn.* 7:12.
בנה *to build.*
בנו 3 pl. pf. 10:4.
בנהו 3 pl. pf. with suff. (l. בנוה?) 9:9.
תבנה 2 s. impf. 3:22.
בנה ptc. pass. 4:8.
בניה ptc. pass. f. 3:5.
מבני inf.? 9:12; 10:2, 3; 12:12, 13.
מבנתא cf. s. v.
בנינא *construction.* 3:22.
בעד prep., *on behalf of.* 11:10.
בעדה with suff. 2:7; 7:21.
בעל; הבעלה aphel inf. 7:33.
בעל *husband.* 7:33.
בעלי 2:9.
בעלה 2:4; 7:4, 24, 26, (35), 40; 14:4.
בר *son, child.* In names and 3:14, 15, 17, 18, 20, 21; 4:13, 18; 5:5, 11, 13; 7:28, 34; 8:4, 5, 6; 9:18; 10:12; 12:2, 7.
ברי 6:3; 8:5, 8, 9.
ברך 5:12, 14.
בני 4:17, 18, 20; 11:8, 9, 10; 12:20.
בניך 3:12, 16, 19; 12:23, 26, 28, 30.
בניכי 4:5; 9:19, 20, 21; 10:9, 13, 14.
בנין 3:21.
בנן 11:11.
בר (מן) *except.* 2:14; 3:21; 7:33.
ברא adv., *outside.* 6:14.
ברה *daughter.* 3:14, 15, 17, 18, 20, 22; 4:13; 5:5, 11; 8:4, 5, 6; 9:18; 10:12; 12:27.
ברת 3:2; 4:3, 17; 6:18; 12:3, 33.
ברתי 5:4, 6, 9, 10; 6:8, 17, 19; 9:5, 6, 8, 17; 10:8.
ברתך 5:7.
ברתה 5:11; 9:2, 27; 10:2, 21.
ברתן 12:18.
בנתן 12:26.
בשם 2:5.
מ[ב]שים 7:20.
גבר *man.* 3:3, 19; 4:16, 19; 5:9.
גברא 4:20.

גו *midst.* בגו 1:4, 7, 10; 2:15; 3:23; 4:23; 5:16; 7:5, 43; 8:10; 9:23; 10:18; 11:13; 12:6, 26.
גוא 12:24.
גמא 7:17.
גמירה 7:7.
גנן *gardener.* 9:10; 10:6.
גרה *institute a suit.*
גרו 3 pl. pf. 3:18.
גרין 1 pl. pf. 3:14.
גרך 3 s. pf. 1:8.
גריתכי 1 s. pf. with suff. 4:14.
גרוך 3 pl. pf. with suff. 3:18.
גרינכי 1 pl. pf. with suff. 3:14.
יגרה 3 s. impf. 3:19.
נגרה 1 pl. impf. 3:14.
יגרנך 3 s. impf. with suff. 3:17, 19; 4:16.
יגרנכי 3 s. impf. with suff. 4:14.
אגרנך 1 s. impf. with suff. 1:4.
נגרנך 1 pl. impf. with suff. 3:12.
גשר *beam.* 3:5.
גשרן 3:5.
גשורן 4:8; 6:4; 9:13; 10:2; 12:13.

דבב *process.* 1:5; 3:13, 14; 5:15; 10:12; 12:25.
דבח *sacrifice.*
דבחי 16:H.
דבק *adjoin.* 3:9; 4:9, 11, 13; 9:9, 10; 10:4, 5, 6; 12:18, 19.
דבר *word.*
עלדבר 13:(1), (6).
עלדברה with suff. 4:13.
דגל 2:3; 3:2; 5:2; 7:2; 11:2; 12:3; 14:2.
דגלא 7:2; 11:2.
דחה ptc. pass. 9:14.
די 3:12; 12:30, 31. See זי.
דילך 9:14.
דין *judge.* 1:6; 12:28.
דין *suit.* 3:12, 14; 4:13, 14, 15, 16, 22; 5:15; 7:32, (37), 38, 39, 40; 9:18, 19, 20; 10:12; 12:25, 27.
דן 1:5; 10:15; 11:8, 12.
דך *that.* 9:10; cf. זך.
דכם *that.* 7:2. See זכם in *A.P.* index.
דכר *male.* 7:34. See זכר.
דמות *likeness.* 3:21.
דמן pl., *price.* 7:18.

דמי 1:3; 2:6; 3:6; 7:8, (12), (13), 14, 15, 23; 12:5.
דמיא 3:7; 12:6, 14.
דמוהי 1:4, 7; 3:6; 9:3; 12:13, 25, 32.
דנה *this*. 5:3; 10:3. See also זנה.
דנח *rise*.
מדנח 6:7.
דם; דסי 10:3.
דרגא *stairs*. 6:10, (13); 9:4, 7, 10, 15.
דרגה 10:3.
דרימיי ? 9:3.
דש *door*. 9:13.
דששן 10:3; 12:13.

הא interj., *behold*. 3:7; 4:5, 8; 9:8; 12:8.
הו pron. 1:1, etc., in dates. 2:11; 4:4, 15; 6:4; 7:16, 35, 42; 9:3, 4, 9. 14, 15, 22; 10:3, 4, 6, 17; 11:7; 12:4, 5, 13.
הוה *to be*.
הוה ptc. 4:6; 6:4.
הות 3 s. f. pf. 12:24.
הוית 1 s. pf. 9:17.
הוין 1 pl. pf. 5:12.
יהוה 3 s. impf. 8:5, 8, 9 [6:d].
תהוה 3 s. f. impf. 7:22.
אהוה 1 s. impf. 7:25.
יהוון 3 pl. impf. 2:11, 12.
הי pron., 3 s. f. 2:3, 11; 3:5; 7:4, 29, 34, (39); 9:11.
הירא (?הידא) 1:3, 5, 6, 9.
הלך *to go*.
יהך 3 s. m. impf. 10:15.
תהך 3 s. f. impf. 7:24, 28.
יהכן 3 pl. impf. 3:23.
המו pron., 3 pl. m. 4:17, 18; 7:42.
הן conj., *if*. 1:5, 8; 2:13b; 3:14, 18, 19, 20; 4:14, 16, 17, 18; 5:13; 7:24, (28), 33, 37, 38, 40, 42; 10:10; 11:5, 8, 9.
הנבג 5:5; 9:18; 10:12; 12:27.
הנגית 5:5; 9:18; 10:12; 12:27.
הנפנא 9:9; 10:4.
הפתחפתא 8:2, 3.

ו conj., *and*, *or*. *passim*.

זבב 3:17; see דבב.
זבן peal, *to buy*; pael, *to sell*.
זבנת peal, 1 s. pf. 4:3; 9:3.
זבן peal, 1 pl. pf. 12:4, 12.
זבנה peal, 3 s. pf. with suff.? 13:5.
זבן pael, 3 s. pf. 3:25; 12:32, 35.
זבן pael, 1 pl. pf. 3:3, 7, 10, 13; 12:3, 6, 9, 15, 17, 25, 29.
זבנהי pael, 1 pl. pf. with 3 f. suff. 3:5.
תזבן pael, 2 s. impf. 12:24.
זבנתא *purchase*. 12:31.
זול; מזלכי, inf. w. suff. 5:7.
זי rel. pron., *who*, *which*. 1:3, 5, 6; 2:2, 3, 4, 8, 9, 13, 14, 15, 16, 22, 23, 25; 4:3, 5, 9, 11, 12, 17, 20, 25; 5:3, 4, 6, 7, 8, 11, 12, 18; 6:16; 7:22, 23, 28, 31, 36; 8:4, 7; 9:3, 5, 8, 9, 11, 15, 16, 17, 19, 21, 22, 27; 10:4, 7, 11, 12, 14, 16, 21; 11:4, 5, 7, 8, 9, 10, 10b, 11; 12:3, 4, 6, 8, 9, 12, 14, 15, 17, 22, 23, 24, 25, 26, 27, 28, 29, 31, 32, 35; 13:5; 15:1.
כזי 5:12; 13; 11:5; 13:2; 16:C.
לקבל זי 9:17.
מן זי 2:13; 12:23.
זילי 9:4, 18; 10:6; 12:13.
זילך 1:3; 3:16, 19; 9:11, 14; 10:4; 11:8; 12:30.
זילכי 4:4, 16.
זילה 10:5.
זילן 12:27.
זילהם 4:22.
זי genitive particle. 2:2, 4; 3:2, 4, 8, 9, 16, 19, 21, 22, 23; 4:2, 3, 4, 5, 10, 11; 5:2; 6:2, 8; 7:2, 6, 7, 11, 13, 14, 17, 18, 19, 31; 8:2, 3; 9:9, 10, 15, 23; 10:1, 6, 17; 11:2; 12:1, 2, 11, 18, 19, 20, 33; 13:4; 14:2.
זין 3:17. See דין.
זית *olive* (*oil*). 7:(19), 20.
זך *that*. 3:7, 12, 23; 4:5, 8, 14; 8:7, 8; 11:2. Cf. דך.
זכר 3:21; 7:28. See דכר.
זלוע *bowl*. 7:15.
זלוען 7:18.

זנא 9:16 (=זנה).
זנה *this*. 1:5, (6), 9; 2:4, 14; 3:11, 13, 17; 4:4, 8, 11; 5:16; 7:4, 32, 43; 9:5, 11, 12, 15, 16, 22, 23; 10:7, 8, 11, 13, 14, 15, 16, 17; 11:10, 12; 12:6, 8, 15, 16, 22, 23, 25, 28, 29, 32; 14:4.

ח abbrev. for חלר(ן). 7:14, 15, 27.
חד *one*. 7:40; 9:13; 10:2?; 11:6; 12:5, 6, 11, 14, 33.
  חדה 7:38.
חדת *new*. 4:8; 7:6, 7, 8, 9, 11, 17; 9:22; 10:15; 12:29.
חוב *be liable, be in the wrong*.
  יחוב 3 s. impf. 10:13; 12:29.
  אחוב 1 s. impf. 4:14; 10:10; 11:6.
  נחוב 1 pl. impf. 5:14.
  חיב ptc. pass.? 7:42.
  מיחב (read מחיב pael, ptc. pass.?) 9:22.
חוט 2:9, 10.
חוצן 7:17.
חטיב 7:7; (14:a).
חי *life*.
  חיי 5:4; 9:2; 10:11, 13.
  חייך 5:12, 13.
חיל *army*. 13:7.
  חילא 8:2, 3. See רב.
חלק *portion*. 4:11.
  חלקא 4:9.
  חלקי 4:19.
חלר a weight, *one-tenth shekel*.
  חלרן 2:5, 7; 7:6, 14, 16, (23).
חם 2:8, 10.
חמד; חמדיה 7:19.
חמשה *five*. 4:15.
חסן; מהחסן Haph. ptc. pl. 12:5.
חפן 7:20.
  חפנא 2:6.
  חפנן 2:6; 7:20, 21.

טיב *be content*. 3 s. pf. 1:(4); 3:6; 7:(5); 12:6, 14, 26.
טלא: מן טלא ל: 5:9.

יד *hand*. 13:4; 17:8.
  ידין 7:8; 14:a.
  ידי 9:17.
  ידה 2:4; 8, 10, 16; 5:3.
יהב *to give*.
  יהבת 2 p. s. pf. 1:3, (7?); 3:5, 7; 4:2; 8:4; 11:3; 12:5, 13, 15, 25.
  יהבת 1 s. pf. 1:(7?); 6:(14), (16); 7:4, 41; 9:2, 3, 5, 6, 8, 18; 10:2, 9; 11:5, 8; 12:9.
  יהבן 1 pl. pf. 3:3, 10, 13; 12:3, 7, 9, 12, 15, 17, 25, 29, 31, 32.
  יהבתה 2 s. with suff. 7:3.
  יהבתה 1 s. with suff. 4:4, 12; 9:3, 12, 16; 10:7.
יהודי *Jew*. 5:2; 11:2.
יום *day*. 1:1, etc., in dates. 2:7, 9, 10, 12, 13; 7:21, 24, 28.
  יומא 2:4; 3:11; 4:4; 7:4; 10:8; 12:23; 14:4.
  ימן 9:17.
  יומן 3:20; 11:7.
יוף; יזפת 1 s. pf. 11:3.
יחב? מיחב 9:22. See חוב.
יכל *be able*. See כהל.
  אכל 1 s. impf. 2:13.
  יכלון 3 pl. impf. 10:15.
ילד *bear*.
  ילדתי 2 s. pf. 4:5, 17, 20.
  ילתי 5:5, 8.
  לידתי 5:6.
ימן *right*. 5:3.
יעא *go forth*.
  מועה 3:9; 4:7, 10; 9:3, 6, 8; 10:3; 12:7, 9, 15, 17.
יצב *valid*. 10:17.
ירח *month*. 1:1, etc., in dates.
ירת *inherit*.
  ירתנה 3 s. impf. with suff. 7:35.
ישר; הושרת haphel, 2 s. pf. 13:4.
יתב *sit*.
  יתב 3 s. pf. 13:3.
  תתב 3 s. f. impf. 7:26 (cf. also תוב).
ית sign of acc.
  יתה 3:22.

כ abbrev. for a measure. 4:7; 12:7, 8, 16.
כ prep. 3:23; 4:22; 5:3, 12, 16; 8:9; 9:23; 10:17; 11:12; 12:33.

לכי 4:3, 4, 6, 9, 12, 15, 16; 5:3; 6:3; 9:2, 3, 20, 22; 10:2, 13, 16.
לה 3:8, 9, 22; 4:9, 10, 11; 6:6; 7:22, 24, 25, 28, 29, (31), (32), 35, 36, 37, 39, 40, 42; 9:8, 9, 11, 18; 10:3, 4, 5, 6; 12:9, 17, 18, 19, 22, 24, 26, 28, 31, 32; 13:2.
לה f. suff. 6:5 ?
לן 3:6, 7, 17; 12:5, 6, 13, 15, 25, 27, 31, 32.
להם 4:21.

לא neg. particle. 1:[4]; 2:13; 3:5, 12, 13, 16, 20, 21, 22; 4:12, 13, 15, 20, 22; 5:6, 9, 13, 15; 6:14, 15; 7:22, 25, 29, 32, 33, 34, (36), 38, 39, 40, 42; 8:4, 5, 6, 8; 9:17, 18, 21; 10:7, 9, 11, 12, 15; 11:5, 8, 9, 12; 12:6, 25, 26.

לבב *heart*.
לבבי 1:4.
לבבך 2:13; 7:5.
לבבן 3:6; 12:6, 14, 26.

לבוש *garment*. 11:11.
לבש 2:4; 7:6, 8, (10).
לבשיה 7:17, 23.
לבשן 7:13.

להן adv., *but*, *except*. 4:16, 20; 7:33; 8:9; 9:22.

לחן *servitor* ? 1:2; 2:2; 3:3, 25; 4:2; 6:2; 9:2; 10:1; 12:1, 10.
לחנא 4:23; 9:23, 27; 10:9, 17; 12:33.
לחנה f. 12:2.

לעד 11:8, =לא עד.

לקח; (יל)קח 3 s. m. impf. 7:36.
תלקח 2 s. impf. 1:10.

מאן *vessel*.
מאני constr. 7:13, 15; 11:11.

מבנתא 11:17.

מגשיא *Magian*. 4:24.

מדי *Median*. 5:17.

מדשה; see נדש.

מהר *bridal gift*. 7:4.
מהרא 7:15.
מהרה with suff. 7:25.

מוזנא *scales*. 7:26.

מועה *going forth* (of the sun). See יעא.

מות *to die*.
מיתתי 2 s. f. pf. 4:17.
מיתת 1 s. pf. 11:8.
ימות 3 s. impf. 2:11; 7:28.
תמות 3 s. f. impf. 2:12; 6:18; 7:34.
אמות 1 s. impf. 4:18.

מות *death*.
מותי 4:21; 5:4; 9:17, 18; 10:11, 13.
מותך 5:12, 14.
מותכי 4:18.

מחזי *mirror*. 2:5; 7:13.

מחר *tomorrow*. 2:7, 9, 10, 12, 13; 7:21, (30); 11:10.

מטא *reach*.
[מ]טאת 3 s. f. pf. 13:7.
[ימט]אני 3 s. m. impf. with suff. 13:2.
תמטנך 3 s. f. impf. with suff. 13:2.

מין *water*.
מיא 12:20.

מלה *word*. 13:6.
מליא 13:5.
מלוהי pl. with suff. 9:16.

מלח *boatman*.
מלחן 12:20.

מלכא *king*. 1:1, etc., in date formulas.
אבני מלכא 3:6, 8, 9, 10; 4:10, 11, 15, 22; 5:8, 15; 6:7; 7:17, (32); 8:8; 9:20; 10:4, 5, 11, 14; 11:4, 6; 12:10, 19, 21, 30; 13:3, 4; 14:d.

מן (+זי) interrog. pron., *whoever*. 3:12, 14, 15, 16.
למן זי *to whomsoever*. 9:21; 12:23.

מן prep., *from*. 2:4, 8, 10, 13, 14; 3:11, 16, 19, 21; 4:3, 4, 5, 6, 7, 21; 5:9; 6:9, 16; 7:29, 30, 35, 38; 9:3, 6; 10:8, 13; 11:4, 6, 10; 12:4, 6, 7, 8, 12, 15, 16, 22, 23.
מנך 1:7; 2:13b; 7:3; 10:10; 11:3.
מנכי 6:15.
מנה 3:11, 13; 7:26; 9:4, 10.
מניומא 7:4.
מנעל *above*. 3:18; 6:(9); 10:11, 16; 11:5, 7, 8, 9, 10, 11; 12:29.

מנדת 5:7.

מנין *number*. 12:14.

מסורע pr. n., Egyptian month *Mesore*. 9:1.

עבדת 1 s. pf. 9:22.
יעבד 3 s. impf. 7:32, 37, 38, 39, 40.
תעבד 3 s. f. impf. 7:33, 40.
יעבדון 3 pl. impf. 7:34.
עבדן ptc. pl. 5:12.
מעבדה inf. with suff. 8:6, 7, 9.
עבור *corn.* 11:11, 15.
עבורא 16:A.
עבץ; נעבצן 7:18.
עד prep., *until.* 2:4, 9, 10; 3:11; 4:5, 6; 5:12; 7:4; 10:8, 10; 11:11; 12:23; 14:4.
עד *yet.* לעד 11:8 (=לא עד).
עדה (?) See בעד.
עדה haphel, *to take away.*
העדיה inf. 10:13.
עדן *time.* 13:1.
עדר; מעדר *torn?* 7:8 (Or מעדד?)
עטיק *old.* 9:22; 10:15. Cf. עתיק.
עטיקא 12:31.
על prep., *upon, concerning, unto, beside.* 3:23; 5:3, 7, 10; 7:26; 8:7; 9:19, 20; 10:7, 9, 13, 14; 12:9a, 18; 13:(2), 7; 14:3.
עלדבר 13:2.
עלדברה 4:13.
עלי 1:4, 5.
עליך 1:6?; 2:3; 7:5; 10:12; 11:2; 12:6, 28, 29.
עליכי 5:7, 10; 6:16; 9:19, 20, 22; 10:15.
עלין 13:7.
עלא *above, concerning it.* 6:13; 8:4.
עלה 12:21.
עליה *upper end.* 4:6, 9; 12:16, 19.
עליא 9:6, 9; 10:5; 12:8. לעליא 13:5.
עליה ל 4:9.
לעליה ל 3:7.
עלימא *slave.* 8:3?
עלל *to go in.*
על 3 s. pf. 7:5, with the prep. על.
הנעלת haphel, 3 f. pf. 2:4, 8, 10, 16; 7:5, 22.
תנעל aphel, 2 s. impf. 12:22.
עלם *everlasting.* 2:4; 4:5; 7:4; 10:8; 14:4.
עלמן 3:11; 12:23.
עם prep., *with.* 7:26; 10:8.

עמר *wool.* 2:4. See קמר.
עק *wood.* 7:19.
עשת *think, take thought of.*
עשתת 1 s. pf. 5:3; 9:2.
עשתא *one(-cubit-measure).* 4:7; 6:4; 9:6, 7; 12:7, 8, 16.
עשרן *twenty.* 7:32; 11:7.
עשרתא *ten(-shekel-piece).* 3:16; 7:17; 8:8.
עשרתה 16:G.
עתיק *old.* 12:29. Cf. עטיק.

פאוני pr. n., Egyptian month *Paoni.* 3:1; 8:1.
פטר; [יפטרו[ן, 3 pl. impf. 13:7.
פיק 2:6; 7:18.
פלג *a part, portion, half.* 2:5, 6, 7; 4:3, 6; 6:13; 9:4, 6, 7, 15.
פלגא 6:12; 9:14.
פלגה with suff. 6:12; 9:8.
פלח *to work.*
יפלחנך 5:11. Error for נפי, 1 pl. impf. w. suff.
פם *mouth.* 1:10; 3:23; 4:22; 5:6; 7:8, 10, 43; 8:9; 9:23; 10:17; 11:12; 12:11, 33; 14:a.
פמנחתף pr. n., Egyptian month *Pamenḥotep: Phamenoth.* 1:1; 5:1.
פס 10:7, 9; 12:9, 18.
פצל *recover?*
פצלן 1 pl. pf. 3:20, 22a.
[אפצל] 1 s. impf. 1:9.
נפצל 1 pl. impf. 3:20.
פריפת 12:11 (or פדיפת?).
פרזל *iron.* 11:11.
פרמותי pr. n., Egyptian month *Pharmouthi.* 2:1; 6:1.
פרס *a measure.*
פרסן 11:3.
פרסין 7:20.
פרסא (בית) 9:4, 8.
פשך *handbreadth.* 7:8.
פשכן 7:6.
פתח ptc., *to open.* 9:13.
פתיח ptc. pass., *open.* 12:21.
פתי *width.* 4:7; 7:6; 12:8, 16.
פתפא *ration.* 11:4, 5.

צבה *to wish.*

צבית 1 s. pf. 3:12, 14, 15, 16; 7:24, 41.
צבע ptc. pass., *dye*. 7:8; 14:a.
צבע *finger*.
צבען 7:10.
צדי; מצדית (?) 6:5; 9:4.
צדק *win a suit*.
יצדק 10:15.
צל 7:20.
צרף *refined*. 10:11; 12:30.
צריף 5:15; 9:20; 11:6.

קבל prep., *before, against*. 9:17.
קבל *complain* (with על), *invoke*.
קבלת 2 s. pf. 1:4, 5.
קבלת 1 s. pf. 1:5, 6 (?).
יקבל 3 s. impf. 9:19, 20; 10:12; 12:28.
קדם *before*. 8:2, 3.
קדמיכי 10:13.
קום *to arise*.
קמן 1 pl. pf. 5:13.
יקום 3 s. m. impf. 2:7; 5:7; 6:16; 7:21, 30; 8:7.
תקם 3 s. f. impf. 2:9. See תקם for noun.
נקום 1 pl. impf. 3:20; 8:6.
קימן ptc.? 3:4.
קוף 7:17.
קמר *wool*. 7:6, 7, 13. See עמר.
קנין *possessions*.
קנינה with suff. 7:27, 30, (31), 35.
קצת *end, part*. 9:3.
קרב *near, next of kin* (?). 1:9.
קריב 5:5.

ר abbrev. for רבע or רבעת, *quarter*. 3:6, 15, 18; 4:15; 7:17, 26, 32; 8:8; 14:b. For רגל ? 7:7, 9.
ראש *head*.
ראשה with m. suff. 2:8; 7:22.
ראשה with f. suff. 2:9; 7:25.
רב *master, chief*.
רב חילא *commander of the army*. 8:2, 3; 13:7 (?).
רבתא 4:3, 6; 9:4, 11; 10:6; 12:13, 21.
רחם *to feel affection toward*.
רחמת 2 s. pf. 12:23.
רחמתי 2 s. f. pf. 9:21.
רחמה *affection*. 6:14.
רחמן 4:4, 12; 7:41; 9:5, 12, 17; 10:9.
רחמת adv. 12:26, 31.
רחק *to be far, removed from*.
רחקת 1 s. pf. 1:7.
רחקן 1 pl. pf. 3:11, 13.
מרחק inf. 5:18.
רחק *far* (*far relative? or unrelated person?*).
רחיק 5:5.
רק 1:9 (error).
רשה *to bring an action*. With double accusative.
ירשה 3 s. impf. 9:19; 12:27.
נרשה 1 pl. impf. 12:26.
ירשנך 3 s. impf. with suff. 12:27.
ירשנכי 3 s. impf. with suff. 9:18, 19; 10:12.
ארשנכי 1 s. impf. with suff. 4:13.
נרשנך 1 pl. impf. with suff. 12:25.

שאל *to ask*.
שאלת 1 s. pf. 7:3; 14:3.
[ישאלון] 13:1.
שאל ptc. 16:E.
שאר *to remain, be left over*.
אשתאר ethpeel, 1 s. impf. 12:6.
שארת *remainder, rest*. 7:23, 26, 27.
שביט 7:9.
שבע *seven*. 6:4.
שבעה 7:23.
שבק *set free*.
שבקת 1 s. pf. 5:4.
שבקתכי 1 s. pf. with suff. 5:4.
שביקה ptc. pass. f. 5:9, 10.
שניא 13:1.
שהד *witness*. 2:15; 3:23, 24; 5:17; 8:10; 9:23, 24, 25, 26; 10:18, 19, 20; 11:13, 14; 12:33, 34.
שהדיא 1:10; 2:14; 3:23; 4:23; 5:16; 7:43; 8:10; 9:23; 10:18; 11:13, 14; 13:33, 34.
שוה *be equal to, be worth*.
שוה ptc. m. 2:4, 9; 7:7, 8, 10, 11, 12; 14:A.
שויה ptc. f. 2:5.
שוק *street*. 3:8, 10; 4:10, 11; 6:(6); 10:4, 5; 12:19, 21.

שכח *to find.*
תהשכח haphel, 2 s. impf. 11:10b.
שכן ptc., *to dwell.* 12:2.
שלט *to have power over.*
ישלט 3 s. impf. 4:20.
שליט *endowed with power.* 2:12; 3:11; 4:20; 5:6, 9; 6:9; 8:9; 11:10; 12:23.
שליטן 4:17, 19; 8:5; 9:21; 10:9; 12:23.
שליטה f. 2:11; 6:10; 7:33, 9:11, 13, 21; 10:8, 11, 14.
שליטא 4:17, 19; 8:5; 9:21; 10:9; 12:23.
שלם *peace.* 13:1, 4, 6.
שלם pael, *to pay back.*
שלמת 1 s. pf. 11:5, 8.
שלמו 3 pl. pf. 11:9.
תשלם 2 s. impf. 11:11.
אשלם 1 s. impf. 11:4, 7.
ישלמון 3 pl. impf. 11:9.
שם *name.* 1:5, 6, 9; 3:13, 17; 4:14; 10:15; 12:25, 28, 29.
שמה with suff. m. 8:3.
שמה with suff. f. 2:3; 5:2, 4; 6:3; 7:3.
שמע *to hear, to listen to.*
ישתמע ethpeel, 3 s. impf. 7:42.
שמש *sun.* 3:9; 4:10, 11; 6:7; 9:3, 8, 11; 10:3, 4; 12:7, 9, 15, 17, 18. See סמשא.
שנא *to hate, to divorce.*
שנאהי 3 s. pf. with suff.? 7:37, 40.
שנאת 1 s. pf. 2:7, 9.
שנית 1 s. pf. 7:21.
שניתך 1 s. pf. with suff. 7:25.
תשנא 3 f. impf. 7:24.
שנאה ptc. pass. f. ? 7:34, 39.
שנאה *divorce.*
כסף שנאה 7:22, 25. כ' שנא 2:8 error?
שנה *year.*
שנת 1:1, etc., in date formulas.
שנן 4:17, 18; 6:(18).
שנטא 7:11.
שנן ? 2:5; 7:20.
שנת *to mark, tattoo.*
שניתה ptc. pass. with suff. 5:3.
משנתכי inf. with obj. suff. 2 f. s. 5:7.
משנתה inf. with obj. suff. 3 s. m. 8:6, 7, 9.

שף 17:3, 4, 5.
שקל *shekel.* (See also תקל.) 7:12, (13), 14; 12:6, 14.
שקלן 1:3, 7; 2:5, 6, 10, 16; 3:6, 22; 7:6, 7, 9, 11, 12, 16, 23, 26, 27; 12:5; 16:C.
שרת 10:7, 9; 12:9, 18.
שש *six.* 7:18.

תוב: תתב 7:26? more probably from יתב, q. v.
ת[וי] ? 7:17.
תונה *chamber.* 4:3, 6.
תחום *limit, boundary.*
תחומי 4:8; 9:8; 12:8.
תחמי 3:7; 12:9.
תחומוהי 4:12; 9:12; 10:3, 7, 11, 14, 16; 12:17, 22.
תחמוהי 3:17.
תחומוה[י] 6:9.
תחות pr. n., Egyptian month *Thoth.* 11:1; 12:1, 10.
תחות prep., *under, for.* 6:10.
תחת 2:13; 6:9; 7:17, 19; 9:4.
תחית *lower portion.* 6:13; 9:4, 13, 15.
תחת See תחות.
תחתי *lower.* 4:8; 6:(5); 9:13; 10:2; 12:12, 13.
תחתיא f. s. 9:6, 10; 10:6; 12:8, 16, 20.
תחתיה f. s. 3:8; 4:6, 9.
תחתיתא 6:11.
תכונה *substance.* 7:5.
תכונתא 7:15.
תכונתה w. suff. 7:22, 27.
תלתה *three.* 12:5.
תלתין *thirty.* 8:8.
תמואנתי ? 9:9.
תמוז pr. n., Babylonian month *Tammuz.* [2:1], 6:1.
תמא ? 4:10.
תמי 3:8.
תמניה *eight.* 7:16, (23).
תמסא ? 7:13.
תמה (מן) *there.* 12:22.
תנה *here.* 13:7.
תעבי pr. n., Egyptian month *Tybi.* 14:1.

תקל see שקל.
תקלן 2:8.
תקם 2:6; 7:20.
תרך pael, *to drive out.*
תתרך 2 s. m. impf. 2:14.
תרכתכי inf. with suff. 2 f. 6:16.
תרכותה inf. with suff. 3 f. 7:30.
תרע *gate.* 9:15.
תרעא 12:21.
תשרי pr. n., Babylonian month *Tishri.* 4:1; 7:1; 8:1.
תרבצה *court, yard.* 3:4; 10:3.
תרבצא 9:4, 7, 14, 15.
תרין *two.* 7:6, 40.
תרי 4:3, 6; 9:4, 11; 10:3, 6; 12:13, 21.
תרתין 7:38.

PLATES

I. PAPYRUS 1 (47.218.152)

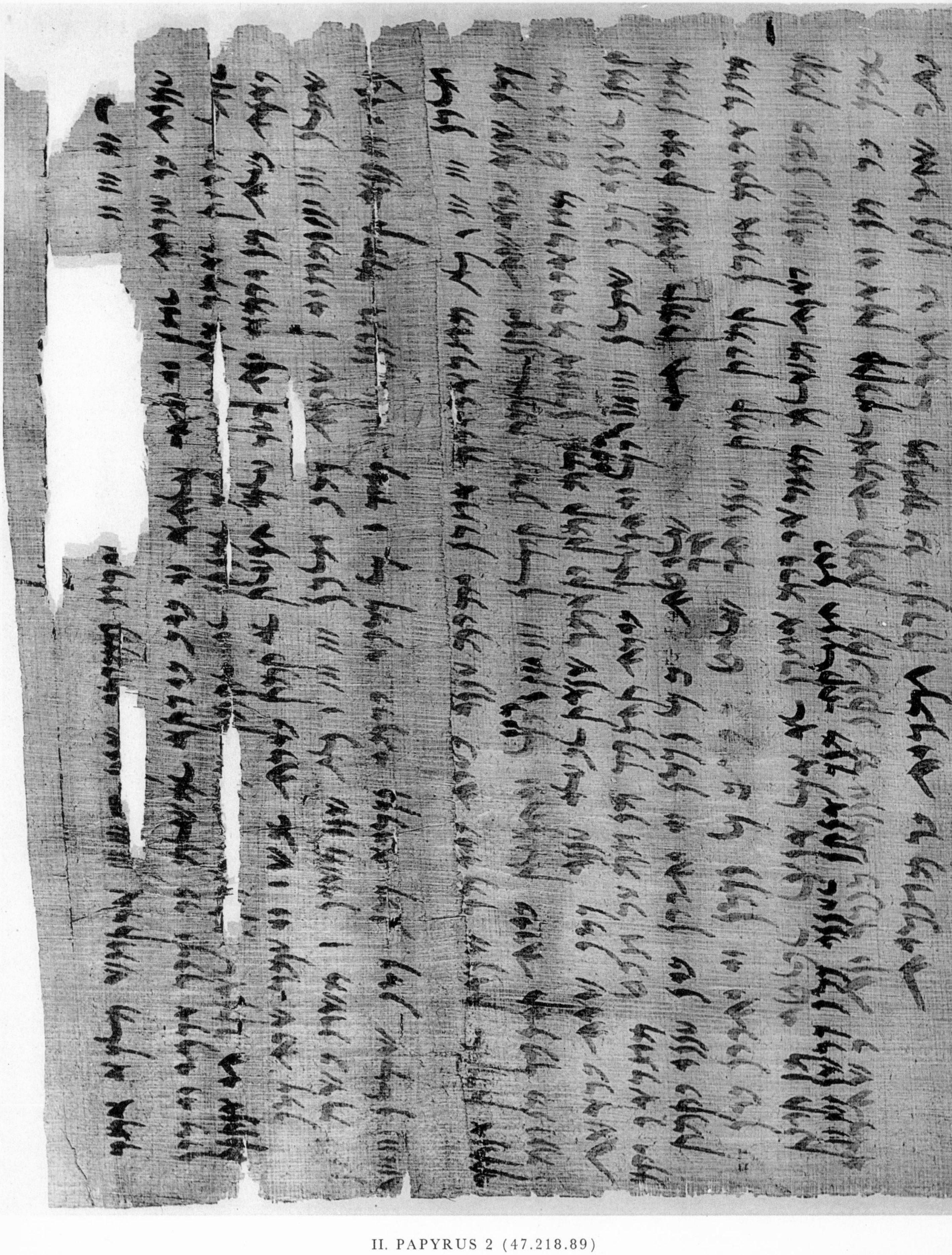

II. PAPYRUS 2 (47.218.89)

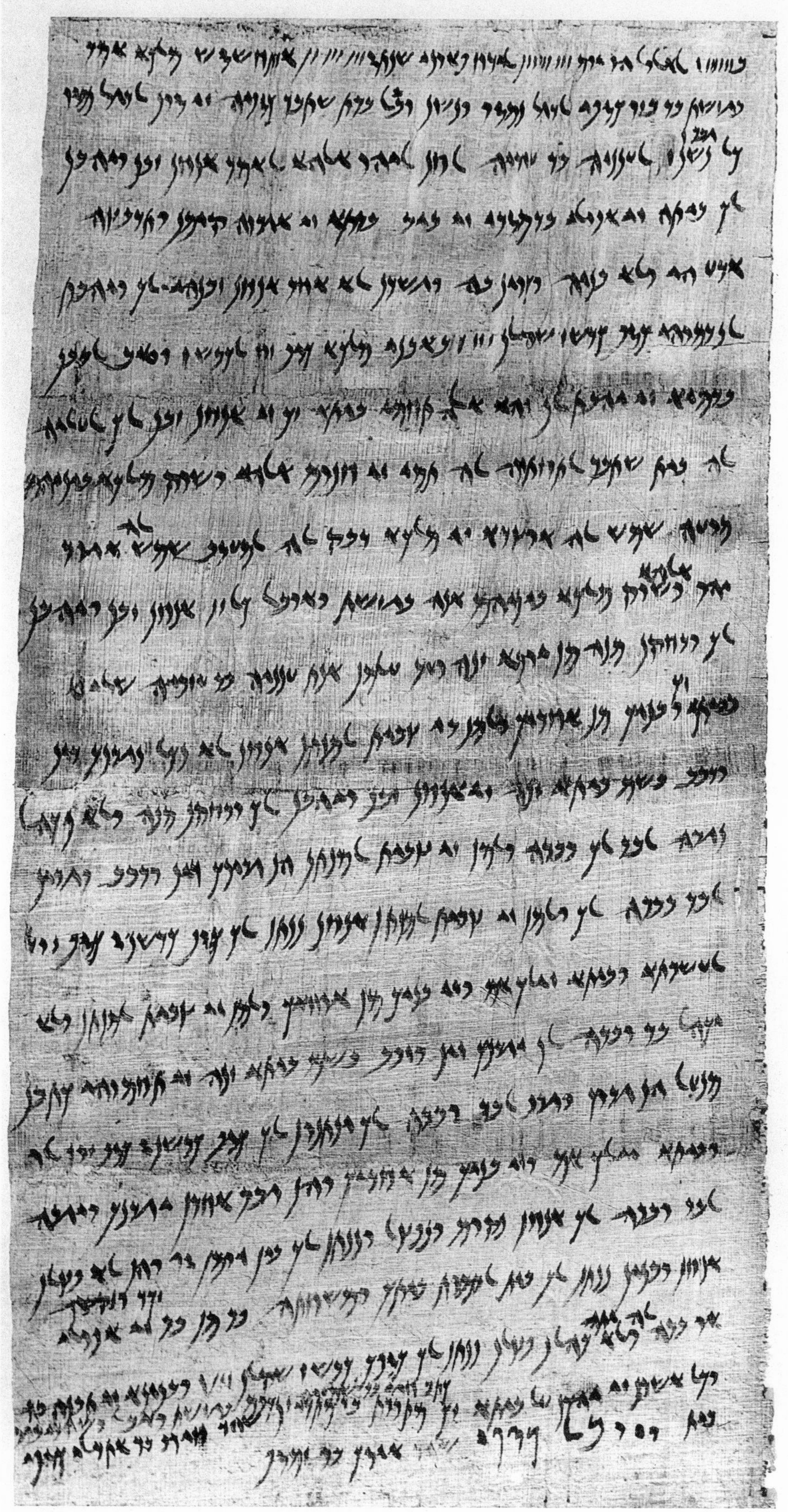

III. PAPYRUS 3 (47.218.95)

IV. PAPYRUS 4 (47.218.91)

V. PAPYRUS 5 (47.218.90)

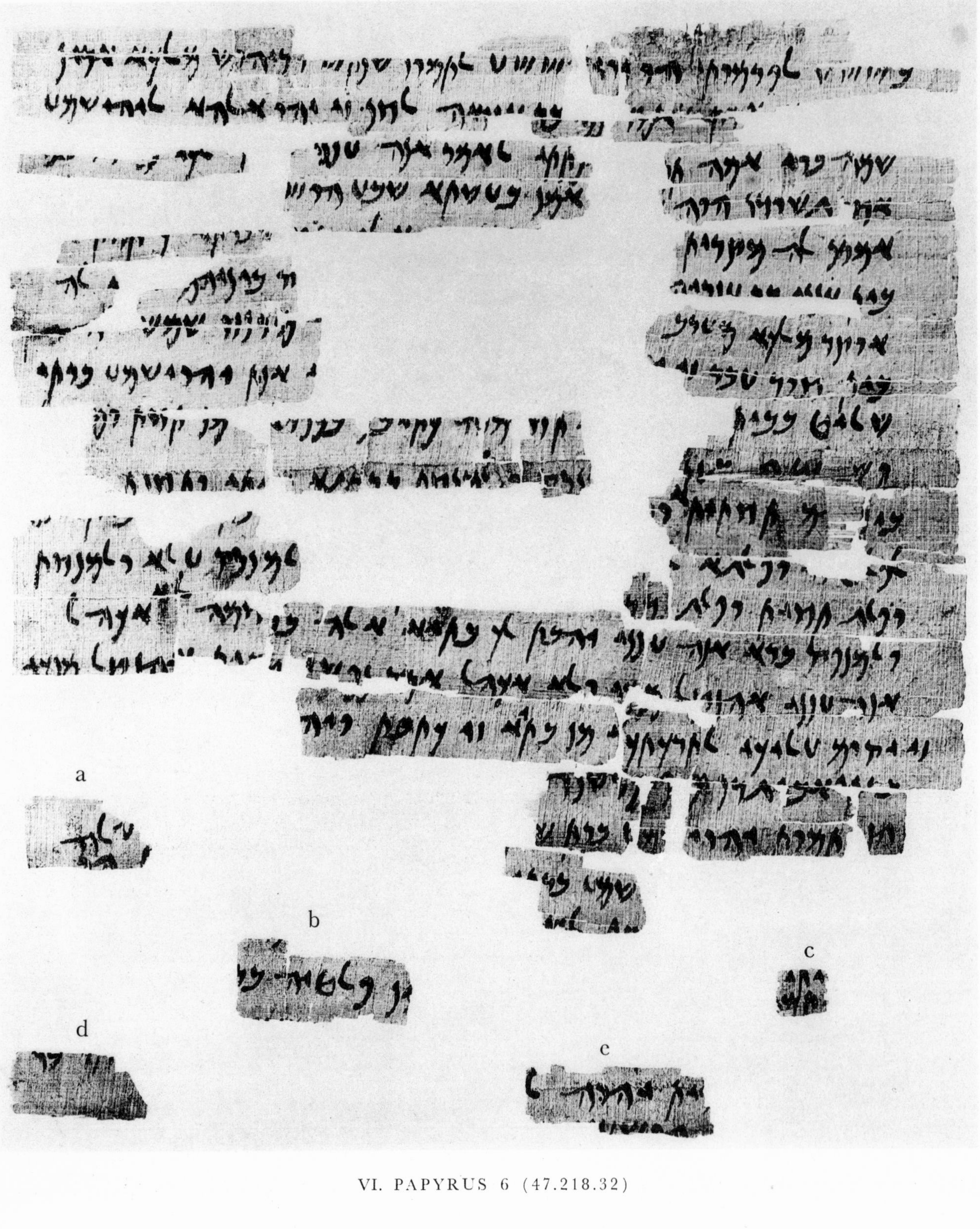

VI. PAPYRUS 6 (47.218.32)

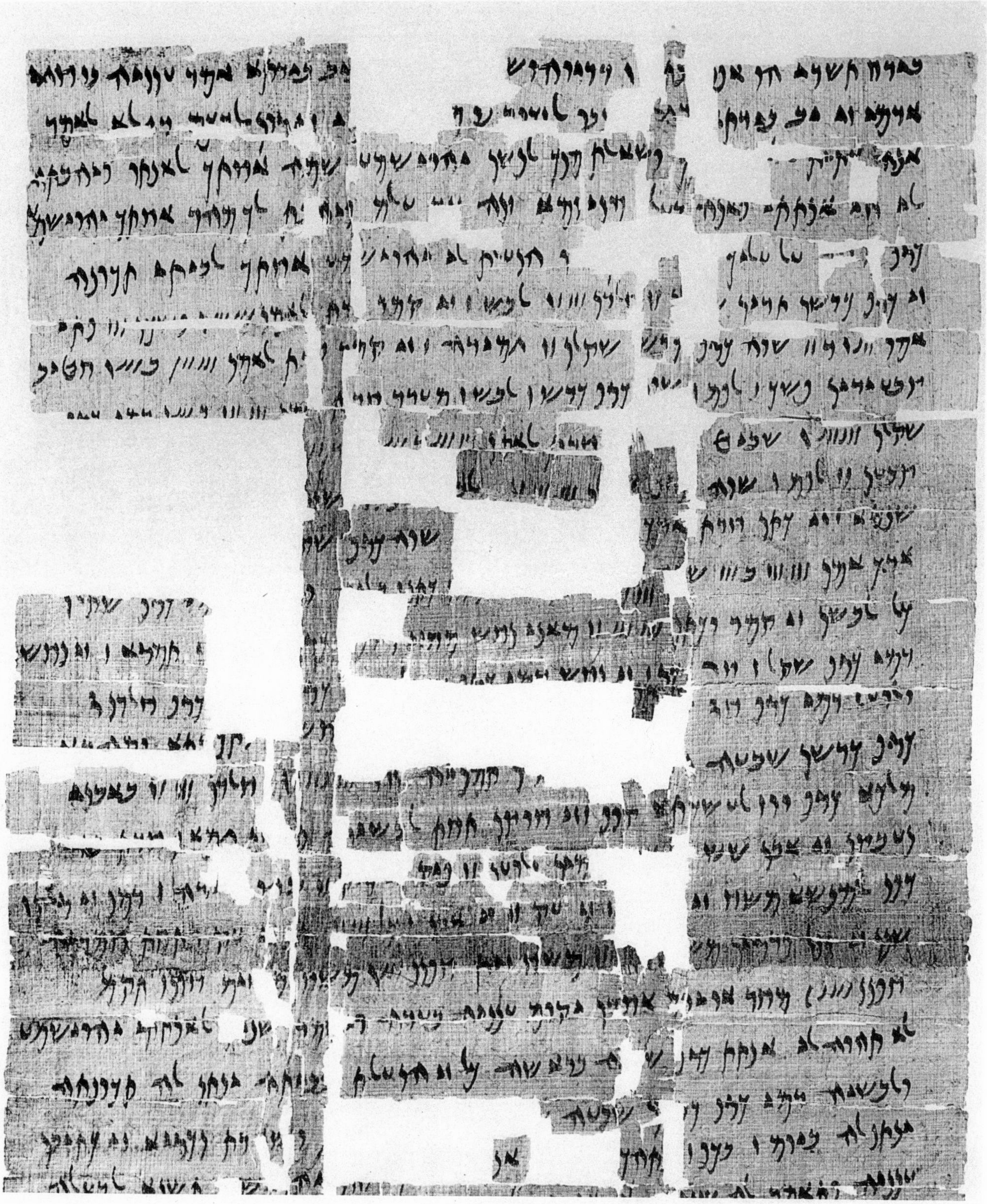

VII a. PAPYRUS 7 (47.218.150)

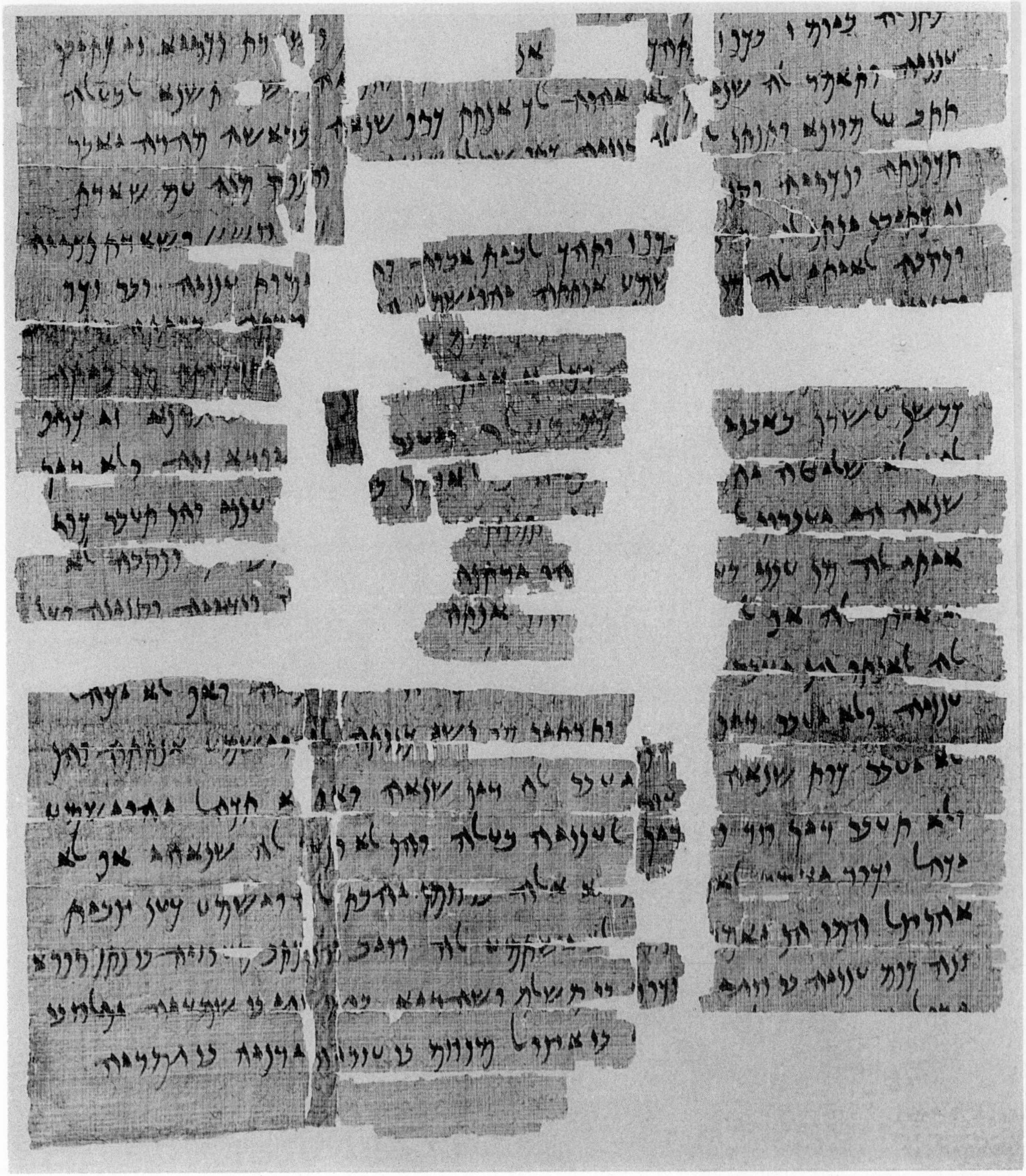

VII b. PAPYRUS 7 continued

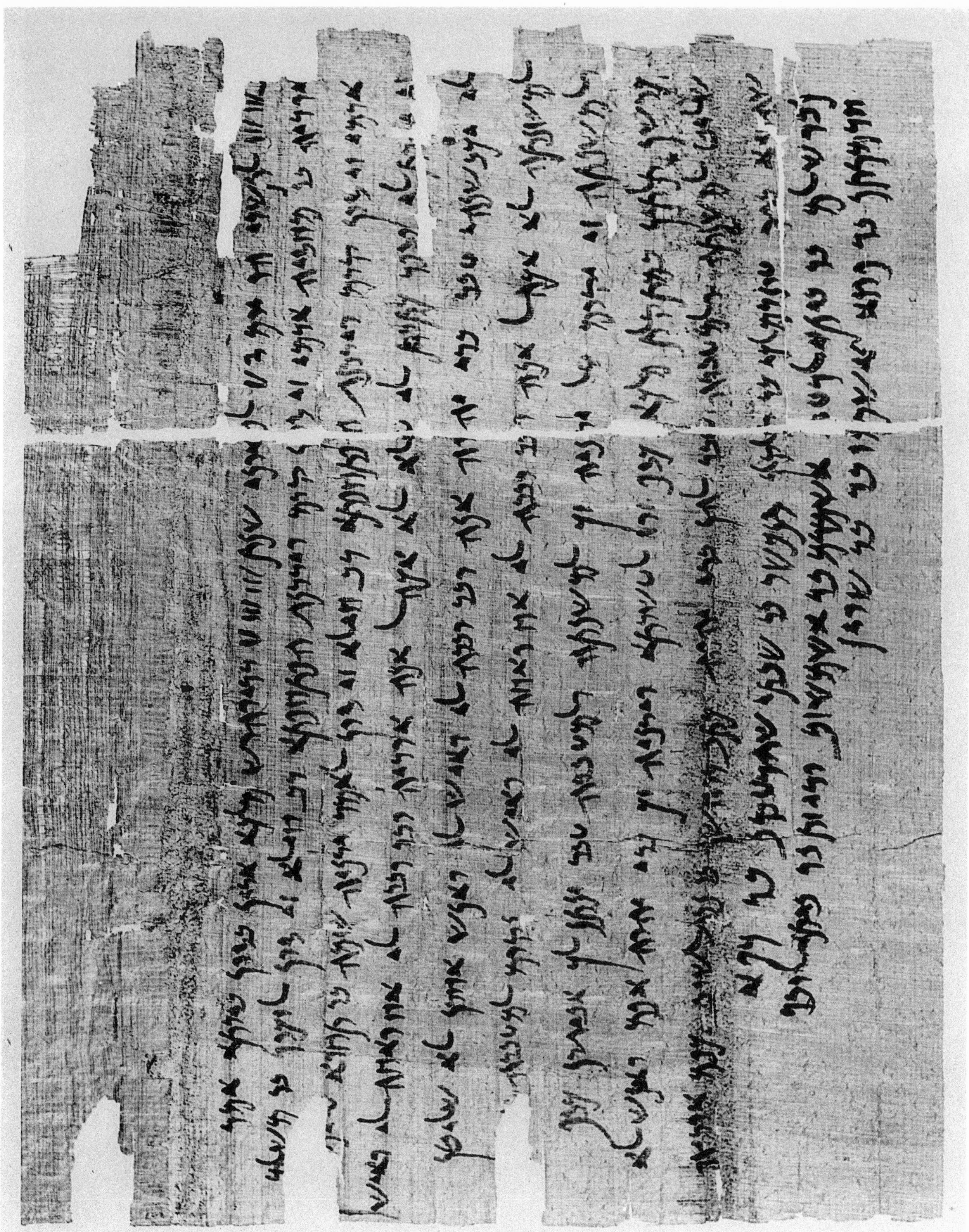

VIII. PAPYRUS 8 (47.218.96)

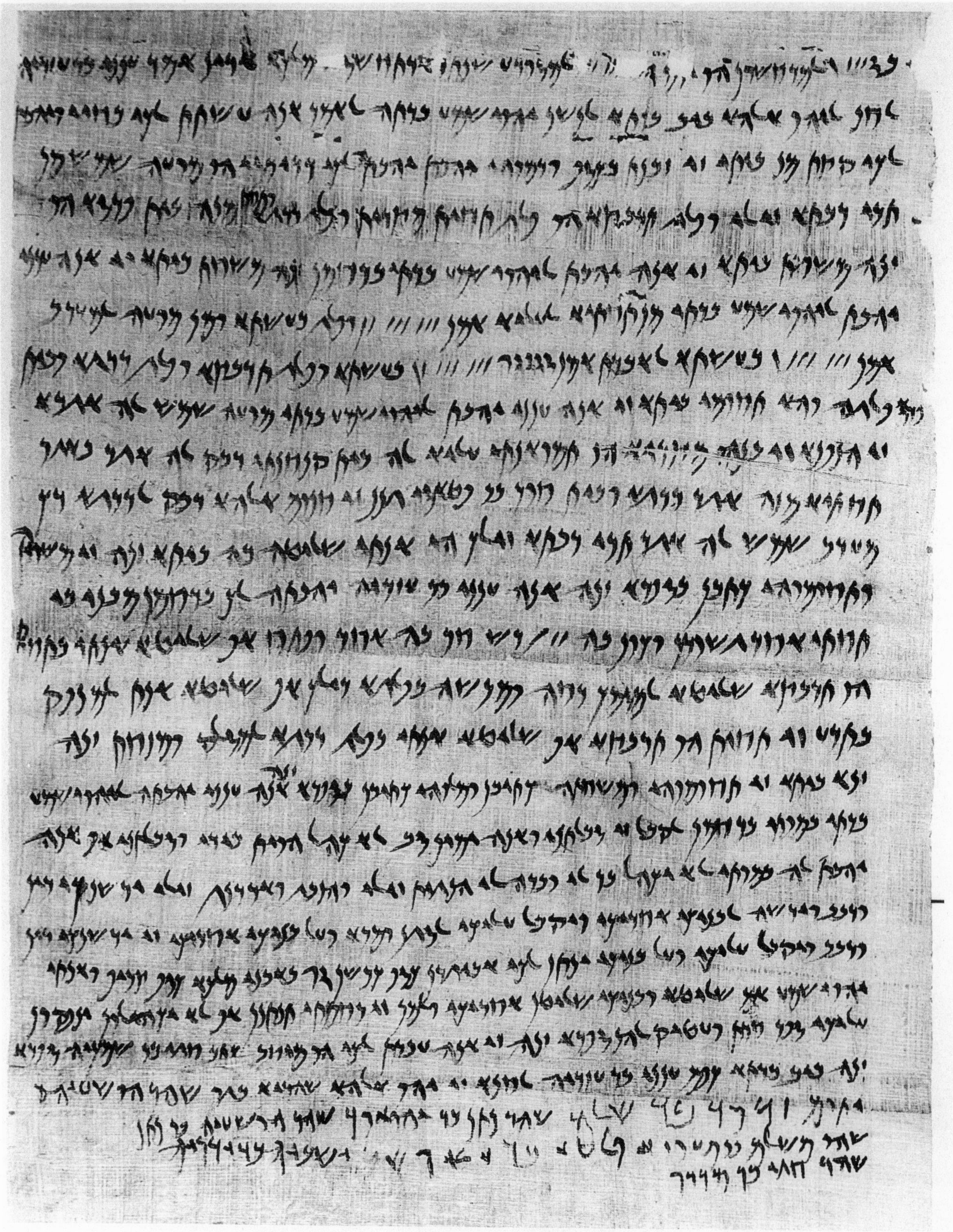

IX. PAPYRUS 9 (47.218.92)

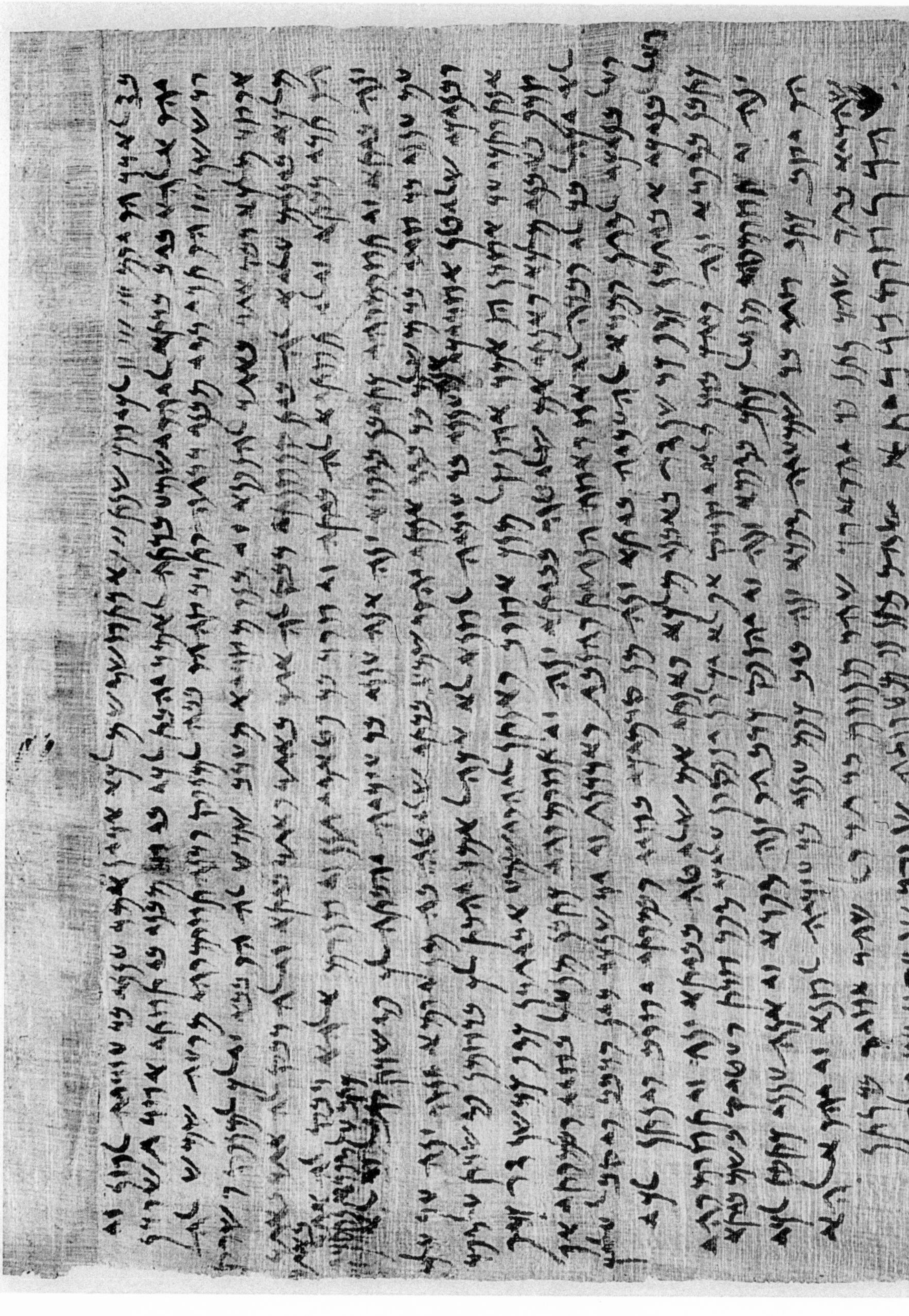

X. PAPYRUS 10 (47.218.88)

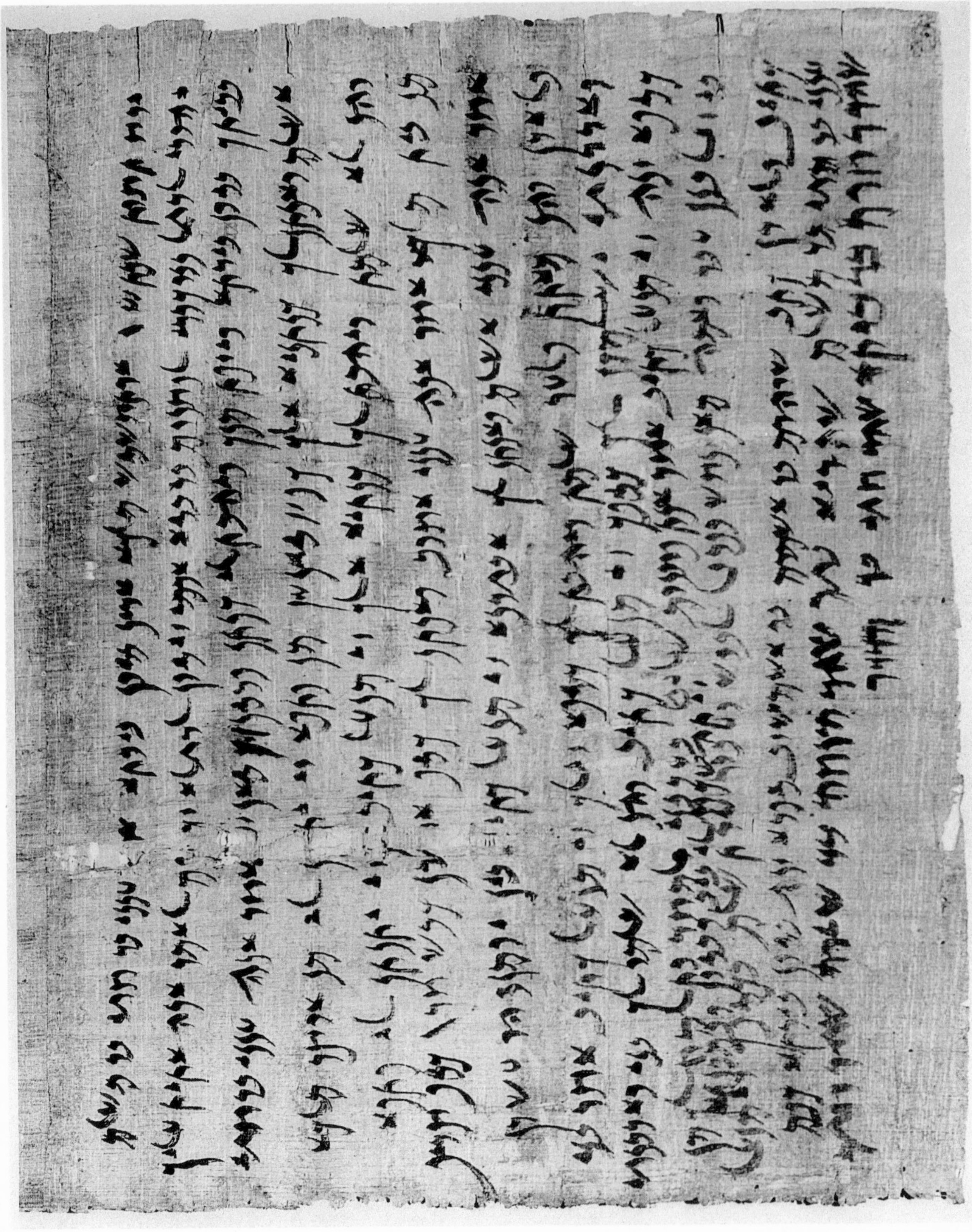

XI. PAPYRUS 11 (47.218.93)

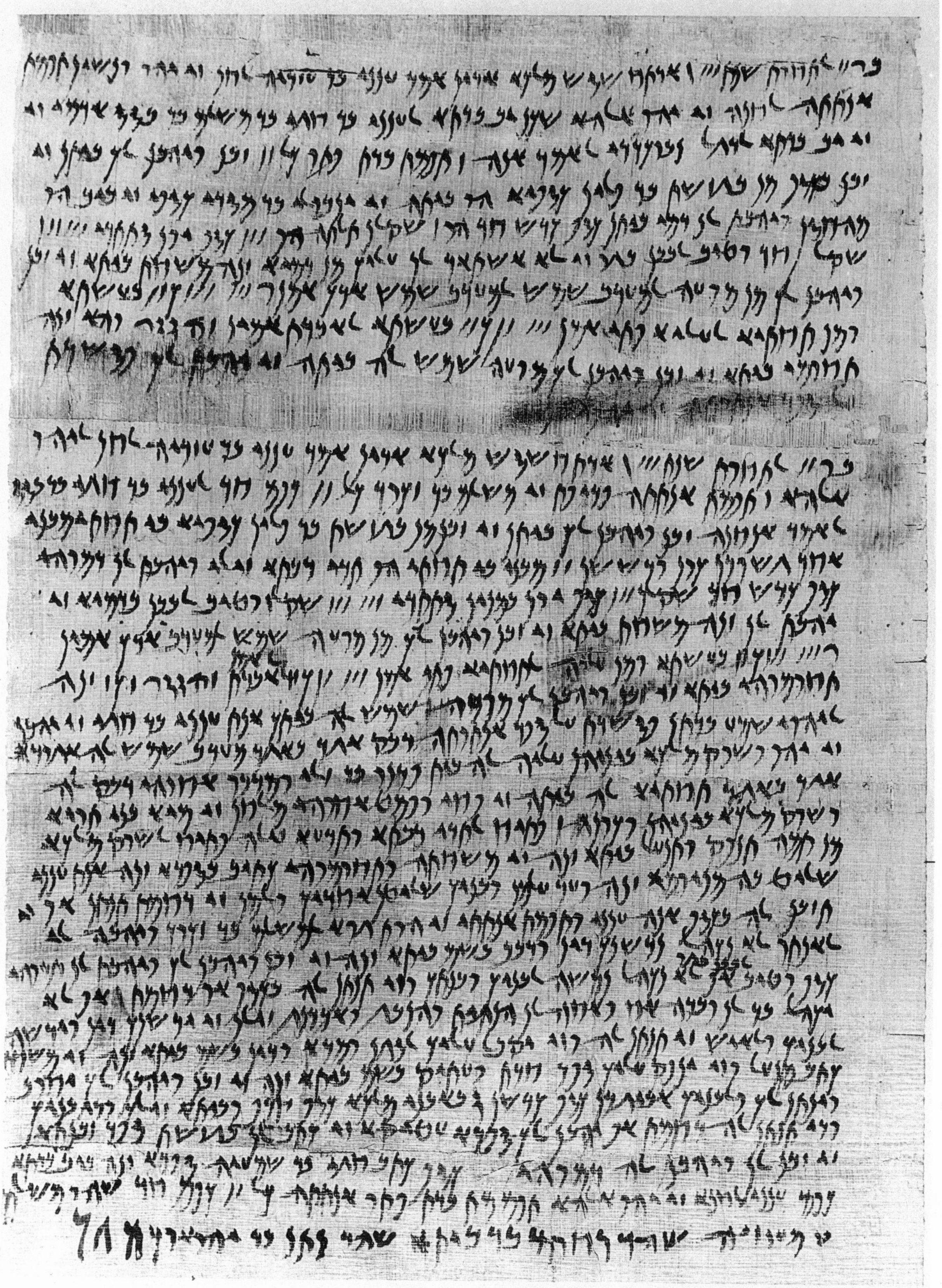

XII. PAPYRUS 12 (47.218.94)

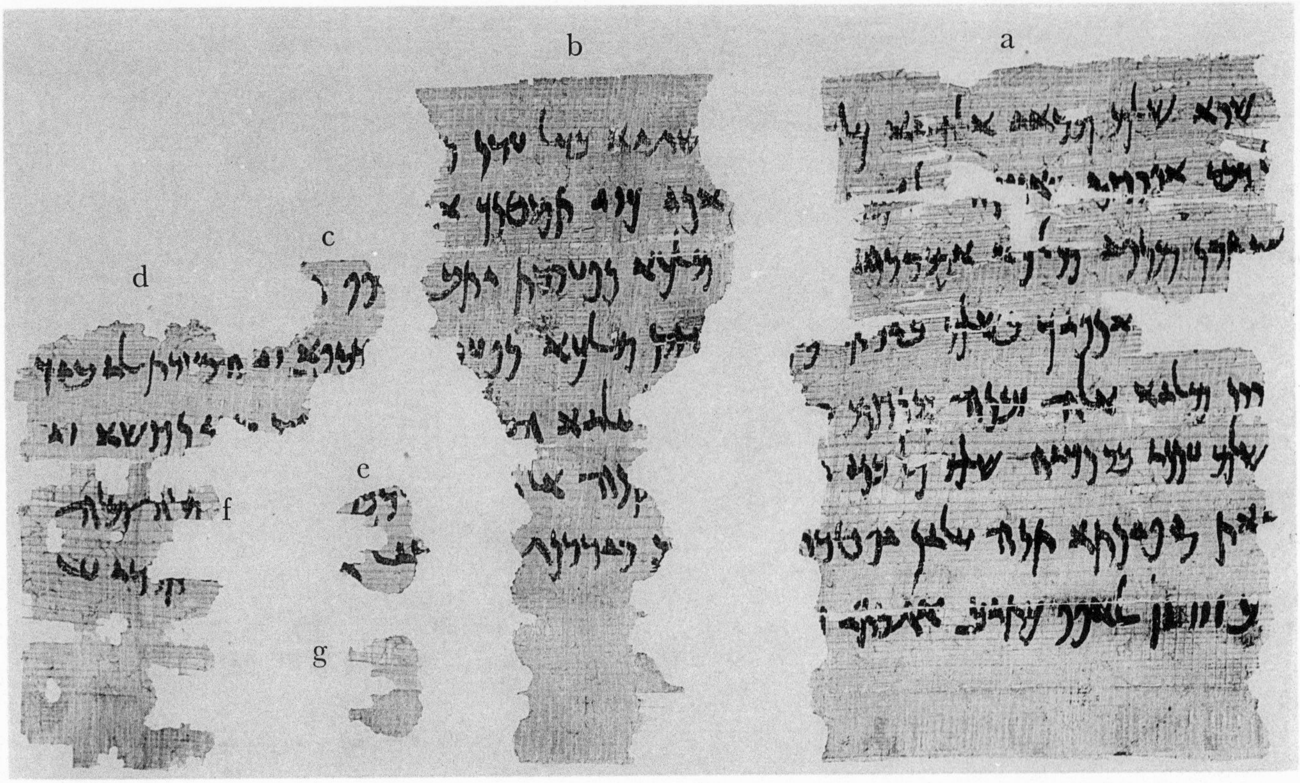

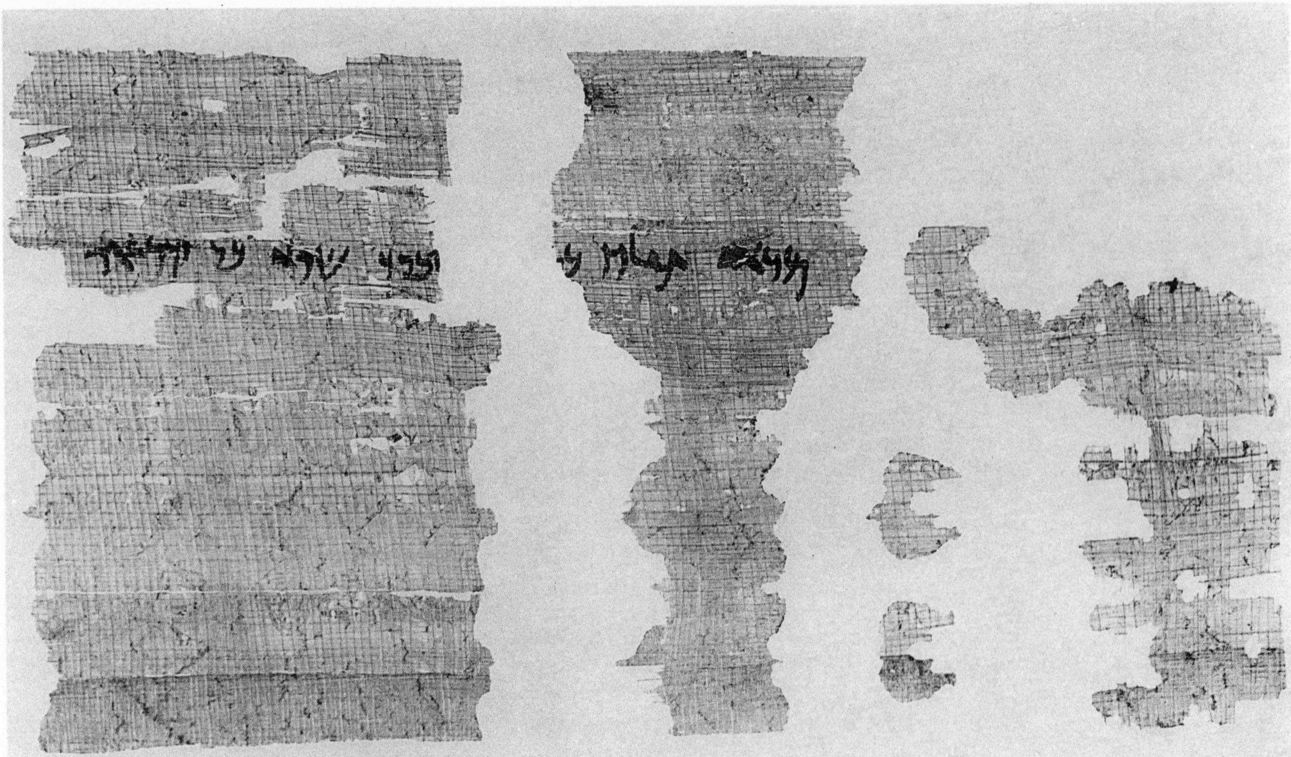

XIII. PAPYRUS 13 (47.218.151)

XIV. PAPYRUS 14 (47.218.12)

XV. PAPYRUS 15 (47.218.97)

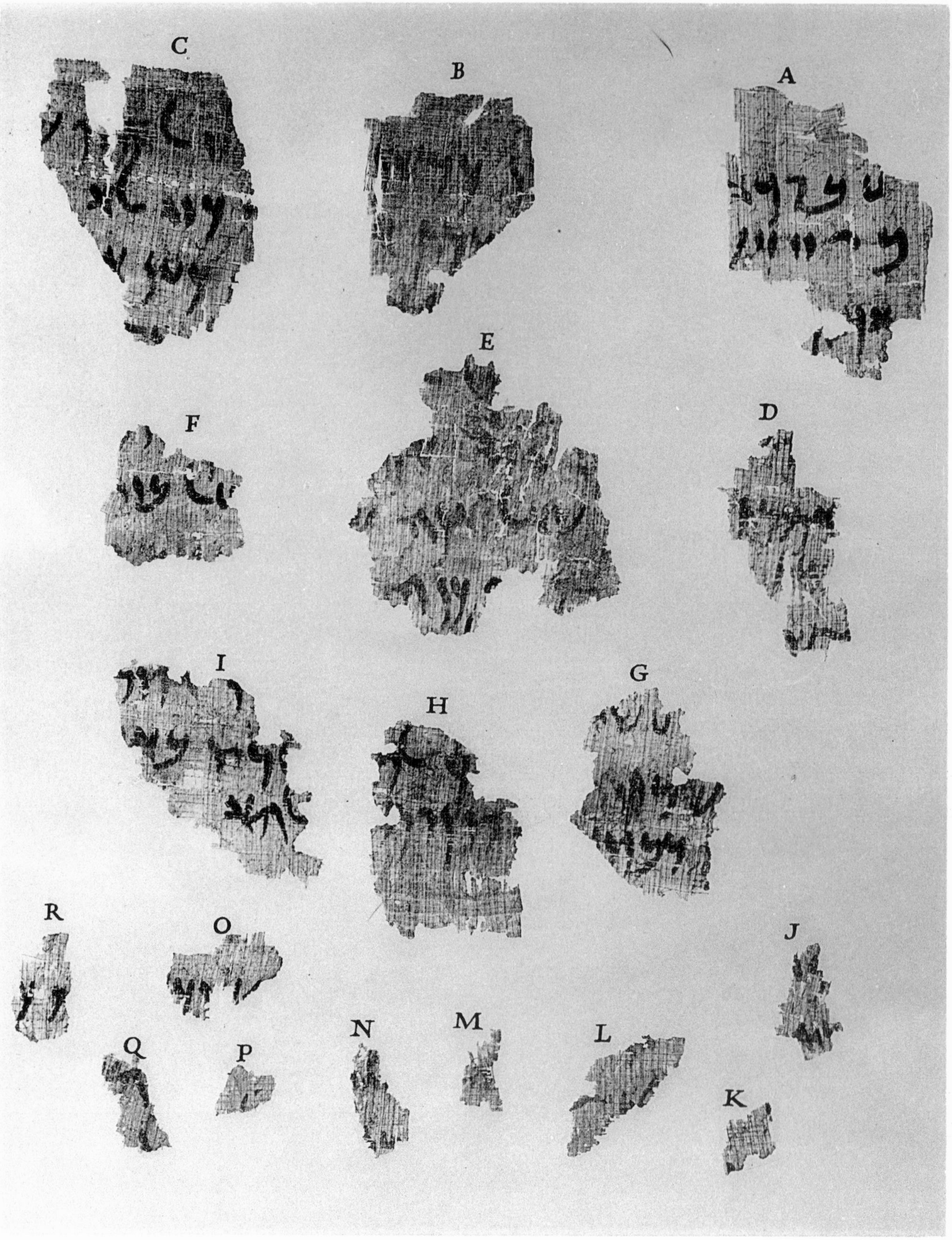

XVI a. PAPYRUS 16 (47.218.13)

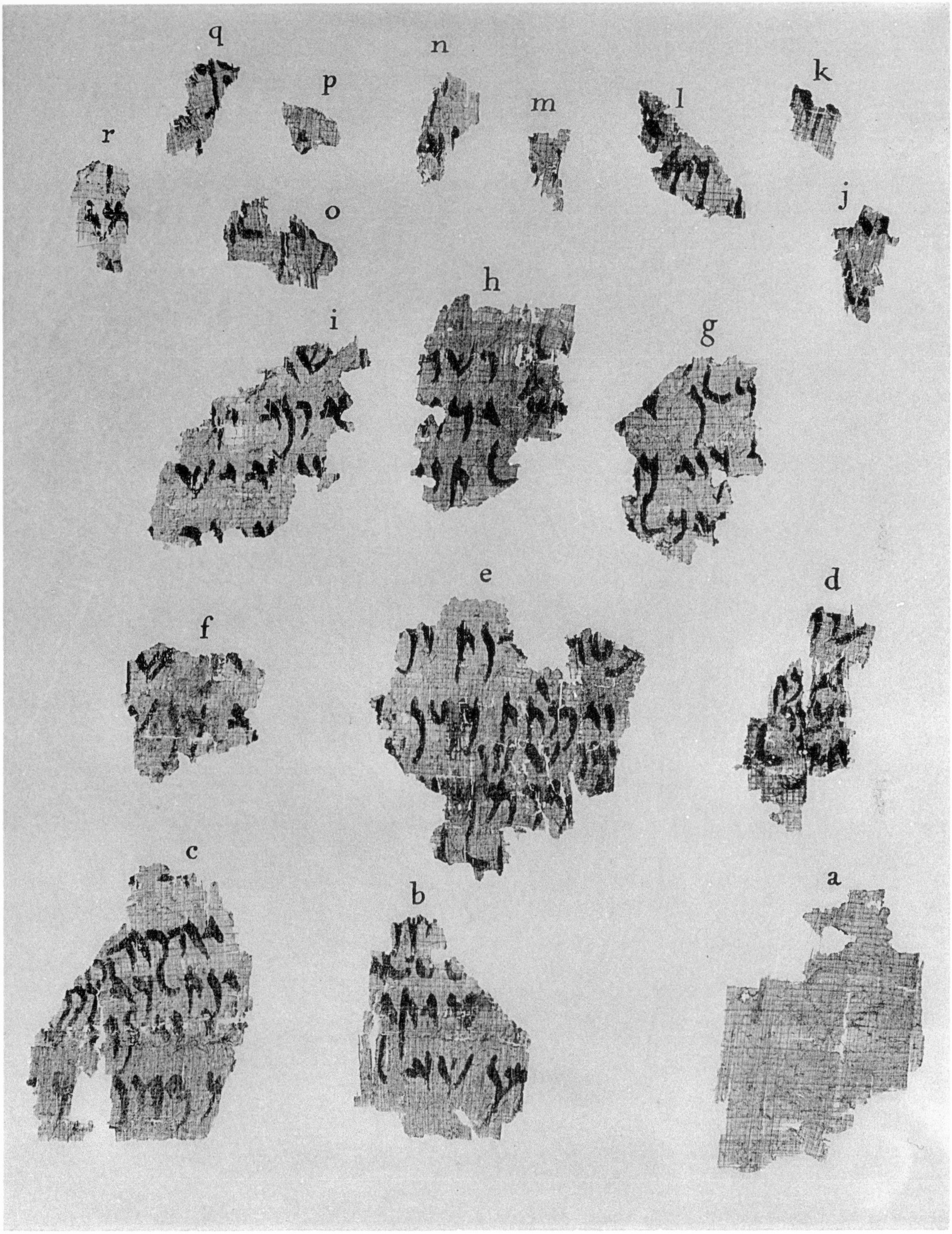

XVI b. PAPYRUS 16 continued

XVII. PAPYRUS 17 (47.218.153)

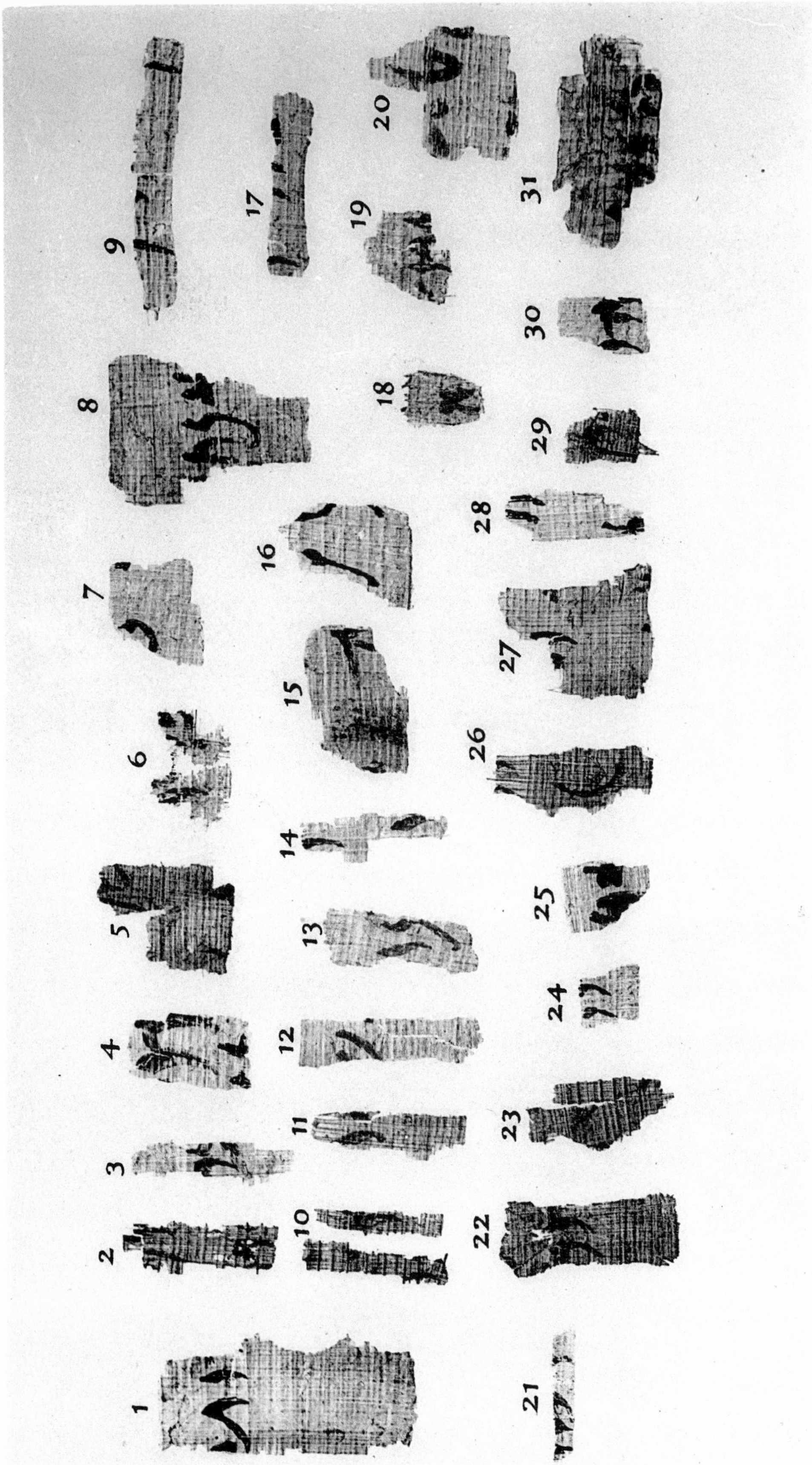

XVIII. UNPLACED FRAGMENTS (47.218.155)

Papyrus 2

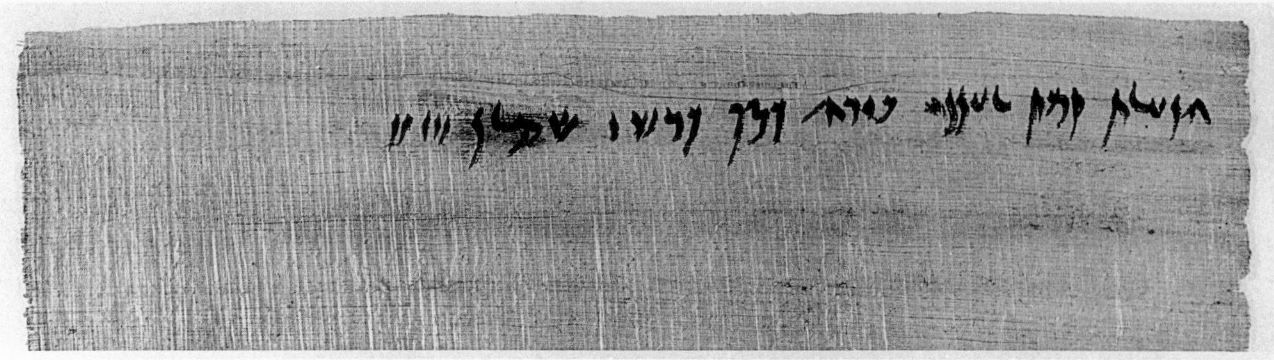

Papyrus 3

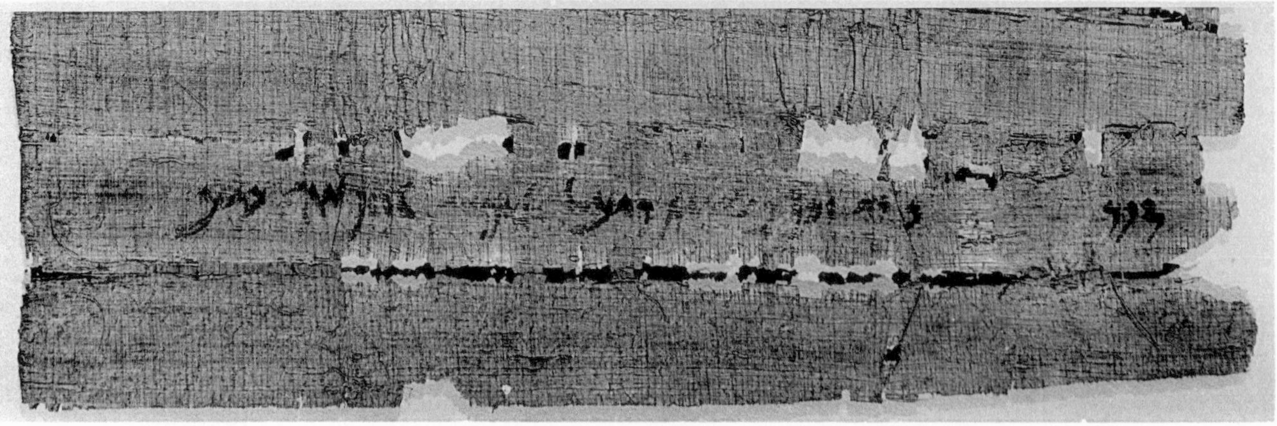

Papyrus 4

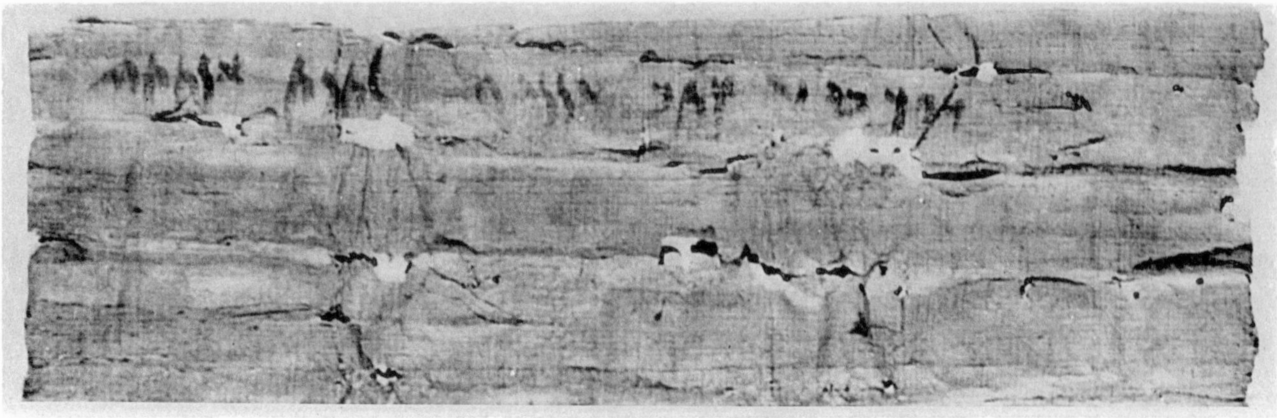

Papyrus 5

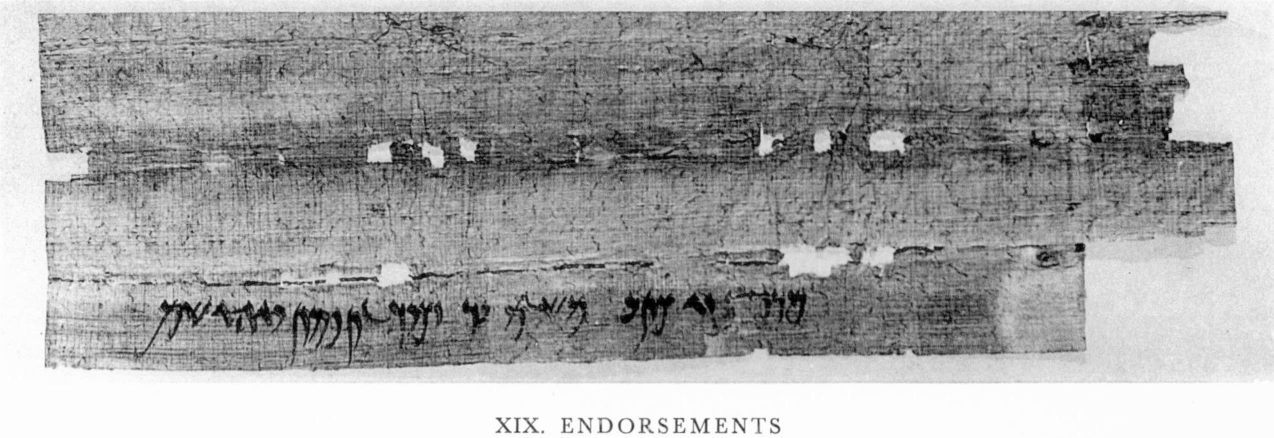

XIX. ENDORSEMENTS

Papyrus 9

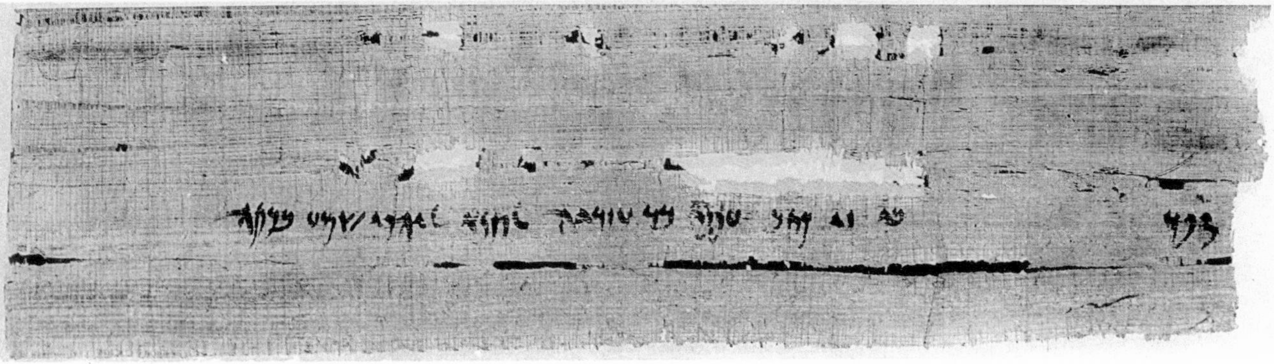

Papyrus 10

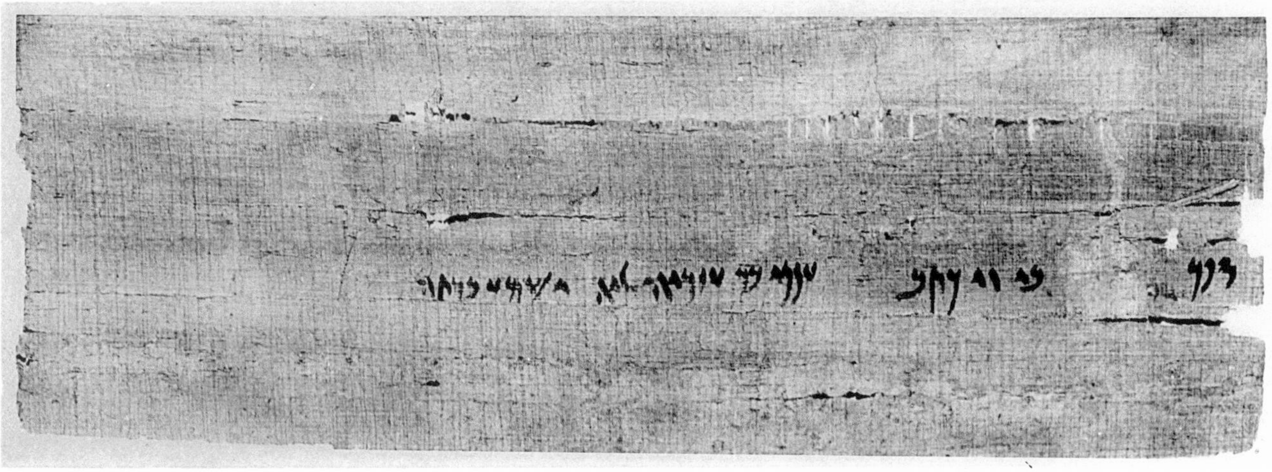

Papyrus 11

Papyrus 12

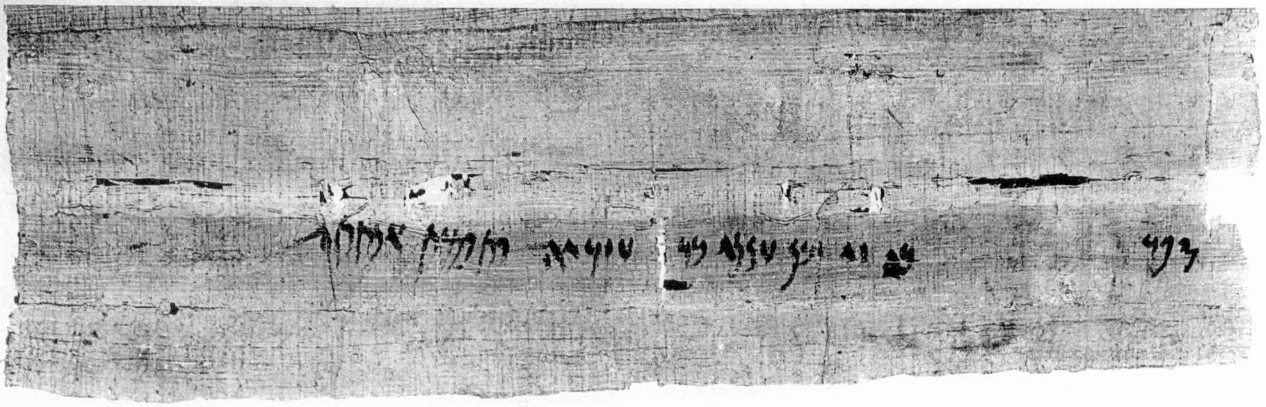

XIX. continued

Palette 1

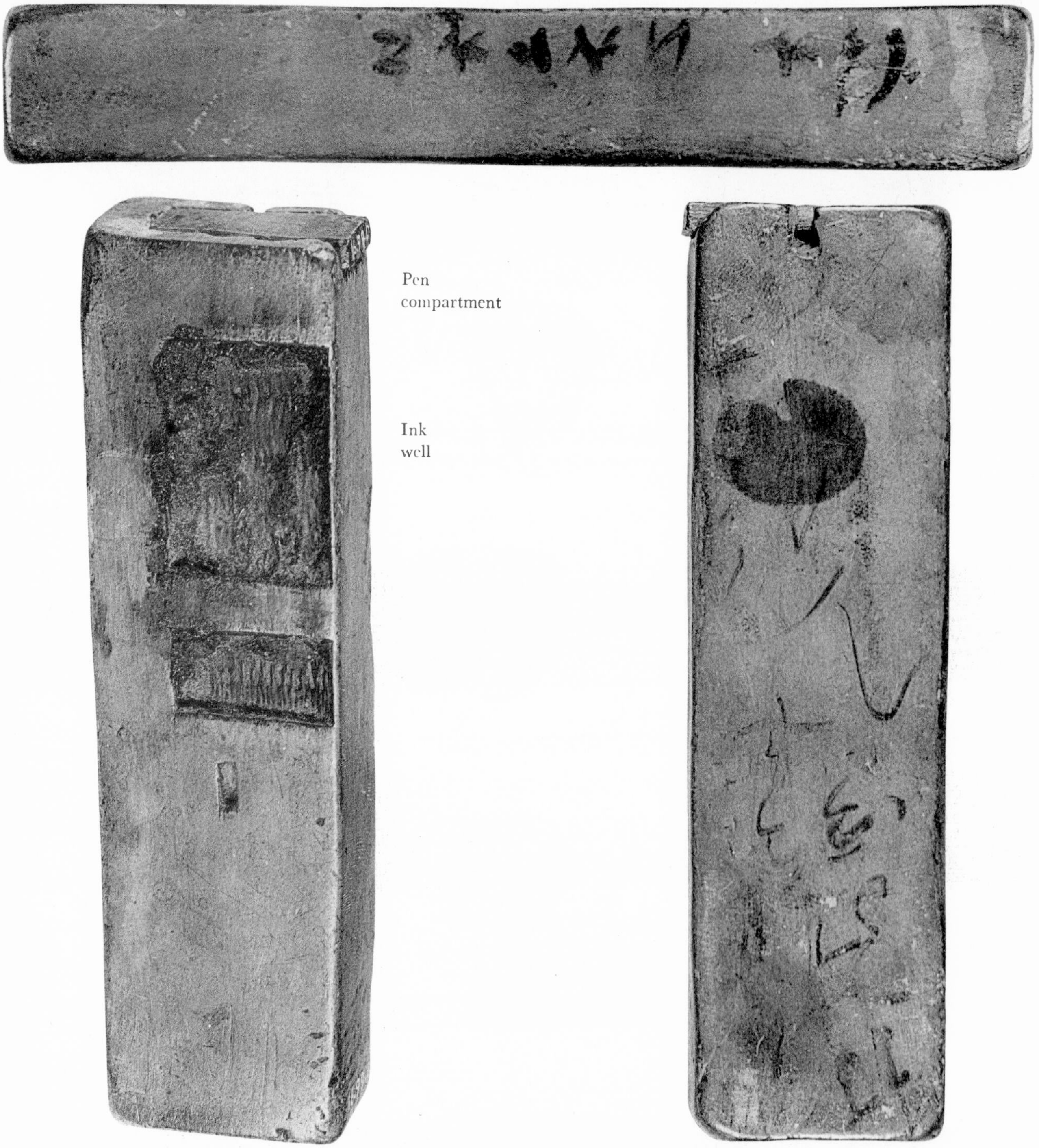

Palette 2

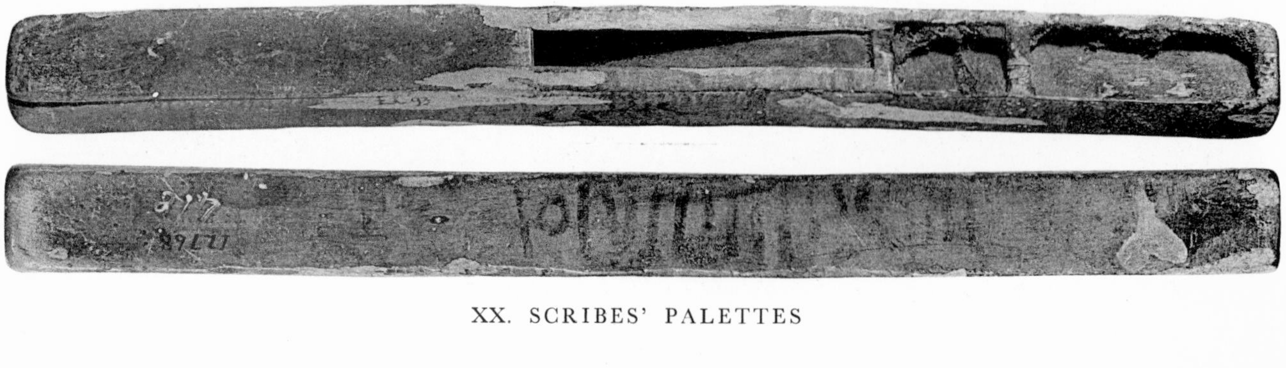

XX. SCRIBES' PALETTES

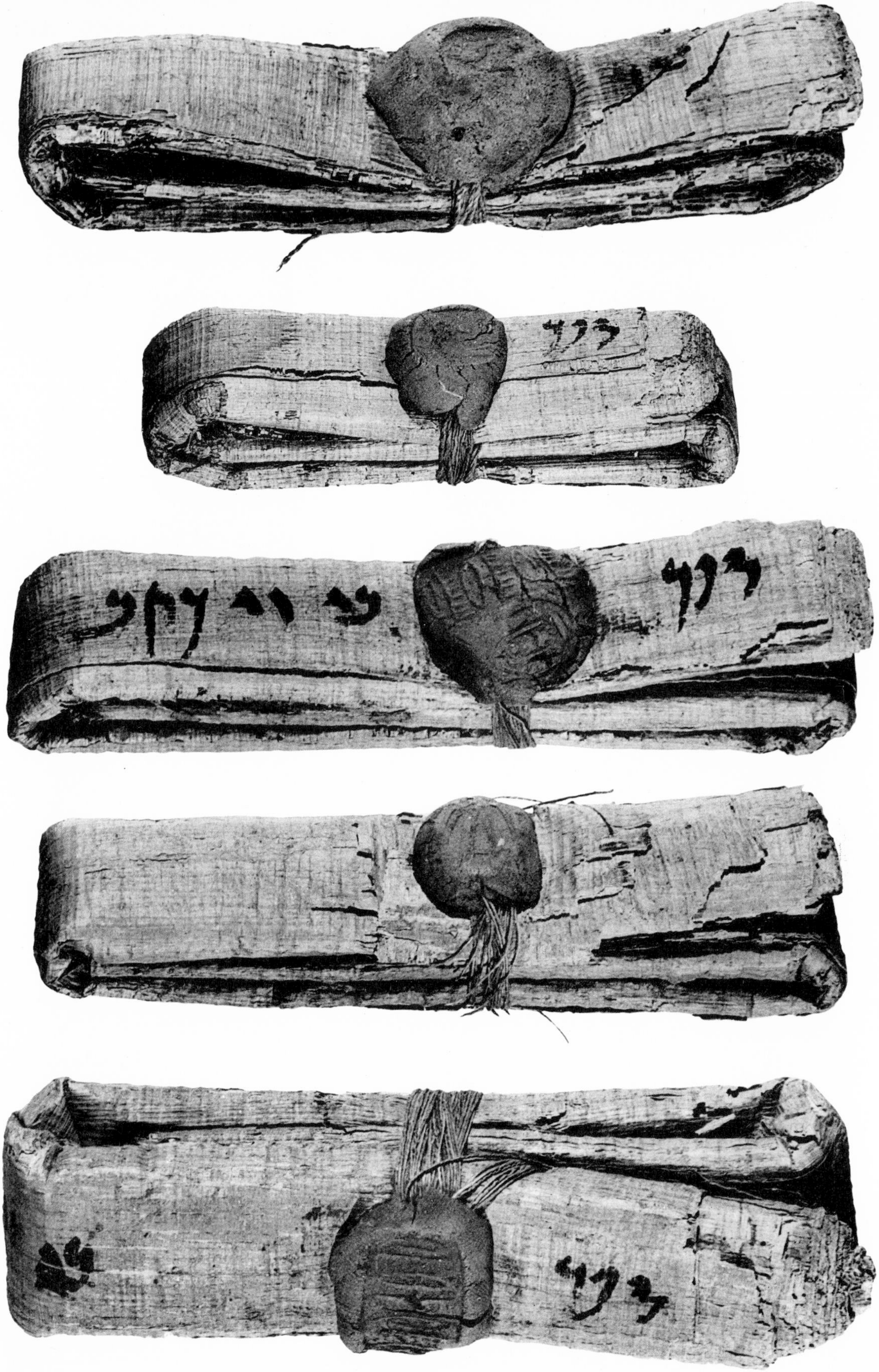

XXI. UNOPENED PAPYRUS ROLLS

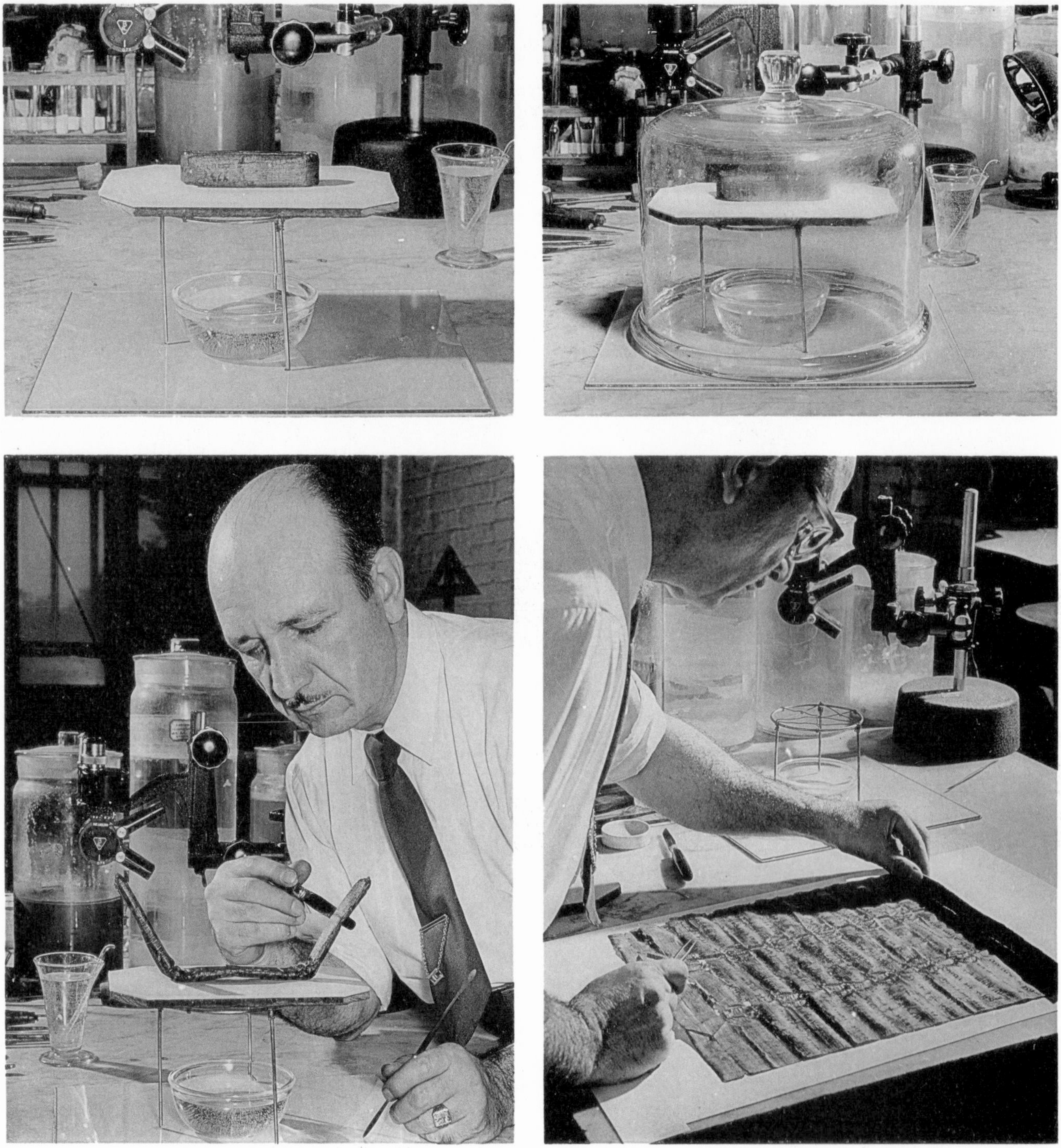

XXII. FOUR STEPS IN THE OPENING OF THE PAPYRI

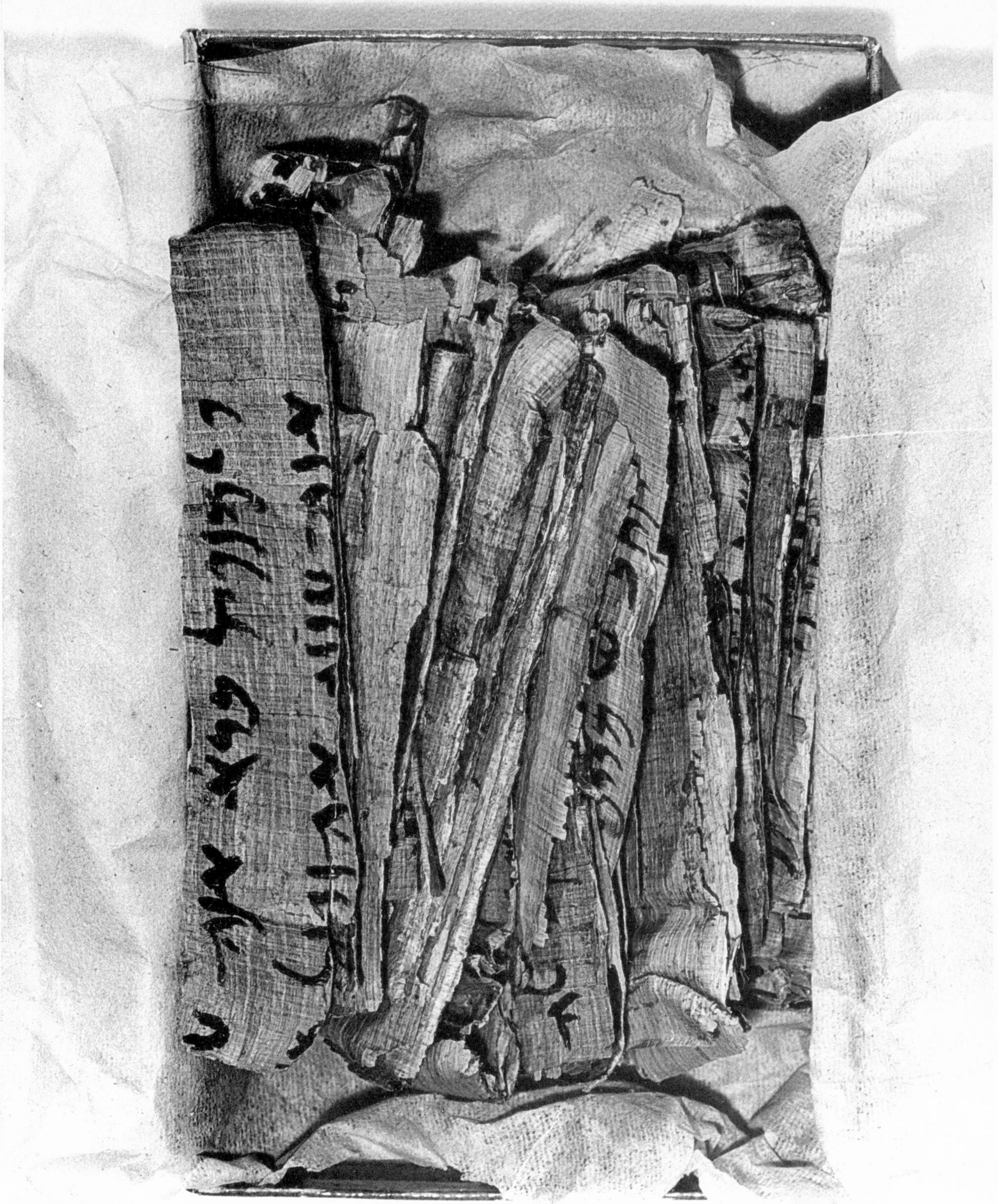

XXIII. PAPYRUS 7 as Received

(12)

C 141 882